PATENTS IN CHEMISTRY AND BIOTECHNOLOGY

by

PHILIP W. GRUBB

European Patent Attorney

CLARENDON PRESS · OXFORD
1986

Oxford University Press, Walton Street, Oxford OX2 6DP

Oxford New York Toronto
Delhi Bombay Calcutta Madras Karachi
Petaling Jaya Singapore Hong Kong Tokyo
Nairobi Dar es Salaam Cape Town
Melbourne Auckland
and associated companies in
Beirut Berlin Ibadan Nicosia

Oxford is a trade mark of Oxford University Press

Published in the United States
by Oxford University Press, New York

British Library Cataloguing in Publication Data
Grubb, Philip W.
Patents in chemistry and biotechnology.
1. Patents   2. Chemistry
I. Title   II. Grubb, Philip W. Patents for chemists
608   T211
ISBN 0-19-855222-X
ISBN 0-19-855221-1 Pbk

Library of Congress Cataloging-in-Publication Data
Grubb, Philip W.
Patents in chemistry and biotechnology.
Rev. ed. of: Patents for chemists. c1982.
Includes index.
1. Patents.   2. Chemistry—Patents.   I. Grubb,
Philip W. Patents for chemists.   II. Title.
T211.G78 1986   346.04'86'02466   86-5306
ISBN 0-19-855222-X   342.648602466
ISBN 0-19-855221-1 (pbk.)

Set by Hope Services, Abingdon, Oxon
Printed in Great Britain by St Edmundsbury Press,
Bury St Edmunds, Suffolk

PREFACE TO THE SECOND EDITION

Since *Patents for chemists* was written, patent laws have continued to change, and the book has rapidly become out of date in a number of respects. Furthermore, the field of biotechnology has rapidly grown in commercial importance, and the special problems of patents in this area have received a great deal of attention.

Accordingly, *Patents for chemists* has been completely revised to take account of new developments up to the beginning of 1986, and three new chapters have been added on the patenting of pharmaceutical and biotechnological inventions. To emphasize the inclusion of this new material, the title has been changed to *Patents in chemistry and biotechnology*.

Most of the changes in the last four years have been positive ones for the patent system. The USA has relaxed some of its formal requirements, and now allows extension of pharmaceutical patents to compensate for regulatory delays. Within Europe, Spain and Portugal have joined the EEC and introduced new laws to strengthen their patent systems and to enable them to join the European Patent Convention. Greece also plans to join the EPC in 1986 and Belgium is strengthening its national patents. Patent erosion in the developing countries seems to have been halted, and the People's Republic of China has introduced a new patent law. Authorities such as the US Department of Justice and the EEC Commission now are more favourably disposed to patents than they were only four years ago.

The greatest challenge to the patent system at present is that of adequately protecting research investment in the field of biotechnology. Many companies have a short-term interest in weakening biotechnology patents to the point where the entire field could be effectively patent-free; others would like to monopolize wide areas on an inadequate basis. Unless the right balance can be found, the result will be unfortunate for industry as well as for the patent system.

As well as the colleagues mentioned in the Preface to the first edition, whose continuing help is much appreciated, I should also like to thank Dr P. Mekler for reviewing the scientific aspects of Chapters 11 and 12 and Mr A. van Wessem for checking Chapter 19. Thanks also to Ian Grubb for suggestions for the paperback cover design.

Inzlingen   P.W.G.
April, 1986

PREFACE TO THE FIRST EDITION

Patents for chemists does not attempt to give a comprehensive account of patent law and practice. The authoritative text books and compilations which do so are intended for the legal specialist and have little interest for the lay reader. This volume is intended rather as a guide to patent matters for laymen, particularly, but not exclusively, for chemists. Chemists, whether in the universities, industry, or government service, may themselves make patentable inventions (perhaps without realizing it), or may be involved in the development and exploitation of chemical inventions. It is hoped that *Patents for chemists* will make its readers more alert to the possibilities of patenting their work, more able to understand and work together with patent practitioners, and more informed about how patents fit into the different types of economic and political systems in the world.

The last three or four years have seen extensive changes in the patent system in many countries, not least in the United Kingdom. The Patents Act 1977 came into force on 1 June 1978 and brought British patent law into conformity with the new European Patent Convention. On the same day the European Patent Office in Munich began to accept applications, and it can now grant patents in ten countries (including the United Kingdom) on the basis of a single application. Simultaneous application in a number of countries has also been made easier by the Patent Co-operation Treaty, ratified by the United Kingdom, USA, USSR, and over thirty other countries. *Patents for chemists* describes these new developments and sets them in the context of the older British law, which to a great extent continues to apply to patents filed before the 1977 Act came into force.

Although the period of most rapid change may be over, patent laws in many countries are still changing. Furthermore, even if the law itself is not changed, its interpretation may develop as a result of court decisions. It is therefore important to remember that neither this nor any other book can replace the professional advice of a patent practitioner (in the United Kingdom, a chartered patent agent) when actual problems arise in connection with patents.

I should like to express my thanks to Dr W. G. Richards, whose idea it was to write a book of this type, and to Messrs B. A. Yorke, C. S. Morris, G. D. Sharkin, M. M. Kassenoff, and other colleagues in the patents department of Sandoz Ltd, Basle, and Sandoz Inc., Hanover, New Jersey, for their correction of factual errors and for their helpful comments. However, the opinions expressed are my own and not necessarily those of Sandoz Ltd, or any other body.

I acknowledge with thanks the permission of the British Patent Office to reproduce Figures 1–4, 7 and 8, the source of which is H.M: Stationery Office, and that of the Hagley Museum, Wilmington, Delaware, to reproduce the photographs of Figure 6. Finally, particular thanks are due to my wife Kay who typed the manuscript and without whose help and support this book would not have been written.

Inzlingen   P. W. G.
January 1982

CONTENTS

PART II INVENTIONS IN CHEMISTRY, PHARMACEUTICALS, AND BIOTECHNOLOGY

LIST OF ABBREVIATIONS

ANDA	Abbreviated New Drug Application (USA)
CA	*Chemical Abstracts*
CAFC	Court of Appeals for the Federal Circuit (USA)
CCPA	Court of Customs and Patents Appeals (USA)
c.i.p.	continuation in part
COMECON	Council for Mutual Economic Assistance (East Bloc countries)
COPAC	Community Patents Appeals Court
CPA	Chartered Patent Agent (UK)
CPC	Community Patent Convention
DAS	*Deutsche Auslegungsschrift* (German patent application published on acceptance)
DOS	*Deutsche Offenlegungschrift* (German patent application published before examination)
DPS	*Deutsche Patentschrift* (German patent)
DSIR	Department of Scientific and Industrial Research (UK)
ECJ	European Court of Justice
EEC	European Economic Community
EFTA	European Free Trade Association
EPC	European Patent Convention
EPO	European Patent Office
ESARIPO	English-Speaking Africa Regional Industrial Property Organisation
FDA	Food and Drug Administration (USA)
IIB	Institut Internationale des Brevets (now part of the EPO)
IND	Investigative New Drug (USA)
INPADOC	International Patent Documentation Centre
IPC	International Patent Classification
ITC	International Trade Commission (USA)
NDA	New Drug Application (USA)
NIH	National Institute of Health (USA)
	Not Invented Here
NRDC	National Research Development Corporation (UK)
OJ	*Official Journal (Patents)* (UK)
OPI	Open to Public Inspection
PCT	Patent Co-operation Treaty
SIC	Standard Industrial Classification
SRL	Science Reference Library (UK)
TOT	Transfer of Technology
TTP	Transfer of Technology Patent

UNCTAD	United Nations Conference on Trade and Development
UNIDO	United Nations Industrial Development Organization
USC	United States Code
USPTO	United States Patent and Trademark Office
WARF	Wisconsin Alumni Research Foundation
WIPO	World Intellectual Property Organization

PART I
THE GENERAL PRINCIPLES OF PATENTS

THE NATURE AND ORIGINS OF PATENT MONOPOLIES

One man should not be afraid of improving his possessions, lest they be taken away from him, or another deterred by high taxes from starting a new business. Rather, the prince should be ready to reward men who want to do these things and those who endeavour in any way to increase the prosperity of their city or their state.

Niccolò Machiavelli: The Prince (1514)

What is a patent?

A patent may be defined as a grant by the state of exclusive rights for a limited time in respect of a new and useful invention. These rights are in general strictly limited to the territory of the state granting the patent, so that an inventor wishing protection in a number of countries must obtain separate patents in all of them. The name 'patent' is a contraction of 'letters patent' (Latin *litterae patentes*, 'open letters') which means a document issued by or in the name of the sovereign, addressed to all subjects and with the Great Seal pendant at the bottom of the document so that it can be read without breaking the seal.

Letters patent are still used in the United Kingdom, for example to confer peerages and to appoint judges, but will no longer be used to grant patents for inventions under the latest Patents Act. Prior to 1878, letters patent for inventions were engrossed on parchment and bore the Great Seal in wax. Subsequently paper was used and a wafer seal of the Patent Office replaced the Great Seal, but the wording of the letters patent document (not to be confused with the printed patent specification) was still very impressive. As can be seen from Fig. 1, British patents were still being granted in 1981 in the form of a command from the Queen to her subjects to refrain from infringing the patent under pain of the royal displeasure. Unfortunately for the patentee with a taste for this sort of thing, under the Patents Act 1977 all that he gets is a certificate of grant from the Patent Office.

It is important to realize that the rights given by a patent do not include the right to practise the invention, but only to exclude others from doing so. The patentee's freedom to use his own invention may be limited by legislation or regulations having nothing to do with patents, or by the

Patent No. 1575423

Foreign Application
23 September 1976

Date of Patent....20...September...1977

Date of Sealing ...**21**...January...1981

Elizabeth the Second by the Grace of God of the United Kingdom of Great Britain and Northern Ireland and of Her other Realms and Territories, Queen, Head of the Commonwealth, Defender of the Faith: To all to whom these presents shall come greeting:

WHEREAS a request for the grant of a patent has been made by

SANDOZ LTD., of Lichtstrasse 35, 4002 Basle, Switzerland, a Swiss Body Corporate,

for the sole use and advantage of an invention for

Cationic monoazo dyestuffs based on pyridone coupling components:

AND WHEREAS We, being willing to encourage all inventions which may be for the public good, are graciously pleased to condescend to the request:

KNOW YE, THEREFORE, that We, of our especial grace, certain knowledge, and mere motion do by these presents, for Us, our heirs and successors, give and grant unto the person(s) above named and any successor(s), executor(s), administrator(s) and assign(s) (each and any of whom are hereinafter referred to as the patentee) our especial licence, full power, sole privilege, and authority, that the patentee or any agent or licensee of the patentees and no others, may subject to the conditions and provisions prescribed by any statute or order for the time being in force at all times hereafter during the term of years herein mentioned, make, use, exercise and vend the said invention within our United Kingdom of Great Britain and Northern Ireland, and the Isle of Man, and that the patentee shall have and enjoy the whole profit and advantage from time to time accruing by reason of the said invention during the term of sixteen years from the date hereunder written of these presents : AND to the end that the patentee may have and enjoy the sole use and exercise and the full benefit of the said invention, We do by these presents for Us, our heirs and successors, strictly command all our subjects whatsoever within our United Kingdom of Great Britain and Northern Ireland, and the Isle of Man, that they do not at any time during the continuance of the said term either directly or indirectly make use of or put in practice the said invention, nor in anywise imitate the same, without the written consent, licence or agreement of the patentee, on pain of incurring such penalties as may be justly inflicted on such offenders for their contempt of this our Royal Command, and of being answerable to this patentee according to law for damages thereby occasioned :

PROVIDED ALWAYS that these letters patent shall be revocable on any of the grounds from time to time by law prescribed as grounds for revoking letters patent granted by Us, and the same may be revoked and made void accordingly :

PROVIDED ALSO that nothing herein contained shall prevent the granting of licences in such manner and for such considerations as they may by law be granted : AND lastly, We do by these presents for Us, our heirs and successors, grant unto the patentee that these our letters patent shall be construed in the most beneficial sense for the advantage of the patentee.

IN WITNESS whereof We have caused these our letters to be made patent

as of the   twentieth   day of   September

one thousand nine hundred and seventy-seven   and to be sealed.

*Comptroller-General of Patents
Designs, and Trade Marks.*

FIG. 1.   Letters Patent granted under the Patents Act 1949.

existence of other patents. For example, owning a patent for a new drug clearly does not give the right to market the drug without permission from the responsible health authorities, nor does it give the right to infringe an earlier existing patent. In the very common situation where A has a patent for a basic invention and B later obtains a patent for an improvement to this invention, then B is not free to use his invention without the permission of A, and A cannot use the improved version without coming to terms with B. The right to prevent others from carrying out the invention claimed in a patent may be enforced in the courts; if the patents is valid and infringed the court can order the infringer to stop his activities, as well as providing other remedies such as damages.

A patent, carrying with it these rights of exclusion, is a piece of property, and may be a very valuable one. Although intangible property, it may be dealt with in the same sort of ways as tangible property such as a house. Just as the owner of a house may live in it himself, sell or rent it to another, mortgage it, or even have it demolished, so a patentee may keep his patent rights, assign the patent to someone else, grant someone else a licence to do something covered by the patent, mortgage the patent (although this is unusual), or of course abandon the patent to the public. Abandonment of patent rights is very common in the majority of countries in which renewal fees must be paid each year to keep a patent in force; these renewal fees often rise steeply as the age of the patent increases, and only those patents which are of real commercial importance are kept alive for their full term. For United States patents applied for before 12 December 1980, no renewal fees are payable and positive action must be taken in order to 'dedicate to the public' such a US patent. This has the disadvantage that there are a great many US patents in force in which the patentees have no real interest but which may still impede the commercial activites of others. For US patents applied for after that date, however, renewal fees will be payable, and so in the course of time the number of US patents in force will decrease. Canada is one of the very few remaining countries which still require no renewal fees.

In any event, no patent can go on indefinitely. It is a point basic to the whole concept of patents that the exclusive rights are granted only for a limited period of time and that once this term has expired the general public is free to use the invention. British patents used to be granted generally for a term of 14 years, this being the time required for two generations of apprentices to be trained in the invention; in 1919 the term became 16 years. Extensions were possible, for example if the patentee was unable to exploit his invention because of wartime conditions, or if he had a particularly deserving invention on which, through no fault of his own, he had not made sufficient profit. A combination of these two grounds enabled the British patent for a pioneering invention relating to colour television to be extended to a total term of 32½ years: unfortunately for the patentee, his infringement action against producers of colour television sets was unsuccessful, the patent being finally held invalid.

In the USA and Canada the term of a patent is 17 years from the date of grant, which means that the longer the Patent Office takes to grant the patent, the later will be the expiry date. In most other countries, the term runs from the date of application and so the expiry date is fixed irrespective of how long the process of grant may take. It may be argued that the US system can operate unfairly in that an applicant whose invention is so clearly patentable that it is granted by the US patent office right away gets a patent which expires before that of an inventor applying on the same day with an invention which requires years to convince the patent office of its patentability. Although the term of protection is the same in both cases, protection at a later stage of commercialization of the product is normally far more valuable than protection in the early years, and the inventor whose patent issues later is in a better position. On the other hand, in some countries in which the term is fixed from the application date and there is no fixed limit to the prosecution time, an unusually long prosecution of the application can mean that only a few years of protection are left by the time the patent is actually granted, and only when the patent is granted can an infringer be sued. Extensions of US patents used to require a special Act of Congress, and were understandably very rare; extensions of pharmaceutical patents of up to 5 years are now possible (see p. 171).

The trend in most Western countries is towards a standard patent term of 20 years from the date of application, and this was adopted in Britain by the Patents Act 1977, which came into force on 1 June 1978.

So far in discussing the basic nature of patents we have avoided using the word 'monopoly', a word which has acquired many negative connotations. This is intentional, because there is a clear distinction to be made between a monopoly of an existing commodity and the exclusive rights given by a patent for a new invention. The old definition of monopoly given in Blackstone's *Commentaries* is still a good one:

. . .a licence or privilege allowed by the King, for the sole buying and selling, making, working or using of anything whatsoever; whereby the subject in general is restrained from that liberty of manufacturing or trading which he had before.

According to this definition, exclusive patent rights are not a monopoly because, being for a new invention, they cannot possibly take from the public at large any right which the public previously had. Even when the term 'monopoly' is given the broader meaning of any exclusive right to make, use, or sell, the distinction between a monopoly in an existing commodity and a patent monopoly in respect of a new invention should be kept in mind. The two were clearly distinguished in English law as long ago as 1624.

Early history in England

In the reign of Queen Elizabeth I, monopolies in common products such as salt, coal, playing cards, and many others were frequently granted by letters patent either in return for a cash payment as a means of raising revenue, or as a convenient method of rewarding royal favourites at the public expense. Such monopolies were a continuing cause of unrest, since not only were prices of everyday articles artificially raised, but also the patent holders were given wide powers of enforcement of their rights, including power to search premises for infringing articles and to levy fines on the spot. The popular outcry against these depredations reached such a pitch that in 1601 Elizabeth, who always knew how to give way gracefully when no other course was open to her, issued a proclamation revoking the majority of grants of monopoly (Figs. 2 and 3). Perhaps more importantly, whereas previously the grant of monopolies had been a matter of royal prerogative which could not be challenged by the subject, the proclamation of 1601 allowed matters concerning such grants to be contested in the common law courts.

The next year, Edward Darcy, who had been granted by letters patent a monopoly in the importation, making, and selling of playing cards, attempted to enforce his right in the courts against an infringer named Allein. The court held that the monopoly was illegal and the patent was declared invalid. In the course of this case, it was clearly stated that patents for new inventions should form an exception to the general rule against monopolies:

When any man by his own charge and industry, or by his own wit and invention doth bring any new trade into the realm or any engine tending to the furtherance of a trade that was never used before; and that for the good of the realm; in such cases the King may grant him a monopoly patent for some reasonable time, until the subjects may learn the same, in consideration of the good that he doth bring by his invention to the Commonwealth.[1]

This classic statement of the law introduces the legal concept of the 'consideration' for the patent grant.

In law, a contract between two parties will normally be valid only if there is a consideration on both sides, for example in a contract of sale A transfers property to B in consideration of a sum of money paid by B to A; conversely the consideration for B's payment is the property transferred. It may be considered that a patent for an invention is in the nature of a contract between the inventor and the state in which the state ensures that the inventor will have a monopoly for a limited time in consideration for the benefit to the state which is expected to arise from the invention.

In spite of the judgment in the case of Darcy's patent, illegal monopolies continued to be granted by King James I, and to curb this

❧ By the Queene.

❧ A Proclamation for the reformation of many abuses and misdemeanours committed by Patentees of certaine Priuiledges and Licences, to the generall good of all her Maiesties louing Subiects.

Hereas her most excellent Maiestie hauing granted diuers Priuiledges, and Licences, (vpon many suggestions made vnto her Highnesse, that the same should tend to the common good and profit of her Subiects) hath since the time of those Grants receiued diuers Informations of sundry grieuances lighting vpon many of the poorer sort of her people (by force thereof, contrary to her Maiesties expectation, at the time of those Grants : All which being duely examined, by such as her Maiestie hath directed to consider, and report the state of such complaints as haue bene made in that behalfe, It doth appeare that some of the said Grants were not only made vpon false and vntrue suggestions contained in her Letters Patents, but haue beene also notoriously abused, to the great losse and grieuance of her louing Subiects, (whose publike good shee tendereth more then any worldly riches :) And whereas also vpon like false suggestions, there haue beene obtained of the Lordes of her Highnesse priuie Counsell, diuers Letters of assistance, for the due execution of diuers of the said Grants, according to her Highnesse gracious intention and meaning. Forasmuch as her most excellent Maiestie (whose care and prouidence neuer ceaseth to preserue her people in continuall peace and plenty doth discerne that these particular Grants ensuing, namely, of or in any wise concerning Salt, Salt vpon Salt, Vineger, Aqua vitæ, or Aqua composita, or any liquor concerning the same, Salting and packing of fish, Trayne Oyle, Blubbers or Liuors of fish, Poldauyes, and Mildernixe, Pots, Brushes, and Bottels, and Starch, haue beene found in consequence so farre differing from those mayne groundes and reasons, which haue beene mentioned in the Grants, and haue also in the execution of the said Letters Patents bene extremely abused, contrary to her Highnesse intention and meaning therein expressed : She is now pleased of her meere Grace and fauour to all her louing Subiects, and by her Regall power and authoritie to publish and declare (by vertue hereof) all the said Grants aboue mentioned, and euery clause, article and sentence in the Letters Patents thereof contained to be void. And doth further expresly charge and command all the said Patentees, and all and euery person and persons, clayming by, from or vnder them, or any of them, that they or any of them, doe not at any time hereafter presume or attempt to put in vre or execution, any thing therein contained, vpon paine of her Highnesse indignation, and to bee punished as contemners and breakers of her royall and princely Commandement.

And whereas her Maiestie hath also granted diuers other Priuiledges and Licences, some for the better furnishing of the Realme with such warlike prouisions as are necessary for the defence thereof (as namely that concerning Saltpeter) and some of other kindes to particular persons, which haue sustemed losses and hinderances by seruice at Sea, and Land, or such as haue bene her Maiesties ancient domesticall Seruitors, or for some other like considerations, as namely, New Draperie, Irish Yarne, Calues skins, Felts, Cards, Glasses, Searching and Sealing of Leather, and Steele, and such like; In which Grants also her Highnesse hath beene credibly informed, that there hath beene abuse in the execution of them, to the hurt and preiudice of her louing Subiects (whereof she meaneth also that due punishment shall follow vpon such as shall bee found to haue particularly offended) Her Maiestie doeth by these presents likewise publish, notifie and declare her gracious will and pleasure to bee, That all and euery her Highnesse louing Subiects, that at any time hereafter shall finde themselues grieued, iniured or wronged by reason of any of the sayd Grants, or any clause, Article or sentence therein conteined, may bee at his or their Libertie to take their ordinary remedy by her Highnesse Lawes of this Realme, any matter or thing in any of the said Grants to the contrary

Fig. 2.   Proclamation of Queen Elizabeth I, 1601.

not witstanding. And forasmuch as her Maiestie (with the aduise of her priuie Counsell is now resolued, that no Letters from henceforth shall be written from them to assist these Grants, seeing they haue serued for pretexts to those that haue had them, to terrifie and oppresse her people (meerely contrary to the purpose and meaning of the same) Her Maiestie doth straitly charge and command, that no Letters of Assistance that haue bene granted by her Counsell for execution of those Grants, shall at any time hereafter be put in execution, or any of her louing Subiects be therby inforced to do or performe any thing therin contained. And that no Pursuiuant, Messenger of her Highnesse Chamber, or other officer whatsoeuer doe at any time hereafter presume or attempt any thing against any of her louing Subiects, by pretext or colour of any such Letters of assistance, for execution or putting in vse of any of those aforesaid Grants, or any thing therein contained. And as her Maiestie doth greatly commend the ducty and obedience that her louing Subiects haue yeelded in conforming themselues to the said Graunts, being vnder the great Seale of England: So her Maiestie doth notifie and signifie by these presents, That if any of her Subiects shall seditiously, or contemptuously, presume to call in question the power or validitie of her prerogatiue Royall annexed to her imperiall Crowne, in such causes, all such persons so offending, shall receiue seuere punishment, according to their demerits.

And whereas she hath also bene informed, that diuers of her Subiects are desirous to be set at libertie for the sowing of Woad, restrained by a Proclamation in the fortieth and two yeere of her reigne, at which time it was thought by many men of good experience, that such restraint would be a meane to preuent sundry inconueniences, forasmuch as her Maiestie had neuer other purpose by that restraint, then to doe that which might be for the greatest and most generall benefite of her Subiects: Her highnesse is also pleased (and so shee doeth) by this Proclamation set at liberty all such persons as shall thinke it for their good, to imploy their grounds to the vse of sowing of Woad, notwithstanding any such prohibition in any former Proclamation. Prouided alwayes, that it shall not be lawfull for any person or persons whatsoeuer, to conuert any ground that shall be within three miles of the Citie of London, or neere any other Maiesties houses of accesse, nor so neere to any other great Citie or Towne corporate, whereby any offence may grow by the noysome sauour of the same. Giuen at our Palace at Westminster the 28. day of Nouember, in the fourtieth and foure yeere of her Maiesties most prosperous raigne.

God saue the Queene.

❧ Imprinted at London by Robert
Barker, Printer to the Queenes most
excellent Maiestie.
1601.

FIG. 3. Transcription of Proclamation of Queen Elizabeth I, 1601.

continuing abuse. Parliament enacted on 25 May 1624 the Statute of Monopolies, which formed the basis of the law on patents in England for over 200 years. It consisted of a general prohibition on the grant of monopolies, qualified by certain specific exceptions. Section 6 exempted patents for new inventions from the general prohibition, in the following words:

Provided also, and be it declared and enacted, that any declaration before mentioned shall not extend to any letters patent and grants of privileges for the term of fourteen years or under, hereafter to be made, of the sole working or making of any manner of new manufactures within this realm, to the true and first inventor and inventors of such manufactures, which others at the time of making such letters patents and grant shall not use, so as also they be not contrary to the law nor mischievous to the state, by raising prices of commodities at home, or hurt of trade, or generally inconvenient.

It will be seen that section 6 contains exceptions to the exception, providing that patents which raised prices, hurt trade, or were generally inconvenient could be declared invalid. We would nowadays call such provisions 'anti-trust' or 'abuse of monopoly' provisions.

This piece of legislation was not innovative, but simply declarative of the common law as it had already been established. It did not alter the fact that an inventor had no automatic right to a patent for his invention; the grant of a patent was still an act of royal prerogative which had to be sought by petition and which could be refused at will.

Where the Statute of Monopolies speaks of an inventor, the term means not only an inventor in the modern sense of the originator or creator of a new idea, but also extends to a person who brings something new into the country for the first time. Many of the early patents granted before the Statute of Monopolies had been to inventors of this type; for example the first and second English patents for invention (in 1449 and 1552) both related to glass-making techniques which were known on the Continent, but not established in England. Here the consideration for the grant of the patent was the establishment of the new industry in England, or, in modern terms, the transfer of technology to a developing country.

The first English patent granted to an inventor in the modern sense of the word appears to have been that to Giacopo Acontio in 1565 for a new type of furnace. In Venice, however, patents for inventions had been granted at least since 1470, and the patent system there appears to have been quite highly developed by 1594 when Galileo was granted a patent for an irrigation machine. The conditions of the 20-year patent grant included a requirement that the machine be actually constructed within one year, and that the machine had not previously been thought of by others; in modern terminology, compulsory working and novelty requirements. In spite of this early degree of sophistication, however, the Venetian patent system fell into disuse as the power and importance of Venice declined, whereas the English system has remained continuously in effect to the present day.

Early English patents for inventions contained no more description of the invention than the title, and as long as the pace of technological progress remained snail-like and the number of patents granted was small, this was no doubt sufficient. As the number of patents increased, however, and as patents began to be granted for specific improvements rather than for the setting up of whole new industries, it became common to add a short description of the invention to the letters patent. By the early eighteenth century it had become the rule that patents were granted on condition that the patentee filed a detailed description of his invention within a fixed period after grant (see, for example, Fig. 4, which shows a patent specification of 1718). Gradually the concept arose that the disclosure of the invention in the patent specification was the consideration for the grant, a concept which is still much in vogue.

According to this view of the patent system, an inventor has the choice of keeping his invention secret or of applying for a patent. In the first case he may succeed in keeping his invention to himself for a very long time, but if it becomes known to others, or others invent it independently, he has no redress. In the second alternative the state guarantees him his monopoly for a limited time but afterwards anyone is free to carry out the instructions published in the specification and practise the invention, to the general benefit of the economy.

This theory presupposes that the technological development of the society in question is sufficiently advanced that there are enough people able to put the invention into effect on the basis of a written description – a condition that is by no means always met in many countries which grant patents. Furthermore, while it can be logically advanced in respect of an invention such as a process, which can be kept secret within the walls of a factory, it is clearly not valid where the invention is a new article or a new chemical compound which is published to the world as soon as it is sold. The question of the consideration for the grant is more complex than would appear from this simple 'disclosure theory'.

Early history in America

The development of patents in North America was, understandably, based largely on concepts developed in England. Although the colonies before independence lacked the sovereign power to grant letters patent, they nevertheless had legislation such as that of Massachusetts in 1641 giving exclusive rights for limited periods to persons introducing new industries to the colony. After independence, South Carolina, for example, introduced

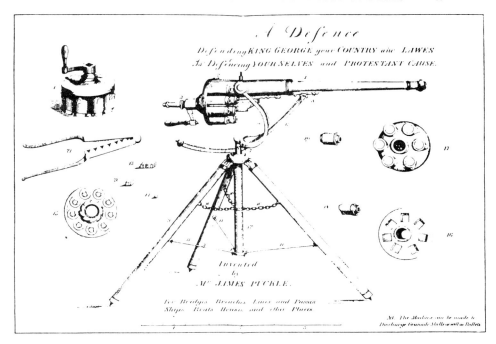

No. 1 The Barrel of the Gun
2 The Sett of Chambers Charg'd put on
   ready for Firing
3 The Screw upon which every Sett of
   Chambers play off and on
4 a Sett of Chambers ready charged to
   be Slip'd on when the first Sett are
   pull'd off to be recharg'd
5 The Crane to rise fall and Turn the
   Gun round
6 The Curb to Level and fix the Guns
7 The Screw to rise and fall it

8 The Screw to take out the Crane when
   the Gun with the Trepeid is to be
   folded up
9 The Trepied whereon it plays
10 The Chain to prevent the Trepieds
   extending too far out
11 The hooks to fix the Trepied and
   Unhook when the same is folded
   up in order to be carried with the
   Gun upon a Man's Shoulder
12 The Tube wherein the Pivot of the
   Crane turns

13 a Charge of Twenty Square Bullets
14 a single Bullet
15 The front of the Chambers of a Gun
   for a Boat
16 The plate of the Chambers of the Gun
   for a Ship shooting Square Bullets
   against Turks
17 For Round Bullets against Christians
18 a Single Square Chamber
19 a Single round Chamber
20 a single Bullet for a Boat
21 The Mould for Casting Single Bullets

Whereas our Sovoraign Lord King George by his Letters pattents bearing date the Fifteenth day of May in the Fourth Year of her Majesties Reign was Graciously pleas'd to Give & Grant unto me James Puckle of London Gent my Exers Admors & Assignes the sole priviledge & Authority to Make Exercise Work & use a Portable Gun or Machine (by me lately Invented) call'd a Defence in that part of his Majesties Kingdom of Great Brittain call'd England his Dominion of Wales, Town of Berwick upon Tweed and his Majesties Kingdom of Ireland in such manner & with such Materials as shou'd be Ascertain'd to be the sd New Invention by writing under my Hand & Seal and Inrolled in the High court of chancery within Three calendar Months from the date of the sd pattent as in & by his Majties Letters Pattents Relation being thereunto had Doth & may amongst other things more fully & at large appear NOW I the said James Puckle Do hereby Declare that the Materials whereof the sd Machine is Made are Steel Iron & Brass and that the Trepied whereon it stands is Wood & Iron And that in the above print to which I hereby Refer the sd Gun or Machine by me Invented is Delineated & Described. July the 25 1718.

48 180

Fig. 4.   Puckle's specification, 1718.

a statute (1784) dealing with inventions on the same basis as artistic copyright, and providing a 14-year term. Finally in 1788, the Constitution of the United States was ratified containing Article I, section 8:

The Congress shall have power . . . to promote the progress of science and useful arts by securing for limited times to authors and inventors the exclusive right to their respective writings and discoveries.

There are two points worth noting in this brief statement. First, although it merely gave Congress power to enact a patent law without seeming to place any restrictions on what form such a law might take, nevertheless the wording '. . . to inventors . . .' is probably the reason why today the USA is the only country in which a patent must be applied for by the inventor himself and not by an assignee such as the inventor's employer. It is for this reason that, as we shall see, correct designation of inventorship plays such an important role in US patenting, whereas in most other countries it has little or no effect on patent validity although it may be important for other reasons such as compensation for employee inventors.

Furthermore, these words of the Constitution appear to be the basis for the practice that whereas in most countries questions of precedence between two patent applications claiming the same invention are resolved on the simple basis that the first to file an application has priority, in the USA the patent is granted, subject to certain conditions, to the person who first made the invention. As this is by no means an easy matter to sort out, a lengthy and cumbersome procedure known as 'interference' has had to be developed to resolve priority in conflicting applications.

It has been suggested that because of the wording of the Constitution, any change in the US law in these respects would require a constitutional amendment. Other authorities discount this view, pointing out that copyright in the US may be applied for by an assignee although artistic copyright is covered by the same section of the Constitution as is patent protection. In any event, as these features of US patent law have existed for a long time and there is little or no pressure to change them now, we must assume they will remain for some considerable time to come.

The second point of interest in the constitutional provisions on patents is the statement that the purpose of granting exclusive rights to inventors is to promote scientific and technical progress. This brings us again to the question of the consideration for the grant, which is here expressed not as the narrow exchange of protection in consideration of disclosure but rather as the broad concept that a patent system encourages progress. Although the mechanism of how it is supposed to do so is not stated, the association in the USA over a long period of time of a strong patent system with an enormous degree of scientific and technological development appears to confirm the view of the framers of the Constitution.

The consideration for the grant of a patent

The consideration for the grant of a patent should not be regarded for individual patents in isolation. It is not the establishment of new industry, although in a few very rare cases a single invention will base an entire new industry. It is not the disclosure of the invention, since in most cases the invention will be made public if and when it is commercialized. It is not the working of the invention, since it is only commercially feasible to work 10 per cent or less of the inventions which result in patents.

The consideration for the granting of patents, in general, is the benefit which results to the state by technological progress as represented by the commercialization of inventions. The connection between the granting of patents and the commercialization of inventions is simply that the existence of patent rights removes part of the risk involved in investment in a new development. Who, after all, would be willing to invest large sums of money in a new project if he knew that an imitator could copy his product as soon as it was marketed, without incurring any research costs? The justification for the patent system is that it provides an incentive for investment in new ideas, without which technological development would be much slower and and more difficult.

HISTORICAL DEVELOPMENTS AND FUTURE TRENDS

I began with the Queen upon the Throne. I ended with the Deputy Chaff-wax.

Charles Dickens: *A poor man's tale of a patent*

United Kingdom: 1800–1949

By the beginning of the nineteenth century, the system for granting patents in England had progressed to the point where a specification describing the invention had to be filed within a certain time after grant. The actual process of getting the patent, however, was an incredible rigmarole of petty bureaucracy which has been immortalized by Dickens in *A poor man's tale of a patent*. The sequence involved, at one stage or another, obtaining the signatures of the Home Secretary, one of the two Law Officers, the Sovereign, and the Lord Chancellor, and sealing various documents with the Signet, the Privy Seal, and finally the Great Seal on the letters patent document itself. All this took time and money; approximately six weeks and £100, equivalent to approximately £1500 today. What is more, the patent extended only to England and Wales, and separate patents had to be obtained for Scotland and Ireland so that the total cost of United Kingdom patenting was over £300, a sum which only a wealthy man could afford.

A major reform of the patent system was enacted in 1852, when the Patent Office was set up which could grant a single patent to cover the whole of the United Kingdom. For the first time a description of the invention had to be filed on applying for a patent; this could be a complete specification, giving a full description; or a provisional specification giving merely an outline to be completed later, within a fixed period after grant. The costs of obtaining a patent were greatly reduced, but renewal fees had to be paid in order to keep the patent in force for its maximum term. An important step forward was that the patent was dated from its application date, so that a disclosure of the invention during the application procedure would no longer invalidate the patent.

Now that specifications describing the invention were required as part of the application procedure and not as an afterthought, more care began to be given to the drafting of the descriptions, and in particular, to pointing out what were considered the new and important parts of the invention. As more and more patents were granted it became necessary to clarify what the patentee thought was the crux of his invention, for which he claimed a monopoly, and the practice grew up of doing this by means of a separate part of the specification referred to as the claims. At that time, infringement actions were still heard before a jury, who had to decide on the basis of the specification what was the scope of the monopoly, and the claims served only to point the jury in the right direction.

Claims grew in importance with the reorganization of the courts in 1875, which transferred jurisdiction in patent cases to the Chancery Division of the High Court, and with the Patents Act of 1883, which required specifications to contain at least one claim. Even so, the claim could be of the type 'the . . . substantially as herein described', which in effect abdicated any responsibility for defining the invention and left the question for the court to determine as before. Gradually, however, it became settled law that the patentee set the boundaries of the monopoly by the wording of his claim, and that 'what was not claimed was disclaimed'.

We shall discuss in more detail later (Chapter 15) how claims are drafted and interpreted and what protection is given by various types of claims. At this point all that need be mentioned is that a patent claim may claim a product (for example a machine, a manufactured article, a chemical compound, or a composition comprising a mixture of substances) or a process (which may be a process for manufacturing an article or synthesizing a compound, or may be a method of using a product). The law differs from country to country as regards what types of claims are permissible and what legal effect they have; thus in the United Kingdom a process claim is infringed not only by carrying out the process in the United Kingdom but also by selling in the United Kingdom the direct product of the process, whereas in the USA the claim does not as yet extend to the product of the process. A claim to a product may be a product *per se* claim, which is independent of how the product was obtained, or a product-by-process claim, which covers the product only when made by a specified method.

Further developments made by the Act of 1883 included the provision that a complete specification had to be filed before the patent was granted, the establishment of a Register of Patents, and the possibility for third parties to oppose the grant of a patent, for example on the ground that the invention was not new. At the same time application costs were further reduced, and it became possible to file an application with a provisional specification for the sum of £1. This nominal application fee amazingly enough remained unchanged until 1978, being probably the only example in history of any charge, official or otherwise, remaining stable for 95 years. When the 1977 Act came into force an application could be filed for a fee of £5, which was still cheaper ın real terms than it was in 1883. However, this fee has not had the permanence of its predecessor; by 1985 it had reached £10 and no doubt it will increase further.

The increasing importance and complexity of drafting patent specifications and claims encouraged certain consulting engineers to specialize in this new art, and to set up in business as agents for inventors in the drafting and procuring of patents. In 1882, an Institute of Patent Agents was founded, and in 1888 a Register of Patent Agents was established by the Board of Trade under the control of the Institute, which obtained its Royal Charter in 1891. The profession of Patent Agency in Britain is still controlled by the Chartered Institute, which sets examinations for admittance to the Register of Patent Agents, a necessary condition in order to practise as a patent agent.

Throughout the nineteenth century, patents were granted in the United Kingdom without anything more than a purely formal examination. Only in 1902 was a novelty examination provided for, and not until five years later could the Patent Office actually refuse an application on the ground that the invention was not new. Even then, the search was limited to British patent specifications not more than 50 years old, and only after 1932 were foreign publications considered. Such publications, however, could be considered only if they were shown to be published within the United Kingdom, an approach consistent with the old concept that patents could be granted for bringing into the country an invention already known elsewhere, as well as for making a completely new invention.

In 1919, the British patent system, which up to then had increased gradually in strength (illustrated graphically in Fig. 5), took its first backward step. Up to then patents had been granted as a matter of course for new chemical substances. However, the British chemical industry felt itself technologically inferior to that of Germany, which for some years before the First World War had dominated the dyestuffs market. British industry pressed for the abolition of patent protection for chemicals as such, and limitation of patent protection to that for specific processes for the preparation of chemicals. In this way, British firms hoped to be free to imitate a German dyestuff appearing on the British market so long as they could find an alternative process for its preparation, a task a good deal easier than that of inventing a new and better dyestuff themselves.

This change in the law was duly made in 1919, together with the further weakening of patent protection for pharmaceuticals by allowing compulsory licences to be granted virtually on demand for patents relating to medicine. The first of these retrograde steps was abolished after the Second World War in 1949, the second only in 1977. One small positive development in 1919 was that the term of a patent was increased from 14 to 16 years.

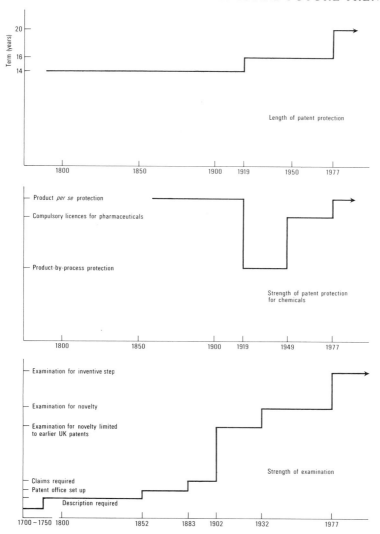

Fig. 5.   The development of the British patent system.

The Patents Act of 1949 was mainly a codification of gradual changes in the law which had been brought about by the courts, and apart from the restoration of protection for chemical substances *per se*, contained little which was really new. For the first time all the grounds on which a patent could be declared invalid by the Patent Office or (a wider set of grounds) by the court were set out in full, and priority dates of claims were defined.

The priority date of a claim was essentially the date on which the subject matter of the claim was first disclosed to the British Patent Office or to a foreign patent office in an application from which priority was properly claimed. No publication of this subject matter could affect the validity of the claim so long as it took place later than the priority date of that claim.

The Patents Act 1949 will be with us for some time yet, since although the new Patents Act 1977 came into force on 1 June 1978, the old Act will continue to apply, with some modifications, to all patents applied for before that date, some of which may remain in force until 1998.

The Patents Act 1977 has introduced major changes to British patent law, but as these are closely related to international developments it cannot be considered in isolation. We shall come back to these new developments after looking briefly at the history of the patent system of some other major countries.

USA: 1790–1980

The constitutional provisions on the protection of inventions first took form in the Patent Act of 1790. This established a very strict examination system under which all patent applications had to be scrutinized by a committee of three cabinet ministers, consisting of the Secretary of State, the Secretary of War, and the Attorney General, at least two of whom had to be present. Incidentally, the first US patent, bearing the signature of George Washington, was for a chemical invention relating to the manufacture of pearl ash (potassium carbonate).

At that time Thomas Jefferson was Secretary of State. Himself an inventor, he took a keen personal interest in the examination and granting of patents, and, with the possible exception of Albert Einstein (who was once an examiner in the Swiss patent office), must surely be the most distinguished patent examiner in history.

It took only three years for the complete impracticality of this system to become clear. Cabinet ministers tended even then to have more important duties than to examine patent applications, and when only 55 patents had been granted in three years, the USA moved to the other extreme of a pure registration system. The Act of 1793 allowed the grant of a patent upon request without any examination, even after the Patent Office was set up in 1802. The confusion caused by the grant of a great many overlapping patents led to a Congressional report by Senator Ruggles on the basis of which a systematic examination system was introduced in 1836 under the direction of a Commissioner of Patents. This system, set up at the time when the Dickensian ritual described earlier was the only way of getting a patent in England, is still the basis of US patent law today.

The 1836 Act retained the original patent term of 14 years, but enabled extensions of 7 years to be obtained. A register of patents was established, and an appeals procedure was set up. The applicant was required to supply a model of his device, and these models were on display at the patent office. This general requirement to supply models was not abolished until 1880, and although many thousands of models were destroyed by fire or otherwise lost, many are now in museums or private collections, and give a fascinating insight into patenting activities in the mid-nineteenth century (see, for example, Fig. 6).

Various amending Acts were passed in the years after 1836, which were consolidated in the Act of 1870. Among these was the extension of the patent term to 17 years (1861). By the Act of 1870, the Commissioner was given power to issue regulations for the administration of the patent law.

The development of US patent law has been strongly influenced by decisions of the courts, particularly of the US Supreme Court. As an example of this we may consider the difficult question of how much invention is needed to support a patent. It is clearly wrong that patents should be granted for improvements so minor that any competent mechanic or chemist could make them as a matter of course, for this would restrict all the normal day-to-day work of the workshop or laboratory. On the other hand, it is also wrong that patents should be granted only for outstanding inventions which revolutionize society. Many inventions are ingenious and at least potentially useful without being world-shattering, and one great merit of the patent system is that the value of the patent grant is left to be determined by market forces. It is not as if the state, in granting a patent, guarantees to the patentee that he will profit by it; by and large a patent for a poor invention will not be very valuable.

The extreme position that only outstanding inventions should be patentable was nevertheless adopted by the Supreme Court in the case of *Cuno Engineering Corp.* v. *Automatic Devices Corp.* (1941),[1] in which Justice Douglas condemned the grant of patents for 'gadgets' as being contrary to the constitutional requirement that the grant of patents should 'promote science' and thus 'push back the frontiers of knowledge', clearly forgetting that the constitution also spoke of promoting 'the useful arts'. After this and similar cases,[2] a very high standard of inventiveness was set by the courts for US patents. A patent could not be granted unless there was 'invention' and there was no 'invention' if there was not a 'flash of genius'.

The amendment of the US patent law made in 1952 – which with relatively minor changes is still the law today – attempted to reverse this trend by shifting discussion from the word 'invention' to the word 'obvious'. Under the new law, an invention not only must be new but also must not be obvious over the 'prior art' (a term used for all earlier

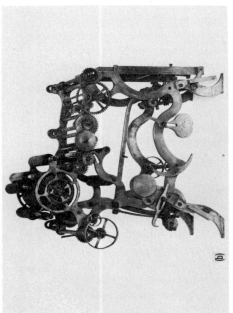

Fig. 6. Early United States patent models; (a) for a hat conformator (1868; patent no. 75 760); (b) for a wool drawer and spinner (1869; patent no. 95 580); (c) for a cesspool cleaner (1873; patent no. 142 840); and (d) for a potato bug remover (1880; patent no. 225 870). All photographs courtesy of the Hagley Museum, Greenville, Wilmington, Delaware.

publications or knowledge which can be cited against a later patent application). To some judges the concept of an 'obvious invention' appeared to be a contradiction in terms, but the change in the law did eventually lead to the replacement of a purely subjective criterion of invention (did the inventor have a flash of inspiration, or was it routine work?) by a more objective and less stringent criterion (would the inventive step have been obvious to an average skilled workman or chemist in possession of all the prior art?).

The last five years have seen a range of far-reaching changes in US patent law which are discussed in detail in later chapters. At the end of 1980 an Act was passed which for the first time introduced renewal fees as a condition for the maintenance in force of US patents. It also made it possible for the patentee or another party to request re-examination of a granted US patent on the basis of prior art which had not been considered during prosecution. Other provisions dealt with the ownership of rights in inventions made with the help of US government funding.

In 1982 the US Federal Courts were re-organized by the creation of a new Court of Appeal for the Federal Circuit (CAFC) which took over the functions of the Court of Customs and Patent Appeals and some of the functions of the Court of Claims and, more importantly, assumed the jurisdiction previously held by separate Circuit Courts of Appeal to hear appeals on patent matters from the Federal District Courts.

In October 1984 a number of bills to amend the US patent law would have lapsed had Congress dissolved when it should have done. However, an impasse on other matters kept Congress in session for another week, and most of the proposals were passed into law. Among the changes were a relaxation of the strict rules on joint inventorship, the formation of a new Board of Appeals and Interferences, and provision for 'Statutory Invention Registrations', a type of defensive patent which would constitute prior art against later patent applications, but give no monopoly rights.

More important than any of these was the Waxman/Hatch Act, which provided for extensions of patent term for drugs whose commercialization had been delayed by regulatory procedures (in the Food and Drug Administration) and at the same time made registration easier for competitors when patent protection expired and provided that testing for regulatory approval involving a patented drug did not amount to patent infringement.

Continental Europe

In the Middle Ages there were infrequent grants of patent monopolies in France, of the same general type as those in England at that time. However, the system gradually fell into disuse, and it was not until after the revolution, in 1791, that a regular patent system was introduced. For many years, France has had a patent system in which only formal examination has been carried out. Since 1969 the French Patent Office has carried out novelty searches on patent applications, and for some years it was up to the applicant to decide whether he wished to amend or withdraw his application as a result of the search. Only recently has the patent office had the power to refuse the application if the search shows the invention to be old.

Prior to the unification of Germany in 1871 there were 29 different patent laws in the various independent German states. Some historians consider that the origins of the patent laws in the German states go back at least as far as in England and Venice, but that the disruption caused by the Thirty Years' War destroyed practically all traces of the early German patent system. The first unitary patent law was passed in 1877, largely as a result of representations made by the industrialist and inventor Siemens. There are now, of course, two German laws, those of the Federal Republic of Germany and the German Democratic Republic (DDR). An important development in German† patent law was the introduction of a standard system for the remuneration of employee-inventors (1957). Protection for chemical substances *per se* was first introduced in Germany in 1968.

The Netherlands is an interesting case, as the patent law introduced in 1817 was repealed in 1869 and no patents were granted from then until 1912, when the patent system was reintroduced. Similarly in Italy no patents were granted for pharmaceutical inventions from 1939 to 1978 (see p. 45).

International developments

The Paris Convention
The International Convention for the Protection of Industrial Property was signed in Paris in 1883, originally by eleven countries. The United Kingdom acceded in 1884. The Convention is now adhered to by the majority of the countries of the world which have any form of patent protection, and, since the Convention also deals with trade marks and designs, even by some countries which have no patents. The basis of the Paris Convention is one of reciprocal rights, so that an applicant or patentee from one Convention country shall have the same rights in a second Convention country as a national of that second country has.

† In this work when the word 'German' is used without qualification, the Federal Republic of Germany is referred to.

The most important practical result of the Convention is the possibility of claiming Convention priority for applications made outside one's home country. The system is such that if an application for a patent is properly made in one Convention country, corresponding applications may be filed in other Convention countries within one year from the first filing date, and if certain conditions are met, these later applications will be entitled to the priority date of the first application. This means that they will be treated as if they were filed on the same day as the first application, so that a publication of the invention after the first filing date but before the filing date of the later application will not invalidate the later filing.

For example, suppose that XYZ Ltd files a patent application for a new compound A in the United Kingdom on 1 June 1980. At any time before 1 June 1981 they may file corresponding applications in France, Germany, Japan, USA, and as many other Convention countries as they choose, claiming priority from the British application. If in the meantime compound A is published by another company (or, which is more likely, by themselves), this publication will not affect the validity of their patent rights. On the other hand, if before 1 June 1981 XYZ Ltd decide that they have no real interest in selling compound A, they can save themselves the trouble and expense of filing in other countries. If it were not for the Convention, a decision whether or not to file in, say, ten countries would have to be taken at the time of first filing, and a great deal of money and effort would be wasted on protecting inventions which within a few months turned out to be old or commercially uninteresting.

The 12-month term for Convention priority must, however, be rigidly kept. If the period is exceeded even by one day, priority will be lost and any intervening publication of the invention will invalidate the foreign application. (The only exception to this is that when the Convention year ends on a Saturday, Sunday or public holiday the application may in most countries be filed on the next working day.)

The later (Convention) application need not be an exact equivalent of the original (priority) application; thus our XYZ Ltd could expand the scope of their foreign applications to cover the related compound B, but as a general rule claims to B would not be entitled to the priority date of the British application which disclosed only A. It is noteworthy that both the British and US patent systems have for some time allowed a form of 'internal priority' by which a later patent application could take the date of an earlier application in the same country. In the United Kingdom under the old patent law this was done by filing an application with a provisional specification, followed by a complete specification up to 12 months later, extensible to 15 months on paying an extra fee. Claims 'fairly based' on the provisional specification were entitled to its filing date; new matter took the date of filing the complete specification. A similar system still applies under the 1977 Act, although there are now two separate applications instead of a single application with two specifications, and no extension of the 12 month period is possible.

In the USA, a 'continuation-in-part' (c.i.p.) application may be filed containing the same description as an earlier application, together with new matter. A c.i.p. may be filed at any time before the earlier application is granted, but there are complex rules which could lead to claims based on the new matter being invalid if filing has been left too late. In Germany also it is now possible to claim priority from an earlier German applicaton filed within the previous 12 months.

All of these systems allow improvements to be incorporated in a patent application within a certain time, and are much to be preferred to a system in which one is held to the original form of one's first filing. In many countries, where there is no such internal priority, a resident applicant may end up with worse protection in his home country than in all others, in which the Paris Convention has allowed him the opportunity to enlarge upon his original disclosure.

The European Patent Convention and the Community Patent Convention

In 1963 a number of European countries signed the Strasbourg Convention, which recommended certain common standards for novelty, inventiveness, and the type of invention which may be patented. This later formed the basis for the European Patent Convention (EPC) of 1973, which has led to the establishment of the European Patent Office (EPO).

The European Patent Convention was originally negotiated by 19 countries and, as of 1985, has been ratified by ten. These are the countries of the European Economic Community (EEC) except Denmark, Ireland, and Greece, together with Austria, Sweden, and Switzerland. It is expected that Spain and Greece will accede by July 1986, and Portugal at a later date. It provides for the grant of patents in any or all of the contracting states by means of a single patent application examined by the European Patent Office in Munich. We shall examine in a later chapter how the EPC works, but the main point to bear in mind is that the European patent is not a single unitary patent but is more like a bundle of national patents in each of the countries which the patentee has chosen. As these national patents are subject to the national laws as regards validity and infringement, it is obviously desirable for the contracting states of the EPC to make their national patent laws conform more or less to a common standard.

By the time the European Patent Office opened its doors to applications on 1 June 1978, most of the contracting states had already changed their laws to the extent necessary to provide standard grounds for invalidity (according to the Strasbourg Convention as adopted by the EPC), a 20-year patent term and product *per se* protection for all chemical substances, including pharmaceuticals. In the United Kingdom, the change was made by the Patents Act 1977, which also came into force on 1 June 1978. Among other changes, this Act lengthened the term of patents from 16 to 20 years adopted the simplified grounds for invalidity as in the EPC, defined precisely what constitutes infringement, strengthened the examination procedure of the British Patent Office by allowing examiners to raise objections of obviousness, and introduced provisions for compensation to employee inventors in some circumstances.

The general effect of the EPC upon the patent systems of Western Europe has therefore been a trend towards longer and stronger patent protection. Even countries which have not at the time of writing ratified the EPC have made their national laws conform with it at least to some extent. Norway and Finland, for example, are adopting a 20-year patent term, although they still exclude pharmaceutical substances from compound *per se* protection, and Denmark has introduced *per se* protection for pharmaceuticals.

This tendency will be reinforced if the Community Patent Covention (CPC) comes into force as planned. According to the CPC, a unitary Common Market patent will be granted by the European Patent Office on any allowable European application which designates at least one EEC country. The Convention provides that although questions of infringement of a Community patent will be dealt with by national courts of the member states, its validity can be challenged only by an application for revocation at a special division of the European Patent Office. However, it is now proposed that national courts should be able to deal with questions both of infringement and of validity, but that their decisions on validity should be appealable to a new Community Patents Appeal Court (COPAC), which could be set up as a special chamber of the European Court of Justice, or as an independent body.

As the Convention now stands, it cannot enter into force until ratified by all EEC member states, and proposals to change this so that it could be implemented by a majority of member states came to nothing. Problems exist for Ireland and Denmark, who have constitutional difficulties, and for the new member states Greece, Spain, and Portugal, who must first upgrade their presently weak patent systems to European levels. Spain and Portugal have concrete plans to do so, and it is a condition of their admission to the EEC that they ratify the CPC no later than 1992. Somehow or other, Greece managed to avoid any such conditions upon its entry, but may nevertheless ratify.

The Patent Co-operation Treaty

A further recent development in international patenting is the Patent Co-operation Treaty (PCT) which entered into force in January 1978 and by

1985 had been ratified by over 39 countries including all ten EPC states, USA, Japan, and the USSR. The PCT, which like the Paris Convention, is administered by the World Intellectual Property Organization (WIPO), does not set out to erect a supranational patent office, nor to grant a 'world patent', but rather attempts to simplify the process of filing patent applications simultaneously in a number of countries. The old procedure, which can of course still be used, requires a completely separate application in each country, which has to be translated into the local language before filing. Under the PCT, a single application may be filed in one of the official receiving offices, designating any number of PCT contracting states. This international application may claim priority from an earlier national application if filed within the normal 12-month period of the Paris Convention.

The application is passed to an International Searching Authority, which carries out a novelty search on the invention, and the application is published, together with the search report, 18 months after the priority date. The application then has two further months in which to prepare all necessary translations, and within 20 months from the priority date the application is delivered to the national patent offices of the designated states and treated from then on as a national application in each country. As a second phase, a preliminary examination on patentability, novelty, and non-obviousness may be carried out by a Preliminary Examining Authority and the results sent with the application to the national patent offices within 30 months from the priority date.

From the point of view of the applicant the chief advantage of the PCT is that although the list of designated countries must be filed on application, and a relatively small designation fee paid for each country, the major expense of national fees and translations is not incurred until nearly a year later, after the search report has been received, and the applicant has had more time to think about the commercial value of the invention. At this point some or all of the designated countries can be dropped, and no large amount of money will have been wasted. The PCT procedure is particularly useful when a decision to file in foreign countries cannot be taken until a short time before the end of the priority year, so that there would be insufficient time under the normal procedure to prepare the necessary translations. However, it costs more than the normal route, and until recently its procedures were complex and inflexible and it could not be used for filing in all countries of interest to most applicants. It therefore tended to be used by many applicants as an emergency procedure rather than as a matter of routine. However, the situation has improved recently as procedural matters have been simplified, and with the accession of Italy it is now possible to include all countries of the European Patent Convention.

The PCT is being used primarily by American applicants to file in Europe and Japan. Out of approximately 5700 PCT applications filed in 1984, 39 per cent came from US applicants. Applications in English predominate (61 per cent), followed by German (13 per cent), Japanese (11 per cent) and French (7 per cent).

Future trends

As we have seen, the effect of the EPC upon Western European countries has been to raise their patent system towards a norm of 20-year protection for all chemical substances including pharmaceuticals: The same tendency exists in other industrialized countries; thus Japan made these changes in its Patent Law of 1976, and South Africa recently extended the term of new patents to 20 years.

Although the USA has for many years had a very strong patent system, a disturbing feature of US patent law has been the eagerness of some US courts to hold patents invalid if at all possible. Recent developments in the USA, including changes in practice introduced by the US Patent and Trademark Office on its own authority as well as the new legislative changes, are aimed at strengthening examination procedures so that granted patents will have a higher 'presumption of validity', that is, will be more likely to be held valid. At the same time recent Supreme Court decisions have also tended to be more favourable to the patentee.

The general trend in all industrialized free-market countries is therefore a strengthening of patent protection. However, the opposite is true for the developing countries, where, for reasons which we shall go into in Chapter 24, patent protection is being generally weakened, particularly for chemical and pharmaceutical inventions. Thus within the last fifteen years, important developing countries such as India, Brazil, and Mexico have either abolished patent protection entirely for pharmaceuticals or have weakened it by one means or another to the point where it is practically nonexistent. Furthermore, international organizations such as UNCTAD (United Nations Conference on Trade and Development) are exerting considerable pressure in the same direction.

The third major group of countries, the industrialized socialist countries of the COMECON (Council for Mutual Economic Assistance) group, have patent systems of moderate strength, largely based upon what was the norm in countries such as Germany some fifty years ago. In addition, many socialist countries have a system of 'inventor's certificates' which provide incentives for inventions made by their own nationals, but leave the right of exploitation to the state. In these countries, the present trend is confused, with a disturbing tendency towards stricter patent prosecution resulting in patents too narrow in scope to be of much value.

One of the most interesting developments in the last five years has been the adoption of a patent law by the People's Republic of China, which previously had no patent system whatsoever. It is particularly noteworthy that the Chinese authorities did not approach the problem of setting up a wholly new patent system in an ideological manner, but on a very practical basis. They invested a great deal of effort in visiting other countries to study how their patent systems worked and in training of future patent office examiners. The system which they decided upon has many positive features although it has the major weakness that it offers only process protection for chemical substances (see p. 44). It remains to be seen how well it will work in practice.

A further trend in recent years has been the decline in importance of national patent offices in European countries because of the attractive alternative offered by the European Patent Office. In countries such as Holland where national applications are expensive and examination is strict, the number of applications filed is down to a third of what it was a few years ago, and the continued viability of the Dutch patent office is in question.

Looking forward to the year 2000, we may expect to see a unified patent system for Western Europe, comprimising the EEC unitary patent together with, in non-EEC countries, national patents conforming with the EPC. There may well no longer be any national patents in at least some European countries. The PCT may become the standard method for foreign filing patent applications, and it is even possible that the USA may change some of the basic points which presently set its patent system apart from those of most other countries.

The Eastern European countries may develop further their own version of the European patent, so that protection in all COMECON countries could be obtained in a single application by western applicants as well as by their own nationals (see p. 301).

The developing countries of the Third World may abandon the traditional form of patent protection completely, but may find alternatives which suit their needs without destroying the basis for co-operation with industralized countries. Finally, China may have developed its patent system in the direction of stronger protection, emulating Japan and Korea rather than India and Mexico.

The future of the patent system depends not only on the attitudes of governments, but also on its continued relevance to new technological developments. The two most important new areas of technology are those of electronic data processing and biotechnology, and it is a fact that patents are not appropriate for the protection of computer software and that their usefulness for the protection of biotechnological inventions is questioned in some quarters. In the former case new forms of protection are being developed, such as the Semiconductor Chip Protection Act of 1984 in the USA. In the latter case the patent system must overcome certain difficulties if it is to be useful (see Chapters 11 and 12).

Meanwhile, in the more traditional industries the high cost of subjecting patent applications to a full examination procedure has led to proposals such as those in the British Government's Green Paper on the patent system ('Intellectual Property Rights and Innovation' Cmnd 9117 HMSO Dec. 1983) to the effect that an alternative system of Registered Inventions or 'Petty Patents' should be set up. Such petty patents would be cheap, have a shorter life than normal patents, and would be granted without examination, but could be enforced only after examination. Similar proposals have been made in Switzerland and in other countries.

The 1983 Green Paper was followed in April 1986 by a White Paper ('Intellectual Property and Innovation', Cmnd. 9712) containing some definite proposals for legislation to be introduced as soon as possible. In the White Paper the idea of a Registered Invention system was turned down, as it was thought that an examined (and thus enforceable) registered invention would have to cost as much or more as a normal patent. The Government felt that it was not the cost of obtaining British patents, but that of enforcing them, which was the real problem, and to make patent litigation cheaper, it proposed that most infringement actions would in future be heard by the Patent Office rather than by the courts (see p. 105).

It remains to be seen whether this far-reaching proposal will become law (many lawyers will not like it, and there are many lawyers in Parliament), and if so, how well it will work in practice. At any rate it represents a bold move to try to make the British patent system represent better value for money. The Government has recognized that the continued existence of the patent system depends ultimately on its continued acceptance by its users. They pay for it, and will continue to pay only so long as it is felt to be useful to them. Having a patent which one cannot afford to enforce is of little use to anybody.

WHAT CAN BE PATENTED

Is there any thing whereof it may be said, See, this is new? it hath been already of old time, which was before us.

Eccles, i.10

In this chapter we shall consider what kinds of invention are patentable. The question of how an invention which basically is patentable can be protected by a valid patent, which meets conditions such as sufficiency of description, is dealt with in Chapters 8 and 15.

The requirements of the European Patent Convention

There are three simple requirements for a patentable invention as set out in the European Patent Convention and in the laws of those countries which have acceded to it; as for example in the British Patents Act 1977. These are that the invention must be new; that it must involve an inventive step; and that it must be capable of industrial application. The same three requirements are met with in one form or another in the USA, Japan, and indeed in practically every country which has a patent system at all. There are in addition certain matters which are specifically excluded from patent protection both in the EPC and in the Patents Act 1977, but these exclusions are not necessarily to be found in the laws of other countries outside the EPC, while many other countries have more extensive ranges of subjects which are barred from patent protection.

Novelty

The first and clearest requirement is that nothing can be patentable which is not new. If a patent were to be granted for something already known, then, on the classical theory of patent protection in exchange for disclosure, the patentee would be receiving something for nothing: there would be no consideration for the grant. Quite independently of this theory of the patent system, if the public at large, or even any part of it knew of the information and were free to use it, then the grant of a patent in respect of this information would deprive the public of rights which it previously had. Such a patent monopoly would be unjust for the same reason as Queen Elizabeth I's monopolies on salt and playing cards.

Considering that the concept of novelty is so basic to patentability, it may seem odd that there are several different concepts of novelty which have been applied to inventions. The most straightforward is that of 'absolute novelty' applied by the EPC and by the British Patents Act 1977; that is, that an invention is new if it is not part of the 'state of the art', the state of the art being defined as everything that was available to the public by written or oral publication, use or any other way, in any country in the world, before the priority date of the invention.

Although some countries, for example France, have applied the absolute novelty criterion for many years, the concept is new to British patent law. Under previous Patents Acts, 'local novelty' was the rule, which meant that a prior publication or use had to occur within the United Kingdom in order to damage the novelty of a patent application. This concept goes back to the early days of patents in England, when, as we have seen, patents were frequently granted for inventions which, although known abroad, were brought into the kingdom for the first time by the patentee. Under the 1949 Act, it was still possible to apply for a patent as an inventor by importation; for example, a person in the UK to whom an invention was communicated from abroad had the right to apply for a patent.

Under the old British rule of local novelty, it was fairly well established that it was enough to destroy the novelty of a later patent application if only one person in the UK was in possession of information amounting to a description of the invention and that person was free to do what he liked with the information. This may not be sufficient under the 1977 Act, which may be interpreted by the courts to require a spread of the information wider than to a single person. Be that as it may, it seems clear that a prior publication in, for example, a local newspaper in Lhasa would destroy the novelty of a British patent application even if the publication was never read outside of Tibet; a situation just as anomalous as that under the old law according to which a printed US patent could be an effective publication only from the day on which copies of it or its abstract arrived in the UK.

Some countries also have, or have had, a system intermediate between absolute and local novelty. According to this 'mixed novelty' system, a later patent application is rendered invalid by written publication anywhere in the world but by use of the invention only in the home country; that is, prior use in a foreign country would not invalidate if there was no written description. Under the absolute novelty system which is now the law in the UK, prior use of an invention anywhere in the world would invalidate a British patent application, if that use made the invention available to the public. The situation is clear if the invention is a machine, a gadget, or a simple chemical compound which can readily be analysed and its structure determined. It is not so clear whether the use, or even the widespread sale to the public, of a complex mixture which cannot be precisely analysed will make the invention which it represents 'available to the public'.

A situation which occurs quite frequently in chemical inventions is that in which an earlier publication discloses a broad group of compounds, and the invention is a narrow subgroup of these compounds. So long as no members of the narrow subgroup are *specifically* disclosed in the publication, it is generally considered that the compounds are novel, even though they may have been described in general terms. The narrow subgroup of compounds will, however, only be patentable if it has some unobvious advantage over the other members of the broad class, that is, if there is an inventive step in choosing that particular subgroup from all those generally disclosed. Inventions of this type are referred to as 'selection inventions' and will be discussed in more detail in Chapter 9.

An important question in considering novelty and inventive step is the position of earlier patent applications which were not published at the priority date of a later application. Unpublished patent applications are not available to the public; and on this basis one would expect that they should not be considered as part of the state of the art. On the other hand it has been a principle of patent law from the earliest times that not more than one patent should be granted for the same invention, since if this were not the rule, licensees could be forced to pay twice over the same rights, and the term of patent protection for one invention could be extended beyond the statutory period.

In the old British law, this problem was dealt with by making it a separate ground of invalidity of a patent if the invention claimed had been claimed in a granted British Patent of earlier priority date. This approach was sound in theory, but in practice gave rise to a great deal of uncertainty. The situation often arose where the disclosure in the specification of an earlier application would clearly have been an anticipation if it had been published before the priority date of a later application, but where the invention was claimed in somewhat different terms in the two applications. There were a number of cases in which the courts held that there had to be substantial identity between claims in order for this objection of prior claiming to be established, which greatly reduced the effectiveness of this approach.

Under the EPC and the Patents Act 1977, the so-called 'whole-contents' approach is adopted. Under this system, the whole contents (not only the claims) of an earlier unpublished application are considered. This is brought about by the simple expedient of defining the 'state of the art' to include unpublished patent applications of earlier date. This should greatly simplify the situation, although some uncertainties still remain. Thus whereas under the old British 'prior claiming' law, the application containing the prior claim had to become a granted patent (and a valid one at that) in order to be effective; under the 1977 Act it seems that all that is necessary is for the earlier application to be published at some stage even if it is later withdrawn or refused. It is not very clear what happens if the earlier application is a European or PCT application designating the UK, and is withdrawn after publication. Unpublished European patent applications designating the UK can be prior art against a later British application, and an earlier unpublished British application is prior art against a granted European patent (UK) under British law. In the European Patent Office, however, earlier unpublished national applications are not considered as prior art against European applications.

Japan also has a system in which earlier unpublished Japanese applications are part of the state of the art, but with the difference that earlier unpublished applications of the same applicant are excluded.

Although under the whole-contents approach the earlier unpublished application is considered to be part of the state of the art, this applies only to considerations of pure novelty, and not to the question of whether or not there is an inventive step. The existence of an earlier unpublished application can destroy the novelty of an invention, but cannot be used to argue that the invention is obvious. This possibility means that under the Patents Act 1977, lack of novelty and obviousness must be clearly distinguished from each other. In early reported cases in England this was often not the case, and many patents were found invalid for lack of novelty or 'anticipation' whereas the real reason was lack of an inventive step. Nowadays the term 'anticipation' is normally used to mean lack of novelty, and is considered to occur when a piece of prior art (that is, a publication or use which was part of the state of the art before the priority date of the patent application in question) either is or describes something which would be an infringement of one or more of the claims in the application. That is,the test for anticipation is essentially the same as the test for infringement, and is met in the case of a written publication if the publication clearly describes something having every feature of the claim, or gives instructions to do something which if carried out would give something falling within the scope of the claim. Thus a claim to a chemical compound may be anticipated by a description of a process, if carrying out the process will inevitably give that compound, even if the compound itself was not described.

Inventive step

The concept of novelty should be basically a simple matter, which can be tested rather easily once the claim in question has been 'construed', that is, has been logically analysed to determine its scope. The question of whether or not something for which a patent is applied for involves an inventive step is one that is intrinsically much more difficult, since to some extent judgment of what is or is not obvious must be a subjective matter.

Because the question is such a contentious one, there have been a great many patent cases in which obviousness has been at issue, and a great many judges have tried at various times to define what is meant by 'obviousness', or to pose questions such as 'Is the solution one which would have occurred to everyone of ordinary intelligence and acquaintance with the subject matter who gave his mind to the problem?'[1] or, more bluntly, was it 'so easy that any fool could do it'? Finally, however, it should come down to the simple dictionary definition of obvious, i.e. 'very plain', bearing in mind that the reason for requiring the presence of an inventive step before granting a patent is that the ordinary worker in that field should remain free to apply his normal skills to making variations of known products.

Thus the person to whom the invention must be non-obvious if it is to be patentable is 'the man skilled in the art'; a competent worker but without imagination or inventive capability. In the days when the great majority of patents were for relatively simple mechanical devices it was common to describe the man skilled in the art as an 'ordinary workman'. This is no longer appropriate in view of the increasing technical sophistication of industry. For chemical patents the man skilled in the art may normally be considered as the average qualified industrial chemist, and the question is whether an invention is obvious, or very plain, to such a man – not to a Nobel prize winner.

Among the principles which have been established in the course of the many cases on obviousness are that there is no quantitative restriction on the size of the inventive step; i.e. the invention is patentable if it involves any inventive step, no matter how small. How the invention was made, whether as a result of planned research, a flash of inspiration, or even pure chance, is not relevant to the question of obviousness. An invention may be simple without being obvious, indeed producing a simple solution to what appears to be complex problem is often highly inventive. It is often very easy to reconstruct an invention with the benefit of hindsight, as a series of logical steps from the prior art, but it does not necessarily follow that the invention was obvious, especially if there is evidence that the invention was commercially successful, or supplied a need. The question 'If the invention was obvious, why did no one do it before?' is usually a relevant one to ask.

It is clear that unless there are particular difficulties to be overcome, an 'analogous use' is not patentable. That is, if something is known for one use it generally involves no inventive step to use that thing for a new but similar purpose. An early example was a case in 1890 in which the invention was the use of a form of composite spring, already known for the rear axle of four-wheeled carriages, on the front axle. The House of Lords held the patent invalid.[2] Similarly, the use of a new material to replace existing materials in applications for which its known properties make it suitable will not be patentable; for example, a patent for dart flights made of polyethylene was invalid for obviousness, darts with rubber flights being known.[3]

In considering obviousness, anything in the state of the art, other than unpublished earlier patent applications, may be taken into account. It was not permissible under the old British law to 'mosaic' together a number of different publications, reconstructing the invention by taking a piece from one and another piece from another, unless for example one document directly referred to the other. The practice under the 1977 Act is that documents can be combined together in considering obviousness if a man skilled in the art would naturally consider them in association; thus it may be enough if they simply relate to the same technical field.

Whether a single publication can be disregarded in considering obviousness because it was so obscure that the man skilled in the art would never be aware of it is not clear. Under the old British law the Court of Appeal in *General Tire* v. *Firestone* (1972) gave an *obiter* opinion (i.e. one which was not necessary to decide the point at issue, and which is not binding at a precedent) to the effect that the man skilled in the art had to be thought of as a real person and not as 'a hypothetical person who read and remembered every piece of published literature'. Under the 1977 Act the problem will be more acute, since the state of the art includes publications anywhere in the world, and the remedy may not be so easy to apply, as the wording of the Act seems to leave less room for the approach suggested by the Court of Appeal.

A useful device which used to be part of British patent law but which was unfortunately abolished by the 1977 Act, in line with the EPC, was the so-called patent of addition. A patent of addition could be granted for an improvement or modification of the invention of an earlier patent owned by the same person, and this improvement or modification did not have to be inventive (non-obvious) over the disclosure of the earlier patent. A further advantage was that no renewal fees were payable on a patent of addition, although it had to expire when its parent patent expired.

Patents of addition are still granted by a number of countries, although some, such as Japan, require the same degree of inventiveness as for a normal patent, which makes the whole exercise rather pointless.

Industrial application

The third basic requirement of the European Patent Convention is that the invention should be capable of industrial application, and this requirement is also stated in the British Patents Act 1977. Industrial application is broadly defined, and includes making or using the invention in any kind of industry, including agriculture. Methods of medical treatment or diagnosis performed on the human or animal body are defined as being incapable of industrial application, although substances invented for use in such methods are patentable. (See Chapter 10.)

This concept of 'industrial applicability' of an invention replaces the old and rather vague concept of 'manner of manufacture' which was applied in British patent law before the 1977 Act. In none of the earlier Patents Acts was it stated what constituted an invention; the criterion was one developed by the courts, which asked 'Is the invention a manner of manufacture for which patents could be granted under the Statute of Monopolies?' (see p. 11) In the early years of this century, this approach led judges to adopt a restrictive attitude as to what type of invention could be patentable. The word 'manufacture' had acquired the connotation of the production of something tangible, and many cases arose of patents being denied for inventions which although industrially applicable, did not produce or restore a 'vendible product'. More recently, the courts have recognized that the increasing diversity of technology requires a less rigid approach, and the new definition of 'industrial applicability' coupled with the specific exceptions to patentability discussed below will represent very little change from the practice immediately before the 1977 Act came into force.

Specific exceptions

The European Patent Convention, and the Patents Act 1977, make certain specific exceptions to patentability, which apply whether or not the invention is capable of industrial application. Artistic works and aesthetic creations are not patentable, and are generally not industrially applicable either; but scientific theories and mathematical methods, the presentation of information, business methods, and computer programs are also unpatentable, although they may very well be applied in industry.

Animal and plant varieties are not patentable in countries adhering to the EPC, although there are in the USA special plant patents for plant varieties and in Hungary the normal patent law gives protection for new varieties of both plants and animals. In the United Kingdom and certain other European countries new plant varieties, although not patentable, can be protected by plant breeders' rights akin to copyright.

A further exception to patentability under the 1977 Act is constituted by inventions 'the publication or exploitation of which would be generally expected to encourage offensive, immoral or antisocial behaviour'. It is not clear just what types of invention are intended to be excluded by this provision, but it seems to be somewhat wider than the corresponding provision in the 1949 Act that an application could be refused if the use of the invention would be contrary to law or morality. There are no reported cases on 'immoral' inventions, and although at one time patent applications for contraceptives were routinely refused, this was done by invoking the royal prerogative to grant or refuse patents at will, thereby neatly avoiding any discussion of the matter.

A certain amount of alarm was caused some years ago when it was disclosed in the British press that patents for chemical warfare agents were available to the public in the Patent Office library. Originally applied for by the Ministry of Defence (for what purpose it is hard to imagine) and granted under a secrecy order, these patents had been published years later and gave details enabling any competent chemist to prepare highly lethal nerve gases using readily available chemicals and simple apparatus. The patents were duly withdrawn from the library, but it would seem more appropriate that any patent applications for this type of invention should now be refused on the ground that their publication would encourage antisocial behaviour.

The 1949 Act also provided that a patent application could be refused because it claimed as an invention anything obviously contrary to well-established natural laws, for example a perpetual motion machine. That this provision was not always applied may be seen from British Patent Specification 970 091 (the first page of which is reproduced as Fig. 7) which claims the formation of helium by reaction of aluminium powder with caustic soda and water in a steel vessel. The Patent Office no doubt took the pragmatic view that no one was likely to be much inconvenienced by the existence of such a patent, and presumably this is still the official attitude, as the new Act does not contain any corresponding provision. In the USA, inventors of perpetual motion machines are apparently discouraged by the Patent Office using the power which it still has to require the inventor to produce a model 'to exhibit advantageously' his invention.

The requirements of United States law

The three basic requirements found in the EPC and in British law are present in the US system, although they are expressed somewhat differently. Three consecutive sections (101–103) of the US Patent Law (Title 35, United States Code) deal with patentable inventions, novelty, and obviousness.

Patentable inventions

These are defined as any new and useful process, machine, manufacture, or composition of matter, or any new and useful improvement thereof. The requirement that the invention be useful is rather stronger than the EPC requirement that it be capable of industrial application, and is more like the old British utility requirement (see p. 115).

Novelty

As we have seen, a US patent is granted to the first to invent and not the first to file, and as a result the novelty requirements in the USA are far more complex than those in systems in which the filing date is crucial. The first requirements are that the applicant must himself have invented the subject matter of the application, and must not have abandoned it at any time. The invention is not novel if before the applicant's invention date, the subject matter was:

(i) invented in the USA by someone else – hence the need for interference proceedings to determine priority of invention in the case of conflicting patent applications;
(ii) described in a US patent application which is subsequently granted;
(iii) known or used by others in the USA or patented or described in a printed publication anywhere in the world – i.e., what we have described earlier in this chapter as 'mixed novelty' requirements.

For all of these criteria the invention date can be established by evidence such as laboratory notebooks for inventions made in the USA, whereas for inventions made in other countries only the US filing date or the date of a convention priority filing can be used.

The matter does not rest there, however, because where the invention date is more than one year before the US filing date there are the additional requirements that the invention must not have been in public use or on sale in the USA, or patented or described in a printed publication anywhere more than one year before the US filing date, and that it must not have been the subject of a patent application made abroad more than one year before the US filing date and granted before the US filing date. The first of these requirements means in effect that a US inventor has a 'grace period' of one year in which he can publish his invention or put it on public sale without prejudicing his subsequent US patent application even though in most other countries such action would invalidate any later patent application. Publication by another less than 12 months prior to the filing date also does not affect the validity of the application, but here it is necessary to show that the date of the publication was not before the date of the invention. Although a foreign applicant cannot establish an invention date other than a US filing date or priority date under the Paris Convention, he is at least assured that his own publication of his invention within 12 months before the US filing date will not invalidate his application: this is because US law takes the sensible approach that you

PATENT SPECIFICATION

NO DRAWINGS

970,091

Date of filing Complete Specification: Sept. 10, 1963.

Application Date: June 19, 1962.　　　No. 23586/62.

Complete Specification Published: Sept. 16, 1964.

© Crown Copyright 1964.

970,091

Index at acceptance:—G6 P1

International Classification:—G 21

COMPLETE SPECIFICATION

Transmutation of Elements

I, NOEL IGNATIUS RAFFERTY, of 120 Evering Road, Stoke Newington, London, N.16, formerly of 62, Florence Road, Archway, London, N.4, of Indian nationality, do hereby
5　declare the invention, for which I pray that a patent may be granted to me, and the method by which it is to be performed, to be particularly described in and by the following statement: —
10　This invention relates to a process for the synthesis of helium and the simultaneous generation of energy.

The present invention provides a process for the synthesis of helium and the simultane-
15　ous generation of energy which comprises admixing in the following order, aluminium in a form presenting a large volume/surface area ratio, sodium hydroxide and water in the presence of air and in a steel pressure-tight
20　vessel, the proportion of the reactants, being 4:8:8.

The actual amounts of the reactants are dependent on the condition of the substances and the composition of the pressure vessel.
25　The basis of the process of the invention is the thermonuclear reaction which takes place within the steel vessel. The thermonuclear reaction is initiated and intensified by the electromagnetic radiation which occurs
30　as a result of the ionisation of the reactants. The electrons liberated during ionisation are available for bombardment of the material within the vessel, which bombardment results in the disintegration of the reactants. As a
35　result of the disintegration of the reactants helium and carbon are formed in the reaction in accordance with Bethe's Theory which is expressed as follows:

$$C^{12} + {}_1H^1 \rightarrow N^{13}$$
$$_7N^{13} \rightarrow {}_6C^{13} + {}_1e^0$$
$$_6C^{13} + {}_1H^1 \rightarrow {}_7N^{14}$$
$$_7N^{14} + {}_1H^1 \rightarrow {}_8O^{15}$$
$$_8O^{15} \rightarrow {}_7N^{15} + {}_1e^0$$
$$_7N^{15} + {}_1H^1 \rightarrow {}_6C^{12} + {}_2He^4$$

40

Once the reaction has started the walls of
45　the reaction vessel increase in temperature and the pressure within the reaction vessel increases.

Gas removed from the vessel is found to be highly combustible and spectrographic
50　analysis shows the presence of N, H, CN, and CO and He. No oxygen is present in the gaseous product. After the reaction is finished carbon and ammonium carbonate are found within the vessel.
55

It is to be emphasised that no external energy, heat or pressure, is applied to initiate or maintain the reaction.

A further feature of the process is that, although the exterior of the reaction vessel
60　becomes hot, a temperature of 200 to 235°C. has been recorded, gas released from the vessel by way of a valve is cold, and pressures of up to 1450 lbs./sq.in. have been recorded. This cannot be explained on the basis of the
65　Joules-Thompson effect since hydrogen, one of the main constituents of the gas mixtures produced does not, as other gases do, cool, when released under pressure through a small orifice. It is to be assumed, therefore, that
70　the interior of the vessel is at a much lower temperature than the exterior.

FIG. 7.　British Patent Specification 970 091.

cannot publish an invention before you have invented it, so that any self-publication may by definition be after the invention date.

Non-obviousness

As we have seen, there has tended to be a very high standard of inventiveness set by US courts, and even though this has been somewhat relaxed, it is still a formidable undertaking to convince the US Patent Office and courts that the average invention is not obvious. One of the greatest difficulties is that, in contrast to British practice, it is permissible in the US to 'mosaic' together a number of prior art documents and, often with a generous measure of hindsight, to piece together the invention as a sequence of logical steps. Another problem is that whereas in the EPC the whole contents of an unpublished application of earlier date can be used to attack novelty but not to allege obviousness, in the USA an earlier-filed application can base both types of attack.

Grace period

The 12-month period granted by US law during which publication of an invention does not invalidate a subsequent filing becomes a two-year term in Canada, which also has a first-to-invent system. As in the USA, such publication must be later than the invention date. Of the first-to-file countries, Japan is one of the few countries which still has a grace period: this has a term of six months, is limited to the applicant's own publications and must be claimed within 30 days of filing. Germany used to have a similar provision, which, however, was abolished in 1980.

Under the 1949 Act, British law also provided a six-month grace period for certain limited types of publication, such as disclosures in the proceedings of a learned society, but under the 1977 Act, these have been restricted to display at certain certified international exhibitions (of which there are very few) and to publications resulting from a breach of confidence.

At the time of writing, it is being proposed in some quarters that a grace period should become a feature of the European patent system. It is felt that the present system is unduly harsh to individual inventors and academic scientists who may publish their results before realizing that they may be commercially interesting. On the other hand the possibility that patent applications could still be validly filed even after an invention had been published would greatly increase the difficulty of estimating whether a manufacturer's proposed action would infringe any other party's patent rights.

Special categories of inventions

Chemical compounds

Although most major countries having industrialized free-market economies now grant patents for chemical compounds *per se*, this has been a relatively recent development in many cases. Countries such as Germany, Japan, the Netherlands, and Switzerland have made this change only in the decade 1968–1978. A great many countries still do not grant patents of this type, and allow only claims to processes for the production of chemical compounds. This is the situation in most East European and Latin American countries, together with some West European countries such as Austria, Spain, and Greece (see Table 1).

How useful process patents are depends chiefly upon two factors; whether or not there is derived product protection (product-by-process protection) and whether or not there is reversal of the onus of proof. To illustrate these concepts, let us suppose we have invented a new chemical compound which is a ketone, and the most commercially feasible way of making it is to produce an intermediate alcohol and then oxidize this to the ketone. In product protection countries we can simply claim the ketone itself; such a claim is infringed by someone else selling the ketone, however he may have made it.

In process countries we should claim the last step of our process: oxidation of the alcohol to the ketone. It does not matter that such oxidations are well known; the process is patentable if the end-product is new, unobvious and useful. Such non-inventive processes are often called analogy processes; in general they are patentable only if the end-product is novel and unobvious. In a country in which there is product-by-process protection, sale of the ketone will infringe the patent if it is has been produced by oxidation of the alcohol, and this will generally be true even if the ketone has been imported from abroad. The difficulty here is that we are usually not in a position to prove that the imported ketone has been manufactured by our process – unless perhaps careful analysis can detect traces of the intermediate alcohol in the final product. This is where reversal of the onus of proof is extremely valuable. Normally in a patent infringement action the onus is on the patentee to prove to the court that his patent has been infringed. Reversal of the onus of proof means that where the compound is new the court will assume that it has been produced by the patented process unless the person accused of infringement can prove otherwise.

We can therefore distinguish three groups of process countries in decreasing order of patent strength:

  (i) product by process with reversal of onus;
 (ii) product by process without reversal of onus;
(iii) process only.

Examples are listed in section C of Table 1.

In the third group, the patent is not infringed by sale of imported product even if made by the patented process, but only by actually carrying out the claimed process within the country.

In any case, no matter how strong the process patent may be, it will normally cover only one method of making the compounds in question, and cannot be used to stop anyone from making the compounds by a completely different method. This may not be a serious problem for certain

Table 1 *Protection for chemical and pharmaceutical inventions*

A Examples of countries having product *per se* protection for all chemicals, including pharmaceuticals:

Australia	Israel	Singapore
Belgium	Italy	South Africa
Denmark	Japan	Sweden
France	Netherlands	Switzerland
Germany	New Zealand	UK
Hong Kong	Nigeria	USA
Ireland	Philippines	

B Examples of countries having product *per se* protection for chemicals other than pharmaceuticals:

Argentina	Finland	Norway
Canada	Ghana	Peru
	Greece	Turkey

C Examples of countries having process protection for chemicals
(i) product by process protection with reversal of onus of proof

Austria	DDR	Hungary

(ii) product by process protection without reversal of onus of proof

Brazil†	Nicaragua	Spain‡
Chile	Pakistan	Taiwan
Guatemala	Portugal‡	

(iii) process only protection

China (P.R.)	Mexico	Venezuela
Czechoslovakia	Rumania	
India	USSR	

D Examples of countries having no protection whatsoever for pharmaceutical inventions

Brazil	Ghana	Turkey

E Examples of countries having no patent protection for any inventions

Indonesia	Saudi Arabia

---

†Not for pharmaceuticals. ‡Reversal of onus to be introduced in stages.

types of compounds for which there is only one commercially feasible manufacturing process (for example, diazo coupling for azo dyestuffs), but for most classes of compound there will be many different synthetic routes available. If the inventor can think of ten different processes, then to cover all of these would, in most process protection countries, require ten separate patents – and then someone else will come along with an eleventh. For this reason complete protection is seldom possible in a country which does not grant product *per se* protection.

Pharmaceuticals (see Chapter 10)

Special rules apply in many countries where the invention is a new chemical compound which is useful as a pharmaceutical. An understandable concern for public health has often led to the conclusion that patents for medicines are contrary to public policy and that medicines would be cheaper and more readily available if they could not be patented. As we shall see, such evidence as there is tends to the opposite conclusion, and the trend in the patent laws of developed countries is to treat pharmaceuticals no differently from other compounds.

Where pharmaceuticals are singled out for special treatment this may take a number of different forms. One approach is that some countries which normally have product *per se* protection allow only product-by-process protection for pharmaceuticals. Such is the situation for example in Canada, Norway, and Finland. At the other extreme, some countries have no protection whatsoever for pharmaceutical inventions; for example Turkey, Brazil, and, until recently, Italy.

For many years Italy had a law prohibiting patent protection for pharmaceuticals, which made the country a haven for small pharmaceutical companies whose products imitated those of research-based companies which were still patented elsewhere. In 1978, as Italy was debating how best it could change this law in order to be able to ratify the EPC (for which at least process protection for pharmaceuticals would be necessary), a surprise decision of the Constitutional Court held that the old law was unconstitutional because it discriminated unfairly against inventors in the pharmaceutical field. Thus whereas most people had expected a lengthy transition period of process protection for pharmaceuticals in Italy, the country went in one step from no protection at all to full product *per se* protection, together with protection for a new pharmaceutical use of a known compound (see p. 146).

A large number of countries which allow product-by-process or process-only protection for pharmaceuticals have further special provisions such as shorter terms for pharmaceutical patents or compulsory licences. Until the 1977 Act came into force in Britain, compulsory licences could be granted at any time on pharmaceutical patents. However, the more recent licences which were granted had the royalty set by the courts at high levels which took into account the patentee's investment in research. More to the liking of the imitator are the provisions in Canada, where the royalty rate for compulsory licences is fixed at a maximum 4 per cent of net sales price of the finished product. In India, compulsory licences for pharmaceuticals are at a royalty rate of no more than 4 per cent of the ex-factory bulk price of the compound, which is practically nothing. There are, of course, nowadays very few pharmaceutical patents in India, for the obvious reason that they are not worth the trouble of obtaining.

In most of the countries with special provisions for pharmaceuticals, the same rules apply to foodstuffs, agrochemicals, and in some cases even to insecticides and to intermediates for any of these.

Microbiological inventions (see Chapter 11)

Microbiological inventions which involve the use of a new strain of micro-organism, whether this is found in nature, selected from organisms produced by artificially induced random mutation, or transformed by recombinant DNA technology, present special problems. This is because, for reasons which we shall discuss in a later chapter, the requirements of a full and sufficient disclosure of the invention are interpreted by most countries to mean that the new strain must be deposited in a recognized culture collection and made available to the public. From the point of view of the inventor, this loss of control of his strain may outweigh the advantages of obtaining patent protection in certain cases.

Inventions ahead of their time

An invention, to be patentable, must be ahead of the state of the art. But paradoxically, if it is too far ahead of its time it will generally be unpatentable. This is because the invention has to be capable of being put into effect on the basis of the description in the specification. If the technology to do this is not yet available, the description cannot be sufficient and the patent will not be valid.

An example of this is given by Valensi's patent for a colour television system—the same one which had been extended in term to a total of 32½ years, more than double the normal life of a British patent at that time. Originally filed in 1939, when black-and-white television was in its infancy, the application claimed a colour system based on the separation of luminance and colour signals. This concept was subsequently used in the PAL system, and in 1970 Mr Valensi brought suit against a number of colour TV manufacturers. In the High Court the patent was found valid and infringed, but the Court of Appeal, assisted by the Chief Engineer of the BBC as scientific adviser, held that the patent was invalid – essentially because the reader in 1939 would not have been able to make a workable system based on its disclosure.[5]

As a further example of this type of invention, the science-fiction writer Arthur C. Clarke published in 1945 an article in *Wireless World* describing the use of geostationary earth satellites for communications purposes – this long before the first earth satellite had been launched. Mr Clarke did not apply for a patent for his invention; but had he done so and subsequently tried to sue NASA he would have had little chance of success. At the date of his invention the technology required to put it into effect did not exist, and such inventions are just too inventive to be patentable!

4

FILING A PATENT APPLICATION

I made nothing of my inventions. By degrees, I had the mortification of
seeing others arrive at the discovery which I had made years before. They
contrived to turn it into gold and fame.

Fr. Rolfe: Hadrian VII

Should an application be filed?

When an invention has once been made, a decision must be taken whether
or not a patent application should be filed, and if so, when. A necessary
first step, of course, is that the inventor or his employer realizes that an
invention has been made at all. Very often, work which is done in
university laboratories or in the production or customer service department of
industrial companies may give rise to patentable inventions which are not
recognized as such. In the former case, the academic inventors may not be
aware of possible commercial applications of their work, in the latter, the
inventors may think that only what comes out of the research department
can be an invention. In such cases, it frequently happens that by the time
attention has been drawn to the possibility of patent protection for the
invention publication has already taken place either in the form of a paper
in a scientific journal or by sale of a product or disclosure of a process to a
customer.

Assuming, however, that a piece of work is recognized as being
potentially patentable and that no publication has occurred, should a
patent application be filed, and when? Since a first patent application in
one's own country is inexpensive, and since in most countries priority in
case of conflict goes to the first applicant (not in the USA; see below), it
would seem that the answers are quite clear: yes, and at once.

Some qualification is nevertheless required. It may be clear from the
outset that patent protection is not needed. Thus it could be that all that is
wanted is freedom to use the new development oneself, rather than any
possibility of excluding others. In such a case, a rapid publication of the
results will meet the case, since once a publication has occurred, in most
countries no one else will be able to obtain a patent. Alternatively the
invention may be of a kind such that infringement would be very difficult to
detect and a patent would therefore be almost impossible to enforce, but
would merely give away useful information. In such instances it may be
preferable to keep the invention as secret know-how. Furthermore, the

invention may be so close to the prior art or of such doubtful inventiveness that a preliminary evaluation will lead to a decision that even the small effort and outlay of filing a priority application would not be justified.

As a general rule, however, if an invention appears patentable and may be of some commercial interest, a priority application should be filed. One then has one year provided by the Paris Convention before significant amounts of time and money must be invested in filing in other countries. In this time the invention can be further evaluated and considered, and if it is decided not to proceed further, the application can simply be dropped. No publication of the invention occurs, and nothing has been lost except the small cost of filing the first application. If, however, the decision is made to file in other countries, or even to proceed to obtain a patent in the home country, the first filing gives a priority date which can be relied upon later. When in doubt, file an application!

When to file

The second question is when. We have already given the answer 'at once', but this too needs qualification. Whereas it may be possible in the case of a simple invention for the inventor to explain it to a patent agent one day, the patent agent to draft an application the next, and the application to be on file at the Patent Office on the day following, this sort of urgency is seldom practicable and usually undesirable. What the inventor has invented can usually be described as one or more embodiments of the invention – for example a particular device in the case of a mechanical invention, or, in the chemical context, a small group of new chemical compounds which may have pharmaceutical properties, a new detergent formulation, or a way of getting improved yield from a chemical process by control of temperature and pressure.

It is the first task of the person drafting the patent application to define what is the invention as distinct from the embodiment of it which has been produced so far. Judgment must be used to decide how broadly the invention can be claimed, and this is important even at this early stage. It would be easy merely to write a description of the particular compounds, formulations, and reaction conditions which the inventor has made or tried, but such a description could probably not serve as basis for claims broad enough to give adequate protection. To take the example of the detergent formulation; the inventor may have tried combinations of four ingredients A, B, C, and D and have varied the proportions of the main component A between 50 per cent and 70 per cent with success, while leaving the relative proportions of B, C, and D in the remaining 50–30 per cent unaltered. The patent agent would in addition wish to know whether all four components are essential, whether additional ingredients could be added, within what ranges each component could be varied, and whether each component could be defined as a class of compounds or only as a single compound.

The inventor may be able to answer some of these questions from experience, or at least be able to give an educated guess without further experiment, but in many cases some further experimental work will be necessary before a clear picture of the invention emerges.

It is also very desirable to establish at the time of first filing not only the outer limits of the invention, but also what are the preferred narrower limits to which the application can fall back if the broader scope turns out to be indefensible. It is important for the draftsman to have an idea of the prior art in the field of the invention and to draft his text accordingly, but because he must always bear in mind that closer prior art may be found after filing, he will usually draft the specification broadly and give himself basis to restrict later if need be.

Consideration of all these matters takes time and carrying out of additional experimental work takes even more. A balance must be struck in each case between the conflicting requirements of having enough information to draft a good text, and filing as early as possible to obtain the earliest priority date. A lot depends upon the extent to which competitors are known to be active in the same area; there are many cases in which a single day's advantage in priority date has made all the difference in cases of concurrent invention. While it is impossible to give a firm rule for all cases, as a general guideline 1–2 months between invention and filing may be realistic. In a field where more urgency is desirable, a subsequent application can be filed when more facts are known, and the two combined later (see p. 53).

Inventions made in the USA

It has already been mentioned that the USA does not give priority to the first applicant, but to the first to invent in the USA, and that interference proceedings are set up by the Patent Office to determine priority of inventorship in cases of conflicting applications. Furthermore, publication of the invention before the filing date is not fatal to a US patent application, so long as the publication was not made more than one year before the filing date, or (by another) before the applicant's invention date. For these reasons, there is not so much pressure upon a US inventor to get his patent application on file as quickly as possible. He knows that so long as he has fully documented his invention date (and has not suppressed or abandoned his invention in the meantime), he can rely upon this date in any conflict with another inventor, and to avoid prior art published not more than a year before his actual filing date. The tendency in the USA is therefore to take longer to define and to refine an invention before committing it to paper and filing it at the Patent Office than would be the case for an invention made in Europe.

This course of action is understandable in view of US patent law, but is not without danger. Even in the USA itself, if an interference should be declared between two conflicting applications, the senior party (who has the earlier filing date) has considerable advantages, as the burden of proof lies on the junior party. Even more important, however, is the possible effect of delay in filing upon corresponding applications in countries outside the USA. The US applicant is sometimes apt to forget that his invention date, which is all-important within the USA, is of no importance whatsoever anywhere else (except for Canada). In Europe and Japan all that matters is his US filing date, from which he claims priority. What is more, a publication before the US filing date may not affect the validity of the US application, but will be fatal to applications in most other countries. It is by no means uncommon for US applicants to publish their own inventions before filing, in reliance on the one year grace period, only to discover later that they have thereby destroyed any chance of getting patent protection abroad.

Even if the US inventor files his application as quickly as possible, it is still of prime importance for him to keep records of the work constituting his invention. For the purposes of US interference proceedings, invention is separated into the distinct elements of conception and reduction to practice. Conception is usually defined as a complete mental realization of the invention; reduction to practice consists of physically completing the invention and proving that it is useful for a particular purpose. Thus the preparation of a new compound is not reduction to practice without some test results to prove its utility. As the uncorroborated statements and records of the inventor are not admissible as evidence, everything must be corroborated by an independent witness. Only inventions made in the USA can go back to a date of actual reduction to practice; inventors outside the USA must rely upon the 'constructive reduction to practice' constituted by filing a US patent application, or a foreign patent application from which priority is validly claimed.

This is often seen as an example of discrimination against foreigners on the part of the US Patent Office, and it is certainly inequitable that an American inventor can for this reason obtain a US patent for an invention for which a European inventor not only had the earlier priority date, but also the earlier actual invention date. That interference-type proceedings can be carried out without such a built-in advantage for the home team is shown by the example of Canada. There, priority of invention is determined by conflict proceedings, conceptually similar to US interferences but procedurally much simpler, in which evidence of actual invention date is admissible no matter where the invention was made.

On closer examination, however, the advantage is not without its drawbacks. It is true that, if in an interference between a US applicant and a foreign applicant, the US applicant has a first-filing date earlier than the foreign applicant's priority date, the foreigner must lose. Still, he would also have lost by the normal rule of first to file applied by other countries, and so has no real ground of complaint. If on the other hand he has an earlier first-filing date than the US applicant, and can validly claim priority from his first-filing, he will win unless the US applicant can meet the rather difficult burden of proof of an earlier date of reduction to practice (or an earlier date of conception coupled with 'diligence').

We have already seen that it is not enough for the inventor merely to produce his laboratory notebook to show when he made the invention (synthesized a new compound, for example). It is standard practice in US industrial laboratories for chemists to date and sign each page of their laboratory notebooks, and have each page read and witnessed by a colleague, in order to provide corroboration of their experimental work. And even if the synthesis of a new compound, for example, can be adequately corroborated, this still does not constitute reduction to practice until it has been tested and found at least potentially useful for something. The tests and test results must of course be corroborated just as the initial synthesis was. Furthermore, when 'diligence' must be shown, then evidence of some degree of continuous activity over the relevant time must be given. Thus although non-US companies are discriminated against, they are at least spared the large number of non-productive man-hours which must be spent on record-keeping and witnessing of notebooks in a US research organization.

One important point, however, is that the non-US applicant must be careful if he wants to be able to rely in the USA upon the priority date of his first filing in another country. The US patent law has rather strict requirements about what constitutes a sufficient disclosure of an invention in a patent application. In particular, the application must disclose how to make and to use the invention, and must give the 'best mode', or the best way known to the inventor, of carrying out the invention. American courts have ruled that for a US application to have the benefit of priority from a foreign application, that foreign application must meet the same requirements as apply to a US application.

It is clear that this judgment is contrary to the Paris Convention, which allows one to claim priority from an application which meets the requirements of the laws of the country in which it is filed rather than those of the laws of the country in which priority is subsequently claimed. Nevertheless, this is the present law in the USA, and the effect is that a priority application, whether in the United Kingdom, Germany, Switzerland, or Japan, must be drafted with the requirements of US patent law very much in mind – at least if there is any chance at all that a corresponding application will later be filed in the USA.

The priority year

Once the first patent application has been filed, the 12-month period provided for by the Paris Convention begins to run. During this priority year, work on the invention will normally continue, and further compounds will be made and tested, new formulations compounded, or new process conditions tried. All this material can be used in preparing the patent applications to be filed abroad, and, in countries where it is possible to claim internal priority, the second application to be filed in the home country. It is also possible to file new patent applications for further developments which are made in the priority year, and then at the foreign filing stage to combine these together into a single application. The advantage of this is that the new developments will then have an earlier priority date (the date of filing of the new application) than they otherwise would have (the date of filing of the foreign text). There are, however, some disadvantages: (a) costs are somewhat increased, mainly because copies of all priority applications have to be provided in most countries when priority is claimed, and in some countries translations will be required; (b) administration and records become more complex; and (c) extra care must be taken over inventorship.

The extent to which new filings should be made during the priority year obviously depends upon the importance of the invention and the degree of competition in the field; for certain pharmaceutical inventions it may be justifiable to file a new application for every new compound or group of compounds made and tested, even if this means combining five or six applications upon foreign filing. In most areas, however, it would be unusual to file more than one extra application during the priority year, and the majority of patent applications are based upon a single priority document. The record for the highest number may be held by the European application of a Japanese company which claims priority from no less than 41 Japanese applications.

It may also be desirable to file more than one application at the same time, particularly when the invention is a complicated one. Suppose that the inventor has carried out a limited amount of experimental work, which is sufficient to define an invention of fairly narrow scope, but at the same time he sees the possibility of extending the idea to a wider area which he has not yet had time to test. In a case like this, a single first application restricted to the narrow scope could be inadequate if by the end of the priority year the broader scope of the invention has been tested and confirmed. On the other hand, if the broad scope is described in the first filing and then only the narrow part can be substantiated, then foreign applications can indeed be filed limited to the narrow scope, but at some stage the priority application will be published, and there will then be no chance of filing a later patent application directed to the broader concept.

The answer is to file two first applications of different scope on the same day, and then to claim priority from one and abandon the other. The abandoned application never sees the light of day and so one can choose the scope of the foreign applications, claim priority validly, and not publish any more than is necessary.

The foreign filing decision

Although the period for claiming Convention priority is twelve months, a decision on whether or not to 'foreign file', that is, to file corresponding applications outside the home country, cannot be left too long. When one considers that an application from Europe or North America which is to be filed in Japan must be posted to Japan, translated into Japanese, reviewed by a Japanese patent agent, and filed at the Japanese Patent Office before the end of the Convention year, it is clear that it must be sent off at least a month and preferably five or six weeks, before that date. When one adds to this the time required for preparing the text of the application, including reviewing further developments with the inventor and considering any new prior art which has been found during the priority year, then a decision to foreign file taken any later than three months before the end of the Convention year may lead to time pressure. A better date to aim at is eight months from the first priority date.

At this time, discussions should be held in order to reach a decision on what should be done with the application. There are four main possibilities which are open:

(1) abandon
(2) abandon and refile
(3) obtain a patent in the home country only
(4) file corresponding applications in one or more foreign countries

Let us look at each of these in turn.

Abandonment. The simplest course of action, where there is no commercial interest in the invention at all, or a search has shown that the invention is old or unpatentable, is to do nothing. It is usually unnecessary to write to the Patent Office deliberately to abandon the application. Sooner or later a fee must be paid or some action taken to keep the application in being, and when this is not done the application will lapse. A letter of express abandonment has the disadvantage that it is normally irrevocable; inventors and their employers frequently change their minds.

An application which is allowed to lapse at this stage will not have been published, and so the invention will remain secret. If interest in it revives at a later date, it can be the subject of a later application, provided no one else has published or patented it in the meantime. If the applicant wants to ensure that no one else can patent the invention, he should have it published, either by continuing an application in his home country or elsewhere long enough for it to issue as a published application (see below) or by sending it to a journal such as *Research Disclosure*, in which any disclosure may be rapidly published for a reasonable fee.

In the USA, the application may now be converted to a Statutory Invention Registration and published without examination on payment of a printing fee.

Refiling. It frequently appears that eight months after the first filing date is altogether too short a time in which to reach a decision on whether or not to invest time and money in foreign patenting of a particular invention. It may be that further testing has to be done, it may be that commercial interest is low at the time but could increase, it may be simply that the inventors have been busy with other things and have done no more work on the invention since the first application was filed. In such cases the best solution is to start from the beginning again. The existing application is specifically abandoned, a new application, which may be identical with the old one, is filed, and the 12-month countdown restarts.

This is a very convenient solution, which is frequently used; there are, however, three points which must be kept in mind. First, the correct procedure must be followed. According to the Paris Convention, priority may be validly claimed from a refiled application only if the original application is abandoned, without any rights outstanding and without priority having been claimed from it, before the second application is filed (in the same country). Under the British Patents Act 1949 there was no provision for abandoning a pending patent application; applicants did their best to comply with the Convention by sending a letter of abandonment to the British Patent Office, but it was never clear whether this had any legal effect. Under the Patent Act 1977 it is clear that an application may be specifically abandoned.

The second point is that refiling always entails a loss of priority, usually of 8–10 months, and the risk is always present that someone else may have published the invention or filed a patent application for it in this time. If this happens, the refiled application cannot lead to a valid patent. Consequently, in a field where competitors are known to be active, the loss of priority may involve an unacceptable risk.

Finally, if there has been any known publication of the invention since the priority date, abandonment and refiling is ruled out. Such publication most frequently arises from the inventor himself or from his employers. He may have published his results in a scientific journal, or in a technical information sheet, or samples of a product embodying the invention may have been given to potential customers to test, or even have been openly sold. Most chemists, if they know anything at all about patents, know that they should not publish inventions before a patent application is filed. It is not so generally realized that publication within the priority year can also be damaging, but such publication can destroy the validity of any parts of the final patent which are not entitled to the first priority date, and can limit one's options by excluding the possibility of abandonment and refiling.

Home-country patenting. In some cases, an applicant may be an individual or a small company having no commercial interests or prospects of licensing outside the home country. For such applicants the expense of foreign filing would be wasted, and the most they will wish to do is to obtain a patent in their own country. Even where the applicant is a larger company which would normally file any commercially interesting case in several countries, individual applications may be of such low interest that protection in the home country is all that is needed. The only question then is, if the country is one which allows internal priority, whether a new application should be filed incorporating any improvements made in the priority year, or whether the original text is sufficient. For countries not allowing internal priority, of course, there is no choice in the matter, if the original priority is to be kept.

It may be mentioned here that some applicants based in countries not allowing internal priority choose to file at least some of their applications in countries where internal priority is possible; for example, some Swiss companies now file priority applications in Germany. Some countries insist for security reasons that all applications for local inventions be first filed locally; thus an applicant for an invention made in the United Kingdom must not file his priority application in any other country without special permission. For the United Kingdom, however, the problem does not arise as internal priority has always been a feature of the British patent system.

Foreign filing. Finally, if an invention appears likely to be commercially important, the decision may be to file corresponding applications in a number of other countries. This decision is best approached on purely commercial terms. Filing and prosecuting a patent application in a reasonable number of countries costs a considerable amount of money, and this should be regarded as an investment which, like any other, should be expected to show a profit. It is of course extremely difficult to estimate the cash value of a patent even where a product is being produced under a granted patent, and trying to do so for a product not yet launched and a patent not yet applied for is an exercise in guesswork. Nevertheless, something of the kind must be attempted if the foreign filing decision is to be taken on a rational basis, and the type of question to be asked is what is the expected turnover and profitability of the product in question, and how would these differ if competitors could or could not be excluded.

For the pharmaceutical industry one can assume that patent protection would certainly be worth the outlay for any new product which actually reaches the market, and the question is rather what is the chance that the product in question will progress that far. Usually it is impossible to make any meaningful prediction at the time when the foreign filing decision must be taken, and one must rely upon some rule of thumb such that if the product is being developed further, foreign filing should be carried out as a matter of course. High patenting costs are a necessary part of the high research overheads of the pharmaceutical industry.

The choice of countries

When the decision to foreign file has been taken, the next question is, in which countries. Here, the points to be considered are which countries are major markets or manufacturers of the type of products in question, how important the product is likely to be, and what is the relative value-to-cost ratio for the countries to be considered. Of course, for particular applicants there may be special reasons for filing in a particular country, such as the existence of a subsidiary company there, or licence agreements with a company in that country. Leaving aside such individual reasons, however, one can say that if an application is worth foreign filing at all, it is probably sensible to file at least in the major industrial countries such as the USA, Japan, West Germany, France, the United Kingdom, and Italy. With increasing importance of the invention filing could be carried out in further countries, which will very much depend on the nature of the technical field. For a non-pharmaceutical chemical invention, one might for example consider, in the following order: the remaining countries of the European Patent Convention; Canada, Australia, New Zealand, and South Africa (strong patent protection and not expensive); Scandinavian countries (strong patent protection but expensive); Spain and major Latin American countries (weak protection, inexpensive); various West European and Asian countries (e.g. Greece, Portugal, Taiwan, South Korea); and finally East European countries, where patent protection is relatively weak and extremely expensive.

For a company large enough to have several foreign filings per year, a great deal of repetitive discussion can be avoided by having fixed filing lists of countries for most normal situations; only cases which are out of the ordinary need then be discussed individually.

Non-convention filings

It should not be forgotten that the end of the Convention year is not necessarily the last chance of filing corresponding applications. If a foreign filing has been decided on and carried out in, let us say, six countries, and shortly thereafter it is felt that ten would have been more appropriate, then applications can still be filed in the remaining four countries, although Convention priority can no longer be claimed. This means that if the invention has been published, such new 'non-convention' filings are pointless, and as a large number of countries including the United Kingdom, Japan, West Germany, and France now publish pending patent applications 18 months from the priority date, the last possible date for further non-convention filings is generally 18 months from the priority date, or about 6 months after foreign filing.

European patent applications

If it is intended to foreign file in any of the contracting states of the European Patent Convention, it must next be considered whether to file a single application at the European Patent Office designating the desired countries, or to file separate applications at the national patent offices of those countries. There are two main criteria for this decision: the relative costs of the two different routes and the relative strength of the resulting patents.

Considering cost first, it has been the aim of the EPO from the beginning that an application for a European patent designating more than three or four countries should be cheaper than a series of applications in the corresponding national patent offices, taking into account agents' charges as well as official fees.

It does depend very much upon which three or four countries are designated. At one extreme, an applicant who wishes protection in Luxembourg, Belgium, and Switzerland can do so by the 'national route' quite cheaply, particularly as a single French-language text can be used in all three countries. Here, a European application designating the three countries would clearly be more expensive. On the other hand, filing in Holland, Germany, and Sweden would for the average applicant be cheaper by the 'European route'.

It is also necessary to specify who is the applicant. An individual or small company must rely completely upon the services of independent patent practitioners in each country. A larger company, which employs its own patent specialists, will normally prepare its own patent applications at least for its home country. It is possible for an international company with a large patent department to prepare applications in different languages and to file these directly in some European countries. For such an applicant, who has already greatly reduced the cost of his national filings, there may be little or no further savings to be made by filing a European application, even if all possible countries are designated.

The other main factor to be considered is the strength of patent protection which will be obtained. At present there is still no effective examination in Luxembourg, Italy, and (in most technical fields) Switzerland. The fact that a patent is granted in one of these countries therefore does not help us to judge whether or not it may be valid. On the other hand, a European patent designated for one of these countries will have been subject to a strong examination and has much more chance of being valid.

One can well imagine that in a weak examining country a national patent belonging to a large company may in a few years come to be regarded with suspicion, the implication being that the application was filed by the national route because the applicant felt that it would not stand up to European examination. On the other hand, a certain amount of caution is necessary in approaching the European Patent Office, since rejection of the application there means that no patents will be obtained in any of the designated countries. Although, as we shall see, the examination by the EPO is turning out to be less strict than was at first feared, there is still the problem that a European patent application allowed by the EPO can within nine months be opposed by other parties. If too many European oppositions prove successful, there will be a strong disincentive to file by the European route (see p. 82).

Once a decision has been taken to file a European application, the list of countries should be looked at once again. The major costs of the European application are the high search fees and examination fees; the designation fee payable for each country chosen is relatively small. Thus, for a low additional outlay, protection can be extended to include additional countries. In particular, whereas one might not normally consider filing in Luxembourg, it may be worthwhile adding it to a European application designating the other possible EEC countries, particularly if national applications are being filed in the remaining EEC countries, so that there will be no gap in protection for the whole EEC.

A European application can be filed in any of the three official languages of the EPO – English, French, and German. The language in which the application is filed then becomes the 'language of the proceedings' for the examination of the application.

In 1979, the first full calendar year of operation of the EPO, approximately 12 000 European applications were filed, of which 45 per cent were in English, 40 per cent were in German, and 15 per cent were in French. The proportion of applications filed in English was less than had been expected, reflecting the fact that while most major German companies enthusiastically adopted the European system from the beginning, British and American companies were generally more cautious. These companies tended at first to use a selective approach in which only their better applications were filed at the EPO, whereas the ones for which difficulties might be expected were filed by the national route. A further large factor is that Japanese companies, which might be expected to file predominantly in English, were initially very reluctant to file at the EPO.

Of the EPO applications filed in 1979, 45 per cent related to chemical inventions, compared with 33 per cent to mechanical and 22 per cent to electrical inventions. The high figure for chemical applications reflects the fact that it was the pharmaceutical companies, for whom strong patent protection in many countries is particularly important, which showed the most interest in the European patent system in its early stages.

Five years later, in 1984, the number of applications at the EPO had risen to over 37 000, and the proportion filed in English had risen to 57 per cent. The USA had now become the largest single source of applications, with 27 per cent of the total, compared with 24 per cent from Germany, 15 per cent from Japan, 9 per cent from France and 7 per cent from the UK. However, the proportion of chemical applications had fallen to 34 per cent, compared with electronic 29 per cent and mechanical 37 per cent.

Patent Co-operation Treaty

A further possibility open to an applicant is to file a PCT application designating the countries for which he wants protection. The PCT application may designate the European Patent Office in order to obtain a European patent for any EPC countries, all of which have now ratified the PCT.

It is not possible to obtain certain national patents by the PCT route; if France, Belgium, or Italy is designated in a PCT application, this is treated as a designation of the European Patent Office and a Europatent for these countries will be obtained. In 1984 about 4250 out of the total 37 000 were 'Euro-PCT' applications.

A PCT application is always published with an English language abstract, but the text may be in English, French, German, Russian or Japanese. The language in which the original application may be filed depends upon the receiving office, and in some countries a choice is possible (see Table 2). However if the original text is not in one of the above five languages, a translation is prepared by the International Searching Authority (for which the applicant is charged a fee) and the translated text is published.

Table 2

Receiving Office – *Patent Office of*:	*Language of filing*
Australia	E
Belgium	E,F,G, or Dutch
Brazil	E
Bulgaria	E or R
Denmark	E or Danish
Finland	E, Finnish, or Swedish
France	F
Germany	G
Hungary	E,F,G, or R
Italy	E,F, or G
Japan	J
North Korea	E,F, or R
South Korea	E or J
Luxembourg	F or G
Malawi	E
Monaco	F
Netherlands	E,F,G, or Dutch
Norway	E or Norwegian
Romania	E,F,G, or R
Sudan	E
Sweden	E or any Scandinavian language
United Kingdom	E
United States of America	E
Union of Soviet Socialist Republics	R
European Patent Office	E,F, or G

E = English, F = French, G = German, J = Japanese, R = Russian.

Registration and patents of importation

It should also be mentioned that it may be possible validly to file patent applications in certain countries even after the invention has been published. One method is the registration of granted British patents in certain British colonies and former colonies, another is the obtaining of a patent of importation in certain countries, mainly in Latin America, based on a granted patent in another country. These are both discussed in more detail in Chapter 6.

5

OBTAINING A GRANTED PATENT

For how do I hold thee but by thy granting?
And for that riches where is my deserving?
The cause of this fair gift is me is wanting,
And so my patent back again is swerving.

William Shakespeare: *Sonnet 87*

Types of examination

Formal

Once a patent application has been filed, it must at some stage be examined. Every country which grants patents has some type of examination, however rudimentary. At the bottom of the scale are countries in which the only examination is a purely formal one, to check that the papers are in order and the fee has been paid. Belgium, for example, had until very recently such a registration system. In Belgium, a patent was automatically granted for anything for which an application was made, and all questions of validity were left to the courts.

Non-unity

Some countries, while having essentially a registration system, do at least check that the application describes an invention of a type which is legally patentable, and rather more go one step further and examine for unity of invention. It is a common feature of nearly all patent systems that a single patent should not be granted for more than one invention. This is not so serious a situation as two patents being granted for the same invention, but is objected to perhaps because the patent office will receive only one set of fees instead of two or more. The interpretation of what constitutes a single invention varies considerably from country to country; typically, however, objections may be raised if the applicant attempts to claim end-products and intermediates in the same application, or claims a new use of a group of compounds at the same time as claiming *per se* a subgroup of compounds which are themselves new. Some countries, including the USA, may raise this type of objection if a group of compounds being claimed would fall into more than one classification group; for example different heterocyclic ring systems with the same novel side-chain, which would be classified separately according to the type of heterocycle.

The EPC and the UK Patents Act 1977 allow more than one invention to be present in an application provided that they are linked together to form part of the same inventive concept, although the British Patent Office seems to be reluctant to make any changes in its previous practice. Once a patent has been granted, its validity cannot be attacked on the grounds that it contains more than one invention.

When two or more distinct inventions are present and a patent office raises a well-founded objection of non-unity of invention, the remedy is for the applicant to file a divisional application. This is a new application, which may have the same text as the original ('parent') application or which may have a shortened text, but which must not include any new matter – i.e. anything which was not present in the original specification. Only the claims will be changed, so as to claim the matter which is being 'divided out'. The requirements as to when the divisional must be filed vary; in some countries a fixed term is set from the date of the official objection of non-unity, in others a divisional can be filed at any time before the parent application is allowed or granted. Whenever it is filed, however, and provided no new matter is introduced, it will be treated as if it had the same filing date as the parent application, so that publication of the invention after the filing date of the parent and before that of the divisional will not affect validity.

Novelty
Approximately half of the countries which grant patents carry out some form of novelty examination, in which the prior art, or part of it, is searched for anything which could be an anticipation of the invention. Some patent offices, for example those in the United Kingdom, Germany, and Japan, carry out a search entirely by themselves, with varying degrees of efficiency; others, for example those in Canada and Denmark, in addition may require the applicant to notify them of prior art which has been cited during examination in other specified countries. A further group of countries – France, The Netherlands, Turkey, and Ireland, for example – do not carry out searches themselves, but require a search to be carried out by an international searching office such as the EPO office at The Hague (formerly an independent searching agency known as the IIB – Institut Internationale des Brevets), or accept the results of a novelty search carried out in another country. There are also countries in which although the law provides for a novelty examination, the lack of technically trained examiners (or even in some cases the lack of any patent office facilities whatever) means that in practice such searches cannot be carried out. For countries in this category, the provisions of the PCT will be particularly useful, since it will enable them to grant national patents which have been subject to a novelty search by a competent searching authority. In Switzerland, only applications in certain technical fields (textile

treatment and time measurement) are subjected to a novelty examination, which is also carried out by the EPO at The Hague.

The USA is in a special position as regards prior-art searches. Although a number of countries may require the applicant to state the prior art cited by certain other patent offices, there is no obligation to give anything more than is asked for. Not so in the USA. Since 1977, the rules there have made it compulsory for the applicant to bring to the notice of the US Patent Office all relevant prior art of which he is aware, and deliberate concealment of relevant prior art is regarded as 'fraud on the Patent Office' and will result in the patent granted as a result of such fraud being incurably invalid, as well as the possibility of the attorney responsible being disbarred and the patentee being sued for anti-trust violations (see p. 293). The whole relationship between the applicant and the patent office should thus be on a different basis from the old 'us-versus-them' approach which is still common in most other countries, and this can be rather hard to adjust to for some applicants.

Inventive step

Only a relatively small number of countries go beyond a novelty examination and look into the question of whether or not the invention is obvious over the prior art. Among those which do are Germany, Japan, the Scandinavian countries, The Netherlands, the USA, and, since the 1977 Act, the United Kingdom. The European Patent Office also examines for the presence of an inventive step. The degree of difficulty in overcoming obviousness objections varies. It seems that it should be relatively easy to persuade both the British Patent Office and the EPO that an invention is non-obvious, but countries such as The Netherlands and the USA present more serious difficulties.

Deferred examination

The idea that the applicant could voluntarily postpone examination of his application for a period of years originated in The Netherlands as a method of relieving some of the pressure upon the overworked Dutch Patent Office. The idea was that postponing examination would not only relieve the immediate overload, but would also have a long-term effect in that many applications would never need to be examined because the applicants would have lost interest in them by the date at which they would finally have to decide whether to request examination or abandon. The system was introduced in 1964, and was followed by Germany in 1968 and Japan in 1971. Some other countries have systems with similar features.

In the basic Dutch system, the application is received, subjected to a formal examination only, and published as filed 18 months from the filing date, or from the priority date if priority is claimed. No further action is taken until the applicant or a third party requests examination and pays the examination fee, which must be done within seven years from filing or the application will lapse. Annual maintenance fees are required to keep the application in being during this seven-year period. After the examination, the patent is published again in its final form. By this time there may well be only 10 years or less of the 20-year term of the patent remaining, since this is counted from the filing date and not from the date of grant. Nevertheless many inventions are not commercialized, or imitated, until after several years from the time they were made, and it is only then that a granted patent is needed. In the pharmaceutical industry in particular, where registration of a new drug often takes at least seven years, it is standard practice for applicants to defer examination for as long as possible. If in this time development of the drug is abandoned, then not only has the Patent Office been saved the trouble of examining the case, but the applicant has saved the cost of the examination fee and the effort of prosecuting his application in that country.

The German system is similar to that of the Dutch, except that examination is in two stages: a prior-art search followed by a substantive examination in which an examiner applies the cited prior art to determine whether or not the invention is patentable. These two stages may be carried out quite separately, so that an applicant may request a search upon filing his application, and then wait seven years before requesting substantive examination of it. Japan, like The Netherlands, has a single request for examination, also within seven years, but no maintenance fees are payable.

Early publication

When examination and grant of patents may be delayed in this way for many years, it was felt necessary to insist upon early publication of pending applications. This was because it would be unfair if a manufacturer could be stopped from doing something he had been doing for years by the sudden appearance of a patent which had been lying dormant in the system for even longer. Early publication enables one to see what patent applications competitors have in the pipeline, and to plan accordingly. The applicant is given certain rights from early publication; he cannot (except in Italy) sue for infringement, but generally has the right to compensation equivalent to a fair royalty for any infringement which takes place before the patent is granted – always assuming that a patent ultimately is granted.

Early publication is also a feature of the patent system in a large number of countries which do not have deferred examination, as well as in the European patent system. It is now part of the British system under the Patents Act 1977. Early publication may take various forms; thus for example in the United Kingdom and Japan the specification and claims are printed, in West Germany and the Netherlands the specification and claims are copied by photolithography, in Australia a printed abstract is available but the full text is only laid open to public inspection (OPI in patent jargon), while in the Scandinavian countries, the specification is laid OPI but nothing is actually printed. In Belgium, up to 1986, the patent was granted so rapidly that final publication there could be earlier than 'early publication' in other countries. On request the publication could be postponed until six months from filing, so that publication of the Belgian patent would be approximately simultaneous with early publication elsewhere.

Portugal publishes in its Official Gazette an abstract of all pending patent applications. Previously this publication did not occur until after the entire application had been published in other countries, but recently it has been made only three months or so after filing. Postponement can be requested, but costs money.

Early published patent applications are an important source of up-to-date technical information, and will often constitute the closest prior art against subsequent applications. Up to 1980, the most important category of early publications has been the *Deutsche Offenlegungschriften* (German publication documents), generally abbreviated to DOS. The DOS are important because Germany is a country in which almost all applicants will file, if they file outside their home country at all; because German industry is a prolific source of applications which will be published as DOS even if they are not filed outside of Germany, and because the DOS document is rapidly available and includes the whole of the specification as filed. The same considerations apply to Japanese early published applications (*Kokai*), although the Western reader has to rely upon English-language abstracts such as Derwent (see p. 263). The early published British and European applications are now also important source materials.

Procedure in the United Kingdom

Filing

In order to establish a date of filing for a patent application in the United Kingdom, the applicant must file at the Patent Office (directly or by post) a description of the invention accompanied by the application form (Form 1/77) and the current application fee. The description may be a very simple one and need not contain any claims; it may therefore be like a provisional specification under the old law. The applicant receives a filing receipt which states the filing date and the application number. The application number is a five-digit number following the last two digits of the year; thus the first application filed in 1986 has the number 8600001.

Preliminary examination and search

The next stage is that within 12 months from the application date the applicant must supply claims and an abstract, and must request, and pay the fee for, the preliminary examination and search, if he wishes to continue with the application. He may, of course, file a new application claiming priority from the first one and proceed with that instead of with the earlier one, thereby taking the opportunity to add new matter and broaden the scope of the original disclosure. There is no need to wait 12 months before requesting preliminary examination; this may be done on filing so that the applicant can consider his decision whether or not to foreign file on the basis of the search report. If he then files a second United Kingdom application claiming priority from the first, the new application must also have a preliminary examination and search report but the closely related search which has already been made may be accepted as sufficient.

The preliminary examination deals with various formal matters, and also with unity of invention; if the examiner considers that two or more inventions are present, he may search only one of them, or may search more than one and require additional search fees to be paid. The search report provides a list of prior art considered relevant, divided into the categories of prior art published before the filing date and United Kingdom applications of earlier filing date which were not prior publications, but which will be part of the state of the art under the 'whole contents' approach. At this stage, no comments are made by the examiner, and no opinion is expressed as to whether the cited prior art is relevant because it destroys the novelty of the invention or because it renders it obvious. About one month after the search report issues, the applicant is informed of the date set for early publication of the application, which will be as soon as feasible after 18 months from the filing date. At the same time, the application is allocated a serial number which will in due course be the patent number; this is a seven-digit number whose first digit is 2.

A further requirement before publication is that before 16 months from the filing date, the applicant must submit a statement of inventorship, a copy of which is then sent by the Patent Office to all the named inventors in British originating applications.

If the application originally claimed priority from an earlier United Kingdom or foreign application, then the time limits for supplying abstract, claims, and statement of inventorship and requesting preliminary examination and search run from the priority date, except that the abstract and claims may be supplied up to one month from the filing date. In practice applications filed with a claim to priority will normally contain an abstract and claims on filing, and the statement of inventorship and request for preliminary examination will be filed at the same time as the application.

Publication occurs about 18 months after the filing date of the application from which priority is claimed.

Publication

After receiving the search report, the applicant may amend his specification (for example to reduce the scope so as to distinguish the invention from the cited prior art) or, if his invention turns out to be totally anticipated, he may decide to abandon it altogether. However, if he wishes the early publication of the specification to include the amendment, or if he wishes to avoid any publication, he must act quickly if, as is generally the case with applications claiming priority, he has requested the search towards the end of the possible period. Once the letter announcing the date of publication has been sent – and it is generally sent within a month or so of the issue of the search report – it is difficult if not impossible to have amendments made to the published specification or to prevent publication by abandonment.

The specification is then set in type and printed as a published British Patent Application, bearing the seven-digit serial number followed by an A. Copies of the specification may then be purchased from the Patent Office, and the file is open to public inspection. The published application also lists the prior art cited in the search report. An example of the front page of such an application is shown in Fig. 8.

Once the application has been published, it is of course prior art against any application filed later than its publication date, and also against applications filed after its filing date, under the whole contents approach. Furthermore the applicant has certain rights against infringers as from the publication date.

At any time after the publication of the application until a patent is granted, any person may send to the Patent Office observations on the patentability of the invention. This provision is similar to one under the old Act, but with the difference that thanks to early publication such observations can be made before the substantive examination of the application instead of only after the application had been examined and accepted. The observations will be considered by the examiner during the substantive examination, and a copy will be sent to the applicant, who can comment upon them. The person making the observations does not become a party to the proceedings, so that he cannot make any further comments and is not informed officially what use, if any, the examiner makes of his contribution. He can, however, check this for himself, since after the publication date the file of the application is open to public inspection at the Patent Office and any person may, for a fee, obtain photocopies of the examiner's reports and the applicant's answer.

(12) **UK Patent Application** (19) **GB** (11) **2 021 437** **A**

(21) Application No **7911925**
(22) Date of filing **5 Apr 1979**
(23) Claims filed **5 Apr 1979**
(30) Priority data
(31) **14321/78**
(32) **12 Apr 1978**
(33) **United Kingdom (GB)**
(43) Application published
5 Dec 1979
(51) INT CL²
B01J 1/00
(52) Domestic classification
B1X 20
(56) Documents cited
None
(58) Field of search
B1X
F4S
F4X *
(71) Applicants
**Sandoz Ltd., 35
Lichtstrasse, CH-4002
Basle, Switzerland**
(72) Inventors
Ludwig Hub, Tomas Kupr
(74) Agents
B. A. Yorke & Co

(54) **Reactor simulator**

(57) A reactor simulator comprises a reactor vessel 1, a heat exchange liquid jacket 2a around the vessel through which heat exchange liquid may be circulated and means 3 for adjusting the level X—X of heat exchange liquid in the heat exchange jacket, the heat exchange area and hence the heating/cooling capacity of the reactor varying accordingly to enable the ratio of heat/cooling capacity of a large scale reactor to the corresponding reactor volume to be accurately simulated in a small scale reactor.

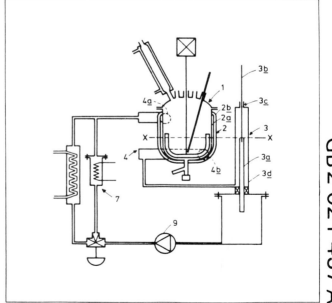

GB2 021 437 A

FIG. 8.   Title page of a published British patent application under the Patents Act 1977.

Substantive examination

The next stage in the proceedings is that the applicant must within six months of the publication date file a request for substantive examination and pay a further fee. In 1986, the search fee was £80 and the fee for substantive examination £100. If the request is not made and the fee not paid in that time, the application is treated as withdrawn, and cannot normally be reinstated. To avoid the serious consequences of missing this deadline, it may be advisable to request substantive examination at the time that the request for preliminary examination and search is made, that is, on filing in the case of an application claiming priority. If it is decided after receiving the search report not to proceed with substantive examination the fee will be refunded provided the examiner has not already begun his work.

The examiner carries out the substantive examination based upon the prior art cited in the search report, but not necessarily limited to this. He then issues an official letter in which he lists whatever objections he has to the grant of a patent on the application. These may range from the serious (for example, an allegation that the invention is not new or is obvious in view of the prior art), to the trivial (for example, a requirement that a registered trade mark used in the description be identified as such). In the fairly numerous cases in which the search report cited no relevant prior art, the official letter will normally concern itself only with formal matters and with the relationship of the claims to each other and to the description, and will in fact be very like an official letter under the previous Act.

There are, however, two significant changes from the procedure under the old law. One is that the examiner used to return a copy of the specification with pencilled comments; the applicant or his agent could then make amendments in ink on the same document and refile it. Now this is no longer done; minor amendments will be made by the examiner upon request in a letter, but for any changes involving more than a few words, retyped pages must be submitted. The other change is that whereas previously the only time constraint was that an application had to be in order for acceptance, with no further objections by the Patent Office, within 2½ years from filing (extensible by 3 months), the Patent Office now fixes a term, generally 3–6 months, within which the applicant must reply. There is still an overall time limit, originally 3½ years from the first priority claimed, or from filing if no priority was claimed. This was in 1980 redefined as 4½ years, but no extensions of the period are possible.

In answering the official letter, the applicant may argue that the objections are not valid ones, or may amend his specification in any way necessary to meet the objections; except that he must be careful not to introduce any new matter not previously disclosed. The introduction of new matter, even if not objected to by the examiner, could lead to the granted patent being invalid. The applicant may also at this time make further voluntary amendments not in consequence of the objections raised; but afterwards such amendments can be made only with the permission of the examiner. If the examiner feels that his objections have not been fully answered by the reply to the official letter, he may issue a second official letter; if disagreement persists the applicant may ask for a hearing in the Patent Office, and has the right of appeal to the Patents Court if the Office decides against him. A further appeal to the Court of Appeals is possible if leave is granted by Patents Court or by the Court of Appeals. The British procedure is summarized in diagrammatic form in Fig. 9.

Grant

Assuming, however, that all objections are met within the 4½-year period, the patent will be granted, the effective date of the patent rights being the date of publication of the notice of grant in the *Official Journal* (*Patents*).

The patent specification is then published for a second time, incorporating any amendments which have been made during prosecution. This time the text is not set in print, but is reproduced directly from the applicant's typescript by photolithography, a procedure which produces a bulkier and less attractive document, but which at least avoids the possibility of printers' errors. There is a printed title page, headed by the seven-digit publication number followed by the letter B, an example of which is given as Fig. 10. The patentee receives a 'certificate of grant' stating that a patent has been granted, but there is no longer any Letters Patent document such as that of Fig. 1. Indeed, it would be true to say that the patent itself, as distinct from the patent specification, has only a notional existence.

Procedure in the USA

Filing

A patent application in the USA must be made by the inventor, even if he has assigned his rights to an employer. The inventor must sign a declaration which is normally attached to the specification, and which sets out, among other things, that he believes himself to be the first inventor, and does not know of any reason why the invention should not be novel under US law. The declaration usually includes an authorization of an agent to act for him before the US Patent Office. If the inventor does not understand English, he must sign a declaration written in a language which he does understand. It is important that the inventor reads the specification carefully and does not regard signing the declaration as a mere formality. It is now possible to file a US application without a declaration by the

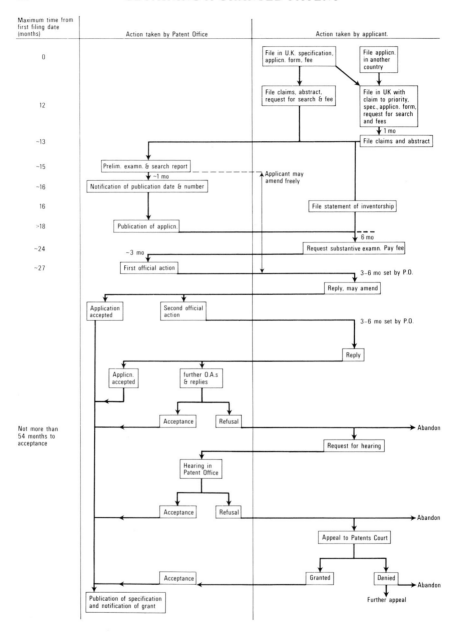

FIG. 9. British Patent Office procedure.

(12) **UK Patent** (19) **GB** (11) **2 038 375 B**

(54) Title of invention

Improvements in or relating to dyed and shrinkproofed wool

(51) INT CL³; **D06P 3/16**

(21) Application No
  7943111

(22) Date of filing
  14 Dec 1979

(30) Priority data

  (31) **12834/78**

  (32) **18 Dec 1978**

  (31) **9366/79**

  (32) **18 Oct 1979**

  (33) **Switzerland (CH)**

(43) Application published
  23 Jul 1980

(45) Patent published
  12 May 1982

(52) Domestic classification
  D1B 2F

(56) Documents cited
  GB 1553811
  GB 1264683
  GB 837950
  GB 835267
  GB 1006787

(58) Field of search
  D1B
  B2F

(73) Proprietor
  Sandoz Ltd
  Lichtstrasse 35
  4002 Basle
  Switzerland

(72) Inventors
  Oskar Ammen
  Hermann Egli
  Karl Zesiger

(74) Agents
  B. A. Yorke & Co.,
  98, The Centre, Feltham,
  Middlesex, TW13 4EP

GB 2 038 375 B

LONDON THE PATENT OFFICE

FIG. 10. Title page of a granted British Patent under the Patents Act 1977.

inventor, and to file the declaration subsequently, on payment of an extra fee of $100.

Once the specification and filing fee (in 1985, $300) have been lodged at the US Patent and Trademark Office (to give it its full title; hereafter we will refer to it, for the sake of simplicity, as the Patent Office or use the abbreviation USPTO), the application is given a filing date and a serial number, and is then allocated on the basis of its subject matter to an examining group. If the declaration was not attached to the application, the applicant will be required to supply it within 1 month of the official notification, or two months from the filing date, whichever is later.

Examination

After a period of anything from four to twelve months, the applicant, or his agent, will receive a first 'official action' from the examiner in charge of the case. Very often this first action will take the form of a 'restriction requirement', which is an objection that the application claims more than one invention. The applicant is normally given thirty days in which to reply; although he may argue against the examiner's position, he must at least provisionally elect one invention, as defined by one group of claims, for further prosecution. He may later decide to drop the other group or groups, or he may decide to file a divisional application to cover them; however, this would normally be left until prosecution of the parent case was complete.

Some months later, a first official action 'on the merits' of the invention will issue. By now the examiner will have carried out a search and will normally cite anything from one to ten pieces of prior art; most usually US patents, but quite often foreign patents or papers from scientific journals. It is normal for all the claims to be rejected on the first official action, and the examiner will carefully list all the grounds upon which each claim is rejected, with reference to the appropriate section of the patent law, which is quoted in full.

The applicant must answer the official action within an inextensible term of six months. However, he is well advised to answer within three months if possible, since additional fees must be paid if the reply is made later than this. As of 1985, a reply made in the fourth month costs $50, in the fifth month $150, and in the sixth month $300. The 'free' term of three months is quite short if the applicant is in Europe or Japan and correspondence must pass over two agents.

The reply may take the form of an amendment to the claims, typically to reduce the scope in order to distinguish more clearly from the cited prior art, coupled with arguments as to why the examiner's rejections should be withdrawn. The applicant may also put in evidence in the form of an affidavit or declaration, either to establish an invention date in the USA earlier than the effective date of a piece of prior art published less than one year before the filing date, or to overcome an allegation of obviousness by showing surprising advantages for the invention over what is described in the prior art (see Chapter 16). If he has not already done so, he should at this stage bring to the attention of the examiner any prior art of which he is aware which is at least as relevant as any cited by the examiner.

The examiner may decide to allow all of the claims at this stage, in which case the applicant will in due course be sent a notice of allowance. Alternatively, so long as at least some of the claims are still rejected, he will issue a further official action. If the issues have not yet been clarified, and in particular if any new prior art is cited or new grounds of rejection are introduced, this second action will be similar to the first. If no new issues are raised, however, the second official action will normally be 'made final', and the claims will be 'finally rejected'. Despite its name, a final rejection does not mean that the proceedings are at an end. It does, however, severely restrict the applicant's opportunities for further prosecution. The applicant may again argue, or offer evidence, but although he may propose amendments, the examiner can refuse to permit them if he feels that they do not put the case in condition for allowance or improve its position on appeal. The examiner may then withdraw his final rejection and allow the application, but if he maintains his rejection of any of the claims he will shortly after the applicant's response issue an advisory action.

The advisory action states that the response has been considered but does not put the case in condition for allowance. It may state that some claims are allowable or would be allowable if amended further, or may conclude that all claims are still rejected. It will also state whether or not any amendments proposed by the applicant in his last response have been entered.

It is desirable to answer a final rejection within two months if possible, as this may reduce the cost of further extensions of time: an advisory action does not give rise to a new term of reply, and further action must be taken by the applicant within the statutory six months period from the date of the final rejection. If the original response to the final rejection was made three months or more after it issued, the further response after the advisory action becomes quite expensive.

In response to the advisory action, the applicant must do one of three things, if he wishes to maintain his application. First, if some claims are allowable, he may accept what has been allowed, and respond by cancelling the non-allowable claims and making whatever further amendments are needed. Secondly, he may lodge an appeal. Thirdly, he may file a new application as a continuation or continuation-in-part of the old. Finally, of course, he may do nothing, in which case the application automatically becomes abandoned when the time limit for response runs out.

Appeal

The procedure for appeal is that the applicant files a notice of appeal within the time for response to the final rejection. Within two months of filing the notice of appeal, an appeal brief must be filed, which sets out in full the claims on appeal, the rejections applied against them and the arguments why the rejections should be reversed. The examiner considers this and will normally write an examiner's answer setting out his reasons for disagreeing with the applicant's arguments, although he may at this stage give way and decide to allow some or all of the claims. If the examiner's answer raises any new issues the applicant may respond to these in a further reply brief.

The appeal is then scheduled to be heard by a three-man panel of the Board of Patent Appeals and Interferences, a board of senior Patent Office officials having the rank of examiner-in-chief. The Board may consider the appeal purely on the written arguments, but the applicant has the right to request an oral hearing at which he or his agent or attorney can argue briefly in person before the Board and answer any questions the Board may put. Because of the large number of appeals to be heard, it may well be about two years from the writing of the appeal brief until the Board gives its decision. It may reverse the examiner's decision in whole or in part, in which case the application will be returned to the examiner for further prosecution or allowance. It may affirm the examiner, in which case the final rejection stands. In practice it is found that the Board reverses the examiner's decision in about one-quarter of the cases it deals with.

If the Board of Patent Appeals and Interferences has decided against him, the applicant may within 30 days request reconsideration, although it is understandably rare for the Board to reverse itself. He may alternatively, or after a request for reconsideration has been unsuccessful, either appeal to the Court of Appeals for the Federal Circuit (CAFC) or bring a civil action in the District Court for the District of Columbia. The CAFC is a specialist court whose judges are experienced in patent matters, and it often produces decisions which appear more sensible than those of the Board of Appeals. The District Court is not a specialist court and it is less often used as a route for appeals from the Patent Office, but has the advantage that it can consider fresh evidence whereas the CAFC must decide on the basis of the record. From the CAFC a final appeal could be taken to the Supreme Court, but only if the Court itself decides to hear the case because, for example, an important point of law is involved, as it did in the Chakrabarty case on the patentability of microorganisms (see p. 152). Appeal from the District Court lies to the US Court of Appeals for the District of Columbia, then to the Supreme Court as above.

Refiling

It has been mentioned that an alternative procedure is that of refiling the application. This can be done at any time during prosecution, and can be a very useful strategy to employ. In a continuation application, the text is refiled unchanged, and the claims may be altered by amendment either concurrently with the filing or at a later time. The continuation application has the effective filing date of the original (parent) application, so that nothing is lost by the refiling. Because no changes are made to the description, the inventor does not have to sign a new declaration. By filing a continuation application, amendments to the claims can be made which the examiner would not permit in the parent case after a final rejection, or time may be gained in which to carry out comparative tests which may be necessary to establish patentability.

A coninutation-in-part (c.i.p.) application contains subject-matter disclosed in the parent case, but also contains new matter. This may be substantial, for example the scope of the claims may be broadened, and new descriptive matter and examples added to support the new claims, or it may involve correction or clarification of mistakes or ambiguities in the parent text. The matter originally disclosed in the parent application retains the original effective filing date, the new matter has the effective filing date of the c.i.p. application. For a c.i.p. application, a new declaration must be executed by the inventor, and care must be taken to get this right when there has been publication or grant of equivalent patents in other countries.

When a continuation or c.i.p. application has been filed, the parent case may or may not be abandoned and the new application will in any event be examined. However, if the parent case had been finally rejected, and essentially the same claims are again presented in the new application, the examiner may make the first official action a final rejection. By a combination of appeals and refilings, the prosecution of a difficult case may last five to ten years or even more, and this may be to the advantage of the applicant since his 17-year term of patent protection runs from the date of grant. Nevertheless, refiling should never be carried out purely to prolong the prosecution, but only if there is a valid reason for it. The Patent Office takes a dim view of deliberate delaying tactics.

When, at any stage of the proceedings, the examiner decides that all claims on file are allowable, he issues a form letter telling the applicant that prosecution 'on the merits' is closed, although formal matters may remain. Once these have been dealt with, which may be done by telephone if appropriate, a notice of allowance is issued; the applicant then has three months in which to pay the base issue fee, and when this has been done the patent is printed a few months later and granted as of its date of publication. The balance of the issue fee, if any, which may include extra printing charges if the specification is long, is payable within three months of grant. The US prosecution process is illustrated in Fig. 11.

At any time while the application is still pending, a divisional application may be filed to claim matter originally claimed in the first application but then withdrawn following a restriction requirement. The form the divisional application takes is the same as for a continuation application, unless new matter is added at the same time. Further continuations, c.i.p.s or divisionals may be filed as long as one application in the series is still pending. However, if these later applications claim matter which the examiner feels is essentially the same invention as claimed by the first application in the series to be granted, they may be granted subject to a 'terminal disclaimer', which means that they cease to have effect when the first patent expires.

If the examiner, after finding some or all of the claims allowable, considers that another pending patent application or granted patent claims substantially the same invention, an interference may be declared to determine which applicant has priority of invention. The procedure involved is extremely complex, and beyond the scope of this book.

Procedure in the European Patent Office

Filing
Generally speaking, a European patent application may be filed directly at the EPO, either at its main office in Munich or its branch office at The Hague, or at the national patent office of a contracting state. In the latter case, the date of receipt by the national office counts as the EPO filing date. In Germany, however, a European patent application must be filed at the EPO and not at the German Patent Office. In the United Kingdom, the secrecy provisions of the Patents Act 1977 prohibit the filing of a patent application abroad unless a corresponding British application has been filed at least six weeks previously, or special permission has been obtained. This means that a European application by a British resident made without claim of Convention priority must be filed at the British Patent Office, although in the more usual case in which priority is claimed from an earlier British application, the applicant has a choice.

A European patent application must be filed in English, French, or German, the three official languages of the EPO, unless the applicant is a national of a contracting state which has an official language different from these. For example, a Swedish applicant may file his application in Swedish, but must later provide a translation into one of the three official languages. The language of the application or the translation becomes the language of the proceedings, in which all the prosecution of the application

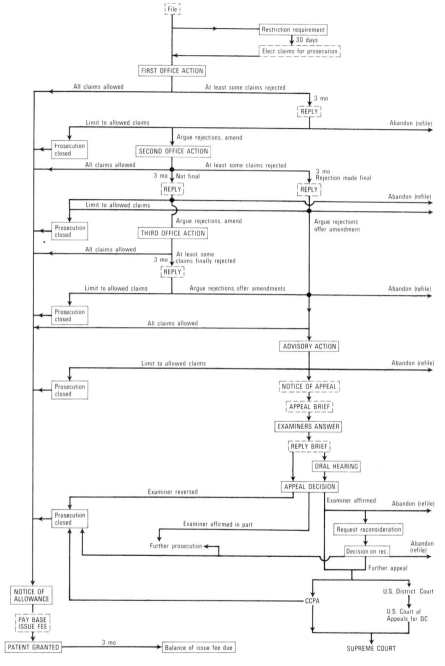

FIG. 11.   US Patent Office procedure.

before the EPO will be conducted (at least so long as no third parties become involved).

In order to obtain a filing date, the application must identify the applicant, indicate that a European patent is sought, designate at least one contracting state and include a description of the invention, with at least one claim. The application should also contain a title and abstract and a designation of the inventor. Fees are charged for the application, for the search, for each country designated, and for each claim in excess of ten, the fees being payable within one month of filing. The correct choice of designated countries is important, as designations cannot be added at a later stage. To be on the safe side one can designate all possible countries in the application, and then cancel one or more of them, although if a designation is cancelled after the designated fee has been paid, there is no refund.

It is possible to have different applicants for different designated countries, although there must be a single representative responsible for communications with the EPO.

Priority may be claimed at the time of filing from one or more earlier European, PCT, or national applications filed within the preceding 12 months. In the case of national applications, these may have been made in any member state of the Paris Convention or in any state having a special agreement with the EPO. Since, for example, a European patent application designating Switzerland may claim priority from a Swiss application, the EPC provides a route whereby 'internal priority' may be claimed in a country such as Switzerland where this is not possible for national patent applications (see p. 56).

The application is sent to the Receiving Section at The Hague, which first checks to see that the requirements for receiving a filing date have been met, and that the fees have been paid, then carries out a formalities examination. The applicant is given a time of 1–2 months to correct minor objections made at this stage.

The application then passes to the Search Division, also at The Hague, which produces the European search report on the invention. As soon as possible after 18 months from the filing date or earliest priority date, the application is published (by photolithography) together with the search report and abstract.

The EPO now encourages applicants to file with their typed specification a diskette carrying the text in a form readable by a word processor, or to type the specification in OCR-B (machine-readable) characters. In this way it is hoped to be able to print early published applications as well as the final patent.

Examination

At this stage the applicant must, if he wishes to proceed, file a request for examination and pay the examination fee within 6 months of publication. Examination is then carried out by a three-man Examining Division in Munich; in practice one member of the Division deals with the application until a final decision is to be reached; the decision to grant or to refuse is then taken by the whole Division.

When each official letter is issued a term is set for reply, but there is no overall time within which the application must be in order for grant, as there is in the United Kingdom. However, there are maintenance fees payable for pending applications which become due after the second year from filing. Divisional applications may be filed at the instigation of the applicant at any time up to the end of the term for answering the first office action, or later if the Examining Division considers it justified. If the Examining Division requires limitation of the claims of the original application because of lack of unity of invention, a divisional application may be filed within two months of that decision. Divisional applications must be filed direct at the EPO, and must be in the same language as the parent application.

If the Examining Division refuses the application, the applicant may appeal to a three-man Board of Appeal, normally consisting of one legally qualified and two technically qualified members; if an important point of law is involved, or if different appeal boards have given conflicting decisions, an appeal may be heard by a five-member Enlarged Board of Appeals. However, unlike the procedure in the British or US Patent Offices, there is no further appeal from the EPO to the courts, for example to the European Court of Justice. Whether the internal appeal procedure will be adequate remains to be seen.

If the Examining Division decides to grant the application, the applicant must pay grant and printing fees; the notice of grant is published in the *European Patent Bulletin*, and the patent is published in printed form, in the language of the proceedings, but with translations of the claims into the two other official languages. The purpose of providing translations of the claims at this stage is to make sure that potential opponents, who may not be familiar with the language in which the specification appears, will have a better chance to appreciate the scope of protection which the EPO has granted.

It should be noted also that the scope of the granted claims may not be the same for all designated countries. One reason for this is that Austria joined the EPC with the reservation that for a limited period (not to exceed 15 years) European patents for Austria, like national Austrian patents, could not claim chemical compounds *per se*. Accordingly where the invention is a new compound, a special set of claims, containing process claims but not product claims, will be required for Austria.

A further possible reason is that an earlier unpublished European application cited under the whole contents approach (see p. 34) is only prior art in so far as it designates the same countries as the later application against which it is cited. Thus, if part of the scope of an application designating all ten EPC countries is no longer new in view of an earlier unpublished European application designating only the United Kingdom, France, and Germany, the claims of the later application would have to be limited in these three countries, but not in the other seven.

Finally, after the end of the opposition period (see below), the granted Europatent is sent to the national patent offices of the designated contracting states, where it has the same effect as a national patent. A contracting state may require that a Europatent does not become effective in the country unless a translation of the full specification and claims into an official language of that country is provided. As the majority of contracting states do insist on this requirement, this means that the expense of translation associated with foreign filing is not avoided by the European procedure, but only postponed. What is more, if the claims of the granted Europatent differ from country to country, then for all countries which require translations the applicant must provide a translation of the specification and each different set of claims; thus special claims for Austria will have to be translated into Swedish, for example.

A diagram of the EPO examination procedure up to grant is given in Fig. 12.

It has been the experience of most patent practitioners that the European Patent Office is very flexible in its formal requirements and does its best to help the applicant to overcome any procedural difficulties. This is in marked contrast to the recent attitude of the British Patent Office and the Patents Court, who seem almost to delight in setting traps for the applicant by applying requirements so strict that trivial acts of omission or irregularity can lead to complete loss of rights.[1] The British Patent Office would do well to remember that it no longer has a monopoly in the granting of British Patents, and that if the customers are not satisfied they will go elsewhere.

Oppositions at the European Patent Office and elsewhere

When a Europatent is granted by the Examining Division, the patentee has still to face what may well be the biggest hurdle; the European opposition procedure. Within nine months of the publication of notice of grant, third parties may oppose the patent on the grounds that the subject matter was not patentable (i.e. it was not novel, lacked an inventive step, or was not

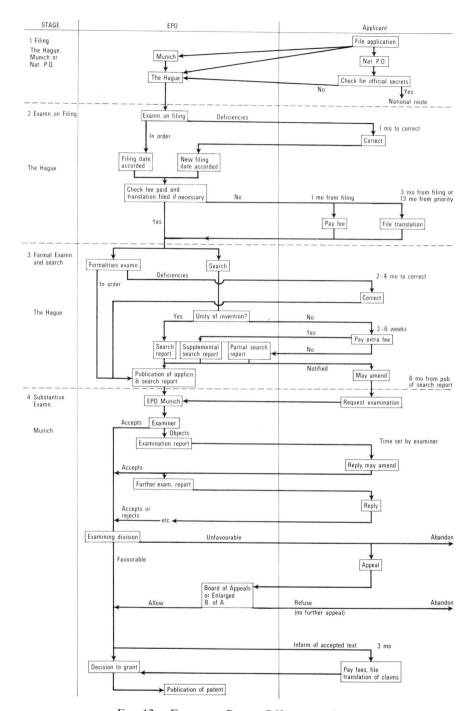

Fig. 12.   European Patent Office procedure.

capable of industrial application), that the disclosure was insufficient or that new matter was added during prosecution. Oppositions are heard by a three-member Opposition Division, one of whom may have been a member of the Examining Division, and appeals lie to the Board of Appeals or Enlarged Board of Appeals, but no further. The opposition may result in the patent being upheld unchanged, amended (in which case the amended specification is reprinted), or revoked. Revocation or amendment normally applies to all designated countries, unless the successful ground of opposition was lack of novelty over an earlier unpublished application which did not designate all countries designated in the opposed patent.

Opposition proceedings have long been a feature of the patent laws of the majority of countries, not including the USA, and in their original form were strictly oppositions to grant; that is a patent application was published after acceptance by the patent office, and within a fixed time other parties might oppose the grant of a patent on that application. If there was no opposition, or if opposition was unsuccessful the application proceeded to grant; if opposition was successful a patent was not granted, so that there was a clear distinction between opposition and an application to revoke a granted patent. Opposition to grant was considered by patent offices whereas revocation of a granted patent was normally a matter for the courts.

This 'standard' pre-grant type of opposition proceedings is still found in many countries, for example in Japan and The Netherlands. In the United Kingdom under the 1949 Act there was not only the standard form of opposition to grant, but also provision for revocation by the Patent Office on application by third parties within one year of the grant. Because the grounds on which a patent could be revoked in this way were the same as the grounds for opposition (and differed from those on which a patent could be revoked by the High Court), this procedure became known as 'belated opposition'.

Strictly speaking, the opposition proceedings at the EPO are belated opposition or revocation proceedings, since they take place after the patent has been granted; however the effect is the same, and the tendency in a number of countries seems to be towards patent office revocation proceeding after a formal grant rather than opposition after acceptance and before grant. For example, Germany had for some years an elaborate procedure in which an application was published three times in all; first early publication of the unexamined application as an *Offenlegungschrift* (DOS), then of the accepted application as an *Auslegeschrift* (DAS) and finally after the opposition stage as a *Patentschrift* (DPS). From the beginning of 1981 the procedure has been simplified so that the DAS stage is omitted, and belated opposition is possible after publication of the

Patentschrift. In Japan, however, there are still three publications; the *kokai* and the *kokoku* (corresponding to DOS and DAS) being published before the patent is granted. Opposition is possible after publication of the *kokoku*. In the United Kingdom, the 1977 Act allows revocation by the Patent Office at any time after grant, the grounds now being the same as those on which the Court can order revocation.

The number of oppositions in the United Kingdom in the last few years before the 1977 Act came into force had sunk considerably, and involved less than 1 per cent of the applications which were published. The reason for this was probably that the Patent Office and the Patents Appeal Tribunal (a High Court judge to whom appeals from the Patent Office could be made) were strongly inclined to give the applicant the benefit of the doubt in any opposition proceedings, the theory being that the patent, if granted, could always be attacked further in the High Court. In practice this meant that it was practically impossible to knock out a patent completely in opposition (or belated opposition) proceedings; usually all that happened was that the applicant made some necessary amendments and ended up with a stronger patent than he would otherwise have had.

Under the 1977 Act the number of belated oppositions (i.e. revocation actions in the Patent Office) has shrunk even more rapidly. In 1982, for example there were only 12 such actions out of over 29 000 granted patents, a percentage rate of only 0.04 per cent.

In contrast, in Germany there has always been a high percentage of oppositions, approximately 20 per cent of all granted applications being opposed. The figure has dropped to about 16 per cent in recent years, but this is still far higher than in any other country. It was supposed that in the EPO, where a single opposition could knock out a patent in up to 10 countries, the opposition rate would be even higher than in Germany, and a level of 25 per cent was predicted. In fact, the percentage of European patents which are opposed is at present only 10 per cent. As of 1984, only 325 oppositions had been finally decided, of which 40 per cent were rejected while in 40 per cent of the cases the patent was revoked and in 20 per cent it was granted with a limited scope of claims.

The 1980 amendment to the US patent law allows a third party to ask for 're-examination' of a granted US patent, which is also a form of belated opposition proceedings. (See p. 121).

6

MAINTAINING A PATENT IN FORCE

'An official of the Patent Office said that many inventors abandon their
parents during their first year of life'.
Surrey paper, quoted by Denys Parsons: *Many a True Word*

Renewal fees

Finally, after periods of time ranging from a new months to several years
from the filing dates, the applicant receives granted patents in the countries
in which he applied. These patents have a fixed legal term, which in the
majority of industrialized countries is now 20 years from the application
date, and in USA and Canada is 17 years from the date of grant. In
Canada, the patentee, as we now call him, need do nothing more. He does
not have to pay any fees in order to keep his patent in force, and it will
automatically run for the full 17-year term unless he takes positive
action to abandon it. The same is true in the USA if the patent was applied
for before 12 December 1980.

In nearly all other countries in the world, however, it costs money to
keep a patent in force. The renewal fee must be paid to the patent office of
the country in question, normally upon an annual basis, although in some
countries payments are made at less frequent intervals. For example US
law now provides for renewal fees payable $3\frac{1}{2}$, $7\frac{1}{2}$, and $11\frac{1}{2}$ years after
grant. If the renewal fees is not paid within a stipulated period from the
due date, the patent lapses. As a general rule, renewal fees are relatively
low in the early years, and rise more or less steeply towards the end of the
patent term. Often the first few years are free; thus in Britain the first
renewal fee falls due at the end of the fourth year from application.

The reasoning behind the requirement for renewal fees is twofold.
First is the purely financial one that it helps to finance the running of the
patent office. In the United Kingdom at least, the Patent Office is
expected to pay for itself out of fees charged to its users. If this were done
only by application, search, and examination fees, these would have to be
set as such a high level that there would be a considerable disincentive to
potential applicants; in particular the individual inventor would be unable
to afford to apply for a patent. It seems reasonable that a considerable
amount of the money should come from those who are making commercial
use of their patents.

This brings us to the second reason, which is that the renewal fee system means that only patents which are of real or potential commercial value to their owners are maintained for more than a few years. In this way inventions in which there is no great commercial interest become public property much earlier than would otherwise be the case.

For European patents, renewal fees are collected by the national patent offices, and are the same as for nationally granted patents. The EPC provides, however, that the European Patent Office shall receive up to three-quarters of these renewal fees, so that the financing of the EPO is not dependent upon application, search, and examination fees alone. For the early years, in which there can be little or no income from renewals of Europatents, the EPO receives direct funding from the contracting states, but in due course it is intended to be self-supporting.

In the USA, by contrast, it was government policy heavily to subsidize the operations of the Patent Office with the object of encouraging inventors. The application and issue fees, together with sundry fees which may be charged during prosecution, for appeals, etc., used to cover no more than a small part of the Patent Office budget, the rest of which came from the funds voted by Congress to the Department of Commerce. In practice this policy resulted in the Patent Office being constantly short of money and in many US patents remaining in force which had nothing more than nuisance value. In 1982, fees were drastically increased (for example the application fee rose from $65 to $300), and by 1992, 100 per cent of actual costs are supposed to be covered by fees, including renewal fees. However, 'small entities' (individuals, non-profit organizations, and small companies) pay only 50 per cent of the normal fees, the difference being made up out of public funds. This increase in self-generated funding of the USPTO has been expensive for applicants, but has had a marked effect on its efficiency: additional examiners have been recruited, backlogs decreased and the average time from application to grant of a US patent has been reduced. The aim is to decrease this average time to 18 months by 1987. It is also planned to institute an electronic data processing system which will make the operations of the USPTO 'paper-free' by 1990. It is to be hoped that this will increase efficiency and not the reverse: it may turn out to be easier to lose an electronic file than a physical one.

It is a somewhat pointless exercise to discuss the absolute amounts of renewal fees in various countries, since fluctuations in exchange rates and inflation levels constantly alter the figures, and in addition if renewal fees are paid through local agents, their charges must be taken into account. For the sake of interest, however, renewal fees in the United Kingdom in 1986 ranged from £76 for the fifth year to £292 for the twentieth year. The costs in the United Kingdom are lower than in many European countries, and there is no particular correlation between cost and value received. The most expensive country in the world in terms of renewal fees is the German

Democratic Republic (DDR), in which a patent is to all intents and purposes worthless.

The need to pay renewal fees to keep patents alive means that a patentee, whether a large company or an individual, should annually review the patents which are held and decide whether or not each patent should be kept in force. If the patent relates to a marketed product, it should be considered for each country involved what would be the commercial consequences of the patent being allowed to lapse. If no market product is involved, it should be asked whether the patent has any useful function as a 'defensive patent' to keep competitors away from an area of interest. For a company with a large number of patents, very considerable sums can be saved by rooting out the patents which have outlived their usefulness.

It is clear that a good record-keeping system is essential in order to ensure that renewal fees are paid when they fall due. Such a system must also be 'fail-safe' – that is, a patent should always be renewed in the absence of a positive decision to allow it to lapse. Patent agents in private practice will normally provide this service for their clients; companies with their own patent departments will do their own record-keeping. This type of system is ideally suited for operation by computer, and recently firms have been founded which specialize in the computerized management of patent renewal fees either directly for industrial clients or on behalf of firms of patent agents.

However good a system may be, the possibility of error cannot be ruled out. For this reason, a large number of countries make provision for the restoration of a patent which has inadvertently been allowed to lapse by non-payment of a renewal fee. In the United Kingdom, restoration of a lapsed patent used to be possible for up to three years after the lapse, but the 1977 Act has shortened this period to one year. The following procedure under the UK Patents Act 1977 applies to all patents, including those granted under the old Act.

The renewal fee for the next year can be paid during the three months before the anniversary of the filing date. The fee is sent to the Patent Office together with a standard form, the counterfoil of which is date stamped and returned as evidence of payment. If payment is not made by the anniversary of the filing date, the patent technically lapses as of that date. Within six weeks the Patent Office sends out a reminder that the fee is still unpaid. The patentee can act on this reminder by paying the renewal fee at any time up to six months after the date on which it was due, but an extra fee must be paid for each month the payment was overdue.

If payment is made within this six-month period, the patent continues in force as if it had never lapsed, and action can still be taken against anyone who infringed the patent while the fee remained unpaid. During the next six months, however, there is no automatic right to late payment of the renewal fee. The lapse of the patent is no longer a technicality but a reality and the ex-patentee, as he now is, must petition for restoration of the patent. In order to do this, he has to show that he took reasonable care to see that the renewal fee was paid on time, or at least within the first six-month period, and that the fee was not paid because of circumstances beyond his control. If the Patent Office allows restoration, a further additional fee must then be paid. What is more, the patent is no longer treated as if it had never lapsed. Anyone who began to do anything falling under the patent claims after the anniversary date on which it lapsed, or even made real preparations to do so, has the right after the patent is restored to go on doing what he began or prepared to do, without having to pay any royalty to the patentee.

In the USA also there are provisions for late payment of a renewal fee during a six-month period, on payment of an extra fee. After this period the Commissioner may still accept a renewal fee if the failure to pay the fee on time was 'unavoidable'.

Extension of term

British patents granted under the 1977 Act have a fixed term of 20 years and cannot be extended. Under the 1949 Act it used to be possible to extend the 16 year term of patents for war loss (up to 10 years) or because the patentee had not made a reasonable amount of money from his patent, taking into account the benefit of his invention to the public. This type of extension could be granted for up to 5 years, or 10 years in exceptional cases. In the 1970s there were a number of successful applications to the High Court for extensions of this type, often involving pharmaceutical inventions. For example: the National Research Development Corporation (NRDC) obtained extensions of six and four years respectively on the patents for cephalosporin C and the cephalosporin intermediate 7-ACA;[2] the Wellcome Foundation obtained a four-year extension of their patent for the drug trimethoprim;[3] and Biorex one of five years on a patent covering the anti-ulcer agent carbenoxolone.[4] In the non-pharmaceutical field, Rolls Royce (1971) Ltd, were able to extend the term of their patent for the Harrier 'jump jet' engine by eight years.[5]

Such extension cases were very costly and involved the preparation of very detailed accounts by an accountant familiar with patent extension work, but for a major commercial product the value of the patent extension would be well worth the trouble and expense of obtaining it.

Under the 1977 UK Patents Act, the term of 'new existing patents', the complete specifications of which were filed later than 1 June 1967, was automatically extended to 20 years, and no further extension of these patents is possible. 'Old existing patents' dated on or before that date could still be extended, but these extensions were limited to a maximum of four years. As the last of the 'old existing patents' expired in June 1983, no more patent extensions are possible in the UK.

This type of extension of a patent term is a feature of patent law which is found only in those countries whose patent law is based on that of the United Kingdom, although certain countries have a variable patent term. Thus it is found in the laws of member countries of the British Commonwealth such as Australia and New Zealand, and former members such as Ireland and South Africa. South Africa has recently adopted a patent term of 20 years, but this was not made retroactive. Patents granted under the old law have a term of 16 years and may be extended by a maximum of five years. In some recent decisions the South African courts have taken a very generous approach to the grant of extensions for pharmaceutical patents, and have granted extensions on the basis that the product could not be sold for some years of the original patent term because approval of the health authorities had not yet been obtained. This is always the case for new pharmaceuticals, which sometimes cannot appear on the market before the patent life is more than half over, so if these decisions are maintained pharmaceutical patents could be extended in South Africa essentially on a routine basis. Elsewhere extensions are generally as difficult to obtain as they were in the United Kingdom.

It is now possible to obtain extensions of US patents in the pharmaceutical field to partly compensate for the time required to obtain regulatory approval from the FDA. This is discussed in more detail in Chapter 12.

Although the term of patents in many countries has in the last few years been increased to a uniform 20 years (for example, from 16 in the United Kingdom and South Africa, from 17 in the Scandinavian countries and from 18 in Switzerland, Germany, and Austria), there has been no uniformity in the matter of what happens to the term of existing patents granted under the previous laws. At one extreme, Germany and South Africa retained the original term for all existing patents, at the other extreme Switzerland made the new term apply to all patents, thereby extending the life of all existing patents by two years.

The Swiss approach operates unfairly for those who are licensees under a Swiss patent and now must pay royalties for an additional two years, as well as for those who were planning to launch a product once the patent had expired. A number of countries have therefore adopted a compromise approach in which only the more recent existing patents have their term automatically extended. Denmark and Sweden for example, granted a 20-year term to existing patents less than 12 years old when the new Acts came into force in 1978. In the United Kingdom, as we have seen, patents dated later than 1 June 1967 now have a 20-year term, but for the last four years of this term the patentee must grant licences upon demand, and a licensee whose licence dates from before the 1977 Act came into force (1 June 1978) does not have to pay any royalty for the last four years.

Working requirements

In the majority of countries, there is an obligation upon a patentee to exploit his invention within the country, and if he does not so 'work' the invention, his rights may be reduced, e.g. by compulsory licensing, or the patent may even be revoked. If a patent becomes liable to compulsory licensing, it means that the patentee no longer has a monopoly; any other person can obtain permission to use the invention, generally upon payment of a reasonable royalty to the patentee.

The Paris Convention for the protection of intellectual property places restrictions on the extent to which signatory countries can take action against a patentee for not working his invention. Compulsory licensing generally cannot be applied until three years after the grant of the patent, so that the patentee has a breathing space in which he can make preparations to work his invention. The patent may only be revoked for non-working if compulsory licensing has failed, and then only after two years from grant of the first compulsory licence.

The patent laws of most countries have more or less elaborate provisions for compulsory licensing of patents which are not worked, but in the great majority of developed countries these provisions are seldom if ever applied. As a matter of practical experience only about 10 per cent of granted patents are ever actually worked; the majority of the others may be allowed to lapse by non-payment of renewal fees, but even those patents which are maintained in force and not worked are very rarely the subject of compulsory licence applications. The reasons for this are fairly clear, the chief one being that if it is not commercially worthwhile for the patentee to work the invention, it is not likely to be so for others either. Even if a patent covers what could be a good commercial product but is being maintained unworked for defensive reasons a compulsory licence would only come in question if the parties were hostile and no agreement could be reached on a voluntary licence. In most cases it would then probably cost more time and money to obtain a compulsory licence against the patentee's opposition than it would be worth.

In a few countries, of which the USA is the most important, there is no statutory obligation to work a patent, and the patentee may, in theory, sit upon his invention and neither work it himself nor be forced to grant a licence to anyone else. Nevertheless, the patentee may be forced to grant licences if he has been guilty of anti-trust violation or patent misuse (see p. 293). Some inventions can thus be effectively suppressed by a US patent but only, of course, for 17 years. Allegations which are made from time to time about patents being used to permanently suppress inventions which might upset established industries are fictitious, since any patented invention must be published and must be available to the public when the patent expires.

In most industrialized countries, therefore, working requirements are either non-existent or a dead letter. It is very different in the case of developing countries, which, as we shall see in Chapter 24, often insist on working requirements to an extent which cannot possibly be met, effectively negating patent protection in these countries. As importation of a patented product generally does not count as working, the patentee must set up local manufacturing facilities, often within an impossibly short time limit, in order to keep his patent from being cancelled for non-working. Some of the most onerous working requirements are found in certain South American countries which are not members of the Paris Convention.

In some countries the practice of 'nominal working' was frequently used when actual working of a patented invention was not being carried out. Nominal working consists in advertising that licences are available under the patent; this was generally done once a year. Only in a very few countries was this practice officially recognized; elsewhere it was doubtful if it accomplished anything other than providing a steady income for local agents. Now increasing numbers of countries stipulate that only actual working is effective, and the practice of nominal working seems to be on the decline.

Licences of right

In the United Kingdom and in certain other countries, including Germany, France, and Italy, a patentee may voluntarily put himself into the position of someone whose patent is subject to compulsory licensing. He does this by stating officially that anyone may as of right have a licence under his patent upon reasonable terms, which will be set by the Patent Office or the courts if the parties cannot agree. His patent may then be useful as a source of royalty income, but can no longer be used to exclude others from carrying out the invention. In return for accepting these restricted rights, the patentee can maintain his patent in force on payment of only half the normal amount of renewal fees.

In Germany this action is irrevocable, but in the United Kingdom and other countries the original position can be restored, if the patentee pays the balance of the renewal fees which he would otherwise have had to pay in full, and if the rights of any existing licensees are protected.

This 'licences of right' provision is also one which is not used as often as one might expect. Even if a patentee wishes to licence his patent he will normally try to do so by direct negotiation with one or more potential licensees rather than by throwing his patent open to all comers. This is because the most important thing which the patentee has to offer is the right to exclude others, and a licensee will often not be interested unless he can obtain exclusive rights. This is not possible if a patent has been endorsed 'licences of right', and a licensee will generally not be willing to pay a high royalty rate for a licence which his competitors may also have on the same terms.

Registrations and patents of importation

The fact of having a granted patent in one country can occasionally give rise to rights in other countries. There are isolated cases in which, by special agreement, a patent granted in one country may extend automatically to another; for example, although Liechtenstein is a sovereign state, a Swiss patent extends also to Liechtenstein, and a British patent automatically covers the now independent states of Swaziland and Botswana.

In a number of British colonies and ex-colonies, and in the Channel Islands, protection can be obtained by registration of a granted British patent. Some of these countries in addition have their own independent patent laws, but in many cases, for example in Singapore, registration of a British patent is the only form of patent protection which is available. The same was true until recently for Hong Kong, but in 1981 Hong Kong acceded to the PCT, which provides an alternative method of obtaining protection there. Registration must normally be done within three years of grant (5 years for Hong Kong), and the registration lasts for as long as the British patent remains in force. Generally no renewal fees are payable.

When European patents designating the UK began to be granted, there was considerable uncertainty as to whether they could be registered in the same way as a national British patent. Some registration countries accepted European patents (UK) from the beginning, whereas a number of others had to amend their regulations in order to make this possible. Although a few registration countries still refuse to register anything other than a national British patent, the majority, including the more important territories such as Hong Kong and Singapore, now accept British patents granted by the European route.

A different group of countries, mainly in Latin America, have a special type of patent known as a patent of importation or patent of revalidation, which like a registration is based on a patent granted in another country. In Europe, Spain and Belgium have until recently also had patents of importation, but these are being abolished to bring the laws of these countries into conformity with the rest of Europe.

The conditions under which such patents are granted vary considerably from country to country; in Spain patents of importation could be granted to persons unconnected with the original patentee, and had a fixed term of ten years from grant. Elsewhere they are normally granted only to the original patentee or his assignees, and have a term equal to the remaining term of the basic patent.

Like the earliest English patents, patents of importation are intended to reward a person who actually introduces the invention into the country, even if it may be known elsewhere. It follows that the basis of the patent is the actual local working of the patented invention, and if this is not done the patent will be invalid.

7

ENFORCEMENT OF PATENT RIGHTS

Many federal appellate judges . . . approach patents with the kind of suspicion and hostility that a city-bred boy feels when he must traverse a jungle full of snakes . . . All patents look more or less strange and threatening to them; and since they are heavily armed with the power of the U.S. Government, they frequently get the idea that it's their duty to kill everything that moves in this dangerous land.

Abe Fortas: *The Patent System in Distress*

What constitutes infringement

Once a patentee has obtained a granted patent, and done whatever is necessary to keep it in force, what can he do with it? As we have seen in Chapter 1, a patent does not give the patentee the right to practice his invention, but only to prevent others from doing so. Although this right is, in the United Kingdom, granted by the Crown, it is not up to the Crown to enforce it. Infringement of a British patent is not a crime for which one can be prosecuted, but a civil wrong (in legal language, a tort) for which one can be sued in the civil courts. Essentially, the right given by a patent is the right to sue for infringement.

While this is true for all countries having an Anglo-Saxon legal system, and also for many others, there are nevertheless a number of countries in which patent infringement *is* a criminal offence, either generally or in special circumstances such as when there is deliberate and wilful infringement.

Although criminal prosecutions for patent infringement are rare even in those countries, the possibility may act as an additional deterrent (in Japan for example an infringer could, in theory at least, be sentenced to up to five years' hard labour), or may give procedural advantages to the patentee (thus in Switzerland, a patentee alleging criminal infringement may be able to obtain a police search of the alleged infringer's premises to obtain evidence of infringement).

Infringement in the United Kingdom before the 1977 Act

The UK Patents Act 1977 is the first Patents Act to define what constitutes infringement. Previously, infringement was defined only by judicial interpretation of the wording of the patent grant (see Fig. 1) which gave the patentee the sole right to 'make, use, exercise or vend' the invention and forbade others to 'directly or indirectly make use of or put in practice the said invention'. For example, when the invention was a new chemical compound the claim to that compound was considered to be infringed by making the compound, using the compound or selling the compound. Because of the territorial limitations of the patent, any such activity had to be within the United Kingdom in order to be an infringement. Thus if the compound was made abroad and imported to the United Kingdom, the manufacture would not infringe the United Kingdom patent, but sale and use in the United Kingdom of the imported product would do so.

If the invention claimed was a method of making an article, including a chemical compound, then it was settled by early legal precedents that the patent was infringed not only by using the process of the invention but also by using or selling the product of that process. Furthermore, this reasoning was extended to situations where the patent claimed a process for making a chemical compound used as an intermediate, and it was held that sale in the United Kingdom of the unpatented final product infringed the patent. Because this principle was laid down in a series of cases involving intermediates for saccharin, it is commonly referred to as the Saccharin Doctrine.[1]

If the claimed invention was a method of using an article or a compound, then the patent was infringed only by carrying out that method of use, and not by making or selling the article used. A patent might, of course, contain claims of more than one type, but if any one claim of the patent was infringed that sufficed to establish infringement of the patent.

In the course of time, a number of court decisions extended the meaning of the simple words used in the patent grant, to cover certain other situations in which commercial use was being made of the invention. For instance, although mere possession of a patented article was not infringement, possession for trade purposes, for example with intention to resell, was considered as 'vending'. The term 'use' was also held to cover situations where a patented article was in position ready for use, for example a fire extinguisher was being used before it was actually operated to put out a fire.[2] Sales of a patented article as a 'kit of parts' to be assembled by the consumer could also constitute infringement.[3]

Case law and statute law

This provides a good illustration of how patent law, as many other branches of law in the United Kingdom and other countries with Anglo-Saxon legal systems, is a blend of statute law and case law. Statute law is what is enacted by parliament; for example the Patents Act 1977. Case law is a set of principles derived from judicial decisions; these decisions may go back to the origins of English law, or may be judicial interpretations of Crown prerogative (such as the words of the patent grant) or of statutory enactments such as successive Patents Acts. What enables a reasonably consistent body of case law to be built up is the principle of precedent, by which a court is bound by an earlier decision of a higher court or a court of equal status to itself. Only the House of Lords is not bound by its own precedents.

At first sight this principle seems to rob judges of any independence of thought and action, but this would be a gross exaggeration. The strict application of precedent applies only when the factual situation is the same, and this is rarely the case. The judge may always 'distinguish' the case he is deciding from an earlier one by pointing out differences in the facts of the case, and it is usually not too difficult to do so when he wishes to reach an opposite conclusion. Thus, there are some patent cases decided by the House of Lords which were clearly wrongly decided, and which have never really been followed since. There may also be two distinct lines of cases taking opposite sides on a particular point, in which case the judge must decide which set of precedents to follow.

What is clear, however, is that if a point of law has been settled by the House of Lords, no lower tribunal, whether it be the Patent Office, the High Court, or the Court of Appeal, can simply decide differently where the factual situation is essentially the same. This means that the outcome of litigation is in many cases reasonably predictable, so that parties who are in dispute, for example a patentee and an alleged infringer, can make a reasonable estimate of their chances of success. If the precedents are clearly against one of the parties, he will be well advised to settle out of court rather than spend large sums on litigation.

In countries having different legal systems, the system of precedent may not always apply. In Spain it appears that only after the third concurring decision does a binding precedent exist, a principle first enunciated by Lewis Carroll.† In certain countries there is no precedent system whatsoever, so that the outcome of litigation is totally uncertain.

In the USA there is indeed a system of binding precedents, but the difficulty there is that the US Federal District Courts, which have jurisdiction in patent matters, are divided into eleven different circuits, each of which has a Circuit Court of Appeals, and a decision of a District Court or Circuit Court of Appeals is a precedent only within the same circuit. It is true that decisions of the Supreme Court are binding upon all lower courts, but the separate independent jurisdictions at circuit level have the result that the same point of law may be decided differently in different circuits. It therefore may be of great importance to the litigants in

---

† 'What I tell you three times is true.' *The Hunting of the Snark*. Fit the First.

which circuit the case will be tried, and a great deal of thought and effort goes into the question of where the action should be brought, and whether the jurisdiction of the court can be challenged and the action removed to a court in a different circuit. Such 'forum-shopping' tactics unnecessarily delay and complicate US litigation.

In patent litigation, however, the situation has now been much improved by giving the new Court of Appeals for the Federal Circuit jurisdiction to hear appeals on patent cases from all Federal District Courts. (see p. 23.)

In countries in which there is the possibility of development of case law built up on judicial decisions, it sometimes happens that a body of case law relative to patents arises which is contrary to the original intentions of the legislature, or which has effects which the legislature wishes to change. When a new patent law is being considered, amendments may then be made with the intention of cancelling that part of the case law. As soon as the statute law is changed, the case law which interpreted the parts of the statute law which have been altered will normally cease to have any value as precedents. Thus although the main object of the Patents Act 1977 was to adapt British patent law to the EPC, the opportunity was taken to correct some minor points where it was felt that the case law was wrong or gave an unintended result.

More frequently, the legislature agrees with the case law developed by the judges, and amends the statute law to make it say explicitly what the judges have held the previous law to mean. The case law is then codified as statute law, and the earlier cases become superfluous as precedents, even though their principles are still followed. This is what has happened to the law of infringement in the United Kingdom. Previously one had only the case law interpreting the cryptic wording of the patent grant; now the Patents Act 1977 for the first time gives a statutory definition of what amounts to infringement. This definition now incorporates much of what had been decided in the earlier case law, and also gives effect to the provisions on infringement which have been agreed as part of the Community Patent Convention. In some minor respects it reverses previous case law, and it also introduces one completely new type of infringement – contributory infringement.

Infringement in the United Kingdom under the 1977 Act

It is now specified that importation of a patented product for commercial purposes constitutes infringement, as does keeping the product for commercial purposes. In these respects existing case law has been written into the new statute law. The same rules as apply to patented products are made to apply to the direct product of a patented process. Product-by-process protection is thus for the first time part of the written law, but here the new law does not go so far as the old case law did. The use of the word 'direct' is clearly meant to do away with the Saccharin Doctrine, so that sale of the final product of a multi-step chemical process is no longer an infringement of a patent for anything other than the last step of that process, and it would seem that sale of the end product will not infringe a patent covering the intermediate. As the list of activities which constitute infringement is stated to be exclusive, there seems to be no room for a court to interpret the new Act any more broadly.

The new aspect introduced in the UK Patents Act 1977 is provision for what is usually referred to as contributory infringement, although it is not called that in the Act. Contributory infringement occurs under certain conditions when someone supplies any of the essential means for putting a patented process into effect, and is as much an infringement of the patent as is carrying out the process itself. The conditions are that there is infringement only if the person supplied is not entitled (e.g. by a licence) to work the patented process, and if the supplier knows, or should know, that the means are both suitable for putting, and intended to put, the invention into effect in the United Kingdom. If the means in question are a staple commercial product, there is no infringement unless the supply is made for the purpose of inducing infringement.

This definition, of which the above is only a summary, incorporates a good deal of legal jargon, but the effect of the provision is that it should now be possible for a patentee who has invented a new use for a known substance to take action not only against unauthorised users but against persons selling the material for the new use. The patentee will generally not wish to sue the end users, who are after all his customers or potential customers. The person he wishes to sue is the rival manufacturer who is using the patentee's invention to increase his own sales of the substance. If the substance has no other significant uses, it is enough if the seller merely knows the substance is intended to be used for the patented use; if the substance is a commercial product with non-infringing uses, there will be contributory infringement only if the seller sells the material with instructions to infringe.

The new UK law on infringement applies to patents granted under the 1949 Act, so that acts constituting contributory infringement of such a patent, which were not infringement before the new Act came into force on 1 June 1978, became infringement on that day. However, so as not to penalize anyone retroactively, it was provided that anyone who started any activity before that date which was not infringement then could continue that act thereafter without infringing a patent, even though the same act started after that date might amount to infringement.

A further change in the law as regards infringement is that there are certain rights given as from the early publication of an unexamined application. The applicant cannot sue anyone until the patent has been granted, but he may then claim damages as from the date of early publication, so long as the infringing act fell within the claims of the application as published as well as the patent as granted. Similar provisions are found in the laws of most countries in which patent applications are published before examination.

It would obviously be unjust if a manufacturer could be stopped by someone else's patent from doing something which he had already been doing before the patent was first filed. Of course, if the manufacturer's activity gave public knowledge of the invention there would be no problem, since the invention would no longer be novel and a later patent could not be valid. However, if this activity was a process improvement which he wished to keep as secret know-how, a subsequent patent would still be novel. The UK Patents Act 1949 got around this problem by making secret prior use a separate ground of invalidity, although not one which could be brought in opposition proceedings. The 1977 Act approaches the problem from the other direction; the validity of the patent is not affected, but the person who began to use the invention before the priority date (or who made serious preparations to do so) has the right to continue what he was doing, or planning to do, after the patent is granted. This seems a fairer solution, as it leaves the patentee with rights which he can enforce against other parties who did not begin to use the invention until after his priority date.

As we have seen, unauthorized sale and use of a patented article constitutes infringement. What is the position, though, of a person who buys the article from the patentee? The answer is that the sale of the article by the patentee gives an implied licence to use and to resell it, and that his right is passed on to subsequent owners of the article. The law in the United Kingdom used to be that the patentee could sell the patented article subject to conditions (for example forbidding export to other countries) which, if properly notified, were binding on the purchaser. Such export prohibitions have essentially been abolished within the EEC (see Chapter 22) and the other main purpose of conditional sale (resale price maintenance) has been abolished by United Kingdom statute law. In most European countries the principle of exhaustion of patent rights applies; once a patentee has put the patented article on the market his rights in it are exhausted and he cannot impose any conditions on its subsequent sale or use.

The purchaser of an article that does not originate from the patentee or someone authorized by him may be liable for infringement by using it. He has, however, a measure of protection in the Sale of Goods Act, which states that a seller gives an implied warranty of the right of 'quiet possession' of the goods. If the buyer is sued for infringement he can in turn sue the seller for breach of this implied warranty and should be able to recover any damages from him.[4]

Infringement in the USA

In the USA the patent law specifies that the patent shall grant to the patentee the right to exclude others from 'making, using, or selling the invention throughout the United States'. Where the invention is a process, however, it is not infringement to use or sell the product of the process, a fact which greatly reduces the value of process claims in the USA. Thus a US patentee, whose patent covers a process, cannot sue for infringement someone who carries out the process in another country and imports the product into USA.

This is the situation as of the time of writing, but legislative proposals have recently been introduced to make it infringement to sell or use the imported product of a patented process, and it is expected that the law will be changed in the near future and will apply to all existing process patents as well as to new ones.

The patent owner, however, may be able to take action of a different kind against such imports by invoking the provisions of the Tariff Act against unfair competition. If it can be proved that the imports are products of a process which would infringe a US patent if carried out in the USA and that the importation would destroy or substantially injure an industry efficiently and economically operated in the United States, or prevent the establishment of such an industry, then the imports may be stopped on application to the US International Trade Commission, which carries out its own investigation. This used to be a very difficult procedure, requiring positive action by the President, but now it has been considerably simplified. Furthermore, it is much faster than a normal infringement action since the ITC is required to give a decision within 12 months in normal cases. This possibility now has to be taken seriously by anyone planning to export goods for sale in the USA; it is no longer safe to ignore US process patents.

The principle of contributory infringement has long been recognized by case law in the USA, but its operation has always been in conflict with another principle of US law, that of patent misuse. Patent misuse is held to occur if the patentee attempts to extend his monopoly beyond the strict limits granted by law, and has the effect of making the patent unenforceable. It is considered patent misuse to 'tie-in', that is, to make a licence contingent upon the purchase of unpatented articles (see p. 295), and it has been held that attempting to prevent contributory infringement is similarly trying to extend the patent monopoly beyond what is claimed and hence to be patent misuse.

The US Patent Law of 1952 attempted to clarify the situation by defining contributory infringement for the first time, and excluding from the scope of contributory infringement the sale of 'staple articles of commerce' for which there was at least one substantial use other than the patented use. Furthermore, the law explicitly stated that enforcing one's patent rights against contributory infringement did not constitute patent misuse. In spite of this seemingly clear statement of the law, the question remained in doubt until it was finally resolved by a decision of the Supreme Court in the case of *Rohm & Haas* v. *Dawson* in 1980.[5] The court agreed that a patentee whose patent claimed the sole commercial use of an unpatented compound could stop others selling the compound for that use and was not obliged to grant a licence to other sellers. The decision on this landmark case (discussed further in Chapter 17) was reached only on a five to four majority, so that if one judge had decided differently, contributory infringement in the USA could not be prevented today. Such use patents in the USA would then be worth very little, since they would in effect be subject to compulsory licensing.

A question which until recently was unclear in the USA is whether experimental use of a patented product or process constitutes infringement. This was the subject of litigation in the case of *Roche* v. *Bolar*, decided in 1984 by the CAFC.[6] Bolar had been making preparations to introduce in the USA a generic version of a Roche pharmaceutical product as soon as Roche's patent expired, and had carried out clinical testing of their product while the patent was still in force, relying on earlier case law which held that experimental use did not amount to infringement. The Court held that the exception for experimental use must be construed narrowly; experimentation for pure speculative research was not infringement, but as soon as the experiments were directed to a clear commercial goal, then infringement occurred.

As part of the compromise between research-based and generic pharmaceutical interests which culminated in the Drug Price Competition and Patent Term Restoration Act of 1984 (see p. 171), Congress overruled the decision in *Roche* v. *Bolar*, specifying that it was not infringement to make, use, or sell a patented invention 'solely for uses related to the development and submission of information under a Federal Law which regulates the manufacture, use or sale of drugs'. It is clear that essentially all pharmaceutical research can be brought under this definition. However, it seems also clear that *Roche* v. *Bolar* is overruled only in the pharmaceutical field, and experimental use for example of a patented agrochemical product would constitute infringement.

Similar decisions have been reached by courts in a number of countries, including the UK and Germany, in litigation between Monsanto and Stauffer.[7] Stauffer planned to introduce a product very similar to Monsanto's patented herbicide 'Roundup', and made very extensive field trials of their substance. Although not literally falling under the claims of Monsanto's patent, at least in the UK, the Stauffer product was arguably close enough to be an infringement if sold commercially. The courts held consistently that the field trials were just as much an infringement as commercial sales would have been.

Infringement actions

Procedure in the United Kingdom

One of the innovations introduced by the Patents Act 1977 is that an infringement action in the United Kingdom may now be heard by the Patent Office. Up to the time of writing, this is only possible if both parties agree, and the Patent Office can in any case refer the matter to the Court, so this procedure has seldom been used.

At present most infringement actions are still heard by the Courts, which now means in the first instance the Patents Court set up under the 1977 Act as a part of the Chancery Division of the High Court to hear all patent matters including appeals from the Patent Office. The two judges of this court are specialist patent judges who have a considerable amount of technical as well as legal knowledge. If the technology involved is particularly complex, the judge may sit together with a scientific adviser.

An infringement action under English procedure can be a very long and complicated business. It begins with the serving of a writ, a formal document in which the plaintiff states the nature of his claim and the relief he seeks, and in which the Queen, through the Lord Chancellor, requires the defendant to enter an appearance or have summary judgement entered against him. After the defendant submits to the jursdiction of the court by entering an appearance (usually through his solicitors), the next stage is the filing of pleadings which are written statements entered by the parties alternately to clarify and define the specific matters of dispute between the parties. The plaintiff starts the pleadings with his statement of claim, which must include particulars of at least one infringing act alleged to have been committed before the writ was issued. The defendant then enters a defence and counterclaims, in which he usually alleges that his acts were not infringement and counterclaims that the patent is invalid. The plaintiff replies, and pleadings are usually closed at that point.

The next important stage is the summons for directions, in which the parties come before the judge, or more usually before an official of the court called the Master, for an Order for Directions regulating the future handling of the case. At this stage the matter of 'discovery' is dealt with; that is, each party must deliver to the other a list of all documents in his possession relevant to the case; the other party is entitled to inspect them and use them in evidence if he wishes. Certain documents may be 'privileged', for example a lawyer's or patent agent's advice to his client, and these may be listed separately and are not made available to the other side.

Finally, the case comes on for trial, which consists of lengthy oral arguments before the judge (no jury is involved in patent cases), and examination and cross-examination of witnesses on either side. These may include independent expert witnesses who have been asked by one side or the other to give opinions on technical matters or to carry out experiments or trials. Finally, the barristers on each side sum up their arguments. The judge may give his decision on the spot, but more usually will reserve judgement and give his decision some two or three weeks later. The losing party may appeal to the Court of Appeal, and the party which loses on appeal may ask for leave to appeal to the House of Lords (strictly speaking, the Judicial Committee of the House of Lords, consisting only of senior judges known as Law Lords. Other members of the House of Lords are *not* involved). Appeal to the Lords is not as of right, however, and if both the Court of Appeal and the House of Lords itself refuse leave, the matter rests there.

Many patent cases do reach the House of Lords, however, and it is not unusual for the case to be decided one way in the High Court, the opposite way in the Court of Appeal, and the original way again in the House of Lords (possibly by a 3:2 majority). As A.P. Herbert has pointed out, a patient who has had his appendix removed by a distinguished surgeon would be amazed if he were then brought before a panel of three more distinguished surgeons who decided that his appendix should be replaced, and astounded if he were then ordered by a panel of five even more distinguished surgeons to have it taken out again; but such procedures are by no means rare in the legal world. Patent litigation in England is an expensive matter; the litigant will normally employ a solicitor and a patent agent as well as at least one barrister; if a Queen's Counsel is briefed, as would be usual for an important case, then junior counsel must also be retained. Costs are chiefly a factor of how many days (or weeks) the hearing lasts and typically may be from £50 000 to £100 000. One consequence of the high cost of patent actions is that a small company may own a valid patent but cannot afford to enforce it, particularly against an infringer who has greater financial resources. Recently, attempts have been made to launch insurance schemes under which a patentee pays a fixed annual premium for each insured patent, and if he wishes to sue an infringer and obtains counsel's opinion that he has a reasonable case, the insurance underwriters will pay the legal costs of the infringement action.

The proposals made in the White Paper of April 1986 (see p. 31) are intended to reduce the costs and delays of patent litigation by making it the rule rather than the exception to have infringement actions heard in the Patent Office. The procedure would be simplified, with more reliance on written evidence. There would be no automatic right of appeal to the courts, and the Patent Office would also have power to grant interlocutory injunctions.

The procedure described above is that of England. It should not be forgotten that Scotland has a separate legal system and that patent actions may also be brought in Edinburgh before the Outer House of the Court of Session, from which appeal lies to the Inner House of the Court of Session and from there (with leave) to the House of Lords. The procedure is similar, but the nomenclature is different. The litigant will now be the pursuer (plaintiff) or defender (defendant), will employ writers to the signet and advocates instead of solicitors and barristers, and may (if he is lucky) get an interim interdict instead of an interlocutory injunction. If the White Paper proposals are adopted, the Patent Office will also be able to hear cases in Scotland.

Remedies

If the decision of the court is that the patent is valid and has been infringed, then the plaintiff may be granted the following remedies:

  (i) an injunction;
 (ii) damages (or an account of profits);
(iii) delivery up or destruction of infringing goods;
 (iv) a declaration of validity;
  (v) costs.

In most cases, the injunction is the most important remedy of all. It is a direct order from the court to the defendant to refrain from future acts of infringement; disobedience of the order is contempt of court which the court can punish by fines or imprisonment. An interlocutory injunction, on the other hand, is an order from the court, issued before the trial, to stop acts alleged to be infringements until the case has been settled. Interlocutory injunctions in patents cases are now more easy to obtain than they used to be, and can be extremely useful to the patentee. On the other hand, if an interlocutory injunction is granted and the patent is subsequently found to be invalid or not infringed, the patentee will have to pay compensation to the defendant for the time during which his activities were halted by the injunction.

Damages may be awarded by the court in respect of past acts of infringement (but not any which occurred more than six years before the writ issued). Damages and account of profits are two alternative ways of reckoning the payment to be made by the infringer to the patentee; damages are based on the loss sustained by the patentee as a result of the infringement, an account of profits is based on the profits made by the infringer. Of the two, damages are by far the most common. At the least, the successful patentee should get the equivalent of a fair royalty plus interest from the infringer.

There are certain restrictions on the payment of damages, however. Damages are not awarded against an 'innocent infringer' who can prove that he was not aware of, and had no reason to be aware of, the existence of the patent. It is practically impossible for a large company, particularly one with its own patent department, to claim to be an innocent infringer. The patentee can also make it difficult for imitators to claim to be innocent infringers by marking the patented articles he makes with the patent number. It is not enough merely to mark 'patented' if the number is not given.

The court also has discretion to refuse damages in respect of a period for which a renewal fee was paid late, and may reduce or refuse damages if the patent was amended after publication or was found to be only partially valid, unless the patent was originally framed 'in good faith and with reasonable skill and knowledge'. Damages could be refused if the patent was originally drafted deliberately far too broadly and had to be cut back in scope later.

Delivery up of infringing goods applies only to articles currently in the possession of the infringer; often it is not asked for, but if the infringer has a large inventory, or if the infringing device is a machine capable of making large quantities of articles, this form of relief can be well worth having. Goods delivered up do not become the property of the patentee; all he can do is destroy them or have them rendered non-infringing.

A declaration of validity of the patent is a useful deterrent to future infringers, and may affect the costs in any future action.

The party which wins an infringement action is normally awarded costs, which means that the other party must contribute towards the expenses he has incurred in the litigation. The party awarded costs must not expect everything to be paid; costs are assessed by an official called the taxing master according to a fixed scale, and normally will amount to less than half of the winning party's actual out-of-pocket expenses. However, if a certificate of validity has been granted in earlier proceedings, and the patentee successfully sues a second infringer, then he may be awarded costs on a higher scale, which might actually approximate to his real outlay.

Who may sue

We have referred to the person suing for infringement as the patentee, but this may not always be the case. The original patentee may have sold the patent to another party; that party, the assignee, now has all the rights associated with the patent, including the right to sue infringers. The patentee may also have granted licences under the patent. We shall discuss licensing more fully in Chapter 18, but it should be noted here that there are basically three types of licence.

1. An *exclusive* licence gives the right to operate under the patent to the licensee to the exclusion of all others, including the patentee himself. 2. A *sole* or *semi-exclusive* licence is one where the licensee is assured that no more licences will be granted, but the patentee retains the right to work the invention himself. 3. A *non-exclusive* licence leaves the patentee free to grant any number of further licences.

British patent law gives to an exclusive licensee, but not to a sole or non-exclusive licensee, the same right to sue for infringement as an assignee has. There is one catch, however. An assignment or exclusive licence is supposed to be registered at the Patent Office; under previous patents acts this requirement was often ignored, but under the new (1977) Act an assignee or exclusive licensee who does not register within six months of the agreement being signed loses his right to claim damages for any infringement before the date on which he does register.

There may of course be more than one patentee, as a patent may be granted to any number of co-patentees jointly. When there is more than one patentee, each co-patentee may sue for infringement without the consent of the others, but is not free to grant licences without the agreement of the other co-owners of the patent.

Threats

A patentee must be careful not to rashly threaten others with an infringement action, as it is possible for any person aggrieved by such conduct to retaliate with a suit for unjustifiable threats. This seems a somewhat anomalous provision of the patent law; after all if I threaten to sue someone for trespass, breach of contract, breach of copyright, or indeed any civil tort other than infringement of a patent (or a registered design), the person I threaten has no statutory right of redress. The reason that patents were singled out was to put a stop to the once common practice of a manufacturer threatening his competitors' customers with an infringement action. The customers, knowing nothing of patents and anxious to avoid any legal problems, were often frightened away from the competitors' goods, even if no infringement actually was present.

To avoid this abuse of patent rights, not only the customers actually threatened, but also the manufacturer whose goods were alleged to infringe could sue the person making the threats (whether or not he was the patentee) and if successful could get an injunction and damages. To succeed, they had to show either that the acts were not infringements, or that the patent was not valid. The possibility of threats actions made it difficult for a patentee to deal in any straightfoward way with anyone he considered to be an infringer, as any warning letter which did more than notify the infringer that a patent existed could be held to be a threat. Even if an infringement action was planned, a warning letter gave the infringer the chance to lodge a threats action, thereby gaining certain procedural advantages and putting the patentee on the defensive. This position has been improved somewhat by the UK Patents Act 1977, which in effect rules out a threats action if the person threatened is a manufacturer rather than a customer.

Procedure in the USA

In the United States, patent infringement actions are heard in the first instance by the Federal District Court in the district in which the alleged infringer resides or has his registered office, or in which he has a regular place of business *and* is infringing. There will generally be the possibility of bringing suit in more than one district, and the one chosen will depend on factors such as the pro- or anti-patent attitude of the courts, geographical convenience, etc. The validity of the patent can, as in the United Kingdom, be contested by the defendant, and a further complication is that where there is an actual controversy, the infringer can take the initial step by bringing an action for declaratory judgement of invalidity, which can be brought in the Federal District Court in which the patent owner resides, or for a foreign patent owner, in the US District Court for the District of Columbia. An exception to the normal jurisdiction occurs when the alleged infringement is a sale to the US Government. The seller cannot be sued for infringement, and the patentee must sue the Government in a special court known as the US Claims Court.

The procedure in US Courts is somewhat similar to that in England, starting in the same way with formal pleadings. Compared to the English system, however, the trial itself is shorter and the pretrial proceedings far longer. The powers of the court to order discovery are exercised more extensively, and there is also much taking of evidence on oath (depositions) before the trial begins. After evidence is taken, one side may move for summary judgement in its favour, which may be granted if there is no unresolved issue of fact, and a decision can be given on legal points alone. The court may also grant a preliminary injunction before trial, but this is rare unless the patent has been held valid in previous suits.

The judge may require a pretrial conference with the lawyers of both sides to try to narrow the issues or reach an out-of-court settlement. If the validity of the patent is being challenged on the basis of prior art not considered by the Patent Office, the judge may stay the infringement action until the validity has been re-examined by the Patent Office, using the reissue or re-examination procedure described in the following chapter.

As well as purely legal defences such as non-infringement and patent invalidity, the defendant may rely on so-called equitable defences, which are based on the old principle of equity that a plaintiff seeking relief must come into court with 'clean hands'. Thus the defendant may allege that the plaintiff has 'unclean hands' because of patent misuse, fraud on the Patent Office, undue delay in bringing suit, and any other reason which the fertile brain of his attorney can come up with.

The trial itself may be heard before a judge alone, or with a jury. In recent years the number of jury trials has increased, largely because juries appear to be more sympathetic to the plaintiff than do judges. The trial will be relatively short by English standards, and the judge will not normally be a specialist in patent law. If the patentee is successful, the remedies he obtains are essentially the same as in England, except that costs (attorney's fees) are awarded only in exceptional cases. Damages must be at least equivalent to a reasonable royalty, and may be reckoned in terms of the patentee's lost profits, in which case they may be very substantial indeed. Furthermore, damages awarded may be tripled if the court finds that there has been 'wilful infringement', for example if the infringing company knew of the patent but went ahead without getting proper legal opinion that the patent was likely to be held invalid or not infringed.

The consequences of losing a patent infringement action in the USA can be very serious, as Eastman Kodak found out to their cost when at the end of 1985 they were held to have infringed patents owned by Polaroid by the sale of their 'instant' cameras and film. An injunction against further sales meant that a factory employing over a thousand people had to be closed down. Millions of Kodak customers all over the world were left holding cameras for which no film would ever be available, and had to be compensated by offers averaging $50 per customer. Finally, Polaroid were at the time of writing seeking damages totalling one billion dollars, and the long-term damage to Kodak's reputation may be even more costly.

The cost of an infringement suit in the USA is very high, normally ranging from $100 000 to $1 000 000 for the first instance alone. Most of the costs are incurred during the pretrial proceedings.

If the patent is found invalid, it is not formally revoked as in England, but merely declared unenforceable. Until recently, such a decision was binding only as between the parties, but the position now is that 'collateral estoppel' exists, meaning that the patentee is barred from asserting his patent against any other infringer. Thus, an unfavourable decision in a circuit which is notoriously anti-patent will, except in rare circumstances, prevent the patentee from enforcing his patent in a circuit in which he would have had a good chance of success.

Appeal lies from the Federal District Court to the new Court of Appeals for the Federal Circuit, which also hears appeals from the Patent Office and from the US Claims Court. The judges of the CAFC, many of whom previously sat on the Court of Customs and Patents Appeals, are experienced in patent matters, and generally have a more positive attitude towards patents than did the judges of the Circuit Courts of Appeals who previously had jurisdiction and who, in the five years from 1966–70, held 70 per cent of all patents coming before them to be totally invalid.

The CAFC will do away with the problem of conflicting precedents in different Circuits in patent cases; but since cases are not heard by the whole court of 12 judges, but normally by three-judge panels, total consistency cannot be expected. Indeed, there have already been instances of the same point being decided in opposite ways by two different panels of the CAFC within a period of two or three months.

Although the US Supreme Court is not an appellate court in the normal sense, it may decide to review cases decided in the CAFC, by granting a petition for a writ of certiorari. This it does only very rarely; when it does its judgments have also tended until very recently to be anti-patentee, but with the Chakrabarty and Rohm & Haas cases, discussed above, there seems to be a change in attitude.

Procedure in Europe

Courts in continental Europe have a different type of procedure from the Anglo-Saxon system of the United Kingdom and the USA. Most of the evidence is written rather than oral, and the role of the judge is seen more as that of an investigator than that of a referee. In some countries such as France and Switzerland, the same court can hear both the infringement action and a counter-claim of invalidity, but in the majority of countries the question of validity is treated as a separate issue which is heard in a different court or is even referred back to the patent office.

In Germany, for example, infringement actions are brought first in one of a selected group of state courts (*Landgericht*), which have a certain degree of specialization in patent matters. Appeal lies to the *Oberlandesgericht* and from there (on questions of law) to the *Bundesgerichthof* (Federal Supreme Court). However, the validity of the patent cannot be considered by these courts, but only by the *Bundespatentgericht* (Federal Patents Court) which is administratively part of the German Patent Office.

The proceedings consist of alternate exchanges of written briefs and short hearings. Often a neutral expert is appointed by the court to give a report on the technical aspects of the case. There is essentially no cross-examination of witnesses as in England. Interlocutory injunctions are rare, but may be granted by the court in clear cases.

Whereas in England the judgement of the court of first instance is normally suspended if the case is appealed, in Germany the plaintiff who wins in the *Landgericht* may compel enforcement of its judgement by depositing a bank guarantee sufficient to compensate the defendant should the defendant win on appeal. A judgement of the *Oberlandesgericht* is enforceable at once without the need to deposit a bond, and if the plaintiff loses on appeal to the *Bundesgerichthof* he is liable only to pay back any damages which he has received.

Infringement actions in The Netherlands are similar to those in Germany, nullity proceedings being a separate issue. There is a very strong presumption that a Dutch patent is valid, and indeed whereas in most countries if a patent is invalidated it is treated as if it had always been invalid, in Holland it is invalid only as from the date of the decision, so that damages may be awarded for infringements made before the determination of invalidity.

There are a number of countries, even within Europe, where it is extremely difficult to enforce a patent even against a clear infringer. As these countries generally do not have product protection for chemical compounds, enforcement is doubly difficult in the chemical field.

Spain used to be a particularly bad example of this. Under Spanish law prior to 1986, holding a Spanish patent gave a positive right to work the claimed invention irrespective of possible domination by an earlier patent. Thus when a foreign patentee tried to enforce his Spanish patent for a process of preparation of a new compound, he would find that the infringer could not be stopped because he had a patent for a process differing only in minor details from his own. This part of the Spanish law is being repealed as of Spain's accession to the EEC, but it is still a feature of the law of certain Latin American countries whose law derives from that of Spain.

Eastern European countries are also notoriously difficult when it comes to enforcing patent rights. An extreme example is the DDR, where in spite of the heavy fees a patent is granted without examination but cannot be enforced until it has been examined. This, of course, takes time, during which the infringer is free to continue his activities. The infringer can then attack the validity of the patent once it has been granted. Finally, it appears from the experiences of more than one chemical company that any really determined attempt to enforce a DDR patent against a state enterprise is regarded as an unfriendly act against which the state is prepared to retaliate by all means possible including police harassment of company representatives when in East Germany. The clear conclusion seems to be that if you have a DDR patent you may frame it and hang it on your wall, but you cannot do much else with it – and, considering its cost, one would be better advised to buy a Picasso instead!

8

INVALIDITY AND AMENDMENT OF PATENTS

That which is crooked cannot be made straight, and that which is wanting cannot be numbered.

Eccles, i.15.

The fact that a patent has been granted is no guarantee that the patent is valid, and the patent laws of many countries state this explicitly. The chance that a patent will be held to be valid if challenged, in other words the presumption of validity of the patent, is essentially a function of the strictness of examination of the patent in the patent office, the chance of opposition by third parties in the patent office proceedings, and the pro- or anti-patent attitude of the national courts. The presumption of validity of an average patent of any given country may be placed on a scale ranging from The Netherlands at one extreme to Italy or Spain at the other, and of course individual patents may have a high presumption of validity if they have already been unsuccessfully opposed or challenged in the courts. At one time, Dutch patents did indeed have guaranteed validity after five years from grant, and after that time could not be challenged; this provision was, however, changed in the early 1960s.

Grounds of invalidity in the United Kingdom

The validity of a British patent granted under the 1977 Act (that is, a patent granted on an application made on or after 1 June 1978) may be challenged at any time during its term by an application for revocation made to the Patent Office or to the Patents Court. The grounds on which the patent can be revoked are the same in each case and are as follows:

   (i) the invention is not a patentable invention;
  (ii) the patent was granted to a person not entitled;
 (iii) the specification does not disclose the invention clearly and completely enough for it to be performed by a person skilled in the art;
 (iv) new matter was added to the disclosure after the filing date; and
  (v) the scope of protection was extended by an amendment which should not have been allowed.

We have already looked at what constitutes a patentable invention

(Chapter 3), and found that a patentable invention is one which is capable of industrial application, is novel, and involves an inventive step. The first of these grounds of attack therefore includes all allegations that the patent is old or is obvious in view of the state of the art, as well as the objection that the type of invention is one which is not capable of industrial application.

The second ground is one which can only be used by a person who alleges that he, and not the patentee, was entitled to the grant of the patent. Normally an application for revocation on this ground must be made within two years of the grant of the patent, unless it can be shown that there was deliberate fraud by the patentee.

Ground (iii) is an attack based on insufficiency of disclosure; the patent specification must give sufficient description for a person skilled in the art to perform the invention without having to do undue experimentation.

The last two grounds are based on the rule that no amendment, whether before or after grant, may add new matter to the specification, or, after grant, extend the scope of protection beyond that as originally filed. Any patent in which this has been done is invalid.

These grounds of invalidity are fewer in number than the grounds upon which it was, and still is, possible to revoke a patent granted under the 1949 Act. As we have seen, there are no longer opposition proceedings for 'old law' patent applications; however, a patent granted under the 1949 Act (i.e. one dated before 1 June 1978) may be revoked at any time during its term by the Patent Office or the Patents Court on any of the following grounds:

(a) the invention was claimed in a valid claim of earlier priority date in another granted patent;

(b) the patent was granted on an application by a person not entitled to apply;

(c) the patent was obtained in contravention of the rights of the person applying for revocation;

(d) what is claimed is not an invention within the meaning of the act;

(e) the invention is not new;

(f) the invention is obvious;

(g) the invention is not useful;

(h) the specification does not sufficiently describe the invention and how to perform it, or does not disclose the best method of performing it which was known to the applicant;

(i) the scope of any claim is not clearly defined or not fairly based on the matter disclosed;

(j) the patent was obtained on a false suggestion;

(k) the primary or intended use of the invention is contrary to law; and

(l) the invention was secretly used in the United Kingdom before the priority date.

Of these grounds, (d), (e), and (f) together correspond to the objection under the new law that the invention is not a patentable invention. Grounds (b) and (c) correspond approximately to ground (ii) under the new law, although there are differences in detail which we need not go into. Ground (h) (first part) corresponds to the insufficiency attack of ground (iii) above. In addition, ground (a) is replaced by the provision that the whole contents of earlier unpublished applications becomes part of the state of the art when considering novelty, and ground (l) is replaced by the provisions on right of prior use.

Grounds which do not apply to new patents

This leaves us with grounds (g) (inutility), (h) (second part) (best mode not disclosed), (i) (ambiguity and lack of fair basis) (j) (false suggestion), and (k) (illegal use) which apply to patents granted under the 1949 Act, but not to those granted under the 1977 Act, and two grounds of invalidity (iv) (new matter added) and (v) (scope of protection increased) which apply only to new Act patents. Grounds (j) and (k) need not be considered further, but the others will merit some closer attention.

Best mode

It used to be a requirement that a patent specification disclose the best method of carrying out the invention which the applicant was aware of at the time of filing. It was never quite clear in what respect the 'best' method had to be the best, although it did not necessarily mean the commercially most successful. Because its interpretation was essentially a subjective one, it was very difficult to establish this ground of revocation, and in effect the only cases in which it was upheld were ones in which it was clear that the applicants were deliberately concealing an embodiment of the invention which was the only one which was commercially practicable. In such circumstances the patentee is trying to have his cake and eat it; to get the benefit of a patent monopoly without disclosing any useful information. It is only reasonable that this should lead to revocation of his patent. Under the 1977 Act, however, there is no obligation to disclose the best method, but only to give a sufficient description. This description may presumably be of any method of carrying out the invention which falls within the claims, even if it is a method inferior to one which is not disclosed. In the USA disclosure of the best mode is still an important requirement, and if priority is being claimed from a British application, that application should also contain a description of the best method of carrying out the invention known to the inventor at that time.

Ambiguity and lack of fair basis

Patents granted under the 1949 Act are invalid if the claims are ambiguous or not fairly based on the specification. When a judge construes a clause of a contract, he must decide upon a meaning for it, no matter how ambiguous the wording, but for a patent claim he can, or could, give up the attempt and declare the claim invalid for ambiguity. In practice, judges have been reluctant to do this, and patents have seldom in recent years been held invalid on this ground, but the fact that the possibility existed was a useful check upon sloppy drafting of claims. The attitude that the public has a right to know what it may or may not do, and that if the patentee does not make this clear then he loses his rights, is basically a sound one. The objection of lack of fair basis was also seldom sustained, but was appropriate in case in which the patentee was trying to obtain a scope of protection broader than that to which his description entitled him.

The Patents Act 1977, however, has abandoned ambiguity and lack of fair basis as grounds of invalidity. The attitude now is that these are matters which the Patent Office should clear up during prosecution, but that whatever gets past the Patent Office cannot be challenged later. In exactly the same way, the Patent Office may raise objections of lack of unity, but lack of unity is not a ground of attack once the patent has been granted.

Inutility

Perhaps the most important omission, because of its possible effect upon how patents should be drafted, is that of inutility as a ground of revocation. The old ground 'that the invention . . . is not useful' was interpreted to mean, at least at one time, that if anything falling within the scope of the claims could be shown not to give the result promised by the patentee, then the patent was invalid. More recently, the inutility provisions were interpreted less strictly, so that invalidity was not found by 'setting problems on the borders of the claims' as one judge put it, but only if there was a clear indication to perform some significant part of the scope which was not useful for the stated purpose.

This had two consequences as regards drafting. First, an applicant was wise to avoid any elaborate statement of what were the advantages of his invention, as failure to achieve any one of these advantages could be held to invalidate. More importantly, the possibility of an inutility attack made the applicant think twice before framing his claims too broadly. This was particularly relevant for claims to a class of chemical compounds defined by a general formula. Such a claim may cover millions of compounds, of which only a few can possibly have been made and tested. Many patent offices will not allow such a broad scope without a great deal of exemplification, a problem which we shall consider in Chapter 15. The

British Patent Office, however, always took the position that it was up to the applicant to define the scope of protection he wanted, and this, provided it was novel and fairly based on the description, would be granted no matter how poorly it was exemplified; but if the applicant was too greedy and claimed compounds which were not effective for the stated use, the patent could be invalid. This principle, which has always worked well, has been abandoned under the 1977 Act. A claim once granted cannot now be attacked on the basis that its scope includes embodiments which are not useful (although it would be invalid if it did not cover anything which was industrially applicable). This throws the burden on the Patent Office to prevent the grant of claims which are too broad, and it is not clear on what basis the examiner can reasonably do so.

It is true that insufficiency of disclosure remains a ground of invalidity, and there is a possibility that the courts will consider objections which are strictly speaking matters of ambiguity, fair basis, or inutility under this heading. Under the 1949 Act insufficiency, but not ambiguity, fair basis, or inutility, could be argued in opposition proceedings, and there were some cases in which ambiguity, lack of fair basis, or inutility were considered as insufficiency. More recent cases, however, drew a relatively sharp distinction between these; for example it was stated that if the specification fails to give directions to enable something falling within the claim to be made, that is insufficiency, but if having made it does not work, that is inutility. How practice will develop under the 1977 Act remains to be seen.

New grounds of invalidity

The two new grounds of invalidity are those of adding new matter to the description, and extending the scope of the claims after grant; the first of these in particular must constantly be kept in mind when amending the specification during prosecution. Neither of these grounds should arise if the Patent Office does its job properly, as amendments introducing new matter during prosecution should not be allowed any more than broadening amendments after grant. The difference is that whereas if the Patent Office mistakenly allows a single application to be granted for more than one invention, or allows claims to be granted which are too broad or ambiguous, the validity of the patent is not affected, Patent Office mistakes in allowing amendments can lead to invalidity.

Revocation by the Patent Office

Under the 1949 Act, validity could be considered by the Patent Office only in opposition or belated opposition proceedings, only for a limited time and only on limited grounds. It was the rule that any doubt should be resolved in favour of the patentee, because the court could always consider validity more thoroughly later. As a result, oppositions became not so much a serious attack upon a patent, but more often a mere delaying tactic to hold up the grant of a patent. Now that the Patent Office can consider validity at any time and on the same grounds as the court, there is no reason why the patentee should have the benefit of the doubt, and the proceedings should become a serious matter in which the patent has a real chance of being held invalid. Nevertheless, the procedure before the Patent Office will still be like the old opposition procedure, with most of the evidence being in written form and only limited opportunity for cross-examination of witnesses.

If someone unsuccessfully applies to the Patent Office for revocation of a patent, he cannot simply try his luck again by making an application to the court, unless the court gives special permission. However, anyone accused of infringement may always contest the validity of the patent by a counterclaim in the infringement action, even if he has already applied for revocation before the Patent Office or the court without success.

It should also be mentioned that the Patent Office may of its own accord revoke a patent in two rather special circumstances, firstly when the patent is found to be anticipated by an earlier application on the 'whole contents' principle, and secondly when a British patent and a Europatent (UK) are granted to the same patentee for the same invention. In the latter case the national patent may be revoked and the European patent remains in force.

Partial validity

It used to be the case that a patent was either totally valid or, if found wanting in any respect, totally invalid. This changed first with the Patents Act of 1883 by which a court could permit a patentee to amend so as to restrict to the valid part of his patent and enforce that part against an infringer. Later, the 1919 Act allowed the validity of each claim of the patent to be considered separately, and each valid claim to be enforced without regard to other invalid claims. The Patents Act 1977 goes further in that the valid part of the patent need no longer even be a complete claim, which, as we shall see, also has implications when we consider how patent claims should be drafted. The validity of a patent may be challenged not only in revocation proceedings but as a counterclaim in proceedings for patent infringement, as well as in threats actions and certain other proceedings of lesser importance. In all cases the grounds which can be relied upon are the same five as can be used in revocation proceedings. In all cases where the validity of a patent is put in issue, it may be found wholly valid, or wholly or partially invalid. If wholly invalid, the patent must be revoked, and is treated as always having been invalid. If it is partially invalid, the patentee is normally given the opportunity to amend his patent to make it valid.

Amendment of British patents

In addition to amendment of British patents in cases where a patent has been found partially invalid, a patentee may of his own accord apply to the Patent Office for permission to amend his patent specification (which includes the claims). If the Patent Office finds the proposed amendment acceptable, it is advertised in the *Official Journal (Patents)* and any other party may oppose the allowance of the amendment. If there is no opposition, or if opposition is unsuccessful, the amendment will be made and the patent will have effect as if it had originally been granted in the amended form. An important point is that there is no right to have the patent amended on request; amendment is at the discretion of the Comptroller and may be refused or made only upon conditions if the patentee's original claim was excessively broad, or if amendment is being made to distinguish from novelty-destroying prior art which the patentee had known about for a long time. A patentee may not apply for amendment in this way if proceedings are pending in which the validity of the patent is being put in issue.

Both 'old Act' and 'new Act' patents may be amended by the same procedure, but the types of allowable amendments are different. Under the old Act, amendments to a granted patent had to be by way of disclaimer, explanation or correction only, and no new matter could be added nor extension of the scope of the claims be made except to correct an obvious mistake in the specification as granted. These conditions still apply to amendments of old Act patents.

Amendments of old patents

Disclaimer has been held to mean any reduction in the scope of the claims, whether or not it can be described as a disclaimer of something specifically claimed originally. The simplest type of disclaiming amendment is one which cancels the broadest claim and limits to the scope of a narrower subclaim, but it is also a disclaimer to make into an essential feature of the claims that which was previously only an optional feature, even if that optional feature was previously never mentioned in the claims. There must of course be basis in the specification for the new claims; thus a feature cannot be added to the claims if it was not previously mentioned in the description. There is some doubt about the position when a numerical range of proportions, temperatures, etc., is to be restricted. If the subclaims or the specification list one or more narrower ranges, there is no difficulty about restricting to one of these, but failing this a limitation derived from numbers in the examples may suffice. There was even a case in which the then Lord Chief Justice gave an *obiter* opinion (not constituting a precedent) that a disclosed range of say 0–100 per cent amounted to a disclosure of all values between these limits which could be narrowed on amendment to any specific range the patentee pleased. This opinion is not followed, however, and it must be said with respect that the Lord Chief Justice was not an expert in patent law.[1]

Perhaps the most extreme case of amendment by disclaimer was that in which American Cyanamid were allowed to limit the scope of their patent covering the antitubercular drug ethambutol from an initial scope estimated at 10^{11} compounds to the single compound ethambutol, the court holding that the original scope was not so recklessly broad as to amount to a fraudulent representation.[2]

Amendment by explanation may be used to clarify the specification or to resolve an ambiguity in the claims, in so far as this can be done without adding new matter. As applied to claims, amendment by explanation is somewhat anomalous, since in order for the amendment to be allowable, the patentee must prove that the true construction of the claim is what he says it is (otherwise the scope of the claims would be extended) and if he can do this on the basis of the unamended claim, amendment would be superfluous.

Amendment by correction is generally a difficult matter, as it is not permissible to correct an error of judgment on the part of the person who drafted the specification. If a correction would introduce new matter (which generally would be the case) or extend the scope of the claims it is allowable only if it is the correction of an obvious mistake. An obvious mistake is present when it is obvious to someone familiar with the field who reads the specification both that a mistake is present and also what the correction should be. Although there was one case in which NRDC were allowed to amend their patent to replace the false chemical formula of their claimed product by the correct formula,[3] this case is no longer followed and such mistakes usually cannot be corrected in this way (but see p. 135). There is also provision in the 1949 Act for the correction of clerical errors arising in the preparation of the specification, and here the prohibitions on introduction of new matter and extension of scope do not apply, although if the amendment would materially change the specification, the amendment will be advertised and may be opposed. A final type of mistake which may arise is that of printing errors in the published specification; these can be corrected upon request by means of a correction slip listing the errata which is fastened to the remaining copies of the specification in the Patent Office.

Amendment of new patents

Under the 1949 Act it is necessary, if an amendment is to be allowed, to persuade the Patent Office or the court that it falls under one of the three allowable categories of disclaimer, explanation, or correction. Under the 1977 Act this is no longer the case, as the Act says nothing about types of amendment. In principle, any amendment is permissible so long as it does not introduce new matter or extend the scope of the claims. Any amendment by disclaimer should therefore be allowable, provided the new narrower scope was already described in the specification. It is not clear, however, whether *any* deletion would constitute an allowable amendment; firstly amendment is still a matter of discretion, and could be refused for this reason if the Patent Office felt that too much descriptive matter was being removed; secondly it could be considered, paradoxically enough, that deletion amounted to adding new matter if it resulted in the emphasis of the disclosure being substantially different from what it was before. The same prohibition about addition of new matter applies to amendments during prosecution, and here British practice is expected to follow that of the EPO, where the Guidelines for Examination indicate that a deletion could be equivalent to adding new matter.

It is not clear to what extent explanatory amendments will be allowed under the 1977 Act, but in view of the possible invalidity resulting from addition of what may later be held to be new matter, patentees will be well advised not to amend in this way without very good reason. As far as corrections are concerned, this seems to be covered by a separate section of the Act dealing not only with clerical errors, but also with false translations and mistakes generally. No mistake can be corrected unless it is obvious what the correction should be, but it would seem that corrections of mistakes do not fall within the prohibitions on adding new matter or extending the scope.

In general, the future practice regarding amendments is one of the most uncertain areas of the new patent law in the United Kingdom. All that is certain is that the provisions are stricter than before, and that whereas under the old law amendments once made could not be called into question, the patent will now be invalid if it is amended incorrectly. Just how serious a problem this will be remains to be seen. It is possible that any such invalidity may be simply corrected by a further amendment to delete the amendment which should not have been allowed; but it may not be as easy as all that. It is fairly common practice under the 1949 Act to apply to amend a patent to strengthen its validity before suing an infringer. Under the present Act any such action might be more likely to harm validity and amendment should probably be left to the infringement action itself.

Anyone who reads a patent specification, whether under the old or the new Act, should be alive to the possibility that the specification may have been amended. If a significant amendment has been made, the specification will normally be reprinted with an indication that it is an amended version; the reader may, however, have an old copy, perhaps photocopied from a library copy of the original version. If the matter is important; for example if possible infringement of the patent is being considered, a new copy should be obtained direct from the Patent Office. Better still, the file of the patent may be consulted to check whether an amendment has been made, as well as such matters as whether the patent is still in force or has been assigned or exclusively licensed.

Invalidity in the USA

United States law until recently had no counterpart to a revocation action in which anyone can attack the validity of a patent before the Patent Office or the court. Until the recent amendment to the law, validity could be challenged only by a counterclaim in an infringement action, or by a suit for declaratory judgment of invalidity; but the latter could only be filed by a party with whom the patentee was in actual dispute, such as someone threatened with an infringement suit.

Re-examination

The amendments to the US Patent Law which became law on 12 December 1980 introduced a completely new possibility. Any person may now, at any time during the life of a US patent, cite new prior art to the Patent Office and request re-examination of the patent. This is at first sight almost like an application for revocation of a British patent before the British Patent Office, but it is a number of respects more limited.

Thus revocation is not possible as a result of re-examination on any grounds other than lack of novelty or obviousness over a printed publication. Furthermore, it is entirely up to the Patent Office to decide whether or not substantial new questions of patentability are raised by the newly cited prior art; if the Patent Office considers that no substantial new issues are raised, the request for re-examination will be refused outright, and no appeal against this decision is possible.

If the Patent Office does order re-examination, the patentee is asked to comment, and the person who requested re-examination may comment in reply. After this point, however, re-examination proceeds in the same way as normal examination and the person requesting re-examination is no longer an active party to the proceedings, although he will receive a copy of each paper issued by or filed in the Patent Office. Finally, and after any appeal has been decided, a certificate is issued cancelling any claim found unpatentable, confirming any original claim which is patentable, and incorporating any newly amended claims found patentable. The scope of the claims may not be broadened by amendment during re-examination.

Grounds of invalidity

The statutory grounds on which a patent may be found invalid by a US court are essentially the same as those on which the Patent Office could have refused grant. Those are that the invention is not patentable because it is not novel, obvious, or useful, or that the specification does not meet the requirements that it must describe the invention, enable any person skilled in the art to make and to use the invention, set out the best mode contemplated by the inventor of carrying out his invention, and contain claims which particularly point out and distinctly claim the invention.

We have already considered in Chapter 3 what are the US requirements for a patentable invention. It should perhaps be mentioned that the US courts from time to time try to invent further tests for patentability which are not to be found in the statute. One of the more recent of these has been the vogue for requiring 'synergism' in mechanical inventions. The concept of synergism may be a relevant one in the pharmaceutical field, where it is held in many countries that a mixture of two or more known substances is patentable only if it shows synergism; i.e. has properties greater than the aggregate of the known properties of the individual components. Certain US cases have, however, applied this concept in such a way as to hold that a mechanical invention which is a combination of old parts is unpatentable unless the components interact in such a way as to give a result somehow greater than that produced by the sum of the parts.[4,5]

This proposition may be regarded as an unjustifiable extension of the sound principle that there has to be some interaction of components to make a mechanical invention patentable. Merely placing together two known machines, each of which does its normal job, is not patentable. For example in an old English case,[6] a patent for a combined sausage machine consisting of a well-known form of mincing machine which fed the meat to a well-known filling machine was held invalid. It covered a mere collocation of two old machines which had previously been used separately.

However, to extend the concept of interaction so as to require 'synergism' is going too far. Practically all mechanical inventions are combinations of old components, and there is no way that they can act other than by the sum of their normal functions. The only relevant question is whether or not it is novel, useful, and unobvious to put them together in that particular way. Fortunately it seems as if the 'synergism requirement', is only a passing fashion and not a permanent feature of US law.

The description requirements for the specification will be considered more fully in Chapter 15. In summary they may be considered as four separate requirements: those of 'description', 'how to make', 'how to use', and 'best mode'. The first three are considered separately with respect to each claim of the specification and are objective requirements, the last refers to the disclosure in general, and is subjective, since it requires inclusion of what the inventor considered to be the best mode at the time of filing. The description requirement corresponds more or less to the British requirement that the claims be fairly based on the description; the 'how to make' requirement corresponds to the British sufficiency requirement; the 'how to use' requirement necessitates a utility statement, particularly in pharmaceutical cases.

The 'best mode' requirement was used successfully as a validity attack in a number of cases around 1977, and gave rise to another of those fashions which make it so difficult to maintain a rational approach to US patent law. The USA suffers from having too many published decisions in patent cases, and too many experts eager to expound upon them. Typically one or two decisions will be published, arising in non-specialist courts and finding patents invalid for some obscure reason. Legal experts then blow the cases up out of all proportion by writing learned articles about them, lecturing about them at conferences, and generally spreading alarm and despondency about the latest threat to the patentee. Such prophecies tend to be self-fulfilling, as more attorneys hear of the new validity attack and try to use it next time they are on the defendant's side in an infringement action; even judges may read the articles and believe mistakenly that the original decisions are correct law. So the poor patentee must take whatever steps, no matter how absurd, the experts decree are necessary to meet the threat; and then a year or two later fashions in invalidity change and the whole exercise is repeated. This type of process has exaggerated the 'best mode' requirement to the point where, in a recent case, the omission of the best mode was regarded as fraud on the Patent Office, and resulted not only in the invalidity of the patent in suit, but the unenforceability of related patents in the same licensing package.

Breach of duty of disclosure
Fraud on the Patent Office has already been mentioned as an equitable defence in an infringement action, but this too has been grossly overplayed. An allegation of fraud is, or should be, a serious matter which is only made if there are substantial grounds for believing that the other side has been guilty of wrongdoing. Nowadays it has become a standard plea brought forward in practically every patent case, and applied to trivial acts of omission which could at worst be regarded as negligence. As Judge Lacey, of the Federal District Court for the District of New Jersey describes it: 'It wasn't until my fifth patent case that I realized that when counsel alleged fraud on the Patent Office, he didn't mean that the other

fellow was a scoundrel. In fact, among the patent bar, "fraud on the Patent Office" isn't even pejorative; it's more in the nature of a salutation.'

The difficulty is that the US Patent Office places a very heavy burden upon the applicant and his agents to disclose all relevant matter to the Patent Office during the prosecution of the application, and not to conceal anything which could be relevant to patentability. Although this duty of disclosure has always been considered to exist, it is only since 1977 that the Patent Office has issued rules which clearly spell it out. As a result, practice today has been tightened up considerably compared with what was normal ten or more years ago. However, patents which were filed long ago in those more relaxed times are now being judged by the stricter standards of today, with the result that many are being found invalid.

There is a breach of the duty of disclosure only if the information withheld is material, material information being facts which a reasonable examiner would regard as important in determining patentability. One difficulty with this definition is deciding what a hypothetical reasonable examiner would think, when so many real examiners often seem to be unreasonable. If this breach is due to inadvertence, mistake, or a minor act of negligence, the situation may be remedied, but if it is due to deliberate fraud, bad faith, or gross negligence, the patent is incurably invalid. What is more, not only is the patent invalid, but related patents may be held unenforceable, and any attempt to enforce a patent obtained by fraud can make the patentee liable under the anti-trust laws for triple damages (see p. 293).

Reissue

If a US patent is wholly or partially invalid or defective because of error without deceptive intent, for example, if it is partially anticipated by prior art which was found only after grant of the patent, the patentee may correct matters by way of a reissue application. This differs procedurally from an application to amend a British patent, since it consists of a new patent application incorporating any proposed amendments, coupled with an offer to surrender the original patent. The whole patent, including any unamended claims, is subject to re-examination in the light of any additional prior art which may be found. If the reissue application is granted, a new patent is issued having a five-figure number prefixed with the letters Re, and expiring on the same date as the original patent. The surrender of the original patent takes effect when the reissue patent is granted.

A reissue application may not contain any new matter, but it is permissible for it to contain claims of broader scope than those of the original patent, provided that the application for reissue was filed within two years of the grant of the original and provided that the new claims had not been deliberately cancelled during prosecution. If a reissue patent issues with broadened scope, it cannot be asserted against someone who started to use the invention before the grant of the reissue unless he is infringing a valid claim of the reissue patent which was also present in the original.

In 1977 the rules governing reissue applications were changed to enable a patentee to apply for reissue without making any alterations in the text or claims, in order to enable the Patent Office to consider patentability in view of prior art not previously of record. The subsequent introduction of re-examination proceedings has rendered this procedure obsolete, and re-issue may now be applied for only if it is intended to amend.

Reissue applications are advertised and the files are open to the public. Any member of the public may 'protest' the reissue, and submit additional prior art and comments, but the protestor is not a full party to the proceedings. It is suggested by many attorneys that a patentee wishing to reissue before suing for infringement should invite the infringer to intervene as a protestor in the reissue proceedings. This puts the infringer in a dilemma: if he declines to intervene, his refusal may be (at least subconsciously) held against him by the judge when he subsequently counterclaims for invalidity in the infringement action; if he does intervene he does so at a disadvantage since he is not a full party to the proceedings and has no opportunity to obtain useful evidence by means of discovery.

One thing which the reissue procedure cannot do is make valid a patent which really has been obtained by fraud. If the 'new' prior art is relevant and if it was in fact known to the patentee during prosecution and deliberately concealed from the Patent Office, then if the facts come out no reissue will be granted and the original patent will be invalid. Reissue applications are scrutinized carefully for any suspicion of fraud; if there is any such dirty linen, reissue cannot be used to launder it.

Reissue is not the only procedure available to amend or correct a US patent; individual claims may simply be deleted by disclaimer without any re-examination of the remaining claims. Minor mistakes such as typographical and clerical errors can be corrected by means of a certificate of correction attached to printed copies of the specification.

The new re-examination provisions should now be used by a patentee who wishes to strengthen his patent by bringing new prior art to the attention of the Patent Office. His can now cite the prior art and request re-examination of his own patent, and if this is refused, or if his original claims are confirmed as a resuult of such re-examination, the presumption of validity of his patent will be enhanced.

Invalidity in other countries

Under the European Patent Convention, the validity of European patents is to be judged by the national courts, but the national laws have largely been harmonized along the same lines as the new British Act. Similarly amendment of European patents after grant can be made only under the national laws. As we have seen, however, the British law adopts the same strict attitude to amendments as is found in the EPO procedure before grant.

Certain countries have unique provisions in connection with invalidity. In Japan, for example, no attack for lack of novelty or obviousness based on foreign publications may be made more than five years after grant, and patents granted under the previous law are incontestably valid five years after grant.

In Spain, unlike most countries, non-unity of invention is a ground of invalidity for patents granted under the old law, and many companies filed large numbers of divisional applications in Spain for this reason. However, it appears that this ground of invalidity cannot be relied upon as a defence in infringement proceedings, and can only be raised by the Spanish Ministry of Commerce. As the Ministry of Commerce is extremely reluctant to do so, such 'invalid' patents are nevertheless treated as valid – not that it helps very much when it comes to enforcing them. In the new Spanish patent law, this ground of invalidity has been abolished.

PART II

INVENTIONS IN CHEMISTRY, PHARMACEUTICALS AND BIOTECHNOLOGY

9

CHEMICAL INVENTIONS

There stood a hill not far, whose grisly top
Belched fire and rolling smoke, the rest entire
Shone with a glossy scurf, undoubted sign
That in his womb lay hid metallic ore,
The work of sulphur.

John Milton: *Paradise Lost*

Novel compounds

There, are different categories of invention in the chemical field; for example, new compounds, new compositions, new manufacturing processes, and new uses. The most straightforward case is that of a new chemical compound of known structure, which will normally be synthesized in a research laboratory. A novel compound, however, cannot be a patentable invention unless it is industrially applicable. In university laboratories thousands of new compounds are made every year, but the great majority of these are only of theoretical interest. It is not enough to make a compound patentable that it is useful in the elucidation of some problem of reaction mechanism or that it has an interesting u.v.-absorption spectrum, but if for example the latter property indicated that the compound would be useful as a u.v.-stabilizer in plastics, then the compound could be patentable.

One interesting point is whether or not compounds can be patentable which have no uses except as intermediates in the preparation of other compounds. The rule is that if the end products are industrially applicable, then so are the intermediates, and that this applies not only to the immediate precursor of the final product but also to the products of earlier steps in the reaction sequence. Such intermediates can therefore be patented so long as they meet the other criteria of being novel and unobvious.

Normally, of course, the invention will not consist of a single compound, but will encompass a group of compounds having some structural features in common and which all have the same end use. It will be the task of the inventor in the research laboratory to synthesize sufficient compounds to form an idea of which compounds will work and which will not, and that of the patent agent to decide in consultation with the inventor what the scope of the claimed invention should be, taking into account not only the inventor's findings but also the prior art.

Obviousness

A compound may be new and useful but still not be patentable because it is so close to the prior art that there is no inventive step involved in making it, or in other words that it is obvious. In considering how close a compound is to a compound described in the prior art one must consider not merely the structural formulae of the compounds, but the compounds themselves, including their properties. Thus, suppose the invention is a certain group of brominated aromatic compounds useful as flame retardants, and the closest prior art is a compound which would fall within the scope except that it is chlorinated instead of brominated. If this chloro-compound was described in an academic publication suggesting no use for it, or if it had a use quite different from that as a flame retardant, then the invention should be patentable in spite of the very close structural similarity, simply because it would not be obvious that the bromo-compounds would be useful as flame retardants.

On the other hand if the prior-art chloro-compound was itself known to have flame retardant properties, then the bromo-analogues would be considered likely to share these properties. In order for the bromo-compounds to be patentable, it would be necessary for them to be surprisingly better flame retardants than the chloro-compound, at least in some respects. If it were known that in similar types of compounds brominated derivatives generally were better flame retardants than the corresponding chloro-compounds, then an improvement over the prior-art compound would be expected and would not suffice to make the bromo-compounds patentable unless the difference was very large. Alternatively, it might be enough for patentability if the bromo-compounds, although no better than the prior art on most substrates, could flameproof one substrate for which the chloro-analogue was ineffective.

It is thus particularly difficult to patent compounds which while new are very closely structurally related to known compounds. Among the closest structural relationships are (in decreasing order): salts of acids and bases, geometrical isomers, positional isomers, homologues (for example, within the alkyl series), and adjacent halogen compounds, as in the example above. If the structural similarities are less close, then the new compounds may be patentable and non-obvious irrespective of whether they have improved properties. In the United Kingdom, for example, a case in 1970 decided that as of 1955 (the priority date of the patent in question) it would not have been obvious to substitute—CF_3 for —Cl at the 2-position of a phenothiazine ring system, even though the prior-art compounds (e.g. chlorpromazine) and the novel compounds (e.g. trifluro-perazine) were both tranquillizers.[1] After trifluroperazine itself was known, however, the substitution of —CF_3 for —Cl in similar types of compounds would be obvious to try, and the results would be patentable only if surprising advantages were found.

Incidentally, there is no general requirement that an invention in order to be patentable must be better than what has gone before. Germany at one time did require an invention to show 'technical progress' but this requirement has now been abolished. It is merely that a surprising improvement in properties may be evidence of the presence of an inventive step, if the closeness of the prior art should cast doubt on this.

A considerable degree of uncertainty exists in situations where a novel compound which is structurally close to the prior art has some advantageous properties which are predictable and some which are not. On the one hand it can be argued that the unpredictable advantages confer patentability; on the other it can be said that the fact that certain advantages were predictable made it obvious to prepare the new compound, and then determination of further advantages is merely discovery of the properties of an unpatentable substance. The latter view was taken by the Technical Board of Appeal in the European Patent Office, where an invention relating to sepulchrate complexes was held obvious over a publication by the inventor of similar complexes.[2] The publication enabled the skilled man to arrive at the claimed complexes without inventive effort, and their predicted advantageous properties would give him an incentive to do so. The further unexpected property which was found was 'not relevant to the issue of patentability'.

This approach does not appear to be followed in the USA, where the properties of the compound are considered as a whole to determine whether surprising advantages exist, and the presence of a predictable advantage would not negate patentability. Even in Europe, the principle of the cited sepulchrate complexes case may not be generally applicable, and the result will depend upon the facts of the particular case.

Selection inventions

Particular problems may arise in patenting compounds which, although individually new, fall within an earlier disclosure of a broader group of compounds. The invention then can only be the selection of a particular compound or relatively small group of compounds from the larger group previously disclosed in broad terms. As an example, suppose C_1–C_{20} monoalkylphenol ethoxylates had been broadly described as being useful non-ionic surfactants, but the only ones which were specifically identified were those in which the alkyl group was methyl, ethyl, or a higher branched-chain alkyl. Then we should be able to protect as an invention the C_8–C_{12} straight-chain monoalkylphenol ethoxylates, provided that this sub-group possesses some advantage over the generality of the broad group of compounds previously disclosed.

It may well be asked how this differs from the normal situation of an invention with close prior art; indeed it could be said that a selection invention *is* the normal situation since all classes of compounds are already known and in that sense any new compound is a selection from some previously described group such as 'steroids' or 'azo-dyestuffs'.

There was however an important case in the UK about 60 years ago (I.G. Farben's Patents[3]) in which special rules for selection inventions were formulated by the judge. Apart from the basic requirement that the compounds must be novel, even though selected from a previously disclosed group, the three 'I.G. Farben rules' were:

(1) there must be some substantial advantage to be secured by the use of the selected members;
(2) all of the selected members must possess the advantage (although a few exceptions would not invalidate the patent); and
(3) the selection must be in respect of a property which can fairly be said to be peculiar to the selected group.

If we look at these requirements in the light of present-day practice, we shall see that the first two are no more than the normal rules whereby any compound which is prima facie obvious over a prior art disclosure may be shown to be non-obvious by possessing a surprising advantage. As regards the third of the I.G. Farben rules, it is by no means clear what is the logical basis behind it. If out of a previously disclosed large group of compounds a smaller group A can be identified having a non-obvious advantage, then the compounds in group A should be patentable as a selection invention. If subsequently a second group B is identified, also having that property, then group B may or may not be patentable (it may of course be obvious in view of A), but why should this affect the validity of the patent claiming A?

There may be rare cases where *no* members of the broad group have been specifically disclosed, and the supposed advantage of the selected group is in fact a property shared by all or nearly all of the large group. In that case the 'invention' really amounts to a mere discovery of a property of a known group of compounds, which is not patentable. In normal cases, however, where at least some members of the broad group are known and do not have the advantageous property of the selected group, I venture the opinion that the third I.G. Farben rule is a dead letter, and one which would no longer be followed by the English courts. Certainly in the USA a disclosure from which the invention is a selection is not treated any differently from other prior art.

There are perhaps two points in which special considerations may apply to selection inventions. The first is that when the earlier disclosed class of compounds is small it may be argued that a general disclosure of the class is equivalent to a specific disclosure of each of its members, thereby rendering every member of the class no longer novel. In England a disclosure of a process involving an 'alkali metal' was held to be a disclosure of the process with lithium.[4] In the European Patent Office, it was decided in a recent case[5] that a description of N-alkylation of a specific compound with a 'C_{1-4} alkyl bromide' amounted to a specific disclosure of the N-methyl compound, because 'C_1' was mentioned as the lower end of the range and C_1 could only be methyl. The implication is that none of the other seven N-alkyl compounds were specifically disclosed, which leads to the somewhat absurd conclusion that if the specification had used the term 'an alkyl bromide having less than 5 carbon atoms' there would not have been disclosure of the N-methyl compound, although to the chemist the two expressions have precisely the same meaning.

A quite different approach was taken by the Court of Appeal and the House of Lords, in the case of *du Pont* v. *Akzo*.[6] In 1950 ICI had obtained a patent for polyesters of terephthalic acid and certain glycols, in which polyalkylene oxide units were incorporated into the chain in order to improve dyeability of fibre made from the material. Although the specific examples all used ethylene glycol, four other glycols including 1,4-butanediol were mentioned by name as possible reactants. In 1972, du Pont filed an application based on their discovery that polyesters of this type using 1,4-butanediol as the glycol had improved mechanical properties making them particularly suitable for example for the manufacture of hydraulic hose. Instead of claiming this new use of the material, however, they claimed the polymer *per se*. The application was allowed, and was opposed by Akzo. In the Patent Office the hearing officer held that the claim was anticipated by the ICI disclosure, since the starting material was named, even though the final product was not specifically disclosed. This decision was overturned on appeal, and further appeals to the Court of Appeal and the House of Lord were lost, so that the du Pont patent was upheld. (see p. 226).

Thus, in the event du Pont were allowed to re-monopolize under the guise of a selection invention a material which had been quite clearly taught by ICI twenty years earlier.

The second consideration applies when the earlier disclosure is a patent, as usually is the case. It can then be argued that once that patent has lapsed its entire scope should be in the public domain, and that a patent for a selection invention unjustifiably prolongs the monopoly, particularly if the same patentee owns both the patents. Based on this reasoning, courts in Israel have recently held certain patents for selection inventions to be invalid. This approach is somewhat extreme and would, if applied logically, have the absurd effect of invalidating all improvement patents, of which chemical selection patents are only a special case. If the earlier disclosure is broad and general it may very well be a meritorious invention to find that a small sub-group has particularly good properties. In consideration for the patent grant the public is being given information it did not have before and which it might be very difficult to find out by trial and error.

On the other hand it may well be an abuse of patent rights for a company to patent a specific group of compounds, obtain 20 yeaɪⅼ monopoly on all of them, and then attempt to get a further 20 years' monopoly just for selecting a preferred group of them. For this reason it is reasonable that in the public interest selection inventions, at least those representing selections from relatively small classes of compounds, should be examined strictly and not granted too readily.

Optical isomers

Perhaps the closest that a new compound can be to the prior art is the situation when the new compound is an optically active enantiomer of a compound previously known only in racemic form. This may be regarded as an extreme form of a selection invention, and it has been argued that the optically active form cannot be regarded as novel if the racemate is known, since the racemate could be considered as an equimolar mixture of the *d*- and *l*- forms. However, in cases both in the UK[7] and the USA[8] it has been decided that optical isomers of known racemates may be considered as novel *per se*.

Usually, however, the problem is regarded as one of obviousness rather than lack of novelty. It is obvious from the presence of an asymmetric centre in the molecule that optically active forms can exist, and it is usually obvious that they can be isolated by one or other of the standard methods of resolution. The only way in which an optical isomer can be patentable is if it has surprisingly superior properties as compared with the racemate, or if it has a use that the racemate did not have.

At one time is was relatively easy to obtain patents for an optical isomer of a pharmaceutical compound on showing superior properties. Nowadays it is more generally realized that it is normal for one optical isomer to have much higher activity than the other, and it has become very difficult to obtain patents for optical isomers of known compounds. For example, in recent litigation,[9] the patent for amoxicillin, an antibiotic which is an optical isomer of a known racemate, was upheld in the United Kingdom only to the extent that claims to an oral composition containing amoxicillin were held valid, it being shown that amoxicillin had particularly high activity on oral administration whereas the racemate did not have this high activity. In France and Germany, however, the amoxicillin patent was held to be invalid.

Physical forms

New physical forms of known compounds may also be patentable chemical inventions. For example certain pigments may exist in different allotropic solid forms, and it sometimes happens that a particular new solid form may have improved stability or better colouring properties than the form in which the pigment was previously known. Even mere reduction in particle size of a known compound may be a patentable invention. The drug griseofulvin was known to be an effective agent against fungal infections of the skin, but could only be used locally because the compound was so insoluble that if it was taken orally none of it was resorbed into the bloodstream. It was found that by reducing the particle size of the griseofulvin to very small dimensions resorption was greatly improved and the drug could be used orally. Griseofulvin in powder form having a surface: volume ratio greater than a specified figure was patentable *per se*.

Compounds of unknown structure

A compound may still be patentable even if its chemical structure is uncertain or unknown. The difficulty lies in defining the compound in such a way that it can be claimed unambiguously. There are two main ways of doing this, firstly by defining the compound in terms of its properties and secondly by defining how the compound is made.

If one is claiming only a single compound, for example a new antibiotic obtained from a mutant strain of a micro-organism, it may well be possible to obtain the compound in pure form and define it in terms of properties which may be: physical, for example melting-point, i.r. spectrum, n.m.r. spectrum, crystal form; physico-chemical, such as solubility in various solvents; chemical, such as its action with various reagents; or biochemical, for example its effect upon various bacteria. The greater the number of such characterizing properties that can be found, the better. The compound can then be claimed in terms of these properties in a so-called 'fingerprint claim'. This is preferable to making a guess at an uncertain structure, since if the guess is wrong the mistake cannot normally be corrected later. In one recent case in the UK the patentee was allowed to replace a compound *per se* claim based on an incorrect structural formula by a 'fingerprint claim' characterizing the compound by the melting-points of a number of derivatives, although he was not allowed to substitute the correct formula.[10] This was rather a special case in that the patent was claiming a single, well-characterized compound. Normally, chemical patents claim a group of compounds and would usually not contain enough data to put together a 'fingerprint claim' for any one compound in the group.

If it is not possible to define the product adequately in terms of its properties, or if it is desired to claim a group of compounds, the product may be defined as the product of reacting certain reagents under certain conditions; that is, by a product-by-process claim. This has the disadvantage that the product is not covered if made by a different process, and it may in some countries be possible to overcome this problem by defining the product as a compound *obtainable by* reacting A with B, etc.; the idea being that this does not limit the scope to the product only when it is obtained by this route. Such claims are of very doubtful effect.

Polymeric compounds

Strictly speaking all polymers are mixtures of various molecular species, so that a precise structural description is usually not possible. If the polymer is completely new, in the sense that it is obtained from monomers never previously polymerized, or by modifying functional groups on a polymer backbone in a new way, the structure can normally be defined in terms of the structural formula of its repeating unit.

Given that this basic formula of the polymer is already known, it is still possible to obtain new and patentable polymers by various kinds of modification, provided these give useful and non-obvious results. Perhaps the simplest of these would be control of the molecular weight to give products of a specific average molecular weight or molecular-weight distribution. However, the correlation between polymer properties and molecular weight is fairly well understood, so that it is difficult to find non-obvious advantages of a particular molecular-weight range.

The nature of the end-groups on a polymer chain may modify the properties of the polymer very considerably, even though the end-groups may represent only a very small fraction of the total structure. In the same way the presence of quite small quantities of comonomers may give a copolymer with surprising advantages over the original homopolymer.

The chemistry of polyoxymethylene, $HO-(-CH_2-O)-_nH$, illustrates both of these points very well. Under suitable conditions, pure formaldehyde can be polymerized into a high-molecular-weight polymer with excellent mechanical properties. The unmodified polymer is quite useless, however, because it has no thermal stability: on heating, the polymer chain 'unzips' and depolymerizes back to formaldehyde.

One approach to this problem was to modify the end groups by converting hydroxy end-groups to methoxy. The resulting polymer, $CH_3O--(CH_2-O-)_nCH_3$ had sufficient thermal stability to be useful, and was a patentable new product. It still had the problem that if the end-group should be cleaved off, the remainder of the chain would rapidly unzip, so that above a certain temperature depolymerization would set in very rapidly.

The problem was solved by the introduction of a small amount of ethylene oxide as comonomer, giving a polymer which after end-capping, had the structure:

$$CH_3O-[-(-CH_2-O-)_{\overline{n}}(-CH_2-CH_2-O-)-(-CH_2-O-)_{\overline{m}}]_{\overline{x}}-CH_3$$

The ethylene oxide units in the chain acted as 'zipper-jammers' so that if depolymerization should set in it would stop at the first ethylene oxide unit and not continue along the whole chain. Here again a patentable new product had been invented.

If larger amounts of comonomer units are present, their distribution in the chain may give rise to different products such as random, regular or block copolymers, and if the polymer chain contains optically active centres, the sterochemistry of the polymer may be used to define new products. For example isotactic polypropylene is an important product, patentable over ordinary atactic polypropylene, and in the USA there has been a conflict lasting many years over the question of who has the rights to this invention.

Cross-linking polymer chains gives products differing markedly from uncross-linked polymers, and again such products may be patentable, although there are increasing difficulties in defining the product once cross-linking occurs.

New synthetic processes

Another major category of chemical inventions is that of new processes for the preparation of known compounds. These may be completely new and applicable to a wide range of end-products, as for example reduction using boron hydrides or alkylation using Grignard reagents were at the time they were invented.

Such a process is patentable since it will be easy to specify at least one industrially applicable end-product which can be made using it, and furthermore such processes may involve the use of novel reagents which could themselves be patentable as new compounds. However, the majority of such advances in general synthetic chemistry are made in university laboratories and are published in the scientific literature rather than patented.

In industrial laboratories, research on new synthetic methods is generally applied to particular commercially important compounds. Such methods may range from an entirely new synthetic route representing the first commercially feasible method of producing a whole new group of compounds to a minor improvement in the established process for a single product. Inventions of this type may be made in the Research and Development laboratory, or by the production chemists.

In deciding whether or not to seek patent protection for such an invention one must balance the relative merits of obtaining patent protection and maintaining the new process as secret know-how. A patent costs money and should be applied for only if a commercial benefit is expected from it. If the process of the invention is such that it cannot be determined from the end product or other evidence whether or not a competitor is using it, then any patent rights will be unenforceable. The patent will then have value only to the extent that the competitors are ethical enough to respect patents which they know they could infringe with impunity. Worse, the publication of the patent application informs competitors, ethical or otherwise, how to carry out the invention.

Keeping a process invention as secret know-how will be feasible only if the invention cannot be deduced from the end-product, but if it is feasible it does have certain advantages. First, it costs nothing over and above the normal overheads of maintaining business security; secondly it gives nothing away to competitors; and thirdly the effective period of monopoly can in theory be prolonged indefinitely and is not limited to the term of patent protection. On the other hand, if the secret is lost other than by theft, or if someone else independently makes the same invention, the original inventor can do nothing about it.

On balance it is preferable in many cases not to patent process improvement inventions, since such patents are extremely difficult to enforce. However, if it is intended to keep a process as a trade secret, it must be made clear to employees that it is secret. If this is not done an employee who leaves and joins a competitor may not feel under any particular obligation of confidentiality with regard to the process, and it is in this way that trade secrets may most easily be lost.

New uses and new application processes

This broad category of chemical invention includes the discovery of a specific new use for a known compound which may or may not have some existing use, as well as all new methods of treating substances or articles with known compounds, for example an improved dyeing process using known dyes and auxiliaries in a new way.

Such inventions may come from Research and Development laboratories in which old compounds are screened for possible new activities, but very often they may arise out of non-research activities such as product development, customer service, or even marketing. Many patentable inventions coming from such sources may be overlooked because they are not recognized as such either by the inventor himself or by management, and yet an invention made in the course of solving a particular problem for a customer, for example, will have more chance of being commercially interesting than many more speculative and less practical inventions arising in the laboratory.

Normally inventions of new uses for old compounds are claimed in terms of the process of using the compound, for example 'A method of preventing corrosion of metals by applying to the metal a compound of formula I' rather than 'The use of a compound of formula I as an anti-corrosion agent for metals'. Special considerations arise when the new use is a pharmaceutical use, and these are discussed in the next chapter.

New compositions and mixtures

A new composition may sometimes be claimed when the invention is really a new compound or a new use of an old compound. For example if a new pigment is useful in paints one could claim a paint composition containing the pigment and a pharmaceutical composition may be a suitable way to claim the invention that a known compound has a pharmaceutical use.

The composition must of course really be new, and one does not make an old composition new merely by giving it a new name or supplying a new use for it. Thus, for example, if a compound of formula X was known to be a u.v.-stabilizer, and had been used in paint compositions for that purpose, then the invention that X could be used as a corrosion inhibitor could not be protected by means of a claim to 'an anti-corrosive paint containing a compound of formula X'. Only if anticorrosive paints differed in composition from paints in which X had been used, and these differences were expressed in the claim, would the claimed invention be novel.

This approach is that of Anglo-Saxon countries and is different from that of Germany, where a claim to an anticorrosive '*Mittel*' (means) could be considered novel even if the composition was the same as that previously used for a different purpose. Pharmaceuticals also constitute an exception, as will be discussed in the next chapter.

There are, however, many inventions where the invention itself lies in the preparation of a composition consisting of two or more components, which is particularly useful for some industrial application. The general term composition covers both simple mixtures and cases in which there is some chemical reaction between the components, for example glass compositions which may be described in terms of their content of various metal oxides, silica, etc.

There are some fields, for example those of detergents and textile finishing agents, in which most commercial products are simple mixtures of various components, each of which is known to have been used in other similar products. To get any kind of patent protection for these mixtures is not easy, firstly because of the difficulty of defining the composition precisely and secondly because of the large amount of close prior art. The difficulty of definition is not helped by the fact that many of the individual components are themselves mixtures, or are commercial products sold under a trade name, whose actual structure or composition is not always known. The close prior art means that most such mixtures will be prima facie obvious, and will have to have some sort of advantage in order to be patentable.

Nevertheless, a great many such mixtures, of very marginal inventiveness, are patented each year, and it could well be argued that in such fields mixtures of known components should in general not be patentable. If certain unpatented components are known to be surfactants, then there is a strong case that anyone should be free to mix any of these in any proportions he chooses, without having to worry about infringing patent rights. Only if the results obtained are really extraordinarily superior to the prior art should there be any question of patenting such mixtures, and this will very seldom be the case.

PHARMACEUTICAL INVENTIONS

> '. . . medical science is as yet very imperfectly
> differentiated from common cure-mongering
> witchcraft . . . one practitioner prescribing six
> or seven scheduled poisons for so familiar a
> disease as enteric fever where another will not
> tolerate drugs at all. . .'
> George Bernard Shaw: Preface to *The Doctor's Dilemma* (1906)

Novel pharmaceutical compounds

In the previous chapter we have outlined the various types of invention which may arise in the chemical field. Where the field of application of the invention is the field of pharmaceuticals, however, some special considerations apply, and these will be considered in this chapter.

Many of these special problems arise from the provision in the British Patents Act 1977 and corresponding provisions in the European Patent Convention and the laws of other states adhering to the EPC that 'an invention of a method of treatment of the human or animal body by surgery or therapy or of diagnosis practiced on the human or animal body shall not be taken to be capable of industrial application', industrial applicability being, as we have seen, a basic condition for patentability. However, it is clearly stated that this does not prevent a substance or composition from being capable of industrial application merely because it is 'invented for use in any such method'.

Accordingly, novel compounds which have a pharmaceutical utility are patentable *per se* in EPC countries (with the exception of Austria, which does not allow claims to any chemical compounds *per se*) as well as in the USA and Japan. There are now relatively few countries of any importance which totally forbid the patenting of pharmaceutical inventions, Brazil and Turkey being among the most prominent.

Metabolites and precursors

It is found that when a compound is administered to the human or animal body, some of the compound may be excreted unchanged but some or all of the compound may instead be subject to more or less complex chemical changes resulting in a series of metabolites which are excreted or broken down further. It frequently happens that one or more of the metabolites is also pharmacologically active, and it is not uncommon to find that the activity of the compound which is administered is entirely due to an active metabolite. In this situation it is more correct to regard the metabolite as the drug and the compound administered as a bioprecursor or 'pro-drug'. Pro-drugs, although inactive in themselves, may be useful for example because they may be more stable or better absorbed by the body than the active compound itself.

At the time a patent for a new pharmaceutical compound is applied for, its detailed metabolism will not normally have been studied. A compound which at the time of filing is believed to have its own pharmaceutical activity may later turn out to be the pro-drug of an active metabolite. This should not, however, affect the intrinsic patentability of the substance; if a pharmacological result is obtained by giving the substance, it is immaterial by what process the result is obtained. It is never necessary to explain in a patent how an invention works; the fact that it does work, whether directly or through an intermediary compound, is sufficient.

However, in this situation it is possible that sale of the pro-drug may infringe any patent rights which may exist for the active metabolite. For example, it was held by the House of Lords[1] that the drug hetacillin infringed Beecham's patent for ampicillin, even though its structure did not fall within the claims of the patent. Hetacillin was the acetone adduct of ampicillin, and as soon as it was ingested it was hydrolysed in the body to ampicillin. Here, of course, the pro-drug in question was considered to be a deliberate attempt to capitalise on ampicillin while evading the letter of the patent claims, and it is not at all clear that this case would be followed if the person selling the pro-drug had acted in good faith without realizing that activity was due to a patented metabolite, or if the 'pro-drug' had any activity of its own.

Following the 'hetacillin' case, Beechams succeeded in obtaining (under the 1949 Act) a patent claiming a novel cephalosporin, its salts and 'pharmaceutically acceptable bioprecursors thereof'. Such claims do not appear to meet the requirement of the 1977 Act that they should 'define the matter for which the applicant seeks protection', since it may require an undue amount of experimental work to determine whether or not a given compound could fall under the vague definition of 'bioprecursor'. Furthermore, it may be argued that in so far as these claims cover the 'hetacillin' situation they are superfluous, since such direct, inactive bioprecursors are already infringements of the claim to the drug itself, and to the extent they cover more than this they are unduly broad and claim more than what the patentee has invented.

Natural products

Very many natural products, both from plant and animal sources, have useful pharmacological properties. One frequently hears it said that naturally occurring products are not patentable, but this is not the case. A claim to a newly discovered natural product may be valid if it is framed in such a way as to distinguish the claimed product from the product as found in nature. This may, for example, be done by claiming the product in pure form, or as having defined physical characteristics which imply a certain degree of purity.

Thus, in an early case in the USA, a patent was granted for pure adrenalin isolated from adrenal gland tissue;[2] the pure substance was medicinally useful whereas the crude gland extract was not. In most countries there have been many such patents granted covering newly isolated hormones, lymphokines, and other substances occurring in the human body. It should also be remembered that many antibiotics are natural products since they were originally isolated from cultures of naturally occurring fungi; there has never been any serious problem in claiming such antibiotics as new compounds.

Indeed, it may not be necessary to include any purity limitation in the claim if the claim is interpreted in such a way that it does not cover the product as found in nature. If the product in its natural state is not an infringement of the claim, then neither should it be an anticipation of it.

If the chemical structure of a natural product X is determined for the first time, and at least one synthetic route to it is found, then it should be possible to claim 'Synthetic X, of formula . . .', however it is made. Such a claim would not however extend to the product isolated from natural sources, and it is clear that merely determining the structure of a product which has already been known and characterized in the pure state cannot give rise to an unrestricted product claim to that chemical structure.

Pharmaceutical compositions

Novel pharmaceutical compositions may be of three distinct types; combination preparations comprising two or more known pharmaceutically active ingredients; new drug delivery systems or galenic forms (for example a new kind of tablet giving a controlled rate of release of drug when swallowed); and compositions comprising a compound not previously used as a drug, together with any conventional pharmaceutical carrier or excipient.

Combination preparations

Whereas in most chemical fields simple mixtures of known compounds can readily be patented, so long as they are novel and unobvious, the practice in the pharmaceutical field in the USA is much stricter; claims to mixtures of two or more pharmaceutically active ingredients are generally refused unless synergism, or a 'superadditive effect' can be shown.

Yet there is no reason for a stricter approach to patentability of mixtures in the pharmaceutical field than for example in the detergent feld. Anyone can put on the market a detergent consisting of a mixture of ingredients which individually have been approved as safe for such use. On the other hand, no one can market a combination product of two old drugs without obtaining approval from the national regulatory authorities, and this generally will not be given unless the combination shows a real advantage over the separate components. Nevertheless, a company which succeeds in convincing the FDA that a new combination product has enough advantages to be marketable may not succeed in persuading the US Patent Office that it has enough advantages to be patentable. By insisting upon too rigid a requirement of synergism, the US Patent Office is trying to do the job of the FDA, not its own job.

Synergism between two drugs can be extremely difficult if not impossible to prove, largely because it is practically impossible to predict what would be expected if there were no synergistic effect. In fact, synergism in the strict sense can be mathematically proved only by comparing dose-versus-response curves for the two components separately as well as for the combination. This can be a long and difficult exercise even for a simple quantifiable measurement such as blood-pressure; when the effect which has to be measured is the rate of incidence of some infrequent occurrence, for example the percentage of patients suffering heart attacks in a given time, and particularly where the results have to be obtained from clinical studies on humans because no suitable animal tests exist, then rigid proof of synergism becomes a practical impossibility.

This should not mean that such compositions are unpatentable. If synergism can be demonstrated, this clearly makes the combination patentable, but even in the absence of synergism, other advantageous and unobvious results should be able to be used to establish the presence of an inventive step. Suppose compounds A and B each have the same pharmaceutical effect at a dose of 100 mg, but at this dosage each gives some undesirable side-effects; and suppose further that a combination of 50 mg A and 50 mg B gives exactly the same desired effect but with reduced side-effects. There is no evidence for synergism between A and B, but nevertheless the advantage of lower side-effects, assuming it was not predictable, should be sufficient for patentability of the combination.

Drug delivery systems

In compositions of this type, the invention lies not in the pharmaceutically active material, but in the other constituents which enable it to be administered in a particular way. Very often such inventions are applicable to a very wide range of drugs. Because it is becoming more and more difficult and expensive to find and develop new drugs, more effort is being put into finding ways of delivering existing drugs more effectively, and inventions of this type are increasing in frequency and in commercial importance.

For example, it is often desirable to have low but more or less steady concentrations of a drug in the body over a relatively long period of time. Alternatives to the frequent swallowing of tablets at regular intervals include, for example, adhesive patches from which a drug is absorbed slowly through the skin, or depot injections of fine particles of a biodegradable polymer which releases a drug over a period of weeks or months. Many hormones such as insulin are peptides which are destroyed by the digestive juices if taken orally and which normally have to be given by injection; alternative methods such as nasal sprays from which the peptide can be absorbed through the mucous membrane of the nose are being developed.

Conventional pharmaceutical compositions

Where a compound is already known for non-pharmaceutical purposes and can no longer be claimed *per se*, the invention that it has a pharmaceutical use may conveniently be claimed by claiming 'a pharmaceutical composition comprising a compound of formula . . . in association with a pharmaceutically acceptable diluent or carrier', which would include all forms in which the compound could be administered, from a complex drug delivery system to a simple tablet, or even a solution in sterile water for injection. This is however a special case of the question of "first pharmaceutical use" protection, which is dealt with more fully below.

First pharmaceutical use

A compound made, tested and found to be useful as a pharmaceutical may, when a search is carried out, be found to be novel. There is then no problem in patenting the substance itself (assuming it is not obvious). It may be, however, that the search reveals the substance to be already known, for example it may be mentioned in an expired patent describing photographic sensitizers, or it may be given as an example in a scientific paper in which no use at all is disclosed for the compound. In both cases product protection is ruled out and an alternative solution has to be found.

As already mentioned, one possibility is to claim broadly pharmaceutical compositions containing the active ingredient. Such claims have the advantage that they are not limited in respect of any specific pharmaceutical indication; they would equally well cover the compound in a cough syrup or in a haemorrhoidal suppository. An alternative approach is to claim the use of the compound as a pharmaceutical. Here there are difficulties to be overcome because the use of a substance as a pharmaceutical is equivalent to a method of medical treatment, which is specifically excluded from patentability by the EPC and by the Patents Act 1977.

However, both the EPC and the Patents Act 1977 contain a provision that for 'an invention consisting of a substance or composition for use in a method of treatment of the human or animal body by surgery or therapy . . .'; the fact that the substance or composition is old does not prevent the invention being taken as new if no previous pharmaceutical use was known. Applying this wording literally, the Technical Board of Appeal of the EPO held[3] that claims in the form 'Compounds of formula . . . for use as an active therapeutic substance' were allowable, and that such claims should cover all therapeutic use of the substances, and not only use for the specific indication which was disclosed.

According to the Guidelines for Examination published by the EPO, claims of this 'for use as' type are regarded as restricted to the substance when presented or packaged for therapeutic use, so that sales of bulk substance could not be stopped by such a claim.

In spite of the long-standing rule in British patent law that a statement of purpose cannot add novelty to an old composition, the British Patent Office now follows the practice of the EPO in this respect. Pharmaceutical uses form a statutory exception to this general rule, which still applies in other areas.

Second pharmaceutical use

From discussion of the protection available for the invention that a known chemical compound may be used as a pharmaceutical follows naturally the question of what patent protection may be obtained for the invention that a compound, already known to have one or more pharmaceutical uses, has a new pharmaceutical utility unrelated to any earlier known use.

A priori, there is no fundamental reason why an invention of this type should be less capable of patent protection than any other. The amount of work involved in making the invention, the potential benefit to the public, and the potential commercial importance may all be as great as for the invention of a new chemical entity having pharmaceutical utility. And, certainly, it is possible to obtain a patent for the dyeing of nylon with a dyestuff previously known to be useful for dyeing wool. So if new uses of dyestuffs can be patented (given that they are novel and unobvious), why not new uses of pharmaceuticals?

The answer, so far as many countries are concerned, lies in the form of wording of the claims. When the only novel feature was the new utility, the claim had to have wording which was essentially equivalent to 'A method of treating disease Y by administering compound X' or 'The use of compound X in treating disease Y'. The problem is that such claims are claims to the medical treatment of humans, and as such were denied patent protection in many countries either by specific wording in the law or by legal precedent.

The rationale for this exclusion from patentability has never been clearly stated, but it seems to derive from the idea that a doctor must be free to treat his patient as he sees fit, without having to worry about being sued for patent infringement. In fact, the likelihood of doctors being sued by pharmaceutical patentees is, for obvious reasons, remote, and certainly never seems to have given any trouble in the USA, where claims to medical treatment of humans have been allowed for a long time.

A typical claim of this type in the USA would read 'A method of treatment of disease Y comprising the administration, to a human in need of such treatment, of an effective dose of compound X'. Claims such as this are also allowable in Japan and in the Philippines, and there were one or two European countries (Belgium and Italy) where, because there was no effective examination, such claims were granted although their validity was never confirmed by the courts.

In the UK, the 1949 Act did not specifically rule out the patenting of methods of medical treatment, but a long line of legal precedents had established that such methods were not considered to be a 'manner of manufacture'. The 1977 Act, like the EPC, appeared to spell out clearly that only the first pharmaceutical use could be patented, and up to 1985 all attempts to get around this restriction failed. For example, claims to a package containing the known drug together with instructions for the new use were refused as being disguised method of treatment claims.[4] The courts indicated that they found the situation illogical and felt that 'second use' inventions deserved protection, but considered this to be impossible without new legislation.

In New Zealand, on an appeal by Wellcome, the High Court overruled the Patent Office and held that under New Zealand law (similar to British law before the 1977 Act), methods of medical treatment were patentable.[5] However, this judgement was in turn overruled by the Court of Appeal, which restored the previous position.

In Germany however, the courts did not feel quite so restricted by what the law actually said. In the case of Bayer's 'Hydropyridine' application, the invention was the use of a known cardiovascular agent (Nimodepine) to treat cerebral disorders. The application was refused by the German Patent Office, and an appeal to the Federal Patent Court was unsuccessful. On a further appeal to the Federal Supreme Court in 1983, however, the Court held[6] that the German law, which also states methods of medical treatment to be unpatentable, did *not* preclude the patenting of new uses of known pharmaceuticals. A claim of the form 'Use of compound X for the treatment of disease Y' was accepted.

The Swiss Patent Office was asked for its views in the light of this German decision, and gave the opinion[7] that although claims of the German type would be forbidden by the Swiss Patent Law, claims of the form 'Use of compound X for the preparation of an agent for the treatment of disease Y' should be acceptable. This means that such claims will now be granted by the Swiss Patent Office, although it does not guarantee that the Swiss courts will hold them to be valid.

The same application by Bayer which was successful in Germany was also filed in the European Patent Office, where its rejection by the Examining Division was appealed to the Board of Appeals. Because it was felt to raise fundamental legal issues, the appeal was remitted to the Enlarged Board of Appeals. After long deliberation, the Enlarged Board of Appeals decided in the Bayer and other related cases[8] that the German form of claim was a claim to a method of medical treatment and was not patentable, but that the Swiss form of claim would be granted by the EPO. Clearly, the Board were very glad to be able to adopt a compromise position originally suggested by a small neutral country and thus avoid offending the UK and France by uncritically adopting the German view or offending Germany by rejecting it totally.

The Swiss form of claim suffers from the logical objection that it lacks novelty, since it claims the use of the compound for preparation of a medicament and normally the medicament itself will be the same as that already used for the first pharmaceutical indication. Accordingly, there was concern that patents granted with such claims by the EPO could be held invalid by national courts in countries such as the UK.

These fears have been allayed by an unexpected decision of the British Patents Court, in which both patent judges sitting together decided that a British national patent could be granted with claims of the Swiss type.[9] The novelty problem was recognized, but it was held that for the sake of a common approach in European patent law it should be considered that the new end use conferred novelty on the claim.

Although this decision could, of course, be overruled by a higher court, it is unlikely that the view of both experienced patent judges would not be respected. Accordingly, it is safe to assume that in the UK, as in the remaining EPC countries, new pharmaceutical uses can now be patented.

These recent developments represent a considerable improvement in the overall strength of pharmaceutical patent protection, and enable research in the field of new applications of existing drugs to be patented in most countries of interest, instead of only a few. It must be realized, however, that this form of claim may be used by the patentee to prevent a competitor from actively promoting the compound for the new use, by advertisements, package inserts, etc., but cannot prevent doctors from prescribing for the patented new use a generic product which is already on the market for an earlier indication.

BIOTECHNOLOGICAL INVENTIONS

The Microbe is so very small
You cannot make him out at all . . .
But Scientists, who ought to know
Assure us that they must be so . . .
Oh! let us never, never doubt
What nobody is sure about!

Hillaire Belloc: 'The Microbe'

What is biotechnology?

Biotechnology may be defined loosely as the production of useful products by living micro-organisms and cell cultures, and as such it has been with us for a long time. The production of ethanol from yeast cells is as old as history, and over 50 years ago the production of various industrial chemicals such as acetic acid and acetone by fermentation processes was well known. Indeed, even the word biotechnology is not recently coined. In 1920 a Bureau of Bio-Technology was established in Leeds, and published a journal dealing with fermentation technology and related topics.

More recently, the antibiotics industry was based upon the isolation of products from selected strains of micro-organisms, and although the majority of antibiotics are now produced synthetically, many are still made from micro-organisms either found in nature or artificially mutated. Not only antibiotics but also other drugs – for example, the immuno-suppressant cyclosporin – are produced by fermentation of a micro-organism.

What may be called the 'new biotechnology', as distinct from the 'classical' fermentation technology, has arisen only within the last 15 years. It relates to the production of specifically modified micro-organisms or cell lines, generally by one or another of two basic techniques. The first of these is recombinant DNA technology (also referred to as gene splicing or genetic engineering), in which genetic material from an external source is inserted into a cell in such a way that it causes the production of a desired protein by the cell; the second is hybridoma technology in which different types of immune cell are fused together to form a hybrid cell line producing monoclonal antibodies.

Patents and biotechnology

The protection of this developing and commercially important new technology constitutes a challenge to the patent system which it must meet if it is going to survive at all in this area. Patenting in this field is beset by many complex problems, which we shall consider in detail in this and the following chapter. It has been suggested that the products of biotechnology cannot be patented because they are natural products, or even that the patent system is inherently incapable of protecting inventions of this type, for which a new form of industrial property should be created.

The first of these suggestions is simply incorrect. As we have seen (p. 143), natural products are, in principle, patentable provided only that the claim is worded or interpreted in such a way as not to cover the product in its natural environment. As to the second, no-one has proposed any feasible alternative to the patent system, and there is no reason why the basic requirements for patentability should not apply in the field of biotechnology as in any other. These are that the invention must be capable of industrial application, must be new, must be non-obvious, and must be described in such a way that a skilled worker in the relevant field can reproduce the result obtained. The difficulty is that the inherent complexity of living systems is such that it becomes more difficult to meet these requirements where living cells are involved, particularly the requirement of a sufficient and reproducible disclosure.

Microbiological inventions

Patentability of micro-organisms per se
Microbiological inventions generally involve the use of a new strain of micro-organism to produce a new compound or to produce a known compound more efficiently (for example, in higher yield or purity). The new organism may have been found in nature (for example, by screening of soil samples) or may have been produced in the laboratory by artificially induced random mutation or by more specific techniques such as genetic engineering.

If the micro-organism produces a novel product, such as a new antibiotic, of which the structure has been determined or which can be characterized by a 'fingerprint claim' (see p. 135), then the novel product may be claimed as any other new chemical compound can, subject to the requirements of a sufficient description being given. However, if the end product is already known, process protection is available, but this protection is weak and it would be preferable to patent the new micro-organism itself.

Most patent laws do not deal specifically with the question of whether or not a new living strain of micro-organism is itself patentable, but the Patents Act 1977 and the EPC do not exclude the possibility. Plant and animal varieties are excluded from protection, as is any biological process for their production, but not excluded is a microbiological process or the product of such a process – which may, of course, be a micro-organism. Both the British Patent Office (under the new Act as under the old) and the EPO do grant patents for micro-organisms as such.

In the USA, it had always been the practice of the Patent Office to refuse claims to living systems as not being patentable subject matter, but in 1980 the Supreme Court decided (by a 5–4 majority) in the famous Chakrabarty case[1] that a new strain of bacteria produced artificially (by bacterial recombination) was a patentable invention. Although Chakrabarty's bacteria did not produce a useful product, they had the useful property that they could feed on, and so disperse, oil slicks. Since the product which would be sold would be the bacterial strain itself, it was particularly important in this case to obtain a *per se* claim to the micro-organism.

The Chakrabarty decision aroused great public interest at the time, many people apparently feeling that by granting patents for living systems, the USPTO was somehow usurping the function of the Creator. In all the fuss, it went unremarked that the British Patent Office had already granted the corresponding British patent in 1976.

Although micro-organisms may now be claimed as such in most countries, it is more difficult to claim a micro-organism isolated from a natural source than one which has been artificially produced. This is due to the 'natural product' objection, which, as we have seen for chemical compounds, can generally be overcome by claiming the product in pure form. In the USA, claims to pure strains or cultures of newly isolated natural micro-organisms are allowed.

Another difficulty is that of the scope of protection which should be granted, and, in particular, whether claims to a new species of micro-organism can be allowed if only a small number of strains of that species have been identified and described. The tendency in the British Patent Office and the USPTO is to allow only narrow claims to what has actually been obtained.

The description requirement and deposition of strains

Whether the claimed invention is a new micro-organism itself or a new product obtained from it, the patent will be invalid unless it gives a disclosure of the invention which is sufficient to enable it to be reproduced. In normal pharmaceutical cases. the claimed substance is a low-molecular-weight compound of defined structure which can be prepared in a few steps from known starting materials by more or less standard chemical reactions, and a reproducible disclosure presents no problems. However, it is practically impossible to define a strain of micro-organism unambigiously by a written description. Observationally, a strain is not of fixed structure and properties, but is a living system, capable of altering its behaviour in response to changes in its environment. It is not always possible to say whether observed differences between two cultures are such as would be expected within a single strain, or if they are large enough to compel identification as two different strains.

Even if a complete description were possible, however, this would not necessarily put the public in possession of the invention when the patent expired. Anyone who wished to carry out the process of the invention would first have to catch his bacterium; he could perhaps tell when he had got the right one, but to get it, by search in nature or random mutation, might take years or might take for ever.

The approach which has been developed to meet this problem is that of deposition of the strain in a recognized culture collection, which will maintain the strain in a viable condition and make samples of it available to the public. In the USA, the CCPA held in the Argoudelis decision[2] in 1970 that such a deposit would suffice to meet the disclosure requirements of the US Patent Law. The deposition had to be made on or before the US filing date, but no access to the deposited strain need be allowed until the patent was granted, whereupon it had to be made available unconditionally to the public. Very recently, however, in the case of *ex parte* Lundak,[3] the CAFC, overruling a decision of the Board of Appeals, held that it was *not* essential that the deposit be made by the date of filing of the application, so long as the applicant had the strain and could make it available to the USPTO upon request. Deposit could be made at any time during the pendency of the application, and addition to the specification of information about the deposit did not constitute forbidden 'new matter'. The requirement that as of the date of grant the strain must be publicly available from a recognized depository remains unchanged.

The majority of developed countries have now adopted the solution of requiring deposit of strains, and the Budapest Treaty of 1977, which came into force in 1980 and has been ratified by 15 countries as well as by the EPO, establishes a list of International Depository Authorities and provides that a single deposit made at any of these will suffice for all signatory states. The Budapest Convention is mainly concerned with formalities relating to the deposit and maintenance of the culture. These provide for the possibilityy of redeposit if a strain becomes non-viable on storage, and for a minimum storage period of 30 years from the original deposit.

However, a serious problem arises from the fact that most developed countries other than the USA now have early publication of patent applications 18 months from the priority date, and consider that, as part of the publication, the deposited strain must be made available from this time. In other words, the applicant must make the means for carrying out his invention available to the public, including his competitors, before there is any assurance that he will actually obtain any patent protection. The traditional concept of patent protection as exchange for disclosure has thereby been distorted so as to require, before any protection exists, not merely disclosure, but what has aptly been described as making available a 'pocket factory handed over to the imitator on a silver plate'.

It is true that in most countries a person who obtained a sample of the deposited strain after early publication had to give an undertaking that he would use the strain only for experimental purposes and would not give it to any third party, but the enforceability of such undertakings was highly questionable, particularly if account is taken of the possibility of minor modifications being made to the strain by mutation, the mutated strain still being useful for the purpose of the invention. In the EPO, the position was improved somewhat by a change of rules in 1980, whereby a deposit would still be acceptable if the depositor stipulated that up to the grant of a European Patent, the strain could be made available not to a competitor directly but only to an independent expert who could carry out experiments on behalf of a third party but not pass the strain on to the party for whom he was acting. In the national patent offices of the UK and Germany, however, the rules still insist that any third party may get his hands on the deposited strain at any time after early publication.

Although Japan also has an early publication system, the rule in Japan is that a deposited micro-organism need not be made available until the accepted application is published for opposition, at which time, unlike that of early publication, the applicant has enforceable rights. This solution was specifically ruled out by the German Federal Supreme Court in the 'Bakers' Yeast' case in 1975,[4] the court insisting that the strain must be available as from the early publication date.

Another serious problem relating to deposits of micro-organisms is that while most states require deposits to be made, most require a written description in addition, and some, e.g. Australia, even consider that a deposit is not sufficient and a reproducible written description is essential. Even within the EPC countries, practice varies greatly; whereas in the Netherlands a deposit suffices in place of a written description, in Switzerland a deposit does not suffice. In Germany, the same 'Bakers' Yeast' decision held that a deposit may be essential to comply with the general rule of sufficiency of the description as a whole, but that a deposit alone is not enough to support a product *per se* claim to the micro-organism. This can only be based on a reproducible written description, which in most cases of course cannot be provided.

Understandably, industry would like to see a uniform practice applied in all developed countries, ideally one in which a deposited strain would be recognized as sufficient description, but the strain would not be released until the patentee had enforceable rights. If this is unattainable, as it may be, then at least the EPO's 'independent expert' provision should be made generally acceptable. It does not help much if some countries have restrictions on the availability of the deposit so long as others allow it to be made available without safeguards. The competitor will simply obtain the strain through the country in which the safeguards for the patentee are least effective. Additional provisions which industry would like to see in connection with deposits of micro-organisms are that the strain should be released only to residents of the country in which patent rights exist, and should not be allowed to be exported; that the release restrictions should extend to cultures derived by mutating the original; and that the doctrine of reversal of onus of proof should be introduced, so that a person who obtains a deposited culture and industrially exploits a result obtainable by this culture should be presumed to have used the deposited culture unless he proves the contrary.

Failing such additional safeguards, a company inventing a process for making a known substance by using a new strain of micro-organism will be well advised to consider keeping the new process as a trade secret instead of trying to patent it. Patenting will require deposit of the new strain, and if anyone obtains this and uses it, it will be practically impossible to prove that he is infringing the patent. The best form of protection in this case is to keep the new strain safely in one's own hands.

Recombinant DNA Technology

Scientific background

Genetic information is carried in the cell by molecules of *deoxyribonucleic acid* (DNA). As elucidated by Crick and Watson, the molecule is a linear polymer in the form of a twin-stranded double helix, each strand of which has a backbone of deoxyribose phosphate, with one of four bases attached to each deoxyribose unit. The four bases are adenine [A], cytosine [C], guanine [G], and thymine [T], and the two strands are held together by hydrogen bonding between pairs of *complementary* bases, an adenine being always paired with a thymine and a cytosine with a guanine.

The sequence of bases along the DNA chain encodes the information for the synthesis of proteins within the cell, each of the possible 64 triplets (*codons*) of the four bases coding for one specific amino acid or for a signal to start or to stop the coded sequence. As there are only 20 amino acids used in protein structure, the code is redundant; that is, there is generally more than one triplet coding for the same amino acid.

The mechanism whereby this code controls the formation of protein is a two-stage one. In the first stage, *transcription*, the twin strands separate, and one strand of the DNA acts as the template for the building up of a complementary and chemically related molecule, *ribonucleic acid* (RNA). In RNA, ribose units replace deoxyribose and the base uracil replaces thymine. This single-strand *messenger RNA* molecule separates from the DNA and is transported to a cell structure known as a *ribosome*, which, in the *translation* stage, assembles amino acids in a sequence corresponding to that of the base triplets on the messenger RNA, which in turn corresponds to that of the original DNA. The resulting protein is the *gene product* of the *gene*; that is, of the DNA sequence coding for its production.

In simple cells such as bacteria which have no distinct nucleus (*prokaryotes*), the genetic material is normally a single closed loop of DNA carrying all the genes required to code for all the proteins produced in the cell. In the more complex cells known as *eukaryotes*, – for example, yeast cells and cells of higher organisms – there is a separate nucleus which contains the genetic material in the form of a number of *chromosomes* consisting of DNA associated with protein.

In eukaryotes, in contrast to prokaryotes, genes are generally not found to exist as one continuous sequence, but consist of sequences called *exons*, which code for parts of the gene product, separated by regions called *introns* which are not transcribed into m-RNA and which do not contribute to the protein. Furthermore, individual genes are usually separated by long non-coding sequences of DNA, which may amount to more than 90 per cent of the total chromosomal DNA. A sequence of one or more structural genes each coding for a specific protein are under the control of *promoter* and *terminator* DNA sequences which do not code for protein but which control the starting and stopping of transcription into m-RNA.

The chromosomes of a complex eukaryotic cell, such as a mammalian cell, contain all the genetic information necessary for the entire organism, but in any one type of cell only a very small amount of this information will be used. For example, a human pancreas cell is specialized to produce insulin, so that the gene for insulin, which is present in all human cells, is *expressed* particularly in cells of this type. In all cells, there is a more or less complex system of regulators and promotors which determines which of the many genes present will be expressed and hence which proteins will be produced by the cell.

Gene-splicing techniques

DNA can be manipulated in specific ways by enzymes which break or rejoin the DNA molecule. A number of enzymes called *restriction endonucleases* are known which cause the DNA to be cut only at specific base sequences. This may occur in such a way that both strands of the DNA are cut at the same place, to give 'blunt ends', or the cut may be staggered so that each cut piece of DNA will have one strand longer than the other by three or four bases, e.g.

$$\ldots\ldots\text{G}\ |\ \text{A A T T C}\ \ldots\ldots$$
$$\ldots\ldots\text{C}\ \ \text{T T A A}|\ \text{G}\ \ldots\ldots$$

The cut portions are said to have 'sticky ends' because the two ends are complementary and can easily rejoin. More importantly, if two separate DNA molecules are cut by the same restriction endonuclease, they can recombine with each other just as easily as with their original partners, to give *recombinant* DNA. Enzymes called DNA *ligases* are also available to join 'blunt ends' together.

Transformation and expression

The above methods may be used to insert a DNA sequence coding for a desired protein into a *vector*, which can then be introduced into a host cell. It is of no use simply to insert the DNA sequence alone into the cell; even if it could express the gene product it would not replicate within the cell, and would be lost when the cell divided as part of its normal growth. A suitable vector has the property of being able to replicate itself within a host cell, thus perpetuating any gene associated with it.

For bacterial host cells such as *E. coli* the most common vectors are *plasmids*, which are circular molecules of DNA that can be transferred from one bacterium to another and that in nature are associated with the transmission of antibiotic resistance between bacteria. A suitable plasmid can be cut at one or more restriction sites, a foreign gene inserted, and the circle re-closed. The plasmid can then be inserted into the host cell by incubating in the presence of calcium ions; the cell containing the plasmid is referred to as a *transformant*. The plasmid will still normally have an intact region conferring antibiotic resistance, so that transformants containing the plasmid can be isolated from non-transformed *E. coli* cells by their ability to grow in a culture medium containing antibiotic. Other types of vectors include *phages* and *cosmids*.

The gene to be inserted into the vector may be obtained by one of three main methods. If the gene is relatively short and its structure has been determined, it may be convenient to make it by chemical synthesis, which is now a fully automated process. Another possibility is that if m-RNA corresponding to the gene product can be isolated, DNA can be produced from it by *reverse transcription*. Finally, the total DNA of a cell known to contain the desired gene can be cut into fragments using restriction enzymes, the fragments selected roughly on the basis of size or the presence of known partial DNA sequences which can be detected by hybridization with radioactive 'probes', and all the selected fragments inserted into vectors.

The last of these methods (*shot-gun cloning*) has the disadvantage that the gene fragments will contain introns, and such genes cannot be expressed directly in a prokaryotic host such as *E. coli*. However, it is also possible to use eukaryotic cells as hosts, and such cells may be able to excise introns and also to produce the protein in the same final form as it is produced in the human body. For this purpose, mammalian cell cultures are most suitable, but these are difficult to grow in large quantities whereas yeast cells can be grown very easily.

Isolation of the gene product

Even if the desired protein is successfully expressed by the transformant, there remains the problem of isolating it in pure form. Yeast cells and some types of bacteria may secrete the product into the culture medium, but concentration of protein from this very dilute solution is by no means easy. In *E. coli* the protein normally remains in the cell, which must be disrupted and the desired protein must then be separated from other cell proteins and endotoxins. The scale-up of such processes to commercial levels also presents serious problems.

Patentable inventions in recombinant DNA technology

General techniques

There are two basic types of patentable invention in this field. The first relates to techniques and methods which are generally applicable to the production of a wide range of gene products; the second relates to specific products.

The basic invention of gene-splicing techniques was made by Cohen at Stanford and Boyer at the University of California. Stanford University filed patent applications to cover their invention, but because publication in a scientific journal had already taken place before filing, patents could be granted only in the USA. If they are valid, the patents cover the great majority of all genetic engineering processes, rather as if in the dyestuff field someone had a patent for the diazo coupling process, used to prepare the majority of all commercial dyestuffs. The first of Cohen–Boyer patents, USP 4 237 224, was issued in December 1980, and claims a method of producing a protein by expression of a gene inserted into any unicellular host. A second patent, USP 4 468 464, was issued almost four years later, but will expire at the same time as the first. It claims biologically functional recombinant plasmids capable of replication in prokaryotic cells, and adds little in terms of effective scope to the first.

Other universities and companies also own patents which are generally applicable to a wide range of products; some of these are pure process patents while others claim novel vector systems, such as plasmids which give particularly good replication in host cells; or, for example, promoter systems which can regulate inserted genes so as to give high expression rates of product.

Novel vector systems

If the invention is a novel plasmid or other vector, the question arises whether it is possible or necessary to deposit it in the same way as a new strain of micro-organism. A plasmid is not a living organism, although it can replicate itself under suitable conditions, but the rules and procedures for making deposits for patent purposes are certainly flexible enough to be applied to plasmids and other vectors. Whether it is necessary to make such a deposit is another matter; if the new plasmid can be prepared reproducibly on the basis of a written description in the text, then no deposit should be necessary.

Specific gene products – natural proteins

The other main type of invention in the field of recombinant DNA technology relates to the production of a specific protein product by a transformed micro-organism. The product may be one whose structure (amino-acid sequence) is already known, one which has been isolated in pure state but whose structure is not yet elucidated, or even a product known only by its activity in some impure mixture. In the last of these cases the product can be claimed *per se* as a new compound characterized by its structure (which will generally be known once the gene has been obtained and sequenced).

Of course, if the product has previously been obtained in pure state a *per se* claim is no longer possible, but the invention can be claimed in a variety of ways having the effect of covering the product whenever made by recombinant DNA techniques. For example, the patentee could claim the isolated gene for the product, a vector containing the gene, the host cell transformed with the vector, the processes for obtaining any of these, and finally the process for obtaining the end product, and the product obtained by that process.

Examples of products which have been obtained by genetic engineering methods include peptide hormones, e.g. insulin and calcitonin, whose structures were previously known. Insulin used by diabetic patients is normally porcine or bovine insulin, which is effective in humans but has the possibility of giving rise to allergic reactions. Human insulin can be prepared by chemical modification of that from other species, but also by recombinant DNA technology. Products whose structures were unknown or only partly known when they were first cloned include larger hormone molecules, e.g. human growth hormone and urokinase (which dissolves blood clots); lymphokines (immune system mediators secreted by white blood cells), e.g. interferons and interleukin–2; and blood-clotting factors, e.g. factor VIII, the hereditary deficiency of which is the cause of haemophilia. Less well characterized are complex factors: for example, colony stimulating factor (which promotes the growth of bone marrow cells), tumour necrosis factor, bone morphogenetic protein, and many others.

A serious question arises as to whether the inventive step necessary for a valid patent is present if the inventor merely uses the standard methods of Cohen and Boyer to produce an obviously desirable product. Certainly, in the early days of genetic engineering the work involved to obtain a product was enormous and there was no guarantee of success, so that the presence of an inventive step could readily be established. However, the rate of progress in this field is so extraordinarily rapid that what was once revolutionary now becomes standard practice within only two or three years. The fact that the state of the art changes so dramatically within the time a patent application is pending makes it very difficult to judge the invention in the light of what was the state of the art at the filing date.

However, the fact is that it is becoming easier to produce proteins by genetic engineering, and thus obtaining patents for the products will become correspondingly more difficult. In particular, the selection of DNA fragments containing the desired gene is made much easier by the probe technique. The DNA is converted to single-strand form and mixed with a synthetic radioactively labelled short single strand of DNA (the probe) which is complementary to a sequence of DNA known to be present in the desired gene. If this target sequence is present, the probe hybridizes with the DNA fragment containing it: that is, the complementary bases pair with each other to form a short length of two-strand DNA, which can be picked out by autoradiography. Using this method, it may be considered as routine (although laborious) work to select and express the gene for any given protein so long as one or two partial sequences of as few as 8 or 10 amino acids in the protein are known, and it may no longer be possible to obtain a valid patent for a recombinant product whose structure was even partially known.

Unnatural protein products

Leader sequences and glycosylation. The protein which is expressed by a transformed host cell containing the correct gene for the desired natural product may not correspond exactly to the natural material, even if it contains the correct amino-acid sequence. For one thing, it may contain a 'leader sequence' of one or more additional amino acids at the N-terminal end of the molecule. Such leader sequences are frequently expressed by the natural gene *in vivo*, but are then split off by enzymes in the cell to give the mature form of the protein. If the transformed host cell lacks the necessary enzyme system, the leader sequence will not be removed in the recombinant product. Such molecules are new compounds which may be patented, even if the natural protein had previously been isolated, but generally they will be less desirable for therapeutic use than the natural product itself.

A simple example is given by human growth hormone, which when first produced by genetic engineering always had an additional N-terminal methionine. This product, Met-HGH, was active as an enzyme, but as a new chemical entity it would be far more difficult to register with health authorities, such as the FDA, than material which was identical to something normally present in the human body. Further efforts succeeded in producing recombinant HGH without the unwanted methionine.

The natural protein may be glycosylated; that is, carry one or more sugar units attached to the amino acid chain. A recombinant protein obtained from a prokaryotic cell will not be glycosylated, and in this case a claim to the protein in unglycosylated form would be novel even if the natural glycosylated protein was known. In many cases, glycosylation does not seem to be important, and the unglycosylated form has the same activity as the natural protein. In some cases, however, the glycosylated form is more active and it may be necessary to use a eukaryotic host in the hopes of obtaining a correctly glycosylated product.

Allelic variations. In any natural protein, there are some regions in which it is possible to change one or two amino acids without affecting the function of the protein, and other regions where any change in the exact amino-acid sequence will alter or destroy the activity. Thus, although porcine and bovine insulin differ slightly from human insulin, they have essentially the same activity in humans. In larger proteins, there may even be differences between individuals in the exact amino-acid sequence. In view of such possibilities, the question arises as to what scope of protection is given by a claim to a recombinant product defined in terms of its amino acid sequence. Some patentees have specifically attempted to draft claims covering all possible variations in structure – some of which go so far as to effectively claim all possible proteins – but even without this, a claim to a specific protein structure should be interpreted as covering also minor variations such as might be expected to occur in nature and which do not alter the properties of the claimed product.

'Engineered proteins'. A different situation exists where the amino-acid

sequence of a protein is deliberately altered with the intent of changing its properties. For example, Cetus has produced a modified form of beta-interferon with the aim of improving the activity and stability of the product. The properties of a protein depend not only on its amino-acid sequence (and glycosylation) but also on its three-dimensional structure: how the amino acid chain is folded in space. An important factor in determing this is the formation of sulphur–sulphur bridges between the —SH groups of two cysteine residues in different parts of the chain. In the case of beta-interferon, the molecule has three cysteine units at positions 17, 31, and 141 of the amino-acid chain. These can form a single S–S bridge, either between 17 and 31, 17 and 141, or 31 and 141, in each case one cysteine unit being left over. It was found that of these three possibilities, only the last (31–141) gave an active product. Cetus therefore modified the recombinant DNA so as to code for the amino-acid serine instead of cysteine at position 17, thereby eliminating the possibility of the two inactive types of S–S bonding involving the 17-position. The resulting product, which Cetus calls a 'mutein' is a novel compound having advantageous properties and is clearly patentable in itself, although it is not clear whether or not it may fall under patents claiming the natural form of beta-interferon produced by recombinant DNA technology.

Factors affecting validity of genetic engineering patents

It is particularly difficult to judge the validity of patent rights relating to products obtained by recominant DNA technology. Early published applications at the EPO and elsewhere generally contain very broad claims which may bear little relation to what will eventually be granted, and competition is so strong that there are usually many co-pending applications with overlapping claims.

Prosecution of such applications is slow in the EPO and almost non-existent in Japan, mainly due to the shortage of examiners who are experts in this field. In the USA, there was a time a few years ago when genetic engineering patents were granted rapidly, with quite inadequate examination; the examining standards of the USPTO in this area have been improved, but this has also led to slower prosecution.

Even when patents are granted, there are often still serious issues of validity unresolved. Apart from the whole question of obviousness when the structure of the product was already at least partially known (see above), there is also the question as to whether there is a sufficient and reproducible disclosure. Here, the question arises as to whether vectors and transformed cell lines should be deposited; some companies do so, while others argue that the techniques which they describe make it possible to repeat the work without the need of a deposited strain.

Perhaps more of a problem is whether there is adequate description of how to work up and isolate the product. Because of intense competition, there are strong pressures to file a patent appliction at as early a stage as possible, often at the point when the product has only just been detected in trace amounts in the culture medium or cell extract. The patent specification will gloss over the whole problem of isolating the pure product, but often this is the most difficult part of the whole process, and a patent which does not adequately describe it may not be valid.

Hybridoma technology

Scientific background

The other main branch of the new biotechnology is based upon the workings of the immune system rather than upon molecular genetics.

The major role in the immune system is played by the white blood cells, or *lymphocytes*. These cells originate as *stem cells* in the bone marrow, and then differentiate and mature either in the bone marrow to *B-lymphocytes* (B cells), or in the thymus gland to *T-lymphocytes* (T cells). The main task of the B cells is the production of *antibodies*. When a foreign substance, such as a foreign protein molecule, enters the body, this *antigen* activates those B cells which carry on their surface receptors that can fit the antigen as a key fits a lock. The activated B cell undergoes rapid division and develops into a *clone* of identical *plasma cells*, all of which secrete antibody molecules which have the same specificity to the antigen as did the original B cell.

The antibodies, or *immunoglobulin (Ig)* molecules, are complex proteins having the approximate shape of the letter Y, and contain, at the ends of the branches of the Y, binding sites specific for a particular antigen. On reacting with an antigen molecule, the antibodies form a cross-linked insoluble structure, thereby effectively removing the antigen from circulation. If the antigen is located on the surface of a foreign cell such as bacterium, the antibodies bind to the surface of the cell, and this process of *opsonization* renders the cell liable to destruction by *macrophages* and other components of the immune system.

The role of the T cells is partially that of acting as regulators of the immune response, through T helper and T suppressor cells which secrete substances called lymphokines which stimulate or suppress, respectively, the action of the B cells. T cells are also involved in the processes which cause inflammation and cytotoxicity; for example, in the rejection of transplanted tissue from a genetically different individual.

Antibodies, in the form of immunoglobulin-G (IgG or gamma-globulin) isolated from the blood of human donors, have been used therapeutically – for example, to supplement the immune systems of patients whose own production of antibodies is impaired, or in cases of viral infection. Of course, IgG taken from pooled blood will contain antibodies to a very wide spectrum of antigens, and will be non-specific in action. *Hyperimmune globulin*, in which the concentration of antibody to a particular antigen is higher than normal, may be obtained from the blood of a donor who has recently been *immunized* with that antigen, and whose B-cells have therefore been stimulated to produce antibodies to that antigen.

Apart from their direct therapeutic uses, the high specificity of the antibody–antigen reaction makes antibodies in principle a very powerful tool in diagnosis and in research; for example, in the identification of antigen sites on cell surfaces. However, up until 10 years ago, the great difficulty was that it was never possible to obtain the desired antibody in a pure state. For example, if a mouse was immunized with human T cells, it would produce antibodies against the various antigens on the cell surface. However, the *antiserum* obtained from the mouse would contain a mixture of all of these. Even if a specific antigen could be separated from the cell membrane and an immunization made with pure antigen, the antiserum would contain all the normal antibodies present in mouse blood, together with the desired one.

If an individual B cell specific for a particular antigen could be isolated and cultured, the culture would produce a single antibody: normal B cells, however, cannot be kept alive in culture. Nevertheless, it was known that *myeloma*, malignant tumours of the immune system derived from B cells, sometimes produced large quantities of a single *monoclonal* antibody. Since all cells in the tumor derived from the same original cancerous B cell they formed a single clone, all producing the identical antibody, and such malignant cells could be cultured indefinitely. However, in a natural myeloma, the antibody actually produced was a matter of chance.

In 1975, Milstein and Köhler, working in Cambridge, succeeded in fusing together a malignant mouse myeloma cell and a normal B cell from the spleen of a mouse. The resulting hybrid cell line, which they called a *hybridoma*, combined the properties of both parent cells. It produced the antibody associated with the normal B cell, but like the myeloma parent it would grow in culture. In effect, the B cell had been immortalized. By choice of a myeloma that did not produce antibodies of its own, only the antibody from the normal B cell was produced. Using spleen cells from a mouse immunized with sheep erythrocytes (red blood cells), *monoclonal antibodies* (MAb's) against sheep erythrocytes were obtained.

Although the importance of this work was not immediately recognized, after two or three years it was seen that the process was of general applicability. To obtain MAb's against a desired antigen, a mouse or rat is immunized with the antigen (which need not be in a pure state). After a few days, lymphocytes are recovered from the spleen of the animal and fused with cells from a suitable myeloma line, in a medium such as polyethylene glycol. The frequency of successful fusion is rather low, and the selection of hybridomas from the mixture is simplified by using a myeloma line with the inherent inability to synthesize an enzyme required for growth in a particular culture medium. The normal spleen cells will have the ability to synthesize this enzyme, and will transmit this property to the hybridomas. On culture in the special medium the spleen cells die, since they are incapable of being cultured, and the myeloma cells die for lack of the enzyme; only the hybridomas survive.

The next step is to separate individual hybridoma cells by dilution and to grow clones from individual cells. Clones that produce the desired MAb may then be selected. The selected hybridoma line may be cultured *in vivo* or *in vitro* to give the MAb in any desired quantity.

Patentability

Whereas Cohen and Boyer at least obtained patents in the USA, the basic work of Köhler and Milstein was not patented. The work was sponsored by the Medical Research Council, and NRDC has been blamed by some persons for failing to protect the invention. This may well be unjust, since it seems that the NRDC were informed only when it was already too late; in any event, the importance of the work was not immediately apparent.

However, patents have been granted to Milstein and his co-workers for specific rat myeloma cell lines which are particularly suitable for fusion with spleen cells, and these patents also claim any hybridoma formed using these myeloma lines. The myeloma cell line, of course, had to be deposited.

General process improvement patents are obtainable in this field as in any other. Developments such as mixed species hybridomas and systems which can produce human MAb's rather than mouse MAb's should be patentable.

The position is less clear when one considers patents claiming MAb's to particular antigens, or classes of antigens. In the UK, the Patents Court upheld the Patent Office in rejecting for obviousness a patent application by the Wistar Institute[5] which claimed broadly monoclonal antibodies to viral antigens. Corresponding applications were however, allowed in the USA and Japan.

On the other hand new specific MAb's, the product of defined and deposited hybridoma lines, must be patentable. The question here is whether the scope of protection obtainable makes it worthwhile to obtain a patent, or if one would not have better protection by retaining absolute control over the producing hybridoma line. A large grey area is that of patents claiming any MAb's directed to specific antigens (e.g. to alpha-interferon) or to certain groups of cells (e.g. certain groups of human T cells). Such patents have been granted, both in the USA and by the EPO, but their validity is questionable. Since 1977, when the general applicability of the hybridoma technique was recognized, it can be argued that there was no longer any invention in producing MAb's to any desired antigen, in the absence of special difficulties which had to be overcome.

Also, in the USA, a patent of Hybritech claiming the use of MAb's in a diagnostic system was held invalid.[6] The court held that there is no invention in using MAb's where, as in this case, polyclonal antibodies were previously used for the same purpose.

12

PATENTS AND THE COMMERCIAL EXPLOITATION OF CHEMICAL PHARMACEUTICAL AND BIOTECHNOLOGICAL INVENTIONS

They say somebody made a mistake when he was
still in the bottle – thought he was a Gamma
and put alcohol into his blood-surrogate. That's why he's so stunted.

Aldous Huxley: *Brave New World*

Patents and the pharmaceutical industry

There can be no doubt that patents are of greater commercial importance in the fields of chemistry, and particularly pharmaceuticals and biotechnology, than in other fields such as engineering or electronics. A new chemical compound may be imitated more easily and with less investment than a complex new machine or semiconductor device, and the patent protection available for the compound is more readily enforced since it is normally easier to establish infringement. For pharmaceuticals, the value of patent protection is even more important than for chemicals in general. To bring a new pharmaceutical on to the market requires a vast amount of investment, the major part of which is spent in testing the compound for safety and efficacy, and only a very minor part on developing the synthesis of the product. It may be possible to produce the compound quite cheaply, but it will still be necessary to charge a high price in order to recover the money spent on testing; not only on the compound which is finally marketed, but also on the others which do not reach this stage. In the absence of patent protection, an imitator who has to carry none of the costs of research and development could offer the compound at a much lower price and still make a handsome profit.

Development of a new pharmaceutical

The period from the first research concept to the marketing of a new drug is presently from 8 to 12 years, which is made up approximately as follows:

1. *Identification of active substance (1–2 years)*
1.1. *Research target*: Research planning, chemical structure planning, literature search, patent search, synthesis planning:

1.2. *Synthesis of active substance*: Laboratory scale preparation, determination of *in vitro* or animal models to test activity.

2.   *Preclinical trials (2–3 years)*
2.1. *Screening*: basic pharmacological and biochemical screening
2.2. *Preclinical trials stage I*: acute toxicity, detailed pharmacological studies (main effect, side effect, duration of effect), analytical methods for active substance, stability studies:
2.3. *Preclinical trials stage II*: Pharmacokinetics (absorption, distribution, metabolism, excretion), subchronic toxicity, teratogenicity, mutagenicity, scale-up of synthesis, development of final dosage form, production of clinical samples:

3.   *Clinical trials (3–4 years)*
3.1. *Phase I*: Toleration in healthy volunteers, pharmacokinetics in man, supplementary animal pharmacology:
3.2. *Phase II*: First controlled trials on efficacy in patents, chronic toxicity and carcogenicity studies in animals:
3.3. *Phase III*: Large-scale trial at several centres for final establishment of therapeutic profile (indications, dosages and types of administration, contraindications, side effects), proof of efficacy and safety in long-term administration, demonstration of therapeutic advantages in comparison with known drugs, clarification of interactions with other medication.

4.   *Registration, launch, and sales (2–3 years)*
4.1. *Registration with Health Authorities*: Documentation of all relevant data, expert opinions on clinical trials and toxicology, preparation for launch, information for doctors, wholesalers and pharmacists, training of sales staff, preparation of packaging and package inserts, dispatch of samples:
4.2. *Launch and sales*: Production and packaging of final form: quality control.

It is, of course, clear that if a strongly negative result is obtained at any stage of this 8–12 year process, the entire project must be abandoned. It is estimated that approximately 8000 compounds undergo initial screening for activity (stage 2.1.) for every one which finally is marketed. The cost of the entire development programme of a market product, for that compound alone, will be of the order of 50 million dollars, and if the total research expenditure of the pharmaceutical industry over a period is divided by the number of new chemical entities introduced to the market in the same time, thus including the costs of the unsuccessful projects as well as the successful ones, a figure of 200–300 million dollars will be obtained.

This enormous investment is finally recouped on the sales of a compound which may be simple enough that any good chemist could produce kilogram quantities of it in a backyard laboratory. In the absence of patent protection for the compound, sales by imitators with no research overheads would destroy any possibility of the innovator recovering his investment, and consequently the investment would not be made. The value of patent protection to the research-based pharmaceutical industry may be seen by the effect of patent expiry upon the market. Thus, for example, Schering-Plough lost 58 per cent of its sales of the antibiotic garamycin in 1981, the year following patent expiry, a loss of $40 million turnover.

Another example of the value of patent protection is given by SK & F's anti-ulcer product cimetidine. When this was introduced in Denmark there was only process protection for pharmaceuticals in that country, and an imitator company with a slightly different process immediately offered the product at a 30 per cent lower price and took half of the market. However, SK & F won their patent infringement case in the Danish Appeal Court, and were able to exclude the competition completely.

Effective term of pharmaceutical patents

The point in the development programme at which a patent application is filed will vary somewhat from company to company, but will normally be at an early stage in the process, where the substance has been made and been shown to be active in early screening. Foreign filing under the Paris Convention will follow only one year later, and in most countries the term of patent protection runs from this date. However, the development of the product will take a further 7–11 years, so that if the patent term is 20 years the *effective* term during which the patentee has exclusive rights to a market product is only 9–13 years. Countries such as certain developing countries which give a patent term of 10 years or less for pharmaceutical inventions are giving in effect no patent rights at all. Similarly, countries which require that the invention must be locally worked within a short period such as three years from grant are denying the possibility of any exclusive rights, since the product can seldom if ever be bought on the market in that time.

In the USA, the term of a patent runs from grant, but since on average the period from application to grant is about three years, the 17-year term in the USA is much the same as a 20-year term from filing in Europe. However, since the FDA in the United States is probably the most difficult health authority in the world from which to obtain marketing approval, the delays in marketing a product are even longer in the USA than elsewhere, and the effective patent life for pharmaceuticals is correspondingly shorter. It has been calculated that the average effective patent life for a drug in the USA fell from 13.6 years in 1966 to 9.5 years in 1979.

Extension of term for pharmaceutical patents

Countries following old British Law

As discussed in Chapter 6, it was possible to extend the term of a British patent under the 1949 Act, and a number of pharmaceutical patents were so extended. Although extensions are no longer possible in the UK, countries such as Australia and South Africa still allow the extension of patents for inadequate remuneration.

For pharmaceutical patents, delays caused by regulatory authorities provide an argument for extension, but such extensions are by no means automatic, and involve a detailed study of the patentee's financial information to determine what profit has been made on the product whose patent is sought to be extended.

USA – the Waxman/Hatch Act

In the USA, a new law has recently been enacted which goes by the unwieldly title of the Drug Price Competition and Patent Term Restoration Act of 1984, but is more familiarly known as the Waxman/Hatch Act after the names of its sponsors in the House of Representatives and the Senate. It originated in pressure from the research-based pharmaceutical industry for an extension of patent term as of right, to compensate for regulatory delays in the FDA. This proposal met with strong resistance from the manufacturers of generic (i.e non-patented) pharmaceuticals, and after considerable lobbying and political in-fighting, a compromise was worked out which granted patent extensions (but with certain important limitations) and on the other hand made it easier for generic manufacturers to market a product after its patent protection expired.

Prior to enactment of the Waxman/Hatch Act, there were three types of NDA (New Drug Application) which could be approved by the FDA so that a drug could be marketed. A normal NDA required full animal and human testing of safety and efficacy, performed by the applicant. A 'paper NDA' had the same requirements, but these could be met by reliance on published data rather than original work. However, the full range of studies required for NDA approval were rarely published in sufficient detail to enable a paper NDA to be filed. Finally, an abbreviated NDA (ANDA) required only equivalence and bioavailability studies to show that the product was the same as a product already marketed, but ANDAs were not available for drugs first marketed after 1961.

The 'Drug Price Competition' provisions of the Waxman/Hatch Act have the effect of making ANDAs available for all new drugs once patent protection (including any extension) expires, provided however, that, irrespective of the patent situation, neither paper NDAs nor ANDAs can be granted for a new chemical entity for 5 years after the date of its first approval by the FDA (10 years if approved between 1 January 1982 and 24 September 1984, when the new Act came into force). As a further benefit to the generic companies, the case of *Roche* v. *Bolar* (see p. 102) was overturned, so that use of a patented invention 'reasonably related to the development and submission of information under a Federal law which regulates the manufacture, use or sale of drugs' is no longer patent infringement. Testing can henceforth be carried out before patent expiry, with a view to obtaining an ANDA approval as soon as possible afterwards. It is not clear if this has retroactive effect, but there may well be litigation to decide the point.

The patent term extension provisions of the Waxman/Hatch Act contain complicated transitional provisions, and for the sake of simplicity these will be ignored and only new products for which both the IND (Investigative New Drug) filing, necessary for permission for clinical trials in the USA, and the NDA approval take place after 24 September 1984 will be considered. In this situation, the patent may be extended for a period corresponding to one-half of the IND clinical-testing time plus all of the NDA approval time, up to a maximum of 5 years, provided that the maximum patent term does not exceed 14 years from NDA approval date. However, the extension period can be shortened if a third party is able to show that delays occurred which were attributable to the NDA applicant himself, and not to the FDA.

Only one patent is capable of being extended in connection with the first NDA approval; if, for example, there were separate product and use patents, then only one of these could be extended. A patent cannot be extended more than once, even if it covers two FDA-approved products, and no extension is allowed if the patent has already expired – a patent once dead cannot be revived. A product patent when extended is limited in scope to the approved product for any approved use; that is, it will no longer cover other compounds within the original scope, nor any non-pharmaceutical use of the approved product.

The patentee must apply for extension of his patent within only 60 days of marketing approval being granted, and must pay a fee (in 1984, $750). Application is made to the Commissioner of Patents, who passes the request on to the FDA for a determination of the regulatory period. The first such determination by the FDA, made on 26 December 1984, was for Sterling Drug's amrinone lactate, which the FDA found to have spent 4 years in the IND phase and 2.7 years in the NDA application phase. Since the IND period counts only half for patent extension purposes, the maximum extension was thus 4.7 years.

One year after enactment of the Waxman/Hatch Act, there are still a good many unanswered questions. It is still uncertain whether patent extensions should be available only for 'products' which are new chemical entities (the view taken by the USPTO), or whether the provisions include pharmaceutical compositions of a new drug which is a known chemical compound, combination products of two known drugs, or new galenic forms. Similarly, the effect of the ANDA provisions cannot be judged until it is known how strictly the provisions on bioequivalence will be interpreted. Generic manufacturers and research-based companies, the FDA, the USPTO, and politicians of all varieties have all put forward their own contradictory interpretations of a law whose confused draftsmanship reveals its origin as a compromise worked out in stuffy rooms in the early hours of the morning.

It seems likely that the generic companies will benefit in the short run as ANDAs become readily available for a number of products whose patent protection has already expired. In the longer term, however, the likelihood of 4–5 years' extension of patent term for the majority of new drugs should greatly benefit the innovative companies.

Proposals for extension of pharmaceutical patents in other countries

Following the enactment of the Waxman/Hatch Act in the USA, there has been considerable pressure for other developed countries to bring in similar measures. In Britain, the ABPI (Association of the British Pharmaceutical Industry) published a study claiming that the average effective patent life for a new pharmaceutical in the UK had fallen from 13.2 years in 1960 to only 4.7 years in 1982 (not counting the additional 4 years with licences of right provided by the 1977 Act). Although the Green Paper on Intellectual Property Rights and Innovation tentatively approved suggestions that patent life should be extended in case of regulatory delay, no government action was forthcoming.

Within the EEC as a whole, support for patent term restoration proposals has rather surprisingly come from a study of the European pharmaceutical industry made on behalf of the EEC Commission. One possible solution which was suggested was to give pharmaceutical patents a term of 15 years from the date of first marketing; a proposal which however well-intentioned would cause chaos in established patent law (would there be no patent rights for substances never actually marketed?) Moves for some form of patent extension also came from the Belgian government: however, there seem to be almost insurmountable problems in obtaining approval from all member state governments, and the fact that the CPC has not yet entered into force does not make matters any easier.

In Japan also there has been some discussion of patent term restoration, but it is too early to say whether there is any real prospect of changes being made.

Patents and the biotechnology industry

The structure of the biotechnology industry

Whereas a large segment of the pharmaceutical industry is made up of a relatively small number of multi-national companies, the biotechnology industry is very much more fragmented, and presents a different picture in the USA, Europe and Japan. In the USA, the industry is characterized by a large number of small venture capital companies, of which there are at least 200 in existence. Of these, about 20 have made public stock offerings, and thus must publish their balance sheets; of these only one company has consistently made a profit, and that is a company which sells equipment to the rest of the industry. Even the largest and most successful of the biotechnology companies, such as Genentech, Cetus, and Biogen, have small profits or actually lose money.

These companies do not have the capability at present to launch products onto the market themselves, and therefore have to license out their products to pharmaceutical companies; as they are chronically short of money, the down payments and royalty rates which are demanded are always high. This situation is unstable and cannot last; the larger biotechnology companies may evolve to the stage of developing their own products, the smaller will inevitably go bankrupt, be taken over by larger companies, or become mere contract research centres for the pharmaceutical giants.

In the UK, the major biotechnology company is Celltech, which was set up with the help of government investment. Elsewhere in Europe there are few purely biotechnology companies; the major European pharmaceutical companies are either active in the field themselves (although far behind the US biotechnology companies in performance) or else are involved in licensing or research co-operation agreements with US biotechnology companies or academic research centres.

In Japan there are few if any small biotechnology companies, but in contrast to the USA and Europe there has been very heavy investment in biotechnology both by government agencies and by large established firms. These are not only pharmaceutical companies, but also companies previously experienced in the traditional fermentation technology of brewing and baking, such as Kirin Breweries, Morinaga Milk Co., and Suntory (whisky), and even companies whose major interests are in textiles (e.g. Teijin) and engineering (e.g. Mitsubishi). Although many such firms began by licensing projects from US biotechnology companies, they are also developing their own projects, which they have the financial and technical resources to develop rapidly within their own company. In the long run these Japanese firms may be the ones most likely to make a commercial success of biotechnology.

Patent conflicts

In the last few years there have been many reports in the scientific and general press about patent conflicts in the field of biotechnology. Whether one reads *Nature*, the *New York Times*, or the *Neue Züricher Zeitung*, headlines about patent battles over interferon or whether or not Cetus will renew its licence under the Cohen–Boyer patents will strike the eye.

The question of whether or not to accept a licence under the basic Cohen–Boyer patents has been a fundamental one for biotechnology companies. Although considerable doubts have been expressed as to the validity of the patents, there has been no serious challenge to them as yet. Stanford's licensing strategy has been to encourage potential licensees by a reasonably low annual minimum royalty of $10 000, and easier licence terms to companies who sign up early. Eventual royalties on a commercial product would be about 1 per cent. This all sounds quite reasonable, until one considers that Stanford has about 70 licensees and so takes in 700 000 dollars a year even without any commercial product. Thus, the patents are commercially very important to Stanford, although for each individual licensee the cost of the licence is much less than the cost of the litigation which would be necessary in order to have a chance of invalidating the patents. In these circumstances it is not surprising that no effective challenge has been made, especially since a commercial firm suing a famous university may find it difficult to win the sympathy of the courts. The situation may nevertheless change when commercial products appear and the stakes really become high.

Stanford has also made a determined attempt to make its US patents felt even in other countries, not only threatening proceedings under the Tariff Act (see p. 101) if products of recombinant DNA technology are imported into the USA from abroad, but also alleging that if a European company has contract research in this field done in the USA and as a result is able to manufacture and sell a product in Europe, the product should be subject to royalties. Most European companies would take the view that in the latter situation it is up to the US firms with which they co-operate to come to terms with Stanford if they see fit, and that they themselves would have no liability. The situation regarding imports to the USA may be different, particularly if, as seems likely, the USA introduces derived product-by-process protection.

The major patent conflicts are, however, those relating to patent rights for individual gene products, such as alpha-interferon or interleukin-

2. In the case of alpha-interferon, Biogen obtained a granted European patent, no. 32134, which was one of the first to be granted for an invention in recombinant DNA technology, and this patent was licensed to Schering-Plough. The patent gave full structural information on the claimed DNA and protein molecules, and the transformed cell lines used were deposited. Genentech, who together with Hofmann-La Roche had a later application also claiming alpha-interferon, lodged opposition to Biogen's European Patent. Genentech's own application, EPA 43980, did not identify deposited cell lines, but according to Genentech their application, but not Biogen's patent, covered the mature form of alpha-interferon free of pre-sequences.

A further complication arose when Hofmann-La Roche was granted a US patent covering pure alpha-interferon obtained not by recombinant DNA technology but by isolation from natural cell lines, based on work done in the 1970s. This patent defines the product by its activity, but does not give structural information; nevertheless Roche claimed that it covered all pure alpha-interferon, however produced.

The situation was finally resolved by a cross-licensing agreement, although the opposition to Biogen's European patent was not withdrawn. Without waiting for the result of the opposition proceedings, Biogen filed suit in Austria (one of the designated countries of the European patent) against Boehringer Ingelheim, who were selling in Austria an eyedrop for the treatment of keratitis caused by herpes simplex virus, and based on recombinant alpha-interferon. Boehringer has also filed a separate opposition to the European patent of Biogen.

In the case of the related compound gamma-interferon the situation was reversed; that is, Genentech had an application with the earlier date, which Biogen alleged to be invalid. As the time of writing, this situation is not yet resolved.

Although not every case is as well publicized as the interferon battles have been, for almost every gene product which has been cloned there will be a series of pending patent applications with overlapping claims. As we have seen in the case of alpha-interferon, the party with the first filing date is not always the outright winner even in Europe, and the situation in the USA, which depends upon proof of the date of invention is often totally unclear. Often the patent application with the earliest filing date may be found to have an inadequate disclosure, having been filed before all the necessary experimental work was done, and a later application giving full structural information may be more likely to be valid.

Reasons for patent conflicts in biotechnology

It may be asked why it is that patent conflicts are more common for recombinant DNA products than for 'classical' pharmaceutical products. A number of different reasons may be given, all of which contribute to this situation.

In the field of classical pharmaceutical chemistry, companies usually pursue quite different research leads. If a patent conflict should arise it is generally recognized at an early stage in the development of the compound, and if it cannot be resolved by licensing, the party who is in the less favourable position can simply drop the compound without much fuss. After all, there are plenty more compounds to investigate, and the chances are that it would have died in any case, as most development compounds do, for reasons of toxicology or lack of efficacy. For the products of genetic engineering, however, the situation is very different, for three main reasons.

First, a large number of companies are chasing essentially the same 'shopping list' of one or two dozen interesting polypeptide products, so that a great deal of duplication of research effort is inevitable. Secondly, as these compounds occur naturally in the body, they can, once isolated, be used directly in clinical trials without long years of toxicity testing in animals. The compounds may therefore already be in the clinical testing stage before the patent conflicts are fully appreciated. Thirdly, and perhaps most important, many of the companies concerned have no products, and indeed no assets other than their patent rights. It therefore becomes of vital importance to them to be able to claim that they have valid patent protection in certain areas, since this is the main way in which they can attract money from licensees and investors. In such circumstances a company which abandoned a project because another firm had a patent application of earlier date would very soon have nothing at all.

Finally, the extreme complexity of the subject matter makes it very difficult to resolve the conflicts which do arise. Faced with numerous overlapping patent applications of differing degrees of sufficiency, rapidly changing state of the art, fluctuating standards of examination in the patent offices, and a lack of court decisions to serve as precedents, the patent agent called upon to give clear and reliable advice to his client or employer finds himself in an unenviable position, even if he is one of the few fortuate enough to have some academic qualifications in biotechnology. He is not altogether helpless, however; the basic rules of patent law with which he is familiar still apply, and there is enough consensus of opinion among patent professionals upon the basic issues that he can still give opinions on the basis of which rational decisions can be taken by management.

Patent conflicts in hybridoma technology
In the field of hybridoma and monoclonal antibody technology there has also been no shortage of patent conflicts; indeed, there has even been, as of 1985, at least one decided case. This was the litigation between Hybritech

and Monoclonal Antibodies Inc. (see p. 166) in which the Federal District Court for the Northern District of California held invalid Hybritech's patent claiming the use of monoclonal antibodies in a diagnostic system for which polyclonals were previously known.

Two further cases pending in the USA are those between Revlon and its licensee Scripps on the one hand and Genentech and Chiron on the other, relating to a patent for the purification of blood factor VIII (anti-haemophilic factor) using monoclonal antibodies; and between Ortho Pharmaceuticals (a subsidiary of Johnson & Johnson) and Becton Dickenson. The latter case relates mainly to cell-counting machines in which cells of a particular type, e.g. helper T-cells, in a mixture of cells, e.g. human lymphocytes, are 'tagged' by a combination of monoclonal antibodies and fluorescent substances. A dilute suspension of the cells is caused to fall in very fine droplets from the end of a vibrating capillary tube illuminated by a laser beam. A fluorimeter detects the presence of a labelled cell in a droplet and each labelled cell is registered on a counter. Alternatively, the principle can be used to effect separation of the labelled cells by specific electrostatic deflection of the droplets containing these cells, but not of droplets containing different cells, or no cells at all.

Ortho have patents not only for such apparatus, but for a number of monoclonal antibodies, defined in terms of which sub-populations of lymphocytes they react with, rather than in terms of specific antigen sites or specific producing hybridoma lines. European patents have recently been granted with claims even broader than those granted in the USA; opposition to these European patents seems likely.

In this field, as in that of recombinant DNA technology, we can expect more litigation as more products come upon the market and the commercial stakes become higher. Success or failure in patent litigation can very well be a matter of life or death for small biotechnology companies; indeed, even the cost of successful litigation in the USA could seriously weaken the immediate financial position of a company, and make it vulnerable to a takeover bid. The task of the courts which must give judgement in litigation will be the same as that of the patent practitioner in giving an opinion – carefully to apply the established principles of patent law to the inevitably complex facts of each case.

PART III

PATENTING FOR THE CHEMICAL INVENTOR

13

INVENTORSHIP AND OWNERSHIP OF PATENTS

What's thine's mine and what's mine's me own.

Yorkshire proverb

Inventorship in the United Kingdom

The inventor is defined in the Patents Act 1977 as the 'actual devisor' of the invention, thereby ruling out the earlier possibility that someone importing the invention to the UK could be considered to be the inventor. It may at first appear a simple matter to decide who the inventor is, but this is really so only in those rare cases where only one person is involved in the matter from start to finish, and can come to the patent agent with a complete working invention and say 'all my own work'. Real-life situations are usually more complicated than this. In a commercial research organization, inventions are seldom stumbled upon by accident (although this can happen). More usually they arise out of planned research in which research scientists are set goals by their management, and are helped to achieve them by laboratory assistants and other technical staff who may run tests, carry out analyses and perform more or less routine operations. Just where in the sequence of operations the invention occurs is something which must be determined specifically for each case, although there are guidelines which may be used to help.

The first basic rule is that invention is the mental act of conception of the inventive idea. The person who makes this mental step is the inventor, and will be the sole inventor if he alone conceived the idea in its full operative form, even though it may require the work of others to put it into effect. If the invention can be put into effect, or reduced to practice, by routine work once the idea is there, then the person who does that routine work may be regarded as the 'extended technical arm' of the inventor, and is not himself an inventor.

Suppose a chemist thinks that compound X may be useful as an insecticide, and instructs his lab technician to prepare it by some standard synthetic method and then sends it for routine screening. If it does turn out to be an insecticide, the invention (which may be claimed in the form of the compound *per se*, the process for making it, an insecticidal composition containing it, a process for killing insects by applying it, or any combination of these) is the invention of the chemist alone and is not the joint invention of him and one or both of the people who made the compound and tested it for the hoped-for use.

Of course, it may happen that unexpected difficulties arise in the synthesis. The reaction may not go in the expected way, and it may be for example that the technician finds a solution to the problem which goes beyond mere routine adjustment of reaction conditions. In such a case the technician will have made an inventive contribution and will be a co-inventor.

Similarly, if the person who carries out the tests finds that compound X is not an insecticide, but has the idea of testing it as a fungicide, then, if X is a fungicide the person who discovers this use is also a co-inventor. Note that he must have the idea himself to do the additional testing; if a new compound is put through a battery of standard tests for a whole range of possible utilities, then it is the person who sent the compound for testing, and not the tester, who is the inventor (if there is any invention at all; of course if the compound is not useful for anything no invention has been made). To be a co-inventor one must contribute to the idea, rather than to the work.

It may be argued that the writing down of a list of compounds to be made and tested may be just as routine a job for a chemist as the running of a standard reaction or the carrying out of a standard test method. Indeed, one could program a computer to print out formulae of random compounds, and one could then synthesize and test the novel ones. If one of them were useful, novel, and non-obvious, there would be an invention – would the computer then be the inventor?

The answer is that there is no necessary correlation between the inventive step needed for a patentable invention and the amount of mental effort required to produce it. The writing down of the compound by the chemist may be the product of a great deal of thought or may be done more or less at random: this does not affect the fact that this is the actual point of invention. Indeed, it is quite possible for the actual inventive step to involve the least mental effort of any of the steps necessary to attain a working invention, and it is a defect of schemes of compensation for employee inventors that they reward only the persons who according to patent law are the inventors, even though others who are not inventors may have contributed more.

In the illustration given above of a computer-generated compound being a patentable invention, the inventor would presumably be either the computer programmer or, if there is such a person, the one who set up the whole project, instructed the programmer and chose which tests should be carried out. This brings us to the question of whether the chemist's supervisor or manager will be a co-inventor. The answer depends on the extent to which the supervisor suggests solutions as well as sets problems. It is not usually an inventive act merely to pose a problem for someone else to solve, but if a particular line of approach is proposed which proves fruitful, that suggestion would probably be an inventive contribution.

It is an oversimplified picture to portray inventions being made only in a hierarchical system of supervisor–chemist–technician. More commonly two or more chemists will work on a single problem, and they will be constantly exchanging ideas with each other, with their assistants and with their supervisors. It is often difficult in such circumstances to determine who contributed to a particular invention, and the task becomes almost impossible when inventions arise out of team meetings or brainstorming sessions where the participants often cannot remember afterwards who said what. Danish law gets around this problem by allowing the company itself to be named as inventor in such cases, but this is unique to Denmark. All other countries require an inventor to be a real person. Correct inventorship is important for several reasons. In the USA, the validity of the resulting patent may be attacked if the patent has not been granted to the correct inventor or inventors, in all countries the ownership of the patent rights will be affected by the inventorship unless all of the possible inventors are such that their inventions would be owned by the same person (usually their employer), and in Germany and the United Kingdom, employee–inventors may qualify for extra compensation from their employers.

Inventorship in the USA

In most countries in the world, although the inventorship of a patent may be relevant to the question of who owns the rights, it is irrelevant to the validity of the patent at least so long as the applicant had the right to apply. In many countries, indeed, the inventor need never be mentioned, and his name does not even appear on the patent. For the USA, however, it is important to have the inventorship correctly determined according to US law. Each US applicant must sign an oath or declaration that he believes himself to be the (or a) true inventor, and a patent for which the inventorship is incorrect may be invalidated. Although it is not essential for the same inventors to be named in the USA as in other countries, any discrepancy between the stated inventorship in the US and for equivalent patents in other countries presents a point of attack which could be used by others to allege invalidity, and it is therefore desirable to name the same inventors in all countries. This in effect means that US practice on inventorship is applied to inventions made in the United Kingdom and other countries, at least if there is any possibility that the case will be foreign-filed in the USA. One advantage of the 1977 British Patents Act is that it is no longer necessary to indicate the inventors at the time of first filing. The matter can now be left to be finally determined at the foreign-filing stage one year later.

For the USA at least, inventorship is a purely legal question, and not one of emotion or company politics. Most patent agents have come across the research manager who insists that his name must go on every patent arising from his group. In some cases, perhaps in most, he may actually be a co-inventor, but the facts must be determined for each case separately. Political choice of inventorship is also evident in many patents originating from research institutes in the USSR, which have been known to carry fiften or more names. It is clearly the policy there to include the whole research group as inventors, which may or may not be a fairer system, but which certainly does not correspond to the legal concept of inventorship in the USA, anymore than the Danish 'company invention' does.

Prior to 1953, it was not possible to change an incorrect inventorship on a US patent. Nowadays, this can be done, so long as the original mistake was made without deceptive intent. It has generally been supposed that at least one inventor had to be the same after the change, that is, one could change A+B into A+B+C, A+C, or A alone, but not into C alone. However, in 1979 one court allowed the substitution of one single inventor by another, and the Patent Office is changing its rules so that any change or inventorship should in principle be allowable. This does not mean, of course, that the patent owner or his agent is relieved of the responsibility of trying to get it right first time.

The inventorship of a patent or patent application in the US may have other consequences. For example, a patent application filed by B before the invention date of A, and subsequently granted, is prior art against a later application of A. In the US, the inventive entity (A+B) is legally different from A or from B; this means that an earlier patent to (A+B) may be prior art against a later application by A alone or by B alone in circumstances in which the earlier patent to (A+B) could not be prior art to a later joint application by A and B together. Another consequence of joint inventorship for inventions made in the USA is that a co-inventor cannot be used to corroborate an invention date for the purposes of an interference – if the whole research group are co-inventors there will be no one left who can give corroboration.

It used to be the case that if it was desired to incorporate a new development into a pending US application by means of a continuation-in-part application, this could be done only if the inventorship for the new development was the same as that for the original application. This has been changed as part of the amendments to the US patent law made in 1984 and it is now possible for a c.i.p. to have different inventorship than the parent case, so long as they have at least one inventor in common.

Joint inventorship in the USA
The same legislation relaxed considerably the previously strict requirements for joint inventorship. Previously there had to be real collaboration

between the co-inventors and some courts had held that in a joint application, all inventors had to be co-inventors for each and every claim, considered separately. This absurd idea has now at last been laid to rest: the amended law now states clearly that inventors may apply jointly even though they did not physically work together or at the same time, each did not make the same type or amount of contribution, or each did not make a contribution to the subject matter of every claim of a patent.

Accordingly, it is now relatively easy to avoid the above-mentioned problem of an application by one inventive entity becoming prior art against a later application by a different inventive entity, when all inventors are employees of the same company. The answer is to combine the applications, while they are still pending, into a joint continuation-in-part application naming all of the inventors.

For a single application, since as a rule US courts are more critical of omitting a real inventor than of including a non-inventor, it is generally desirable in case of doubt to name joint inventors rather than a single inventor. One should not go too far, however; it is a priori unlikely that more than three or four people could really have contributed to a single inventive step, and incidentally, one frequently notes that the more inventors named, the more trivial the invention. Really good inventions tends to be the work of one or two people, not a committee.

Ownership

The ownership of the rights in an invention, whether or not it is patentable, may be regulated by common law, by contract, or by statute. In the USA and for inventions made before 1 June 1978 in the United Kingdom, only the first two of these are relevant; for later inventions in the United Kingdom, the new statutory provisions of the Patents Act 1977 apply.

Common law provisions

Under the common law, the first premise is that the rights in the invention, including the right to apply for and be granted a patent, belong to the inventor. This presumption no longer holds good, however, if the inventor was being paid or commissioned to make the invention on behalf of someone else. Then the principle followed was that the rights belong to the person who paid for the work to be done. When the inventor was an employee, the rights were held to belong to the employer if it was part of the duty of the employee to make inventions or if the employee was in so senior a position (e.g. a general manager or director) that he had a general duty to further the interests of his company.

If the employee was not in either of these positions, then he retained the rights to his inventions, even if these were made using the facilities of the employer and related to the employer's business. In the USA, but not in the United Kingdom, it was held that if the employer's facilities were used then although the employee owned the invention, the employer had a 'shop right' to use it. A shop right was equivalent to a royalty-free non-exclusive licence which could be transferred with the business, but not transferred separately.

Contracts of employment

As the terms of a contract could be used to overrule the provisions of common law, more and more companies began to insert into their contracts of employment clauses in which the employee promised in advance to assign all inventions to his employer. Such clauses became the rule for all employees having individual contracts of employment, whether or not they would normally be expected to invent in the course of their duties. Sometimes such clauses were drawn up so broadly that they required the employee to assign all inventions, even those having no connection with the employer's business, and even those made after termination of the employment.

Both in the USA and the United Kingdom, the courts frequently had to review such contracts as a result of disputes between employers and (usually) ex-employees. Some of the most restrictive terms were sometimes held to be unenforceable as being in unreasonable restraint of trade. For example, a clause requiring assignment of future inventions after termination of employment would, if enforceable, make the ex-employees unemployable anywhere else. Such 'trailer clauses' are in the US considered enforceable only for a limited time (say up to one year), and if the invention arises out of the former employment.

In the United Kingdom, there was an important case on employee inventions in 1977 (*Electrolux* v. *Hudson*).[1] Mr Hudson was employed as a storekeeper by Electrolux, and together with his wife invented an adaptor which allowed a cheap paper dust bag to be used on an Elextrolux vacuum cleaner, instead of the more expensive bag which Electrolux supplied. His standard staff contract of employment stated that the company owned all inventions made by staff relating to 'any articles manufactured and/or marketed by the company or its associated companies in the United Kingdom or elsewhere'. The judge held that this clause was unenforceable. First, Mr Hudson was a storekeeper, not a research worker, and was not paid to invent. Secondly, even a research worker should not be required to assign inventions which might have no relation to the field in which he was employed. No US court has gone so far as this in overturning the terms of a contract of employment, and agreements to assign all inventions in the USA are probably enforceable.

Statute law in the United Kingdom

Parliament had even in 1949 felt that employee inventors were being unfairly treated, and the Patents Act 1949 attempted to remedy matters by making provision for an apportionment of rights between the employer and the employee. This approach failed, however, because in the case of *Patchett* v. *Sterling*, the House of Lords held that this provision could only apply when the invention did not as a matter of law belong wholly to one or to the other.[2] As in the great majority of cases the common law or contract law could be used to give one party or another the whole rights, the apportionment statute was a dead letter.

In the 1977 Patents Act, the matter has been approached differently, and fundamental changes to the benefit of the employee–inventor have been made. As regards ownership of patent rights, the old common law provision is restated: the invention belongs to the employee unless it was made in the course of his normal duties or in the course of duties specifically assigned to him, and the circumstances in either case were such that an invention might reasonably be expected to result from the carrying out of his duties, or the employee had a special obligation to further the interests of the employer's undertaking. What is more, any contract which purports to limit the employee's rights in any future inventions is unenforceable.

In other words no contract of employment for persons employed in the United Kingdom can now legally require the employee to assign to the employer all inventions which he may make. The only inventions which belong to the employer are those made in the course of the employee's duties, if such duties are expected to result in inventions. It is clear that a research chemist will still have to assign to his employer all inventions he make relevant to the research area assigned to him, but if he makes an invention not relating to his own work, even though it be in an area of interest to his employer, the invention is his, not matter what it may say in his employment contract. A person employed in a position, such as storekeeper, in which he would not be expected to make inventions, will own any invention he may make, while the position of people in customer service, marketing, design, production, etc., will generally depend upon how their 'normal duties' are defined.

It is amazing that some companies still require employees to sign contracts which completely ignore the provisions of the Patents Act 1977. What should be the attitude, for example, of someone asked to sign a contract which states 'I hereby declare that any discovery or invention or secret process or improvement in procedure made or discovered by myself during the period of my employment with . . . . (hereafter called 'the company') or within one year after the termination thereof in connection with or in any way affected by or relating to the business of the Company or any subsidiary thereof or capable of being used or adapted for the use therein or in connection therewith shall (whether the same be patentable or not) forthwith be disclosed to the Company and shall belong to and be the absolute property of the Company'?

He would be quite justified in refusing to sign on the ground that in so far as the legalese in which it is written means anything, it is depriving him of his common law rights and is contrary to Section 42 of the Patents Act 1977. However, if he does not want to be regarded as a trouble-maker he can sign the contract secure in the knowledge that it is legally unenforceable.

From the point of view of the employer: first, any such restrictive clauses should be dropped from employment contracts, since their retention implies either that the company lawyers are ignorant of the law, or, worse, that they hope that their employees are. Secondly, in order that there should be a reasonable degree of certainty about which inventions do belong to the company, more thought should be given to a definition of the normal duties of the employee, and this should be reviewed from time to time as the employee moves to different positions or higher levels of responsibility within the company. It is quite reasonable that a sales manager or a production engineer, if they make an invention relating to a product which they are responsible for selling or producing, should have to assign such an invention to the employer, but their contracts of employment should make it clear that their normal duties include making such job-related inventions. Here, of course, it helps if the company had previously patented the occasional invention from sales or production instead of only from the Research and Development department. No matter what is written in the contract, if an invention would not be expected to arise in the course of his duties, any invention the employee makes is his own.

Some light is shed on this point by one of the first cases on employee inventions decided under the Patents Act 1977, that of Harris' Patent.[3] Mr Harris was manager of the Wey valve department of Reiss Engineering Co., who were UK distributors for the Swiss manufacturer of Wey valves. He had no written contract of employment. In the period between being given notice by Reiss and leaving the company he made an invention relating to Wey valves and filed a patent application in his own name. Reiss sued for a declaration that they owned the patent.

It was held that Harris was not expected to make inventions as part of his normal duties (which consisted mostly of sales and customer service) because the facts showed that no inventive activity at all went on within Reiss Engineering, all design problems relating to the valves being referred back to the Swiss company. Furthermore, although he had the job title of manager, his powers and responsibilities were very limited, so that he had no special obligation to further his employer's interests. Accordingly,

Harris retained ownership of the invention he had made while employed by Reiss.

A further consideration is that the right of an employee-inventor to his own inventions does not remove his duty of confidentiality, and he would not be free to file a patent application for the invention if this could not be done without revealing confidential information owned by the employer.

Academic inventors

The same provisions which apply to the employee of a company or an individual apply also to employees of government departments, so that scientific civil servants will also be able to keep for themselves inventions made outside of their normal duties. The position of academic scientists is less clear. They will generally be employees inasmuch as they will have a contract of employment with a university, but the position is often complicated by the receipt of research funds from the government or from private industry. The obligations of the academic inventor to all of these parties should be clearly set out in written agreements, otherwise considerable confusion can result.

An example from the USA was the litigation (eventually settled out of court) about the rights to the invention of 'Gatorade', a commercially successful thirst-quenching drink for athletes invented by an assistant professor at the University of Florida. The rights were claimed by the inventor, the University, and the National Institute of Health, which provided the inventor with some research funding.

It would seem, however, that a contract entered into between a company providing money for research and an academic scientist who is not an employee of the company is not subject to the limitations placed by the Patents Act 1977 on contracts of employment. A consultant may certainly be required to assign in advance any inventions he may make in the field of his consultancy.

Where, in the UK, government research funding is involved, the government used to require assignment of the patent rights to the NRDC (National Research Development Corporation) which tried to commercialize them, usually by licensing to industry. This is no longer obligatory, however, and the funding body – for example, the Medical Research Council – may use the British Technology Group (NRDC), may patent the results themselves, or may leave the rights to the inventors. As far as the universities themselves are concerned, some assert rights to inventions made by their academic employees and some prefer to avoid the trouble and expense of patenting and leave the rights in the hands of the inventors. In the USA, universities seem to be more patent conscious, and the larger of them may employ their own patent lawyers and set up their own organizations like the NRDC to commercialize their inventions. For example inventions made at the University of Wisconsin are assigned to the Wisconsin Alumni Research Foundation (WARF), whose most successful licensed product has been the anticoagulant rat poison, Warfarin. The situation where US government funding is involved used to vary from one government department to another. There are now uniform regulations whereby the university may take title to the patent rights, but the government obtains a non-exclusive royalty-free licence and exercises some control over the types of licence which may subsequently be granted to industry. In continental Europe, academic scientists seem to have greater freedom to own their own inventions, and universities seldom if ever assert title.

The right to apply for a patent and to be granted a patent

In the USA, the inventor, whether or not he owns the patent rights, must apply for the patent. In the United Kingdom, it seems that anyone may apply for a patent, although on the application form he is required to state either that he is an inventor or that a statement of inventorship on Form 7/77 is or will be supplied. Presumably someone not entitled to the grant of the patent could apply and sort out the ownership later, but this is not clear. The Patents Act 1977 is more specific about who has the right to the grant of the patent. This is either the inventor himself, or a person who at the time the invention was made owned the rights in it (e.g. an employer), or anyone to whom either of the first two have assigned the rights. The Act provides for the Patent Office to settle disputes about who has the right to the grant, and it is a ground of invalidity if the patent has been granted to the wrong person.

In addition, the inventor has the right to be named as such on the patent, whether or not he owns any rights in it. Before the patent application is published, Form 7/77 must be filed naming all of the inventors, and unless the inventors are the applicants or the application is one claiming Convention priority from an earlier foreign application, enough copies of this form must be provided for the Patent Office to send a copy to each of the inventors. Presumably this is intended to prevent patenting by an employer without the knowledge of the inventors, since it is no longer necessary for the inventors to sign the application form. There are provisions for any person who considers he should be named as an inventor to apply to the Patent Office for his name to be added.

Incidentally, it should be noted that although an applicant may be a natural person (i.e. a man or woman) or a legal person (e.g. a company, university, government department, etc.) an inventor in the United Kingdom can only be a natural person. Outside of Denmark, a company cannot invent, only a human being can.

Compensation for employee–inventors: United Kingdom

The other main change brought about by the Patents Act 1977 is the provision for compensation for employee-inventors. A scheme of this type has been in effect in Germany for many years, but the British law differs from the German in some important aspects, and it cannot be predicted how it will work in practice. It applies only to inventions made after 1 June 1978, and it will probably be some years before the commercial importance of such inventions becomes apparent, and before any disputes about them come before the courts.

The provisions apply both where the invention is owned by the employer and where it is owned by the employee but the employer has been granted an assignment or an exclusive licence for a lump sum or royalty payment, or other consideration. Where the invention is owned by the employer, compensation is to be paid by the employer to the employee-inventor when a patent has been granted and the patent is, having regard to the size and nature of the employer's undertaking, of outstanding benefit to the employer. When the invention is owned by the employee and assigned or licensed exclusively to the employer, additional compensation is payable if the benefit to the employee from the contract of assignment or licence is inadequate in relation to the benefit derived by the employer from the patent. Here it seems that the patent does not have to be of 'outstanding benefit'. It is not possible for the employee to contract out of his right to compensation, except that rights under the Act may be replaced by rights under a collective agreement made between the employer and a trade union to which the employee belongs. As of 1985, however, no such collective agreement was known to exist.

This is all rather complex, but the main point is that in the UK compensation is not due as a matter of course on all commercialized employer-owned inventions, as it is in Germany, but only on ones of 'outstanding benefit to the employer', whatever that means. Until the Patent Office or the courts have determined some cases, no one can say just how important a patent must be in order for inventor compensation to be a possibility. For example in the pharmaceutical industry a great many patents are granted and abandoned because the compounds they cover are no longer being developed. A patent which covers a market product is the exception rather than the rule. Is the question of 'outstanding benefit' to be considered with reference to the average patent, or to the average market product? If the former, then any patent covering a marketed pharmaceutical would be of outstanding benefit, if the latter, then perhaps only those covering the outstanding products such as Valium®, Ampicillin, or Tagamet®.

And when compensation to the inventor is called for, the Act is equally vague about how much compensation should be paid. It talks only of 'a fair share of the benefit which the employer has derived' having regard to matters such as the nature of the employee's duties, his salary, the amount of effort and skill which went into the invention, the contribution of joint inventors and other employees who are not inventors, and the degree of contributions made by the employer. It will not be an easy job to determine such matters fairly, and the results are at this stage totally unpredictable.

Already at least one organization in the United Kingdom has advertised itself as ready to represent the interests of employee-inventors in any conflict with their employers, in return for fees plus a commission on the compensation to be received. Firms or companies of this type should be looked at with some suspicion, particularly if the persons controlling them are neither lawyers nor patent agents. They may only build up false hopes that every inventor has a right to substantial extra compensation from his employer, and provoke unnecessary conflicts between employer and employee. This is not to deny that conflicts may arise; in particular some employers may refuse to consider payment even when the conditions of the 1977 Patents Act have clearly been met. In such circumstances the inventor should be able to get more knowledgeable advice and assistance by consulting a firm of patent agents, although to avoid conflict of interest it should not be a firm used by the employer.

It is clear, however, that the system could operate unfairly in a number of ways. Given that the object is to provide additional compensation for employees who give the company something above and beyond what is expected of them, it is worth considering whether this end will be achieved in view of the following problems:

1. Only *inventors* can benefit. As we have seen, in the work involved in commercializing an invention, the actual inventive step may involve the least effort.
2. A patent must be granted. If the invention is kept as secret knowhow, or if a patent is refused because of prior art, no compensation will be paid no matter how important the invention.
3. It is the patent and not the invention which must be of outstanding benefit, and the two are not necessarily the same. Is compensation to be paid in respect of a blocking patent which is commercially important although never worked? If so, how can its financial value be determined?
4. As the size of the company is taken into account in considering the question of 'outstanding benefit', it seems that inventors in a large company are less likely to get compensation than those in a smaller one.

5. The compensation is due only from the employer at the time the invention was made, and if the employer sells the business, the employee has no claim against the new owner.
6. The commercial success of an invention bears no necessary relationship to its inventive merits. If A invents a pharmaceutical X and B invents Y, and five years later X is dropped because it is found to be carcinogenic while Y goes on to be a big success, does this mean that B is more deserving than A?

The only sensible way to regard the British law on compensation for employee-inventors is that it gives the inventor a ticket in a lottery. He may be lucky or he may not, but at least he is better off than he was before, when he did not even have the ticket. If one wants a system which leaves less to chance, the German law provides a better example.

Compensation for employee–inventors: Germany

The German law on employees' inventions dates from 1957, and in 1959 directives were issued to provide guidelines to the amount of compensation to be paid. An arbitration board adjudicates disputes between employer and employee, both as to ownership of inventions and as to the amount of compensation. The law recognizes two types of invention; service inventions, which belong to the employer; and free inventions, which belong to the employee-inventor. An invention is a service invention if it arises in the course of the employee's duties, or if it is based upon experience or activities within the firm. Thus even if the employee is not 'paid to invent', his invention may belong to the employer if it is closely related to the firm's business, for example an improvement or development of a product of the company.

An employee who makes a service invention is obliged to report it in writing to the employer. The employer then has a period of four months in which he may lay claim to the invention. If he does so, the rights automatically pass to the employer; if he does not, the invention becomes a free invention and the inventor may dispose of it as he pleases, including, for example, selling it to a competitor. If the employer does lay claim to it, however, he is obliged to file a domestic patent application (unless it is necessary to keep the invention as secret knowhow, or the inventor agrees that no application need be filed), and he must pay compensation to the inventor. Further, if he decides not to file patent applications abroad, or to abandon any applications or patents once filed, he must give the inventor the opportunity to file in his own name, or to take over the patent rights.

The employee–inventor is also obliged to report to his employer any invention which he considers to be a free invention, unless it is obviously incapable of being used in the employer's business. The employer can agree that the invention is a free one, or may allege it is a service invention; in case of dispute the Arbitration Board can be used. The employee cannot exploit his free invention while he remains employed by the company without offering the employer at least a non-exclusive licence on reasonable terms, but the employer must take up this offer within three months. Thus an invention which is originally a free invention cannot be exploited so freely by the inventor as a service invention which becomes free by the employer failing to claim it. Like the new British law, the provisions of the German law on employee inventions are mandatory and cannot be set aside by a contract; unlike the British law, there is no way that a collective agreement with a trade union can take precedence over the statutory provisions. Incidentally university professors, lecturers, and assistants are outside the provisions of the German law, so that any invention they make in the course of their employment by the university is a free invention.

If a service invention is used by the employer, then compensation is payable according to the system set out in the 1959 directives. The first step is to determine the Invention Value (IV), which is usually assessed on the basis of the royalty which the employer would have to pay for an exclusive licence if the invention were a free invention and he had to negotiate for it at arm's length, less overheads such as the cost of patenting. Less frequently, it may be based on the savings made to the company (e.g. by a process improvement which cuts costs), reduced by a factor to allow for the company's overheads and investment. An IV may also be assigned to a defensive patent which is not actually worked. Once the IV has been determined, the next step is to calculate the participation factor (PF). This is done on a point system based on consideration of how the problem was posed, how it was solved, and what was the employee's position in the company. In the first category, the scale goes from 1 point (the employer posed the problem and indicated the approach to be taken) to 6 points (the employee posed himself a problem falling outside of his normal range of duties). In the second category the scale is also 1–6 and depends on how much contribution was made by the employer, including facilities, assistance, etc. towards solving the problem. The less help from the employer the higher the point rating. Finally, the position of the employee is rated on a 1–8 scale: a research director making an invention gets 1 point, a research chemist 4 points, and an unskilled worker 8 points. These three are totalled together to give a point count of from 3 to 20, and the PF is read off as a percentage from a table; for example, 3 points gives a PF of 2 per cent, 8 points 15 per cent, 15 points 55 per cent and 20 points 100 per cent. Multiplying the invention value by the participation factor gives the compensation due to the inventor. In the majority of cases the PF lies between 15 and 21 per cent so that the compensation is 15–20 per cent of a net notional royalty.

This somewhat complicated German system has been described at length because it may be used as a model for the British Patent Office or court to estimate the amount of compensation to be paid, since the Patents Act 1977 mentions the same type of factors to be considered but gives no clear guidelines as to how to apply them.

The German system is less of a lottery than the British, because it applies to all inventions which are of commercial value and not merely to those of exceptional benefit. The philosophy applied here is essentially different. The British and US case law talks of employees being 'hired to invent'. By German thinking this is not possible, since no one can guarantee to produce inventions. Inventions may be made in the course of an employee's duty, and they will then (if claimed) belong to the employer, but they are always 'something extra' over and above what the employee is being paid to do. From the point of view of the employer, too, the German system has the advantages that service inventions are more broadly defined than the equivalent employer-owned inventions in the British Act, and that the employer must be offered a licence for free inventions.

Compensation for employee–inventors: other countries

Germany and the United Kingdom are by no means the only countries which provide for compensation for employee–inventors. Austria has a scheme similar to that of Germany, and the laws of the Scandinavian countries, The Netherlands, Japan, and Switzerland, while differing in the categories of inventions which belong to the employer, all provide for additional compensation for an inventor employed to do research only if the invention is of unusual commercial importance. For example in Switzerland, although Swiss law, like US law, allows a contract of employment to require assignment of all inventions, the Swiss Law of Obligations requires special compensation to the inventor if the invention is of considerable economic value. As far as European patents are concerned, the EPC provides that the right to ownership of the Europatent is according to the law of the state in which the inventor is primarily employed. The inventor has a right to be named as such on the Europatent, although he may renounce this right.

Compensation for employee–inventors: conclusion

Many research-based companies in the United Kingdom fear that the new law on compensation for employee–inventors will bring a number of disadvantages, apart, that is, from that of having to part with some money.

Company patent departments look forward with dismay to the possible disputes about inventorship which may have to be resolved. This can be difficult enough when all that is involved is the honour of having one's name on a patent: when money is at stake it can only make things worse. It is also feared that the free exchange of ideas between research workers will be inhibited because each inventor will jealously guard 'his' invention, which may one day bring him wealth.

If the 25 years of German experience with a similar law is any guide, such fears are exaggerated. The actual amounts of money involved will be very small compared with normal salary costs; in Germany there is substantial tax relief on money paid to employee–inventors, and although this is not provided for in the United Kingdom the fact that no compensation will be payable unless the invention is an exceptional commercial success means at least that the profits to pay for the compensation must be there. It may involve some additional work for company patent departments, but these have always had the responsibility of deciding question of inventorship, and should not shirk it just because it has become of greater importance to the inventor. And German industry has not seen any drying up of collaborative research; rather it is found that the morale of research workers is increased and there is often competition to join a successful research group which is productive of inventions.

14

THE PATENT PRACTITIONER AND HIS FUNCTIONS

. . . when he was in the company of chemists, he spoke as a lawyer, and
when with lawyers, he was a chemist. And when with the chemical patent
lawyers, he didn't mind being just a fifty–fifty chemist–lawyer. They had his
problem, too. It was like group therapy. Patent lawyers had a profound
sympathy for each other.

Charles L. Harness: *An Ornament to his Profession*

The term 'patent practitioner' has been used so far to cover all those
persons whose profession it is to draft and prosecute patent applications
and to advise generally about patent matters. They may be employed by
companies or be in private practice, and they may, in different countries,
have different types of qualification. Basically, however, their job is the
same, and the most important part of the job is to help inventors to obtain
valid patents for their inventions. In order to do this, the patent
practitioner must have both scientific and legal training, so that he can
understand both the invention and the patent law and practice of at least
his own country.

The British patent profession

In the United Kingdom, the patent practitioner goes by the name of patent
agent, a professional title which sometimes leads people to believe that, by
analogy with an estate agent, he is only a middleman in the buying and
selling of patents. As we have seen in Chapter 2, the profession in Britain is
regulated by an autonomous professional body, the Chartered Institute of
Patent Agents. The Institute conducts qualifying examinations, controls
matters of professional ethics, and keeps a register of qualified patent
agents, an up-to-date version of which is published each year. The Patents
Act provides that no one who is not on the register may act as a patent
agent for gain (a non-qualified person can act as agent for someone else so
long as he does not get paid for it), and the Register of Patent Agents
Rules, made under the Patents Act, sets out the regulations for qualifications
for entry into the profession and for the keeping of the register. The great
majority of registered patent agents are also Fellows of the Chartered
Institute of Patent Agents, and designate themselves FCIPA or CPA
(Chartered Patent Agent).

The 1983 Green Paper on 'Intellectual Property Rights and Innovation', already referred to (p. 31), has suggested that the case for the monopoly right of representation held by registered patent agents should be reviewed, and at the time of writing such a review is being carried out by the Office of Fair Trading. The Green Paper considered that this monopoly kept out 'exploitation brokers who could handle patent matters quite competently and also give attention to the crucial matter of raising development finance.'

The Chartered Institute sensibly takes the view that it welcomes any discussion of the professional monopoly, which it considers would be found justified by an impartial review. The Green Paper itself makes the point that 'unwitting inventors could lose their property through poor advice', and while there may well be an important role to be played by 'exploitation brokers' there is a considerable danger that if these unqualified persons also draft and prosecute the patent applications, they will find themselves finally with nothing of any value to exploit.

The training of a patent agent

At one time it was common for new entrants to the patent profession in the UK to be accepted as articled pupils to chartered patent agents, and to work for little or no salary in exchange for their professional training. Today this method of entry has essentially died out, and most new entrants are science or engineering graduates who work as technical assistants to a chartered patent agent for a reasonable salary. In industrial practice it often happens that scientists enter the patent profession after some years in research; their additional scientific experience is helpful in dealing with complex technical fields and in understanding the problems of the inventor.

Whether in private practice or in industry, the new entrant is an assistant to a particular qualified patent agent; a partner in the firm, perhaps, or a more senior employee in the company patent department, who has a responsibility for his professional training. A necessary condition for taking the Institute examinations is to have put in a certain number of years as an assistant to one or more named qualified agents. It is not possible to qualify by studying the subject from the outside; on-the-job training is more important than theoretical knowledge.

One difficulty with this system is that the amount of on-the-job training which a new entrant receives is up to the firm or company for which he works. Some large industrial patent departments have excellent training programmes; in some small firms the trainee may be left to pick up what he can. In private practice, trainees may have the advantage of more varied experience than is to be found in industry.

The Institute holds qualifying examinations in the spring of each years; after one full year in the profession the graduate candidate may take the Intermediate Examination, which tests knowledge of British and foreign patent law as well as the law of trade marks, registered designs, and copyright. If successful, the candidate may become an Associate of the Chartered Institute, and may, after three years in the profession (five years for a non-graduate) take the Final Examination. This is a week-long series of papers on patent, trade mark, and design practice; drafting of patent applications; and interpretation of patents (i.e. giving opinions on infringement and validity); a candidate passing in two of these three subjects need only resit the part which he failed. The pass rate in the Final Examination is generally low (around 25 per cent on average), although it tends to fluctuate significantly from year to year.

The qualified British patent agent, therefore, has had at least three years of on-the-job training and has passed a difficult examination testing his professional skills and knowledge of the patent law not only of the United Kingdom but also of other countries. Some patent agents may have a degree in law, but all must have some academic qualifications in a scientific or technical subject. In spite of this technical training he should not be a specialist; within a broad area such as chemistry, mechanics, or electronics he should be able rapidly to grasp any technical subject which is submitted to him.

Patent agents as members of the legal profession

As well as being technically qualified, patent agents have legal training at least within the specific field of industrial property. Patent agents occupy a somewhat anomalous niche in the structure of the legal profession. They may not draw up documents such as deeds, which are the prerogative of solicitors (although a solicitor may also draft patents, few are bold enough to try). Nevertheless, although normally a party in High Court proceedings must be represented by a barrister instructed by a solicitor, in proceedings before the Patents Court arising on appeals from the Patent Office, patent agents may either instruct a barrister directly or may themselves appear on behalf of their client. Communications between a patent agent and his client on patent matters are privileged documents protected against disclosure in legal proceedings in the same way as solicitor–client communications.

At present there are approximately 1200 patent agents on the register in Britain, the numbers being divided fairly evenly between those in private practice and those employed by industrial companies, government departments, and nationalized industry. The numbers are divided very unevenly between men and women, with women patent agents constituting no more than 2 per cent of the profession. No disrespect to them is intended if the masculine pronoun is used for the sake of brevity when referring to a patent agent of either sex.

The British patent profession is a unitary one, with the same professional titles, the same professional ethics, and the same Chartered Institute for all patent agents. In this it differs from the profession in the USA, where there is a sharp distinction between lawyers and non-lawyers, and in Germany where private practice and industrial practice are kept strictly apart. Most British patent agents feel that they are fortunate in this respect.

The patent profession in the USA

There are two distinct classes of American patent practitioner, known as patent attorneys and patent agents. Both have passed an examination in US patent law and Patent Office practice which is set by the US Patent Office itself, although former Patent Office examiners with at least four years service are exempt. The patent agent has no further legal qualification than this (although he must have scientific qualifications as well), and he is entitled to represent a client in proceedings before the US Patent Office, but not before any court. A patent attorney, on the other hand, is an attorney at law who has a law degree and has been admitted to the bar of the highest Court in any jurisdiction in the USA (e.g. in any state). Subject to the rules of Court and state laws regulating legal practice, he can represent his client in the courts, as well as carry out tasks reserved by state law to qualified attorneys, such as giving legal opinions and drawing up contracts. Some patent attorneys specialize in pleading cases before the courts, as do barristers in England; the majority are patent solicitors in the sense that they solicit patents from the US Patent Office.

Although there are professional associations such as the American Patent Law Association which draw up codes of professional ethics for patent agents and patent attorneys, it is the US Patent Office which exercises disciplinary control over the profession and can disbar agents or attorneys from the Patent Office bar for deliberate fraud on the Patent Office or for breaches of legal ethics in matters such as advertizing and soliciting clients.

The wider range of activities open to a patent attorney restricts the patent agent in the USA to a secondary status in the profession, so that a law degree is a prerequisite to professional advancement. The US patent attorney may therefore be expected to have a broader legal knowledge than a British patent agent, but he will not have been so rigorously tested in the skills of patent drafting and interpretation, nor will he normally know so much about patent law in countries other than his own.

The patent profession in other countries

In Germany, the profession is also split into two categories, but here the distinction is rather between the *Patentanwalt* in private practice and the *Patentassessor* who is employed in industry. Members of both groups have precisely the same qualifications, and need not have a law degree, although they must have a university degree in either law, science, or engineering. The training involves spending time at the German Patent Office and as a clerk in one of the courts which deal with patent matters, and the qualifying examination, which is controlled by the Patent Office, is essentially a theoretical examination in patent law. Two days of written papers are followed by a gruelling oral examination before a nine-member examination board consisting of three Patent Office officials, three patent judges, two *Patentanwälte* and one *Patentassessor*. The result is essentially a legal qualification which does not test the skills of drafting and interprètation of patents.

Both *Patentanwälte* and *Patentassessoren* may represent clients before the Patent Office, the Patent Court (*Bundespatentgericht*) and on appeals from these to the Supreme Court (*Bundesgerichthof*), but must be accompanied by a *Rechtsanwalt* (i.e. a general lawyer) in patent proceedings such as infringement actions which originate in the *Landgerichte*. The main distinction is that whereas the *Patentanwalt* may represent any client, the *Patentassessor* may only represent his employer, which may, however, include his employer's associated companies in Germany or abroad. The two sides of the profession have separate professional institutes, so that a *Patentanwalt* who accepts employment in industry must resign from the *Patentanwaltskammer* and call himself a *Patentassessor*.

In some European countries, for example Switzerland, there is no regulation of the profession, and anyone who likes is free to describe himself as a *Patentanwalt*. Switzerland also distinguishes between private and industrial practice, as indeed do most of the European professions. Only The Netherlands resembles Britain in having a patent profession which is both unitary and well qualified.

In Japan there is a strict examination for qualification as a patent attorney, but there is no requirement that candidates have any prior experience whatsoever. As a result, large numbers of new university graduates take the examination and the pass rate is extremely low: typically only 80 candidates out of over 3000, or less than 3 per cent. However, it is recognized that the newly qualified patent attorney will require practical experience before he is in a position to practice on his own.

European patent attorneys

For practice before the European Patent Office, the EPO maintains a register of professional representatives, divided up according to the contracting state in which they have their place of business. When the EPO was set up in 1978, the rule was that anyone qualified to practice before his home country patent office could automatically go on the European list. In countries such as the United Kingdom, Germany, and The Netherlands, where a register of qualified persons was kept, then anyone on that register could have his name put on the European list; in countries such as Switzerland in which the profession is not regulated, then anyone who could show that he had acted for clients or employers before the local patent office for at least five years could qualify for the EPO list.

Since 1979 there has also been a qualifying examination for entry to the European list, and since October 1981 this is the only method by which new entrants can qualify. Qualification as a patent agent in the United Kingdom now no longer gives the right to be entered on the European list. A patent practitioner who is an employee of the applicant need not in fact be on the European list in order to prosecute a European patent application of his employer before the EPO; however, it will clearly be most desirable, if not essential, for British patent agents in future to be qualified both in the United Kingdom and in Europe, which will mean passing both examinations.

The European examination is based on drafting a European patent application, answering an office action from the EPO, preparing a case for opposition to a European patent, and giving a legal opinion. It may be taken in any one of the three official languages but the candidate must have some knowledge of the other two. For example if he is sitting the examination in English, he will have to consider at least one document (e.g. relevant prior art) in French and one in German. The examination is now held simultaneously in Munich and The Hague, and, provided there are sufficient candidates, also in Paris and London. A further distinction from the British system is that only science or technology graduates or those having an equivalent qualification can take the European examination. Although there is a European Institute of Professional Representatives, this Institute is not a wholly autonomous body, and in particular does not control entrance to the European profession. The qualifying examination is under the general control of the Administrative Council of the EPO, and the direct control of an Examination Board comprised both of officials of the EPO and members of the European Institute.

Patent agents in private practice

The type of patent agent with whom the chemical inventor is likely to come into contact in the United Kingdom will depend on whether the inventor is independent, or is employed by a large or a small company, a university, or a government department. The independent inventor, or the inventor who works for a small company, will normally deal directly with a firm of patent agents in private practice. Firms of patent agents may legally be limited companies or partnerships, although the latter form is far more common. If it is a partnership, all partners must be registered patent agents; it is not permitted to have joint partnerships with solicitors, for example. Firms vary in size from one-man operations to those with twenty or more partners and numerous technical assistants, translators, and clerical staff. Their work will normally be a mixture of work for United Kingdom clients and agency work, i.e. obtaining United Kingdom patents for foreign clients on instructions sent by the client's agents in his home country. Conversely, when a United Kingdom client wishes to file abroad, the firm of patent agents will send instructions to agents with whom they deal and whom they usually know personally, in the countries in question.

Although the private practice section of the patent profession is centred in London, in particular the area around Chancery Lane and High Holborn, within easy walking distance of the Patent Office, the larger firms have branch offices in cities outside London, and many smaller firms are based in cities and towns across the country. Generally wherever there is any significant amount of industry there will be a firm of patent agents reasonably accessible.

Assuming the clients' invention is a chemical one, it will be dealt with by a patent agent or technical assistant who has chemical qualifications. A patent agent should never be a narrow specialist in one particular technical field, but some degree of specialization is essential, and while any patent agent may feel competent to draft a patent application for a relatively simple mechanical invention, no chemical patent agent would consider tackling an electronic invention, or vice versa.

Larger client companies, which may file several patent applications a year, will normally have built up a working relationship with a particular firm of agents, and often with a particular patent agent within that firm, who will have become familiar with his client's technical field and with his particular problems. Similarly, the company will generally find it convenient to designate a single person as contact man with the patent agents on all patent matters; this may be a part-time activity of the research manager or equivalent, but if the company is big enough this will be a full-time job for a patent officer who while not himself a qualified patent agent will know something about patent matters and can for example write a description of an invention which the patent agent can use as the basis for drafting a patent application.

Industrial practice

At some stage, however, as the size of the company increases, it will find it advantageous to employ its own patent agents, who can deal directly with the Patent Office in the United Kingdom and with firms of patent agents in other countries. This step can be advantageous from the company's point of view not only on cost grounds, but because it enables the company patent department to choose its own methods of working without being tied to the methods of an independent firm of patent agents. Furthermore, company patent agents are relatively free from the time pressures inherent in private practice where work has to be charged by the hour, and they have the advantage of closer direct contact with the inventors, who may even be working in the same building as the patent department.

This direct contact, which is of prime importance in establishing a good working relationship between the patent department and the research department, can easily be lost in a large company, in which research is being carried on at different sites, if the patent department is allowed to become a remote branch of the head office. It may be desirable to have patent officers at each site in liaison with the central patent department; the ideal solution of having a separate patents department at each research centre is feasible only for the very largest companies such as ICI.

A large multinational company may have research centres in several countries, and in many of these (e.g. United Kingdom, USA, Germany) it is necessary to file the first patent application in the country in which the invention is made. This can be done through local patent agents, through a central patent department which prepares the application and sends it back to the originating subsidiary company or an agent for filing in the country of origin, or by having a separate patent department in the subsidiary company. A European company with a US subsidiary, for example, can have a patent department in its subsidiary company, staffed with US-qualified patent agents or attorneys, which can file applications for inventions made in the USA and also act as agents for filing in the USA in respect of inventions made in Europe. The reverse of course applies for US companies with European subsidiaries.

The job of the patent practitioner

Drafting

Whether the patent practitioner is in private practice or in a large or small industrial patent department (including those of nationalized industries and government departments) and whether he is in the United Kingdom or elsewhere, his task is essentially the same. First of all he must, from the information given to him, understand what it is that the inventor has done and define what the invention is. To do this, he must above all put a great many questions to the inventor, to explore such matters as which features are essential and which are merely preferred, which features can be generalized, and how far; which reaction conditions work and which do not, what are the advantages offered by the invention and whether all the advantages are shown by all the embodiments of the invention.

For example, suppose the inventor has found that a group of compounds are good flame-retardants on a particular substrate, say cellulose acetate. At this point it is clear what the inventor has done, but by no means clear what the invention is, or indeed if an invention is there at all. If the compounds are new, the invention may be the compounds *per se*; if they are known, the invention could be their use as flame retardants. If they are known as flame retardants in other substrates, the invention, if any, can only be their use in cellulose acetate, and it will be an invention only if there is some unexpected advantage, since *a priori* a flame retardant for one substrate might be expected to be useful for another.

Suppose the last of these situations is the true one; the patent agent must find out from the inventor what is clever about using these compounds in cellulose acetate – is cellulose acetate a particularly difficult substrate to flame-proof? Are there problems associated with the incorporation of the flame retardant into the substrate? Can the flame retardants be used alone in cellulose acetate whereas in other substrates they had to be used in conjunction with other flame retardants? Is the quantity of flame retardant used in cellulose acetate less than in other substrates, or less than that used for other flame retardants in cellulose acetate? How are the physical properties of the end product affected? Only by asking questions such as these can the inventive idea be determined; and often it turns out to be other than what the inventor originally thought.

It is very important for the chemical inventor to realize that it is an essential part of the process for the patent agent to play devil's advocate and to take what appears to be a sceptical and even critical view of his invention. Only by asking the right questions at the beginning can the patent application be properly drafted. If it is not, the questions may be asked by the patent office, at a time when it is too late to put into the application the additional information which may be necessary. Any patent practitioner who simply writes down what the inventor tells him, without asking awkward questions, is doing the inventor a disservice.

Of course, the patent agent must also decide who should be named as sole inventor or joint inventors, and this is another area in which awkward questions may have to be put and answered. A patent agent cannot simply accept without question an edict that so-and-so must be named as inventor, since if he does he not only compromises his professional integrity, but also runs the risk of obtaining an invalid patent in the USA.

Prosecution

Once the application has been filed, the next part of the patent practitioner's job is to prosecute the application through the patent office of the home country plus any countries in which it has been foreign-filed; the latter is usually done through intermediary agents in those countries. Most applications must be reviewed with the inventor from time to time in the light of new prior art which may be cited by patent offices or found internally, and in view of specific objections raised. Normally the agent will check back with his clients or with research management before accepting a significant reduction in the scope of the claims. For the USA it may be necessary for comparative testing to be carried out, and this must be thoroughly discussed with the inventor or other persons who will carry out the testing (see p. 229).

When the patent is granted, the patent agent will be responsible for defending it against opposition or revocation proceedings in the Patent Office, and for ensuring that renewal fees are paid for as long as his client or employer wishes to keep the patent in force.

Opinion work

The other major part of the patent practitioner's job consists in giving opinions as to whether actual or proposed activities of his client or employer would infringe anyone else's patent rights, and if so, whether such patent rights are valid. This is another area which can easily give rise to misunderstanding between patent agents and their clients, or between the patent department and the research, production, or marketing departments of a company. One can always tell the difference between a patent agent and a non-patent chemist by the way they read a patent: the patent agent turns first to the claims, the chemist to the examples. All too often a patent agent will have to report that the sale of some new product would infringe a patent, will meet with the incredulous reply 'but we use acetic acid and they use sulphuric acid!', and have to point out that what the claims say is merely 'acid'.

The danger exists that unless the chemist understands something of patents, the patent agent may be seen as a person who does nothing but put obstacles in the way of company projects. If this attitude prevails, then the tendency will be either to avoid the obstacle by not keeping the patent agent informed or to flatten it by putting pressure on the patent agent to give the 'right' answer. It is better for the company to accept the fact of infringement and change plans or seek a licence before too much money has been invested than to go ahead and be faced with an infringement action once the product is on the market.

Clearance of publications

A further task of the patent agent, at least in industrial practice, is to review proposed publications by employees to make sure that they do not give away inventions which are not yet adequately protected and do not contain anything which could adversely affect existing patent rights. For example, it is not uncommon for inventors writing up their work for publication in a scientific journal to analyse it as a sequence of logical steps, and even to use phrases such as 'it was then obvious that . . .' Meanwhile the patent agent may finally have convinced the US Patent Office that the invention was surprising and non-obvious, and the last thing he wants to see is the inventor contradicting him in print. This is not to say that his representation to the US Patent Office was false; simply that inventions may often appear obvious with the benefit of hindsight, to the inventors themselves as well as to others. A scientist may well value scientific papers as much as, or more than, patents and will naturally feel resentment if his manuscript is blocked from publication for patent reasons unless he understands and accepts the occasional need for such measures.

Licensing (see Chapter 18)

The patent agent will also be involved if his client or company wishes to license its own patent rights or to take a licence from another, and whether or not he is directly concerned in the negotiation or the drafting of a licence contract, he will at least review and advise upon any clauses relating to patent matters, as well as reporting on the extent and validity of the licensed patents. If it should actually come to litigation over patents, the patent agent will confer closely with the solicitors and be involved in the briefing of counsel in all matters relating to patents. It should be mentioned that patent agents may also deal with other industrial property rights such as trade marks, registered designs, and industrial copyright, although these are outside the scope of this book.

Relationships with the inventor

The interests of the chemical inventor and his employer are best served if there is a good working relationship between the chemist and the patent agent. Both should be able to contact each other directly on a friendly and informal basis. Ideally the chemist should let the patent agent know when something interesting is coming along, before it is at the stage of a formal invention report, and when he has new developments or learns of new prior art on a case already filed. The patent agent should always be ready to listen to the chemist and should not treat patent matters as some sort of arcane mystery for the initiated, but should always be ready to explain any technicality in straightforward language. The co-operation must be based on a mutual understanding of each other's job and a mutual recognition of each other's professional competence. After all, each needs the other; if there were no inventors there would be no patent agents, and if there were no patent agents it is hard to see how there could be any patents.

15

THE PATENT SPECIFICATION AND CLAIMS

This harmonic condenser enginium . . . they caused to be worked from a magazine battery (called the Mimmim Bimbim patent number 1132, Thorpetersen and Synds, Jomsborg, Selverbergen) which was tuned up by twintriodic singul valvulous pipelines . . . with a howdrocephalous enlargement, a gain control of circumcentric megacycles, ranging from the antidulibnium onto the serostaatarean.

James Joyce: *Finnegans Wake*

Drafting the scope

When an invention has been made (for example, a group of novel and useful compounds has been prepared), the first step towards drafting a patent specification is defining the scope of the invention. The first main factor to be considered is the size of the group of compounds which can reasonably be predicted, on the basis of those already made and tested, to be useful for the desired purpose. The second is the closeness of the prior art.

In those rare cases where a completely new molecular structure has been invented and the prior art is very remote, the patent agent can cheerfully draft a very broad scope, including all kinds of derivatives of the basic structure which the inventor thinks may be useful. More usually, however, such flights of the imagination will be cut short by some earlier publication of similar structures, which will force the invention to be redefined in more narrow terms in order to avoid claiming what has already been published.

The scope of protection which it is commercially important to achieve varies from one field to another. At one extreme, in a patent application for a pharmaceutical invention it is sufficient to have a scope which includes those compounds which have a real chance of being marketed by the applicant, and once the market product has been decided upon, it is sufficient for most purposes to protect only that single compound. The reason for this is that imitators only imitate the actual market product. To take any other product, even an adjacent homologue, would involve carrying out all the necessary animal and clinical testing to get marketing approval from the regulatory authorities. The imitator does not want to involve himself in this expense any more than he wants to incur research costs, so he sticks to the product on which someone else has already done the work.

On the other hand, if a dyestuff is marketed, then it is quite likely that not only its immediate homologues, but even more remote derivatives, will also be useful dyes. They may differ slightly in shade, or in cost, but they too could be usefully marketed. Consequently the patentee of a dyestuffs patent needs a broader scope of protection than a pharmaceutical patentee, but because all other dyestuffs manufacturers are in the same position, there will be more extensive prior art and the desired scope of protection will be made even more difficult to obtain.

Where the prior art is close, as it ususally is in the dyestuffs field, it is often a pointless exercise to try to carve out a scope which touches the prior art at all points. Such a scope may indeed be novel, but the parts of the scope closest to the prior art will be *prima facie* obvious and usually will not show any significant advantage over the closest prior art compounds. It is much better to try to define a somewhat narrower scope which has a certain distance from the prior art and which will be much more defensible against obviousness attacks.

The structure of the patent specification

Once the draftsman has got a clear picture of the correct scope of the invention, he can begin the task of drafting the specification and claims of the application. Some prefer to draft the full set of claims first; more usually the main claim, defining the scope of the invention, will be drafted first in the form of the statement of invention which is the kernel of the patent specification, then the rest of the specification will be drafted, then the claims.

In whichever order they are drafted, the specification and claims have a certain logical structure, which will be described in the context of a new compound invention. A British patent specification begins with a title; this may be kept deliberately vague on filing, but a descriptive title will be required during prosecution if it is not supplied initially. The text of the specification normally begins with a very brief statement of the field of art to which the invention relates, such as 'This invention relates to anthraquinone dyes'.

It is quite possible to go straight from this to the statement of invention, for example: 'The invention provides compounds of formula I, in which R=. . .' etc., exactly as in the main claim. However, in many cases some introductory description of the background of the invention is desirable, particularly if the essence of the invention is the solution of an existing problem or the improvement of an existing process. This is not essential, at least in the United Kingdom, but if it is omitted it will make it much harder to understand what the invention is, and this makes the prosecution of the application more difficult.

After the statement of invention will generally come an indication of what are the preferred parts of the scope, and one or more formulae may be given defining narrower sub-generic scopes.

The specification must then describe how the new compounds are to be made starting from compounds which are known or which could readily be made by analogy with known compounds. This may be given by a schematic reaction diagram, together with information about suitable reagents and process conditions. It should also be stated whether the compounds may be used as formed, or if they must be purified, and if so, how.

Next comes an indication of what the compounds are useful for, a part of the specification usually called the utility statement. This may be quite brief for many uses, but for pharmaceuticals rather more detail may be required. Any advantageous properties of the compounds should be mentioned at this point.

The body of the specification is then usually followed by a number of examples giving detailed instructions for the preparation of at least one of the compounds within the scope, and for the use of the compounds. Often there will be rather few fully written out examples followed by a tabular listing of further compounds within the scope which can be prepared in the same way.

Finally, after the examples come the claims, which start with 'what we claim is' and are written as if each separate claim completes a single sentence starting with these words. There may be any number of claims, but the Patent Office objects if they are multiplied unduly; 50 or more claims are not at all uncommon although for relatively simple cases 20 or so should suffice.

If the specification relates to a category of invention other than novel compounds, the exact structure will differ from this, but the general logical sequence of statement of invention, preferences, instructions, uses, examples, and claims will normally be followed.

Priority and foreign filing texts

No distinction should be made between a specification for a first filing from which priority will later be claimed and one which claims priority from an earlier application. At one time British provisional specifications used to be very sketchy, and this did not matter as far as providing a priority date for a later complete specification was concerned. However, the ruling in the USA that priority may be validly claimed only from a priority document which meets the full US requirements means that even a first filing in the United Kingdom must be drafted as if it were to be filed in the USA.

On foreign filing it is clearly undesirable to draft different texts for different countries where the language is the same, and since the requirements for the USA are stricter than in most other countries, a text which is suitable for the USA will also be suitable elsewhere. With the requirements of the US particularly in mind, we can consider individually the different parts of the specification. Claims are normally drafted differently in different countries, and will be considered separately.

Background of the invention and prior art

When the background of the invention is to be described, this description may refer to some specific piece of prior art, and indeed a discussion of the prior art in the specification is considered desirable by the US Patent Office. This is not a positive requirement, however, and except in cases where it is really necessary for an understanding of the invention, it is best avoided.

At the time of filing, the closest prior art is not always known, and an elaborate discussion of less relevant prior art serves no useful purpose. Furthermore, the emphasis of the invention may change, or indeed it may be realized only some years after filing what the invention really is. If there is such a change of viewpoint, a prior-art discussion in the text which is based on the original incorrect conception of what the invention was, will only create difficulties.

In the USA particularly, admissions which are made in the specification as to what is actually taught by the prior art may be binding upon the applicant. A particular publication may not even be prior art because it may not exactly meet any of the criteria of 35 USC 102 (novelty), but if it is described as such in the specification the applicant may be unable to argue the contrary later. The safest rule is to admit nothing and say as little about the prior art as possible. Of course, all relevant prior art should be brought to the attention of the US Patent Office, but that does not mean that it has to be mentioned in the specification. And, whether in the specification or in communications to the Patent Office, the term 'prior art' should never be used.

One situation in which some mention of the prior art may be essential is where the invention is a selection over an earlier disclosure. In this case some reference to the disclosure and to the advantage of the selection should be given, for example in a form such as:

It is disclosed in British Patent No. . . . that compounds of formula [broad group] have activity as beta-blockers. It has now been found that a particular group of compounds, in which [definition of narrow group], which are not specifically disclosed in British Patent No. . . ., have particularly selective action and are indicated for use as cardioselective beta-blockers.

In Germany, and in the EPO, the examiner may call for a prior art statement to be inserted if one was not originally present. Care must be taken, however, not to add new matter by such an insertion. In the EPO, the Technical Board of Appeal has decided[1] that an application may be refused unless the applicant inserts a reference to the prior art when requested to do so. The Board stated that this could not reasonably be objected to as adding new subject-matter. It was 'not inevitable' that even adding a discussion of the advantages of the invention over the prior art would constitute addition of new matter, but clearly this possibility would have to be guarded against. Normally, a brief reference to the prior art will be sufficient, as the advantages of the invention should be apparent from the original description.

For the same sort of reasons, statements of the object of the invention, although very common in the USA, should preferably be avoided. They are not required by law, contribute nothing to the disclosure and can give rise to problems if it turns out that some of the objects of the invention are not in fact attained.

US sufficiency requirements

A discussion of the prior art is optional, but for the descriptive part of the specification, there are strict requirements in the US as to what constitutes a sufficient disclosure. These can be labelled as the 'description', 'how to make', 'how to use', and 'best mode', requirements.

Description

The 'description' requirement is essentially a requirement that each claim should be fairly based on the disclosure. This requirement was very strictly interpreted in the notorious case of *In re Welstead*,[2] where it was held that reduction of the scope of a generic claim to a subscope not disclosed as such in the specification or examples as filed was not allowable because the description requirement would not be met with regard to the amended claim. Consequently, it is important that in the US the original disclosure contains a full disclosure of preferred subscopes to which it may be necessary to limit.

Thus, preferred significances should be stated for each variable substituent on the general formula, for example if substituent R_1 is defined as alkyl, alkoxy, cyano, halogen, or hydroxy, one might have a statement such as:

'R_1 is preferably alkyl, alkoxy, or halogen, more preferably alkyl'

In addition, the preferred members of a particular significance may be given, e.g.

'R_1 as alkyl is preferably C_1–C_4 alkyl, more preferably methyl or ethyl, particularly methyl;

R_1 as alkoxy is preferably C_1–C_3 alkoxy, more preferably methoxy;

R_1 as halogen is preferably chloro.'

It will be seen that the word 'preferably' tends to become rather overworked in chemical patent specifications, but the reason is to give as much basis as possible for any restrictions in the scope which may become necessary later.

This should not, however, be carried to the lengths of writing out long lists of individual compounds covered by the scope of the claims. One sees this quite frequently in the patents of US companies, but it does not serve any useful purpose. It makes it much more difficult for any later selection patents to be granted, and since it is far more likely to be the original patentee who makes a selection invention than any third party, the practice actually does more harm than good to the patent owner.

How to make

For new compounds, a process for the production of the compounds from known or obtainable starting materials must be given for all the compounds in the scope, in sufficient detail to enable a chemist to reproduce the work without undue experimentation. If a single process can be used for all of the compounds, it is normally necessary to give only that one, even if a number of alternative processes are available.

It will be necessary to give additional processes if no single process can be used to make all of the compounds within the scope, or if different processes are respectively the best methods for different parts of the scope (see 'best mode' requirements, below). Once the minimum number of processes necessary to meet these requirements has been described, however, it is usually pointless to add more. For the USA itself the process will not normally be claimed at all unless it is inventive in its own right, and in other countries having product protection, process claims, although they may be included, are of little value. For countries having only process protection it is in most cases a hopeless task to try to cover all possible processes (see p. 45). Adding more processes to the text will make divisional applications necessary in some countries and give rise to extra translation costs in others, without any real advantages in return.

How to use

There must be a utility for the entire scope of the compounds, and although in some fields the utility of a claimed product does not have to be disclosed if it would be obvious to the skilled reader, utility can never be inferred for a pharmaceutical product and must always be stated. A pharmaceutical utility statement should state what type of activity the compound has, how this is demonstrated (i.e. a particular test method on a particular animal species), what the dosage should be, and how the compound should be administered. Dosage ranges may be very broad, since the scope will often cover a wide range of compounds of differing activity.

The requirements for patents claiming a new pharmaceutical use of a known compound are stricter than those for new compounds useful as pharmaceuticals. In the former case it seems necessary to insert some data comparing the activity of the compound with that of a standard compound already known for the claimed indication, and this may be desirable even for novel compound cases. In fields other than that of pharmaceuticals, however, it is best not to give any comparative data with prior art compounds. At the time of filing any data available will probably be crude and may be unreliable, and inclusion of such data can cause trouble if it is later found to be incorrect. As we shall see, it is often essential in the USA to prove superiority over a prior art compound, but this need not appear in the specification itself. What should be mentioned, however, are all the properties for which advantages over the prior art might be able to be demonstrated.

If the claimed compounds are useful only as intermediates, then the specification should describe a process for converting them to end-products known to be useful or whose use is disclosed in the specification.

Best mode

The 'best mode' (see p. 52) of carrying out the invention known to the inventor at the time of filing should be given for each aspect of the invention (best compound, process, and use). This requirement can give rise to difficulties if for example one process is best for a certain part of the compound scope and a different process is best for another. However, it is not specified in which respect the process must be 'best'; it need not necessarily be the process giving the highest yield, but could for example be the one which is most convenient or most economical to carry out. It is not essential that the best mode should be identified as such; it is enough if it is in the specification somewhere or other.

If a c.i.p. application is filed in the USA, the best mode at the time of filing the c.i.p. should be given if this is not already present.

Since the best mode to be supplied is that *known to* the inventor, not necessarily *invented by* him, it is considered that if a c.i.p. is filed, a best use or best preparative method invented by someone else subsequent to the original filing should be added. Previously, when the inventorship of a c.i.p. had to be the same as that of the original application, the newly added best mode could not be claimed in the c.i.p. Under the new regulations it is possible to claim it and add its inventor as a new co-inventor in the c.i.p. application.

A patent specification which meets these four sufficiency requirements is an 'enabling disclosure' which can be used to base priority for a US application, and which amounts to constructive reduction to practice, thereby establishing a date of invention in case of interference with another application or patent.

Sufficiency requirements in the United Kingdom

Insufficiency is a ground of invalidity both for old and new patents and is established if the specification, when read as a whole, does not contain such instructions as will enable the reader to produce something within each claim, without any inventive activity of his own. Accordingly, there is no need to describe fully more than one embodiment within the scope of a broad claim, but if further embodiments are specifically claimed they must be fully described.

It has been held that there is no actual requirement that any examples be present in a British chemical patent specification so long as the description as a whole gives sufficient instructions for putting the invention into effect.[3] Normally, however, a specification will round off the description by a number of examples, both of the synthesis of new compounds and of their application. These examples will normally illustrate representative members of the entire scope of compounds claimed, but there is no necessity that all of the examples should actually have been carried out.

Thus, one frequently finds in new compound applications one or two fully written out examples including characterizing data such as the melting point of the product, followed by a list of examples in tabular form prefixed by wording such as: 'Using similar procedures to those described in Example 1, but with suitable choice of starting materials, the following compounds may be prepared. . .'. Note that this does not allege that all of these compounds have been made; those in the list which are given with a melting point or other physical data will have been made, the rest may be 'paper examples' intended to illustrate the scope.

The traditional approach in Britain has always been that there is no need to establish the scope by actual synthesis if the inventor feels he can reasonably predict that the claimed compounds will have the stated utility. If some of the compounds cannot be made or are not useful, the patent is at least partially invalid. This may, however, change now that inutility is no longer a ground of invalidity.

A classic example of insufficiency in a chemical patent in Britain was a case dating from the turn of the century in which BASF claimed a process involving heating the reaction mixture in an autoclave. In fact, although the process worked in the standard iron autoclaves, it did not work in enamelled ones because, unknown to BASF, ferric ions were a necessary catalyst for the reaction. The patent was invalid for insufficiency because the need for an iron autoclave was not specified.[4]

It would not have mattered whether or not BASF understood why iron was necessary, so long as this necessary feature was included. This illustrates the fact that there is no need in a chemical patent to explain reaction mechanisms or to give theories as to why the invention works. Such speculation should be avoided, in case it should be interpreted as limiting the scope of protection in any way, and also to avoid making the invention appear obvious.

A general rule of patent drafting is that the specification is its own dictionary. One may use expressions which would otherwise be unclear, such as 'lower alkyl' so long as these are defined somewhere in the specification, and one can also use an expression to mean other than its normal definition or even coin wholly new terms, so long as these are all defined, and so long as à 'redefined' term does not depart too greatly from its normal meaning.

Sufficiency requirements in other countries

In many countries it seems as if a patent is awarded not so much for an inventive idea as for routine experimental work. In such countries, the claimed scope must be based upon real characterized examples. Such requirements are met with for example in Latin America, Eastern Europe, Japan, and even to some extent in Germany, France, and the European Patent Office.

When such requirements are rigorously applied, as in Argentina or the USSR, it is practically impossible to obtain a chemical patent of any reasonable scope at all. Furthermore, as the compounds themselves cannot be claimed, but only the process for making them, one finds in Eastern Europe that the process claims are limited not only with respect to the scope of compounds to be made, but also with respect to process parameters such as temperatures and solvents used in the examples.

Japan has unfortunately moved towards stricter sufficiency requirements recently, and the Japanese Patent Office now demands characterization for all examples needed to support the scope. In the field of dyestuffs, where melting points often cannot be given, it is not enough to state the colour of the dyestuff; some actual numerical value such as λ_{max} must be given.

Countries such as Japan and Germany in which the patent office may refuse a broad scope if it is not sufficiently exemplified, may allow characterizing data to be added to examples, or may even allow additional examples to be supplied during prosecution, provided that these are within the original scope as filed. This practice can give rise to problems, however. First, it is addition of new matter which in Germany, as in Britain, may now lead to invalidity of the patent. The examiners will allow it, and may even demand it because they have always done so, but this does not mean that a court may not find the resulting patent invalid. Secondly, it is not all clear what is the effective date of an example added in this way, or what happens in the event of conflict with another application claiming an overlapping scope of compounds or a selection from the earlier case.

It was originally feared that in the European Patent Office, the examiners would object to scopes as being insufficiently exemplified, but would not allow examples to be added. In some quarters it was urged that the EPO should be more ready to admit new examples, but as discussed above such a move might have done more harm than good. Instead of this, the practice now is that objections of inadequate support should be made only if the examiner can show prima facie evidence that the invention would not work over all the claimed scope. If such objections are made, the applicant can submit further examples or data to the examiner, which will go into the file and can be used as evidence in support of the scope but will *not* become part of the specification and cannot therefore cause problems due to introduction of new matter.

In Japan, additional examples and descriptive matter may be added relatively freely to a pending application, so long as the 'gist of the invention' is not changed.

The claims

Until 1969 French patents had no claims, but ended with a résumé of the important features of the invention, and until recently this was also possible in Belgium. Now, however, all countries having patents require at least one claim to define the invention. In several patent offices a large number of claims is discouraged by requiring additional fees for claims in excess of a particular number. In the USA there are additional fees for more than three independent claims or more than 20 claims in all, but these fees are relatively small and do not much affect claim drafting. In France and at the EPO there are substantial fees for claims in excess of ten, and applicants will not normally file more than ten claims.

Claims may be written in independent form or may refer back to an earlier claim. This is essentially a form of shorthand to avoid writing out an entire definition many times over; thus if claim 1 is 'A compound of formula I . . . in which R_1 is alkyl, alkoxy, or phenyl, R_2 is . . . etc.' then a later process claim may begin 'A process for the production of a compound of formula I, stated in claim 1, comprising . . .'

A true dependent claim, however, is of the same type (e.g. compound claim) as the claim to which it refers, and includes all the limitations of that claim and adds further limitations. Thus if claim 1 is the example given above, further dependent claims could be:

2. A compound as claimed in claim 1 in which R_1 is alkyl.
3. A compound as claimed in claim 2 in which R_1 is methyl.

If a dependent claim is anticipated or obvious the same must be true of the claim or claims upon which it depends. Conversely if a main claim is novel and unobvious then so is any claim depending upon it, even though the extra feature added in the dependent claim may itself be old or obvious.

In most countries multiple dependencies are allowed; thus a claim may be dependent upon 'any preceding claim'. In the USA and Canada there are complicated rules governing claim dependencies, which we need not go into.

United Kingdom practice

The main claim of a British patent specification will normally correspond to the statement of invention, and one may well wonder why anything more than this is needed. For novel compounds, a claim to the compounds is infringed not only by selling the compounds but also by making or using them. Why then claim the preparation or the use separately?

The answer is that since 1919 a British patent could be enforced against an infringer even if partly invalid, so long as at least one claim of the patent was invalid and infringed. If there was only one claim, it would be invalid if only one compound within its scope was found to be old; whereas a claim to the preparation or the use of the compounds might still be valid.

For the same reason, it is desirable to have a range of compound claims of decreasing scope finishing up with claims to individual compounds of particular interest. If one or more of the broader generic claims are later found invalid, the narrower sub-generic or species (single compound) claims many remain unaffected. It is, of course, possible to claim various combinations of preferences for particular substituents, and it is not difficult to frame 20 or so claims for a compound case of normal complexity.

When claiming new organic compounds which are acids or bases and which may exist in salt form, the claims should make it clear that not only the free acid or base but also salts are covered, at least to the extent that the salts will have the claimed utility. Thus, for a basic compound having pharmaceutical properties, wording such as 'A compound of formula I . . . in free base or pharmacologically acceptable acid addition salt form' would be appropriate. Where relevant, the specification should state that steric and optical isomers, and tautomeric forms of the claimed compounds are included in the scope.

At the same time all other possible aspects of the invention should be claimed. Claims to the process, any novel intermediates, novel compositions containing the compounds, processes for using them, and even when possible the products of such use processes (e.g. textiles dyed with novel dyes) should all be claimed. Similar considerations will apply for inventions other than novel compounds; for example if the invention is a new process then claims to various preferred process parameters should be present, as well as claims to products produced by the process.

Where the invention is a composition of a number of different components, care must be taken both in the description and in the claims to specify which components are essential and whether additional optional components may be present. The wording 'a composition consisting of A, B, and C' means that only A, B, and C, and no other components, may be present. Such a claim may be unduly narrow, since infringement would be avoided by adding a small amount of D. More useful protection is given by claiming 'a composition comprising A, B, and C'. This means that A, B, and C *must* all be present, but further components D, E, etc. *may* also be present. A claim of intermediate (but rather vague) scope is 'a composition consisting essentially of A, B, and C' which covers $A+B+C$, optionally with additional ingredients which are either present in minor amounts or are inactive, so that the properties of $A+B+C$ are not significantly affected.

In expressing the proportions of the components of the mixture, use may be made of ratios, parts or percentages, each of which may be calculated on a weight, volume, or molar basis. Whichever is used, it should be used consistently throughout, and it should also be remembered that in an n-component mixture there are only $(n-1)$ independent variables to consider.

The drafting of a set of claims of progressively narrower scope may no longer be necessary under the UK Patents Act 1977, since a patent may now be partially valid and enforceable even if the valid part is less than a complete claim. However, the present system can at least do no harm and most patent agents quite rightly will not change their drafting methods until the interpretation of the new law by the courts clearly shows that a change to a simpler system will not damage their clients' interests.

There are certain types of claims which are met with only in the United Kingdom and in a few countries having similar jurisprudence. One of these is a claim often found in specifications in which the scope of protection has been expanded on foreign filing. This claim, which is narrower than the main claim, claims precisely the same scope as was in the priority document, and is intended to ensure that that claim at least will certainly be entitled to the priority date. Under the 1949 Act, it was desirable to have such a claim for each priority document, if there were more than one; under the 1977 Act they may not be necessary at all. Such claims are often called Thornhill claims, after the case in which the problem first arose.[5]

Another typically British claim is the 'omnibus claim' which is a relic of the old days in which there were no specific claims and what was claimed was the contraption 'as herein described'. It is still permissible to include a claim of this type, generally as the last of a series of claims. In a mechanical case it refers to the drawings, in a chemical case, to the examples. Such a claim should preferably be in independent form, for example 'A process for the production of polyethylene terephthalate as described in any one of the examples', or 'A bis-naphthalene azo dyestuff as described in any one of examples 1–20'.

Such claims have two main purposes. First, they represent a last-ditch attempt to save something from the patent if all the other claims should be invalid; thus the latter of the above claims could be regarded as 20 separate claims one to each example, at least one of which might be valid even if the generic and subgeneric claims fall.[6] Secondly, they represent a form of insurance against the inclusion of some unnecessary limitation in claim 1. It is possible for an omnibus claim to be broader in some respects than a main claim.

Omnibus claims are not allowed in the USA, nor in the EPO, unless the applicant can show that the parameters of the claim cannot be expressed verbally; for example, when they can be expressed only by reference to a drawing or graph given in the specification.[7]

Claims in the USA

There was a time at which the drafting of US claims, particularly in mechanical cases, was hedged about by a large number of rules of a purely formal nature. For example, integers of a claim had to be recited positively, which meant that one could not use phrases such as 'in the absence of', and that semantic problems arose when claiming an object with a hole in it. Fortunately practice seems to have relaxed considerably in recent years, and it is now possible to include negative features in US claims.

In the chemical field, the major problem area for years has been the extent to which it is possible to put together a claim listing a group of compounds too closely related to be separately patentable, but too distinct to be conveniently expressed by a single generic term. Because of the formalistic approach to US claim drafting at that time, alternatives were not allowed to be stated as such in a claim; one could not therefore claim 'A, B, or C' *per se* or as an integer in a process claim. The solution adopted in the case of *Ex parte Markush* in 1941 was to claim 'a compound selected from the group consisting of A, B, *and* C', the fatal word 'or' thus being avoided.[8] This may seem a mere exercise in semantic triviality, but it produced important effects in US patent practice. Thus it was at one time held that the applicant by putting A, B, and C together in a 'Markush group' was admitting that the compounds were not patentably distinct, so that prior art disclosing A would preclude the patenting of B or C. There have also been a great many cases on the question of the extent to which the Patent Office can object that a Markush group is too broad and must be split up for the purposes of examination. Markush groups could also be made out of substituent groups in a general formula, for example 'a compound of formula I . . . in which R_1 is selected from the group consisting of C_1–C_4 alkyl, nitro, and cyano. . . .'

In chemical cases as in mechanical, the over-formal requirements of 40 years ago have been relaxed, and today it is acceptable to say simply 'where R_1 is C_1–C_4 alkyl, nitro, or cyano', although from force of habit this may still be referred to as a Markush group.

German practice

In Germany, as well as countries such as Holland, Austria, and Scandinavia, claims are normally drafted in such a way as to distinguish what is old in a claimed combination from what is new. Thus a process invention would be claimed in a form such as 'a process for the preparation of A by condensation of B and C under acid catalysis characterized in that (*dadurch gekennzeichnet*) orthophosphoric acid is used as catalyst.'

The first part of the claim, the 'pre-characterizing clause' recites what is already known, namely that one can make A from B and C in the presence of an acid catalyst. Then comes the phrase 'characterized in that' followed by the characterizing clause telling us what is the novel feature of the invention, that is, using orthophosphoric acid as the acid catalyst.

This type of claim is particularly useful in claiming inventions which are clearly an improvement over a well-known product or process, and may be used equally well in the United Kingdom or the USA (where they are known as Jepson claims).[9] They are not particularly suitable for claiming novel compounds, and indeed the German Patent Office does not insist on this format for compound claims. Problems can also arise where it is not clear what the prior art is, and one should always put as little in the pre-characterizing clause as possible, since the applicant by putting a feature in the first part of the claim effectively admits that it is old. Thus in our example, if the applicant later found that the prior art only disclosed basic condensation of B and C to A, he might find himself unable to claim acid catalysis generally.

The German style of claim drafting is favoured, but not insisted upon, by the EPO.

16

CHEMICAL PATENT APPLICATIONS IN THE PATENT OFFICE

> . . . the whole unfortunate situation might have been avoided if Albert Einstein had not 'doodled out' his equation $E = mc^2$ in the Swiss Patent Office around 1905 instead of getting on with the work he was being paid to do.
>
> from *British Patent Specification 1426698* (A. P. Pedrick)

The process of prosecution of a patent application to grant in the United Kingdom, the USA, and the EPO has already been described in Chapter 5. In this chapter we shall consider some of the problems which may arise when objections of lack of unity, lack of novelty, or obviousness are raised against a patent application for a chemical invention.

Lack of unity

Objections of lack of unity are more of a nuisance than a real threat. It is always clear that one can avoid the problem by filing one or more divisional applications, but in most cases this brings the applicant no advantage and simply costs him a good deal more money, since not only must a new set of application and examination fees be paid, but eventually two or more patents will issue instead of one, and renewal fees will be payable on all of them.

In the United Kingdom, examiners who have raised such an objection can sometimes be persuaded to change their mind if one argues strongly that there is a common inventive concept which unifies the parts of the invention which the examiner wished to divide. However, recent practice seems to be adopting a more restrictive line, taking the view, for example, that intermediates and final products may be claimed in the same application only if the structures are very closely related, so that they may both be searched under the same classification, or if the intermediates have the same properties as the end products. Practice in the EPO is more favourable to the applicant. In the USA, although the Patent Office has attempted to liberalize its practice recently, many examiners are still very liable to issue restriction requirements and very reluctant to be persuaded to withdraw them.

Previously, it did not greatly matter if one had to divide an application in the USA, since the extra costs involved were relatively small (one extra application fee and issue fee). There are even some advantages; thus as the divisional application need not be filed until the parent case has been allowed, the grant of the divisional may be delayed and the term of patent protection extended. Furthermore, when the examiner requires restriction between two groups of compounds within the original scope, he is thereby admitting that he considers the groups 'patentably distinct'. Thus, even if one group is anticipated by prior art, the other groups should not be regarded as obvious over that prior art, and prosecution can be made a good deal easier (although if a court later disagreed with the examiner, the resulting patent could be held invalid).

Now that renewal fees are payable on US patents, however, the cost of divisional filings will be higher than before, and it is to be expected that there will be more serious contesting of restriction requirements.

Lack of novelty

In the United Kingdom and the EPO, a search report will be available to the applicant before any substantive examination takes place. The applicant will of course check the citations which have been made, and will particularly look out for anything amounting to an anticipation of part of his claimed scope.

If such an anticipation is found, the applicant should probably amend his application voluntarily in order to cut out the old matter, since this will simplify the course of further prosecution. This is not obligatory, however, and if there is any doubt he may well prefer to wait and see what comments the examiner will make before taking any remedial action.

When the examiner makes an allegation of lack of novelty, this must first be closely examined to check if it is correct. It is possible that the examiner may have misread the prior art, or failed to notice a limitation in the claims which distinguish them from what has been cited. In such cases the response will be to argue that this objection should be withdrawn. It must also be investigated whether the document cited by the examiner is indeed prior art. Thus, for example, in the United Kingdom a scientific paper published before one's filing date would not be prior art if one could rely upon a priority date earlier than the publication. Similarly another British application claiming an earlier priority date would not be prior art under the whole contents approach if one could show that for the relevant subject matter one's own application was entitled to its priority date and the cited application was not.

In the USA a publication less than a year before the US filing date may be overcome by relying on one's priority date, showing that the publication originated from the inventors, or, if the invention was made in the USA, 'swearing back' by means of an affidavit or declaration to establish an invention date before the date of the reference. It may also be necessary to check closely into when a publication was actually available; in the case of a scientific journal this may be some days or even weeks after the issue date on the cover, or may even be before that date.

The question frequently arises as to whether it is enough to destroy the novelty of a compound that its name or structure has been published, even if there is no indication of how it may be made or whether it is useful for anything. In the USA, since the recent case of *In re Donohue* was decided by the CAFC,[1] it seems to be the law that such a publication is enough, provided that the compound could be made by an average competent chemist. It is immaterial in the USA whether a compound has actually been made or not, so that 'paper examples' are just as effective anticipations as real examples (see p. 216).

On the other hand if the reference states that the named compound could not be made, or if working the suggested process does not give the named compound, and no other obvious method of preparation is known, then the disclosure may not be an anticipation. In the latter case, however, it is very difficult to convince the US Patent Office that a method disclosed in the prior art does not work, particularly if the prior art is a patent, which is legally presumed to be workable. If the later applicant gives evidence to the effect that he was unable to repeat the process of the earlier patent, he may be suspected of not having tried hard enough. Evidence from an independent expert may be more credible.

In the United Kingdom there have been decisions to the effect that the mere naming of a compound, without a method for its preparation, is anticipation. This would lead to the logical conclusion that a computer programmed to print out the structural formulae of all possible chemical compounds could prevent all future patenting of chemicals. However, the Court of Appeal decision in *du Pont* v. *Akzo* (see p. 133), which was approved by the House of Lords, went to the other extreme, holding that 'a compound which has never hitherto been made cannot be a known substance' and therefore cannot anticipate a later claim to the substance. On this basis, even a full written disclosure of how to make a named compound would not be novelty destroying in the absence of proof that the compound had in fact been produced.

Since in the patent literature it is usually impossible to tell which examples are real and which are 'paper examples' (see p. 260) the general adoptation of this approach would lead to a chaotic situation. It is to be hoped that the Courts will try to side-step this decision by distinguishing from it on the facts wherever possible.

Restriction of scope

If the cited document does genuinely amount to an anticipation, action must be taken to reduce the scope of the claims so that they no longer claim what is old. Here a distinction must be made between prior art which discloses the same or a similar utility for the compounds as does the application, and prior art which discloses either a different utility or no utility at all. In the latter case the prior art may be regarded as an 'accidental anticipation' since it did not relate to the same inventive idea as that of the application.

For example, if we are claiming antidepressants of general formula X—R where R is C_1–C_6 alkyl (preferably C_1–C_3 alkyl), C_1–C_6 alkoxy or phenyl, and a journal article is found disclosing X—n-C_5H_{11} without any stated use, then in the United Kingdom it would be acceptable to avoid the anticipation simply by adding to the end of the claim 'provided that R is other than n-pentyl.'

The reason for this is that because no utility is disclosed for the n-pentyl compound then it would not be obvious that the butyl, hexyl, or even the other isomeric pentyl compounds would have any use, whether as an antidepressant or anything else. These neighbouring compounds are therefore still patentable even though the n-pentyl compound is known, and a claim which simply excludes the known compound is *prima facie* valid. If the n-pentyl compound was found to be known as an antidepressant, however, or even as having any central nervous system activity, then such an amended claim would not be allowable because the immediately neighbouring compounds would also be expected to have this activity. Limitation to the preferred scope of R = C_{1-3} alkyl, C_{1-6} alkoxy, or phenyl would then be necessary, and even then objections of obviousness might well arise.

In other words, whereas in the case of an accidental anticipation one can go right up to the boundary of the prior art, where the anticipation is in the same field of inventive activity one must leave a gap between what one claims and the prior art.

In the USA, although claims on filing may incorporate provisos to disclaim individual compounds, difficulties will be encountered if one tries to do this during prosecution, because there will usually not be a basis in the specification as filed for the new reduced scope.

At least it does now seem to be possible to restrict to a preferred significance of one substituent while leaving other substituents unchanged. Previously, following *In re Welstead* (see p. 213) the reduced scope was considered to be new matter because it was not described as such in the specification as filed. In some recent cases, disclaimer of specific compounds has been allowed, and, in general, US practice seems to be much less formalistic in this respect than it was a few years ago.

If one must restrict to a scope for which there really is no basis in the specification, one can always do this in the USA by filing a c.i.p.

application containing the new scope. The problem is that this new matter may not be entitled to the filing date of the parent case, with possibly fatal effect upon validity.

Obviousness

Although the British Patent Office is now empowered to raise objections of obviousness, its practice has not so far developed in the same direction as the USA, and applicants will not usually be required to prove non-obviousness by submitting comparative test results as is often necessary in the USA. An objection of obviousness can always be argued, and if the argument is reasonable on its face it will be difficult for the examiner not to accept it. The arguments given by the applicant will of course be on the record and if they can be shown to be incorrect or misleading, the patent will be very vulnerable to any subsequent attack.

If an obviousness objection appears to be at all well-founded, the sensible course is to limit the scope of the claims by adding further features not found in the cited prior art, assuming of course that there is basis for such limitation in the specification or claims as filed.

The practice in the USA on the other hand is well established and follows rules which are simple enough in concept, although they may give rise to great difficulty in individual cases.

The examiner may cite under 35 USC 103 any combination of prior art references in order to allege the obviousness of a claim. In a simple case, for example where the claim covers compounds of a certain formula with a C_2–C_6 alkyl substituent and the prior art discloses the methyl compound, for the same utility, then that single reference will suffice. If, however, the prior art disclosed the ethoxy compound, then the examiner might cite that as the primary reference together with a second reference showing that in similar but less closely related compounds which were also useful for the same purpose, both alkoxy and alkyl substituents were disclosed. He would then argue that in view of the secondary reference it would be obvious to substitute ethyl for ethoxy in the compound of the primary reference, so obtaining one of the claimed compounds.

The examiner may combine more than two references, but when he does so it is a clear sign that his argument is not a strong one. The invention cannot really be very obvious if it can only be reconstructed with the benefit of hindsight, by selecting bits and pieces from three or more different publications.

The first line of defence in response to an obviousness rejection is to argue the matter, if necessary combining this with a suitable limitation of the claims to features not found in the prior art. The argument should first of all point out the differences (the more the better) between the prior art and the claimed invention. If the claimed utility is not disclosed in the prior art, it can be argued that the man skilled in the art would have no reason to suppose that compounds similar to the prior-art compounds would have that utility. If two or more references have been combined it can often be argued that it would not have occurred to anyone to read both references together, for example because they relate to different technical fields; one can also allege that even if they were combined they would not amount to the invention.

It is a strong argument against obviousness if it can be said that the prior art 'teaches away from' the invention, for example by indicating that poorer results were obtained from the compounds closest to the scope now claimed.

Showings in the USA

If none of these arguments are effective, it may be necessary to submit a 'showing', that is, a declaration or affidavit (merely different legal forms for essentially the same thing) which gives the results of comparative testing to show that the compounds of the invention have unexpectedly superior properties to the closest prior-art compounds.

The basis for such showings is that although a claimed compound may be prima facie obvious in view of the prior art because of close similarity in chemical structure, it may nevertheless be legally unobvious and patentable if not merely its structure, but its properties as a whole are taken into consideration, and unexpected advantages are found among these properties.

In carrying out a showing, the number of compounds to be compared depends upon the size of the scope which is claimed. If the scope is narrow it may be enough to compare one compound from the scope with a prior-art compound; a broader scope will require two or more pairs to be compared.

The compounds chosen for comparison should be selected by the following procedure. First find the specifically disclosed or exemplified compound from the prior art which is closest in structure to the claimed scope. Having done this, find the compound in the claimed scope closest to the chosen prior-art compound, whether or not this compound is specifically disclosed or exemplified. If two prior-art compounds are equally close, either may be chosen, but a comparison involving both might carry more weight.

Only in rather exceptional circumstances should this procedure vary. For example, where the prior-art scope includes a compound not specifically disclosed but closer to the claimed scope than any specifically disclosed compound, it may be necessary to choose that compound if the prior art points to it, for example by including it in a narrow sub-scope. It may sometimes be allowable to compare against a compound which is not structurally the closest, for example where the prior art discloses that such a compound has better properties than the closest compound.

Having selected the compounds for comparative testing, the next question is what tests to apply. In some cases this is fairly clear; if the compounds are supposed to have a pharmaceutical utility, then a test for that activity will normally be necessary. If the compounds are dyestuffs, however, a wide range of possible properties could be compared; for example, fastness to light or to various wet treatments, dyeing properties, migration, compatablity with other dyes, stability to pH changes, and many more. Care should be taken in the selection of properties to test, since the duty of candour to the Patent Office means that all test results obtained must be disclosed. One cannot carry out a whole battery of tests and select one or two in which good results have been obtained.

There are no absolute rules as to how many properties must be shown, nor how great the superiority must be. The only criterion is that the superiority should be unexpected, and relatively small improvements may be dismissed by the examiner as being within the normal expected range of variation.

The properties tested must be disclosed in the specification, but if a property relied upon in a showing is not mentioned it may be added by means of a c.i.p. application without loss of priority date.

The person who signs the declaration or affidavit should be the person who either personally carries out the tests reported or supervises directly the person who does. This will often be the inventor, and this is acceptable as long as the declaration sticks to reporting facts. In so far as it gives opinions, the opinions of the inventor are given little weight by the Patent Office, and thus if for any reason an opinion declaration is needed, this should be done by someone other than the inventor and preferably by an outside expert.

Opinion declarations may sometimes be used to establish what are sometimes called secondary criteria of non-obviousness, for example that there had been a long-felt want in the trade which the product met and that this gave rise to commercial success.

In many cases, the prior art will be so close that it is quite clear that the application will never be allowed without a showing. In others, the prior art is remote and a showing is clearly not needed. In between is a large grey area, in which the examiner alleges obviousness, and in which a showing may not be strictly necessary, but would make allowance of the application much easier.

In such cases it is advisable to avoid a showing if at all possible, and to do everything in one's power to convince the examiner by argument. There are three reasons for this. First, a showing requires the investment of time and effort by research workers, which costs money and which diverts them from their main job of making new inventions. Secondly, submitting a showing could be taken as an admission that the invention was prima facie obvious and required a showing to establish non-obviousness. Thirdly, and perhaps most important, a showing presents a point of attack to a competitor who may want to challenge the patent later.

If a showing has been submitted, it can be argued that the patent has been granted only because of the contents of that showing. If these contents can be discredited, the patent may well be held invalid. Worse, if it can be shown that there was any concealment of relevant facts, or any misrepresentation of the results, the patentee will have been guilty of fraud on the patent office, which as we have seen can have consequences beyond the invalidity of the patent. The same patent granted as a result of argument rather than a showing has a much better presumption of validity, since the examiner has been convinced that the invention is not *prima facie* obvious, and that conclusion is difficult to rebut.

For these reasons, submissions of a showing should, where there is any doubt, be regarded as a last resort. The same goes for opinion declarations about commercial success and such matters. It is far better if the patent attorney can work out why there was commercial success and relate this to the nature of the invention in such a way as to be evidence of prima facie unobviousness. It will in many cases be preferable to go on appeal rather than carry out a showing.

Obviousness in the EPO

The practice of the European Patent Office in considering questions of obviousness is still being developed, but some trends may already be discerned. For chemical compounds, practice is similar to that of the USA in that a finding of prima facie structural obviousness may be displaced by evidence of surprising advantages, which must be shown over the closest disclosed prior art, even if these closest prior art compounds were not actually made.

Quite generally, the EPO adopts the 'problem and solution' approach to obviousness: the invention is seen as the solution to the problem of getting from the closest prior art to the advantageous new result. It is for this reason that the EPO wishes the applicant to include a discussion of the prior art in his specification, so that the problem and the solution will be apparent to the reader. This is all very well in theory, but in practice the inventor often does not know what is the closest prior art, and the 'problem' is a fictitious one arrived at by analysis with the benefit of hindsight.

Although surprising advantageous results may demonstrate the presence of an inventive step, this is not necessarily so. Even if there is a surprising advantage, this may be discounted if it is only an extra bonus over and above an obvious, expected advantage, or if the improvement would in any event have been obtained by routine development. A number of recent EPO decisions[2] have adopted the concept of the 'one-way street solution' to find lack of inventive step in a situation where the state of the art obliges a skilled person to adopt a certain solution, irrespective of what advantage may be obtained as a result.

It can be concluded, however, that although there are more theoretical difficulties ('one-way streets' and the like) in establishing non-obviousness in the EPO, the practical difficulties are less than in the USPTO, and the evidence required will normally be less extensive than that for US showings.

17

INFRINGEMENT OF CHEMICAL PATENTS

. . .Not to mention the expert evidence about the scientific stuff – all that fandango about the magnesium alkaloid and the patent vapour-feed. The chemists on the two sides flatly contradicted each other, and so did the accountants.

A. P. Herbert: *Wigs at Work*

From the viewpoint of the patentee

When the owner of a chemical patent becomes aware of commercial activity by a competitor which is in the area of his invention, he will naturally want to know if the patent can be used to stop these activities. The first and most important question is whether what the competitor is doing amounts to an infringement.

This may sometimes be a very easy question to answer, particularly when the patentee has product *per se* protection, and a compound clearly within the claims is being sold without the patentee's permission. It may be that determining whether or not there is infringement is essentially a problem in analytical chemistry; for example where the competitor is selling a complex mixture which may or may not contain a patented compound. If the presence of the compound can be detected, the rest is simple.

The interpretation of claims

In many cases, however, the question of whether or not there is infringement is one which requires careful study. The problem is one of analysing the scope of the claims of the patent in the country in question, and although practically all countries having patents require claims, there are considerable differences from country to country in the way in which claims are interpreted.

There are indeed some general principles of claim interpretation which hold good in all, or nearly all countries. The claim may be analysed into distinct features (e.g. parameters of a process, components of a mixture, or substituent groups on a molecule), the specification being used as a guide to the meaning of terms used in the claim. If, then, a process, mixture, or compound has all of these essential features, then its unauthorized manufacture, sale or use is an infringement of the claim. To take a simple example, a claim to 'A mixture comprising A, B, and C' is not infringed by a mixture of A and B, but is by a mixture of A, B, C, and D – infringement is not avoided by adding extra features. If a patent contains a number of claims, some may be infringed and others not. As we have seen, claims are often written in dependent form, and a dependent claim incorporates all the features of an earlier claim and either further defines one or more of these features or adds some extra features; for example we may have:

1. A process for the manufacture of X, comprising the step of reacting Y and Z in an inert solvent.
2. A process as claimed in claim 1 in which the solvent is water.

Because claim 2 adds an extra feature (sometimes called an extra integer) to claim 1 it is narrower in scope, and it follows that a process which does not infringe claim 1 cannot infringe claim 2. The use of alcohol as a solvent would, however, infringe claim 1 but not claim 2.

Sometimes the presence of a dependent claim may assist in the interpretation of the claim on which it depends. Thus given a claim having 'a fluid' as an integer, it may not be clear whether this really does include a gas as well as a liquid, particularly if only liquids are exemplified. However, if there is a dependent claim adding only the feature 'in which the fluid is a liquid', then because there is a legal presumption that different claims have different scopes, the earlier claim must include fluids which are other than liquids, that is, gases.

Difficulties in interpretation tend to arise not so much when integers of the claim are added or omitted but when they are substituted. Does a mixture of A, B', and C infringe our claim to a mixture comprising, A, B, and C, where B' is very similar to B? It is this question of 'equivalence' which is approached differently by different countries.

United Kingdom. In the United Kingdom, the practice has always been to interpret claims somewhat literally. The attitude has been that it is up to the patentee to define his own claims and it is his own misfortune if he fails to do so broadly enough. On the other hand, the courts have also recognized that it is unjust that someone should be able to take the benefit of a patentee's invention just because of a technicality in claim drafting. These two approaches are in opposition to each other, and practice lies closer to the first than the second. Claims are in principle interpreted literally in the United Kingdom, but the substitution of a simple mechanical equivalent (e.g. using a nail where the claim says a screw) will generally not avoid infringement, and there is still the possibility of infringement being found where the court is convinced that the alleged infringer has taken the essence of the invention (the 'pith and marrow', to use a phrase common in the case law), even if no claim is literally infringed.

A recent example of this was the finding that the drug hetacillin infringed Beecham's patent for ampicillin, even though the structure of hetacillin did not fall within the claims. Hetacillin was an acetone adduct of ampicillin, and as soon as it was ingested, it was hydrolysed in the body to ampicillin. The House of Lords considered hetacillin was 'ampicillin in disguise' and found infringement on the old 'pith and marrow' basis.[1] (See p. 142).

A similar conclusion was reached by the High Court in a more recent case involving steel door lintels. The claim called for the back wall of the lintel to be vertical, whereas in the alleged infringements it was at an angle of 6° or 8° from the vertical. The High Court held that the claim was not literally infringed, but that the 'pith and marrow' had been taken. On appeal, the Court of Appeal reversed this judgment and held that verticality must be taken literally. The case went on to the House of Lords, who restored the decision of the High Court, but for a different reason. They did not distinguish between literal and 'pith and marrow' infringement but simply construed the claim broadly to cover deviations from the vertical small enough not to significantly affect the function of the article.[2] This may be a sign of a general move to less literal claim interpretation in the United Kingdom.

United States. In the USA, the scope of the claims may be extended beyond their literal meaning by application of the 'doctrine of equivalence'. Originally developed by the courts in considering mechanical inventions the doctrine of equivalence enables infringement to be found when an integer of the claim is replaced by a different integer which 'performs substantially the same function in substantially the same way to obtain the same result'. The same principle is applied to chemical cases: for example a claim to a dentifrice composition containing 1 to 10 per cent of urea (plus other ingredients) was held infringed by a composition containing 13 per cent urea, which gave the same result in the same way. This result would not be possible in the English courts, where the patentee would have been bound by the numerical limits which he had chosen to set to the claim.

One restriction upon the extent to which the doctrine of equivalence can be applied in the USA is that the claim cannot be extended to cover anything which is old: consequently the claims will have a greater range of equivalents in the case of a pioneer invention than for one which represents a small advance in an already well-worked field. Another limitation arises from the fact that in the USA, unlike Britain, the claims are interpreted not only in the light of the specification but also in the light of what happened during the prosecution of the patent application. This is a matter of public record in the 'file wrapper' of the patent, and is sometimes referred to as the 'file history'. If this shows that during prosecution the patentee had to limit his claims in a relevant respect and argued that this limitation made the claims patentable over the prior art, then he will not be able to extend his claims by the doctrine of equivalence to recover the ground he gave up during prosecution.

For example, to take the case of the dentifrice composition previously mentioned; let us suppose the patentee originally had a claim in his application to 1–20 per cent urea, with a subclaim to a preferred range of 1–10 per cent. Let us further suppose that the examiner had cited as prior art a composition with 18 per cent urea and as a result the patentee had dropped the broader claim and restricted himself to the 1–10 per cent range. In these circumstances the doctrine of file wrapper estoppel, as it is called, would prevent the composition containing 13 per cent urea from being regarded as an infringement.

Germany. In Germany, claims tend to be interpreted by the courts even more broadly than in the USA. German practice distinguishes two types of equivalents to claimed integers. The first, *'glatte Aequivalente'*, (plain equivalents) are those which are immediately obvious as equivalents (our nail and screw, for example). *'Nicht glatte Aequivalente'* on the other hand are equivalents whose recognition requires careful thought, although no inventive activity. These concepts are then applied to define three scopes of increasing breadth:

(i) the direct subject matter of the invention, which is the literal wording of the claims;

(ii) the subject matter of the invention, which is the literal wording of the claims plus plain equivalents; and

(iii) the general inventive concept, which also includes the *'nicht glatte Aequivalente'*.

Anything coming within the broadest of these scopes may be held to be an infringement, although as in the USA the extent of the range of equivalence will depend upon the degree of unobviousness of the invention.

Other countries. In The Netherlands, the standard of examination is strict, but claims are construed broadly by the courts, much in the same way as in Germany. In France, on the other hand, it is unknown for a chemical claim to be extended beyond its literal scope; indeed if the exemplification is considered insufficient, the actual scope of protection given by the courts may not be as broad as the claim itself. In Japan the doctrine of equivalents is not applied, at least in chemical cases, while Canada is intermediate in its practice between the United Kingdom and USA.

European Patent Convention. The framers of the European Patent Convention found themselves faced with a problem when they considered how the claims of a European patent should be interpreted. There would be a single set of claims to be interpreted by the national courts of any of the member states, whose practice in the interpretation of their own patents ranged as we have seen from essentially literal interpretation in the United Kingdom to wide-ranging equivalence in Germany. As it was undesirable to accept a situation in which a Europatent would have a broader scope of protection in some countries than in others, a protocol on interpretation of claims was added to the EPC which attempts to find a compromise position between those of the United Kingdom and Germany.

Unfortunately, it does this by presenting an exaggeration of the United Kingdom system on the one hand and an exaggeration of the German system on the other, and stating that both of these hypothetical extremes are to be avoided. The result is supposed to 'combine a fair protection for the patentee with a reasonable degree of certainty for third parties'. In fact, all it provides is confusion for everybody, and until some case law develops it is true to say that no one knows how claims will be interpreted according to this protocol.

What is more, the protocol is made to apply not only to Europatents, but also to British national patents granted under the new Act. In so far as it will have any effect at all, this must mean some tendency to go in the direction of a wider and less literal interpretation of claims in the United Kingdom – but how far is anybody's guess.

If the competitor's activity does not fall within the literal wording of the claims, so that the only way in which he can be caught is by relying upon equivalence, then it is essential to obtain the opinion of an expert in patent law in the relevant country before proceeding any further. Only someone thoroughly familiar with local law and practice can give any useful opinion as to whether a court would hold the patent to be infringed.

Process patents and contributory infringement

If the patent is for a process rather than a product, it is of course more difficult to establish infringement. If the process is a process of manufacture of a chemical product, then the manufacturer will certainly do his best to keep secret the process he is using, and one may have to rely upon circumstantial evidence such as analysis for unchanged reactants or by-products which may characterize the process used. It may be possible during an infringement action to obtain information under one form or other of legal compulsion, but the trouble is that one cannot fully evaluate the chances of success before filing suit.

If the claimed process is a process of use of a non-patented product, then it will be directly infringed only by customers who buy the product from an unauthorized competitor. In Chapter 7 we discussed the nature of contributory infringement, which gives the patentee the possibility of taking action against the competitor himself, at least if the product in question has no substantial non-infringing use. The *Rohm & Haas* v. *Dawson* case in the USA referred to briefly in that chapter gives a good illustration of a typical contributory infringement situation and as it is a chemical case, it is worth considering here in more detail.

The case related to the compound propanil, which can kill weeds in rice fields without harming the rice. The compound was known and could not be claimed *per se* (a patent for it issued to Monsanto had been found invalid) and Rohm & Haas had a patent for its use as a selective herbicide; that is, a process for the control of weeds in rice by applying propanil under certain conditions. Propanil had no other substantial use and thus was a 'non-staple', so that although the patent could be directly infringed only by farmers, unauthorized sale of propanil to farmers was contributory infringement.

Rohm & Haas refused to grant licences, but farmers purchasing propanil from them received an implied licence to use the patented process. Dawson also sold propanil and when sued by Rohm & Haas admitted contributory infringement but alleged that the conduct of Rohm & Haas in not granting licences to other sellers constituted patent misuse. The Supreme Court decided in favour of Rohm & Haas, although by only a 5 to 4 majority. An interesting point is that Dawson were not just selling propanil, they were selling it with full instructions for applying it to rice fields so as to kill weeds selectively; that is, with instructions to infringe Rohm & Haas's process patent. This should according to US patent law amount not only to contributory infringement but to direct infringement, since the law says 'whoever actively induces infringement of a patent shall be liable as an infringer'. This point was not argued or decided in the Rohm & Haas case, presumably because Dawson admitted that they were liable as contributory infringers if their defence of patent misuse failed. But it is of vital importance in the more common cases where the product does have other non-infringing uses.

Take, for example, a patent for an improved dyeing process. The process can be applied to old, unpatented dyestuffs sold by a number of manufacturers, all of which can of course be used in many old, unpatented dyeing processes. If a rival manufacturer sold his dyestuffs with trade literature describing how to carry out the patented process, then he is not a contributory infringer in US law since the product is a staple article of commerce. He *should* be a direct infringer, since he is actively inducing infringement by his customers, but how the US Supreme Court would decide such a case if the infringer raised a defence of patent misuse can only be guessed at, in view of the narrowness of the majority in *Rohm & Haas* v. *Dawson*.

An ironic twist to the story of *Rohm & Haas* v. *Dawson* is that in subsequent litigation[3] Rohm & Haas's patent was held to be invalid! Nevertheless, this does not affect the value of the Supreme Court's decision on the issue of contributory infringement.

In the United Kingdom, selling a product with instructions to infringe a patented process will amount to supplying 'for the purpose of inducing infringement' and so fall within the definition of infringement under the 1977 Act. Infringement would not be avoided simply by calling the customers' attention to the existence of the patent.

Contributory, or indirect, infringement was recognized by German case law before 1981, but it was a rule that there could be no indirect infringement without direct infringement. Thus because a claim to a cleaning process using a particular composition would not be directly infringed by a housewife (since private non-commercial use was not infringement) it followed that sale of the composition as a domestic cleaner was not indirect infringement. Since 1981 the law has defined infringement so as to include sale of a product where the sole or main use of the product falls within the patent claim, or where the product is sold with instructions to infringe. It is no longer necessary to prove that direct infringement has occurred. The law does not now make any distinction between direct and indirect infringement.

Exhaustion of rights

The patentee must also remember that if the 'infringer' is selling or using goods which originate from the patentee himself, then such sale or use can generally not be prevented. The original purchaser of the goods from the patentee will have an implied licence to use or resell them, which passes with the goods to subsequent purchasers. Furthermore, within the EEC, sales of imported goods, even though they are infringements under national patent law cannot be prevented if the goods were first put on the market in another EEC country by the patentee or with his consent. (An exception has however, been made for goods imported from Spain or Portugal until 1995.)

To sue or not to sue

Given that the competitor's activity is infringement and that there are no legal barriers to the enforcement of the patentee's rights, the patentee must still consider carefully what his options are. Normally his first step would be to write a warning letter bringing his patent rights to the competitor's attention. In some countries this may be a necessary preliminary to any subsequent claims for damages, but at this stage the main object is to find out the infringer's reaction.

He may agree to stop his infringing activities, or may ask for a licence. If the patentee is willing to grant licences, negotiations about terms will naturally follow. If not, or if the infringer denies infringement or alleges that the patent is invalid, then the patentee has to decide whether or not to sue the infringer.

In making his decision, he must weigh up all the many factors which are involved, one of the most important being the degree of confidence he has in the validity of his patent. A patent of questionable validity may be respected by the majority of the patentee's competitors, but if as a result of attempting to enforce it against one competitor the patent is found invalid, then all the competitors will be free. The indirect effect upon corresponding patents in other countries must also be considered. Furthermore, infringement actions are expensive and if the infringement is small what would be gained by a successful action might not justify the costs.

On the other hand, it is important in order to deter future infringement for it to be known that the patentee is willing to enforce his rights. Certainly a reputation for timidity in such matters can become an open invitation to infringers, and it is probably worth even the occasional unsuccessful action in order to avoid such a reputation. Finally, of course, the patentee may have granted one or more licences by which he is contractually obliged to enforce the patent against infringers, in which case he may have no choice in the matter.

From the viewpoint of the potential infringer

Few companies set out deliberately to infringe the patents of others, but every company which puts a chemical product on the market or uses a chemical process is potentially an infringer of one or more of the tens or even hundreds of thousands of chemical patents presently in force. It is irresponsible, to say the least, to market a new product without carrying out a thorough search for any patents which might be infringed.

A full infringement search requires the joint efforts of a professional searcher familiar with the technical field, who can find the patents which may be relevant, and a patent practitioner who can give an opinion on whether any of the relevant patents would actually be infringed by what it is proposed to do.

Such a search will normally be based on a variety of sources and may turn up a mixture of patents and published patent applications from various countries. The first step will be to correlate them with the countries in which it is actually proposed to market. For example, if it is proposed to sell in the United Kingdom and USA, and a search finds a relevant

German DOS, then it is necessary to check whether equivalents of this exist in the two countries in question. There are various ways, which we shall mention in Chapter 19, of obtaining lists of equivalent patents; that is, patents which all claim priority from the same original application. It will then be necessary to obtain copies of these to check what the claims are in each country; the claims of a published but unexamined German DOS are little guide to the scope of claims allowed by the US Patent Office.

The claims of any relevant patents should then be checked for possible infringement as described above, bearing in mind the possibilities of infringement by equivalence or contributory infringement in some countries. Whereas the patentee is concerned with possible infringement of a particular patent, the potential infringer will often have a number of relevant patents to consider. Nevertheless, he at least does not have the same problems of chemical analysis, since he presumably knows what it is that he proposes to sell.

There may be situations in which it is not clear whether the proposed activity would amount to infringement or not. Apart from the whole question of equivalence, discussed above, there may be problems for example when the patent claims a multi-step process and it is proposed to carry out the steps in a different order, or to carry out the early steps in one country and the later steps in another. The answers will of course depend upon the precise wording of the claims, and on the law of the country in question, but in general unless the claim stresses that the steps must be carried out in a particular order, then altering the order in which the steps are stated in the claim would not avoid infringement. The situation in the second case would probably be that there would be no infringement unless the entire claimed process was carried out within one country.

The question may also arise as to whether the sale of a drug A can infringe a patent which does not cover A but which covers a compound B to which A metabolizes in the body. In the UK at least it may do so in the clear situation where A itself is pharmaceutically inactive, and is totally converted to B, so that all the activity is in fact due to the formation of B. (See p. 142.) In the normal case where A has activity of its own and B is only one of a number of metabolites there is little chance that the sale of A would be held to infringe a patent for B.

If the patent is near to expiry and no commercial sales will take place until after the patent has expired, one may still have to consider whether necessary experimental work such as clinical or field trials conducted while the patent is still in force would amount to infringement and could be stopped by interlocutory injection as in *Monsanto* v. *Stauffer* (see p. 103).

Is the patent in force?

As a result of a rapid check, many apparently relevant patents can be dismissed from consideration, and the potential infringer may be left with a small number for which a serious question of infringement arises. The next step is to check whether these patents are still in force, which can be determined relatively quickly in most countries from the national patent office. In the United Kingdom indeed a simple telephone call will elicit the information, although this should be confirmed in writing to be on the safe side. The quick check should always be done at an early stage, however; many patent agents have at some time or another wasted time in detailed study of a patent, only to learn later that the renewal fees had not been paid for the last ten years.

For the USA, patents applied for before 12 December 1980 cannot lapse for non-payment of renewal fees, but the possibility should not be overlooked that they may have been specifically abandoned by being 'dedicated to the public'.

Is the patent valid?

If a relevant patent is in force and would be infringed by the proposed activity, the potential infringer should then consider whether or not the patent is valid. The original infringement search will have already found patents which are prior art to the patent in question, and the chemists responsible for the proposed activity may know of more. A further search may still be necessary directed towards finding prior art which could anticipate or render obvious the claims of the patent.

Internal grounds of invalidity such as insufficiency should also be considered, and in countries where this is available the prosecution history of the patent should be studied carefully. The potential infringer should also consider whether or not his proposed activity would have been patentable at the priority date of the patent. In the United Kingdom at least it is an effective argument against a charge of infringement to say 'What I am doing was, at the priority date of the patent, either old or obvious in view of the prior art. Therefore either what I am doing does not fall within the claims of the patent, and there is no infringement; or the claims cover what is old or obvious and therefore are invalid.' This argument is known as a 'Gillette Defence' since it was first pointed out by one of the judges in the House of Lords in the case of *Gillette Safety Razor Co.* v. *Anglo-American Trading Co.*[4]

Are there rights of prior use?

As well as considering questions of validity, the potential infringer should check whether he has any rights of prior use. Even if the product has not yet been put upon the market, in many countries making effective and serious preparations to do so before the priority date of the patent can give the right to continue such activity after the patent is granted.

Can one design around the patent?

If after all this, the potential infringer is faced with a patent which he would infringe, which is in force, and against which he has neither grounds of attack nor rights of prior use, his next step must be to consider whether or not he can 'design around' the claims of the patent.

This is hardly possible if he wishes to sell a single compound which falls within the scope of the claims, but with patents covering mixtures of compounds the question arises whether one of the components can be replaced by another compound not covered by the claims, or whether the proportions of the components can be varied outside the claimed range without too great a loss of advantageous properties. He must of course be careful not to be caught by the doctrine of equivalents in countries where this applies, or (although this is unlikely) to be considered as taking the 'pith and marrow' of the invention in the United Kingdom.

One must be careful not to infringe other industrial property rights such as copyright; in the UK there may be, in the mechanical field, copyright in engineering drawings which could possibly be infringed without infringing the claims of a patent, or even after the patent expires; indeed, at present we have the ludicrous situation that, while even the most deserving invention can be protected for only 20 years, the 'design' of a bent piece of pipe is protected for the life of the 'author' plus 50 years – and without even having to make an application or pay a fee.

Although deliberate copying of another's efforts may be regarded as wrong, there is nothing immoral about designing around a patent which stands in the way of one's own developments. No patentee is entitled to any more rights than the law gives him, and has no cause for complaint if another manages to avoid infringement and still to have a commercially successful product. It would certainly be anti-competitive and against the public interest if companies were to agree that each should keep well away from the patented areas oi interest of the others.

Is a licence available?

If all else fails, the potential infringer must decide whether to abandon his plans, seek a licence from the patentee, or to go ahead without a licence. It is usually worthwhile to ask for a licence, unless it is absolutely clear that there is no chance of one being granted. It may be that a mutually acceptable cross-licence may be negotiable, for example if the potential infringer has a patent for a selection invention within the scope of an earlier dominating patent. In this situation the possibility of an application for a compulsory licence in the United Kingdom and certain other countries should not be ignored: the same is true if the patent which would be infringed is not being worked.

In cases where the parties are hostile and no licence will be forthcoming, then if there would clearly be infringement the potential infringer has little choice but to abandon his project. However, when in a situation where there is some real doubt as to the validity of the patent or as to whether there would be infringement, it may be an acceptable business risk to go ahead. Factors such as the remaining life of the patent, the difficulty of analysis of the product, the costs involved if the product had to be taken off the market once launched, and the possible expense of having to fight an infringement action would then have to be considered.

18

LICENSING CHEMICAL PATENTS

In France, British duds falling behind German lines bore the tiny stamp KPz96/04, 1896 being the year Vickers first licensed Krupp's fuse patent and 1904 the year the agreement was renewed.

William Manchester: *The Arms of Krupp*

Patent conflict licences

A manufacturer who finds that a product he wishes to sell or a project he wishes to develop is covered by someone else's patent may have to obtain a licence from the other person in order to be free to go ahead. Such licences may be obtained for a lump sum or for a running royalty, or it may be necessary to grant a cross-licence in exchange. A special case of this type of licence occurs frequently in the USA where two parties find that patent applications assigned to them are involved in interference proceedings. The parties may decide to enter into an interference settlement agreement under which they agree to decide between themselves which party has the earlier invention date and agree in advance that the winning party will grant a licence on reasonable terms to the other. The interference proceedings in the Patent Office can then be terminated by consent, a patent for the claims involved in the interference being granted to the party agreed to have the earlier date.

Commercial licences

A completely different type of licence is one which is entered into not to gain freedom to pursue one's own project but to take over a project or a product which originated elsewhere. Whereas the first type usually involves a non-exclusive patent licence or immunity from suit, without any know-how being involved, the second type may be broadly described as transfer of technology, which normally involves rights to confidential know-how as well as under patents, such rights often being exclusive.

Commercial licences of this type form the major part of licensing activities between industrial companies, and where the licensor and licensee are in different countries, the net flow of royalty payments can have a significant effect upon balances of payments. In 1983 for example, United Kingdom companies paid a total of £482 million in royalties for technology to recipients abroad, but received £615 million in royalties from other countries, that is, a positive technology balance of £133 million. Typically European countries have tended to have technology exports roughly comparable with their imports, whereas the USA has been a large net exporter of technology and Japan a large importer, although Japanese companies now license out more and more inventions. For developing countries, most of which must import all the technology they need and have little or none to export, the strain upon their balance of payments can be very great.

Potential licensees

Within the industrialized countries, however, what types of companies wish to license-in technology, and under what circumstances? One type is the small company which lacks the facilities to do basic research of its own and wishes to buy the products of others' research. This approach was essentially that adopted by Japanese industry in the last 25 years after the war, and proved very successful on the national scale. On the scale of an individual company, however, it is not easy for a small company to find suitable products. If the licensor is another small company or a university, the licensor will normally seek a licensee with the market strength and technological facilities to develop the project rapidly. If the licensor is a large company the small licensee will be in danger of being swallowed up or becoming a mere distributor.

A second type of potential licensee is a larger, research-based company which wishes to expand its product line or investigate areas new to it. No matter how good a company's research department may be, it cannot investigate everything and will naturally concentrate its activities in certain areas of particular interest to the company. If the company wishes to branch out into other fields, there will inevitably be a long lead-time before its own research activities, starting from scratch, can produce anything of commercial interest. This gap can best be bridged by licensing-in a project which is already on the market, or nearly so. Even if a completely new field is not involved, weak points in the research programme can be strengthened by licensing-in projects which may be in a somewhat earlier stage of development.

A third type of situation arises when a company, large or small, is established in a particular business and an invention is made by another company of such basic importance to that business that all companies involved practically must take a licence (assuming the patentee is willing to grant licences). Naturally, this does not occur very often, but a good example is the patent on oil-extended synthetic rubber for vehicle tyres, held by General Tire Co., which was licensed to a number of other tyre companies and infringed by most of the others (an infringement action against Firestone was successful in the United Kingdom).[1]

Potential licensors

Taking again the example of the large research-based company which wants to license-in projects to supplement its own research, where should the company look for such projects? One possibility is from university research, either from individual academic scientists, in so far as they own rights in their own inventions, or from the universities or other organizations which do own the rights. Such projects will often be in a relatively early stage of development, and will require considerable effort and investment by the licensor.

A further possibility is licensing-in from other large companies. Here, however, a certain amount of caution is needed, and the potential licensee should always try to find the answer to the obvious question 'if this project is so great, why aren't they doing it themselves?' Often there is a satisfactory answer, particularly if the licensor company has decided that it has no further interest in a particular area in which it was previously involved, and all projects within that area, no matter how promising, are being offered for licence. It may be, however, that the project is one which has been dropped because it has some defect, and unless the potential licensee knows he can cure it, he is better to decline the offer with thanks.

The best source of licence projects for a multinational company is the smaller, national, research-based company which can cope with its home market adequately but which does not have the resources to launch a product on the market in a number of different countries. Such a company, having a project which looks as if it may be a commercial success, often wishes to enter into a licensing agreement whereby it retains all rights in its home country and grants an exclusive licence to a multinational company for all other countries.

This is particularly true in the pharmaceutical industry, in which marketing a product is a lengthy and very expensive process because the permission of the health authorities in each country must first be obtained. Since no Japanese pharmaceutical companies are yet in a position to sell directly in Europe or the USA (except through a small number of joint venture companies with local partners), Japanese companies are an important source of licence projects. The number of research-based national pharmaceutical companies in Europe is small and is in danger of declining further as the cost of developing new drugs continues to rise.

The NIH syndrome

Wherever the licence project may come from, its further development within the licensee company is often precarious. This is particularly the case where it must compete for resources with other projects which originated within the company. It is a fact of life that very few inventions, even those made within a company research department, succeed purely upon their own merits. If an invention develops into a commercial product it is usually because someone within the company (often, but not always, the inventor) feels strongly enough about it to push it along, to argue for it before the research manager or the board, and to fight for its existence when necessary.

The project licensed in from outside does not so easily find a champion. The inventor, who is the most likely candidate for this role, is not an employee of the company, and the person responsible for finding the project will often be someone in a staff group such as a patents or licensing department who is not directly involved in decisions about the subsequent development of the project.

Not only does the licence project often lack the positive effect of having a champion, it frequently arouses negative feelings from within the company, feelings which may be unconscious but are nevertheless real. It is easy for research workers to feel they are being slighted if their own efforts have to take second place to the inventions of others, and this feeling may spread to other parts of the company too.

All this adds up to what has often been called NIH-syndrome – Not Invented Here. It is a real problem for the development of licence projects, and any company management which plans to use such projects to supplement its own research must give serious thought to how to combat it. One possible method is to involve research workers more closely in the seeking out and evaluation of licence projects. This would help to avoid the impression that such projects are foisted upon research by some remote head office department, and by involving the research worker who found the project in its subsequent development, the necessary champion for the project may emerge.

Finding a licensee

There is unlikely to be a licence agreement unless the potential licensor and licensee are able to get in touch with each other and exchange information on what each party wants or has to offer. Between large and medium sized companies in the same business area this is most usually done by personal contacts and word of mouth. When the potential licence project arises from a small company or a university department, finding a licensee may be more difficult. A small company having patent rights it wishes to license may advertize in the trade literature, or even in the *Official Journal (Patents)*, or write directly to firms which may be interested. It may be more useful to employ the services of a reputable licensing consultant, who may be able to match up licensor and licensee from his previous experience, and who will if requested negotiate the agreement on behalf of his client. Firms of patent agents may also undertake to seek licensees for their client's patents.

For inventions made in university laboratories, the situation will depend upon who owns the patent rights. If, as is usually the case in the United Kingdom, the research was funded by government grants, for example from the Department of Scientific and Industrial Research or the Medical Research Council, then the grant-giving body may require that rights in inventions made in the course of the work be assigned to the National Research Development Corporation (NRDC) which at present forms part of the British Technology Group (BTG). The involvement of the NRDC used to be obligatory, but is now optional, and whereas the NRDC is required to give priority to British companies when licensing out inventions, the university or the inventor may now directly license a foreign company.

Royalties received by the NRDC are shared with the university where the work was done, which may share it further with the inventors. The money retained by the NRDC can be made available as loans to small businesses lacking the necessary funds to develop inventions which they have made.

The NRDC has made a great deal of money by successfully licensing the basic patents on cephalosporin antibiotics, all the more so because it was able to secure an extension of the term of these patents in the United Kingdom. It has been less successful in getting smaller inventions off the laboratory bench and into industrial development, and industrial companies which have dealings with the NRDC often find it to be overly bureaucratic in its approach.

In the USA, the Research Corporation is a privately founded non-profit organization which attempts to do the same type of job as the NRDC in Britain, that is, it can take over from the university the task of patenting the invention, finding a licensee and negotiating a suitable agreement. The Research Corporation does not automatically own the patent rights it deals with, but may take assignment of the patents as part of an agreement whereby any licence royalties are divided between the university and the corporation.

Many larger universities in the USA now have their own patent attorneys and deal directly with their own patents, which may be assigned either to the university or to a foundation such as the Wisconsin Alumni

Research Foundation. There is even an organization called the Society of University Patent Administrators, through which it is possible to obtain information about projects available for license from the member universities. At present there is no such organization in the United Kingdom, although some years ago there were plans to set up something similar at Nuffield College, Oxford.

Where government funding of academic research has been involved in the USA, the government does not as a rule take title to the patent rights, but may insist on certain conditions to any licences which may be granted, and a fully exclusive licence will generally not be possible because the government will retain non-exclusive licence rights. The object of US policy is to disseminate the results as broadly as possible for the general good of the public.

The individual inventor

So far we have not discussed the role of the private individual inventor as licensor, and indeed in the chemical field the chances of a 'back yard' inventor being able to make a significant invention are somewhat remote. This is in contrast to the mechanical field, where the resources required for experimentation are much smaller, and many ingenious devices, some of which are actually useful and potentially commercial are invented by individuals in their own time. Even in the chemical field individual inventors may own the rights to their own inventions, whether they be totally independent, academic scientists whose university does not lay claim to their inventions, or employees whose inventions belong to them under the provisions of the UK Patents Act 1977. Any of these individuals will usually lack the means to develop the invention themselves and will be interested in finding a suitable licensee.

The first step in the process, *before* publishing the invention, is for the inventor to consult a patent agent and get a patent application on file, thereby giving himself a priority date for his invention and protecting himself against the consequences of non-confidential disclosure. This is also a protection for any company which may look into the possibility of taking a licence. Suppose the company itself had a similar project under development and that it was in the process of filing a patent application. The information it received from the outside inventor might be of no use to the company, but if it declined the offer and then shortly afterwards filed a patent application for a closely similar invention, then the outside inventor would certainly feel that the company had stolen the invention from him. To avoid the danger of being unjustly accused of theft or breach of confidence, many companies (particularly those making mechanical gadgets, which frequently receive unsolicited offers from inventors) refuse to look at any invention submitted to them unless it is already the subject of a patent application. In the USA, some large companies try to protect their interests by accepting information only on a non-confidential basis. This is unfair to the inventor, since not only does it leave him without redress if the company should steal his ideas, but also it will prevent him form obtaining valid patent protection outside the USA unless he has already filed a US patent application.

The problem is that from the date of filing the priority application, only nine months or so remains before a decision on foreign filing must be taken and substantial sums of money must be spent on patenting. This is scarcely enough time for the inventor to contact companies which may be interested, or for the companies to evaluate the idea. In case it should be necessary to abandon and refile the application, all communication of the invention should preferably be done under conditions of confidentiality; this of course would preclude the inventor from demonstrating his invention at minor exhibitions, or advertizing it generally to the public in any way. If no licensee has been found by the end of the priority year, and there has been any non-confidential publication, the inventor will have to either abandon hopes of foreign patent protection or else find the money for foreign filing from his own resources.

It is in this type of situation that the NRDC could be very useful to the small inventor. Unfortunately its terms of reference apparently preclude it from supporting minor inventions whose patentability is questionable (as indeed it is in most cases). The NRDC is not set up to meet the needs of the individual inventor, and there is no other organization in the United Kingdom which is.

In Sweden, by contrast, there is a national invention scheme which will lend money to individuals or small companies with new inventions. The loans are repayable at high interest rates if the projects become commercially successful, but are written off if the projects fail.

In 1935, the basic British patent of Frank Whittle for the jet engine was allowed to lapse because a government department refused to pay the renewal fee of £5, and Whittle could not afford to pay it himself. One wonders how many Whittles are in a similar position in Britain today.

Whereas in the United Kingdom the individual inventor finds no one willing to help him, his counterpart in the USA must beware of a form of help which may turn out to be no more than an elaborate confidence trick. A number of organizations recently flourished there which described themselves as Invention Promotion Agencies, and which offered inventors an expert evaluation of their invention as well as assistance in finding a licensee. In fact many such organizations charged the inventor a substantial initial fee, produced a glowingly optimistic 'evaluation' of the invention on the basis of which they persuaded the inventor to part with more money for licensing the invention, and then merely sent some routine promotional material to a few companies selected at random.

Not only did such firms consistently fail to make any money for their clients (one of the more notorious admitted that of 30 000 clients, only three had received in royalties more than they had paid in fees), but by publishing the inventions they prevented the inventor from obtaining valid patent protection. Fortunately the Federal Trade Commission investigated some of these firms and has stamped out the worst of the abuses, but US inventors should remain wary of such organizations.

When an individual inventor does find a company which is interested in the possibility of a licence, he must not expect instant riches from his invention. The invention is likely to be at a relatively early stage of development, and to require a lot of investment and effort before it reaches the market place. The more investment the licensee must make and the more risk it must take the less it will be prepared to pay in royalties.

An extreme example of this is a new compound which might be useful as a pharmaceutical. A company might be willing to pay a royalty of 10 per cent on net sales for a licence for a pharmaceutical which already had regulatory approval. But for a mere new compound which may show some sign of pharmacological activity in some *in vitro* test, and for which a programme of testing and development lasting many years must be undertaken before it could ever be sold, no company would be willing to offer a royalty of more than 0.5–1 per cent. Of course, even a royalty of 0.5 per cent on sales of a successful pharmaceutical would be a very large sum of money for an individual.

Option agreements

If, as is usual, the company will require some time to evaluate the project to the point where it can decide if it really wants a licence, it is common practice to enter into an option agreement, whereby the company has a limited period of time (perhaps 1–2 years) in which to make up its mind and by the end of which it must either enter into a licence agreement or leave the inventor free to offer his invention elsewhere. In return for the option rights, the company may pay the inventor a lump sum, or may for example offer to pay the costs of foreign filing the patent application, or, if the company has its own patents department, to carry out the foreign filing itself, in the inventor's name. Academic inventors may be interested in obtaining funds for further research in exchange for option rights, and essentially any agreement which meets the needs of both parties may be entered into.

Licence contracts

When it comes to entering into a licence agreement, whether between two multinational corporations, or between a small company and an individual, a suitable contract must be drafted which accurately expresses what has been agreed in the negotiations between the parties. The production of a first draft may be no more than a stage in the negotiations, and gives a certain tactical advantage to the party which writes the draft. The other party may require numerous amendments, or produce a draft of his own; at any rate when all disputes have been resolved the final version must be clear and unambiguous.

Drafting a licence agreement

There are different styles of contract drafting in different countries, and a typical contract covering exactly the same terms might be three pages long in Germany, ten in the United Kingdom, and thirty in the USA. A UK view is that continental practice expresses the intent of the agreement in terms which are often somewhat general and imprecise, while American practice runs to excessive legal jargon and unnecessary verbiage. A contract should be written in language which is clear, grammatical, and as simple as possible without losing the main object of precision. As the facts of each licensing situation are different, 'boilerplate', or standard clauses, should be avoided as much as possible.

The worst fault a contract can have is ambiguity. An agreement is clearly on a very shaky footing if it could be reached only because a certain clause in the contract was vague enough to be interpreted one way by one party and differently by the other. This is standard practice in diplomatic joint communiqués, but is a recipe for disaster in a business relationship which will fail unless there is trust on both sides.

It may also happen that a clause is recognized to be ambiguously worded, but it is decided to leave it as it is because the negotiatiors of both sides agree fully what is meant by it. That is all very well at the time, but ten years later the negotiators may have changed jobs, retired, or died and the problem will rear its head when no one remembers what the original intention was.

While one should not use standard clauses to any great extent in drafting agreements, a check-list of what sort of clauses to include may be very useful. The contract should provide not only for what is intended to happen, but also for what may happen if things go wrong – what happens if the parties change ownership, the patents are infringed, the licensee makes no sales, and any other hazards which can be foreseen. A typical straightforward patent licence agreement, without trademarks being involved and with no provision for supply of materials or technical co-operation between the parties, might have a structure something like the following:

A	Preamble	1	Parties
		2	Reasons for agreement
		3	Definitions
		4	Schedule of licensed patents
B	Grant	1	Extent
		2	Exclusivity
		3	Sublicensing rights
		4	Know-how
C	Consideration	1	Down payment
		2	Royalties
		3	Mechanism of payment
D	Patent provisions	1	Maintenance in force
		2	Policing of infringement
		3	Third-party rights
E	General provisions	1	Exploitation
		2	Quality control
		3	Developments
		4	Most favoured licensee
		5	Duration and termination
F	Legal framework	1	Language
		2	Applicable law
		3	Arbitration
		4	Severability
		5	Approval of authorities

The points which would arise under the above headings are discussed briefly below:

A   Preamble

1   *Parties*: names, addresses, legal status.

2   *Reasons*: brief explanation, often in the form of one or more 'whereas clauses', reciting that A wishes a licence from B and B is willing to grant it.

3   *Definitions*: e.g. of terms such as 'subsidiary', 'associate', 'territory' (whole world, United Kingdom only, etc.), as well as the technical field involved. If the licence is for one particular compound, 'compound' can be defined by its chemical name and formula.

4   *Schedule of patents*: normally referred to here and added as an annex to the agreement. Should contain pending applications as well as granted patents.

B Grant

1 *Extent*: is the licence to make, to use or to sell, or more than one of these? Is the whole scope of the patent licensed or just a part of it (perhaps only one compound)?
2 *Exclusivity*: is the licence exclusive, sole, or non-exclusive?
3 *Sublicensing rights*: can the licensee grant sublicences? If so, to anyone, or just to his subsidiaries or customers?
4 *Know-how*: may take the form of operating manuals, test results, registration documents, loan of technical staff, etc. What provisions are there for keeping this know-how confidential?

C Consideration

1 *Down payment*: a licensor may want a down payment sufficient to cover his patenting costs, and perhaps a percentage of his development costs.
2 *Royalty*: (a) a lump sum or running royalty?
   (b) how calculated – price per unit of production, percentage of profit, percentage of net selling price? Should percentage royalty decrease with increasing sales?
   (c) should there be a minimum annual royalty requirement; if so, for how long?
3 *Mechanism of payment*: when payable (quarterly, half-yearly?), where and in what currency. Provisions for exchange rate fluctuations. Licensee should keep accounts, open to inspection by accountant appointed by licensor.

D Patent provisions

1 *Maintenance in force*: the licensor normally undertakes to maintain the patents in force. Alternatively, he may give the licensee the option of taking over any patents he may wish to drop.
2 *Policing of infringement*: the licensee may wish the licensor to take action against any infringer but the licensee may refuse such an open-ended commitment. The parties may agree to consult together about infringement and to share the costs of any action as well as any damages received. An alternative which gives the licensor an incentive to take action but does not commit him to doing so is to provide that the royalty reduces by half in any country in which substantial (to be defined) unlicensed competition appears and is not stopped within a certain time. The same provision allows for loss of exclusivity should patents be found invalid, or patent applications not be granted.
3 *Third party rights*: a licensor will not normally be willing to indemnify

his licensee against possible infringement of third party patents. A possible compromise is for the royalty to reduce by the amount which may have to be paid to third parties, but only up to an agreed limit.

E   General provisions

1   *Exploitation*: the licensee should use his best endeavours to exploit. If he fails, there may be provision for the licence to terminate or to go from exclusive to non-exclusive. Minimum royalty requirements may have the same effect, but the licensor should not be satisfied with a minimum royalty indefinitely, and may provide for termination or non-exclusivity if only minimum royalties are paid for two or three years running.

2   *Quality control*: will the licensor have rights of inspection to control quality of goods manufactured under the licence? Should the licensee mark the goods with the licensor's name, patent number, or trademark?

3   *Developments*: are there cross-licensing rights to developments made by either party during the agreement? Must the parties communicate all developments to the other, or give clearance for any publications?

4   *Most favoured licensee*: if the licence is non-exclusive, such a clause promises that if any subsequent licences are offered on more favourable terms, the first licensee will be offered the same terms.

5   *Duration and termination*: is the duration for the life of a single patent, the last to expire of a series or for some defined longer or shorter term? Under what conditions (e.g. default, change of ownership of a party) can the licence be terminated earlier? What obligations (e.g. confidentiality of know-how) continue after termination?

F   Legal framework

1   *Language*: if there are texts in more than one language, which one is authentic?

2   *Applicable law*: under the legal system of which country (state, canton) will the contract be interpreted?

3   *Arbitration*: should there be provisions for arbitration, e.g. by the International Chamber of Commerce?

4   *Severability*: a clause to spell out the intention that if any clauses be found inoperative or illegal, the remainder of the agreement will not be affected.

5   *Approval of authorities*: if approval from or registration with a national authority, or notification to the EEC Commission is required, which party should apply for it?

Such a list should be no more than a guideline, and it should always be remembered that in many countries, and within the EEC, parties are not wholly free to reach whatever agreement seems best to them, but are subject to anti-trust laws, EEC Commission Regulations, and rules of national authorities. These problems are dealt with in more detail in Part IV of this book.

19

PATENTS AND INFORMATION

Now, what I want is, Facts. . . Facts alone are wanted in life.
Charles Dickens, *Hard Times*

The increasing volume of patent literature

Published patents and patent applications are important sources of information. Primarily, of course, patents which are granted and in force give information by way of their claims about what areas of activity are the subject of monopoly rights and are not free to be used by the public, and published applications indicate potential monopoly rights. This is the information which one needs when carrying out an infringement search to determine whether one's proposed activity infringes anyone else's patent rights.

Secondly, all patent publications are part of the prior art and the information contained in them is relevant to the question of whether or not a later invention is new and non-obvious. This information is necessary for a patentability search. What is more, recently published patents and applications in a particular field can be an important source of up-to-date technical information not only for the scientist employed in industry, but also for the academic chemist. This 'current awareness' approach to the patent literature can of course also be directed to keeping an eye on the patenting activities of competitors, by selecting the literature by name of applicants instead of, or as well as, by subject matter.

The amount of patent literature which may have to be searched is constantly increasing, since every year further hundreds of thousands of documents are added to the mountain of material which already exists. Not only that, but changes in patent systems in recent years have greatly multiplied the number of documents issued each year which may be relevant for search purposes.

In the United Kingdom, for example, at one time the only documents which needed to be considered in an infringement search were British patent specifications. Now one also has published British patent applications, which give early warning of potential patent rights but which do not permit evaluation of the precise scope of such rights, since the claims may well be reduced in scope during prosecution. In addition to early published British applications, one has to consider European patents and published European applications, as well as International (PCT) patents and applications, in so far as these include the United Kingdom among their designated countries.

This additional flood of documents makes the job of a patent searcher more difficult, and makes it more important than ever to have effective means for obtaining information *about* patents. Information about patents may help to identify current applications or granted patents relevant to particular subjects or originating from particular companies, to investigate the status of a patent or application, to find equivalent patents in other countries, or to evaluate the validity of a patent which is in force.

Patents as a source of technical information

A patent is basically a legal document whose main purpose is to define a legal ·right. Because of this, it is usually written in a style which is unfamiliar to most chemists, and which differs considerably from the style of a paper in a scientific journal. Nevertheless, it must contain a legally sufficient description of the invention which it claims, and this may be very useful to the academic as well as the industrial chemist, especially in certain fields in which there is considerable research activity by large companies and where new advances may well be published in the patent literature long before they appear in the journals.

The chemist who is interested in patents purely for their technical information content will find it easier to extract the information he wants if he reads the specification selectively, concentrating upon the abstract, the statement of invention (or the main claim) and the examples and skipping the preferred scopes and sub-scopes.

The abstract of a British patent specification is a useful aid to gleaning technical information. It should be possible for the reader to tell from the title whether he need read the abstract, and from the abstract whether he should read the whole specification. Under the 1949 Act, the examiner wrote an abridgement of the specification which was intended to be used as the basis for future searching within the Patent Office, and which was also very useful for outside searchers. Under the 1977 Act, the applicant must supply an abstract, and although the examiner may re-write this if it is not satisfactory, professional searchers fear that the abstracts will not be so useful for search purposes as the old abridgements.

Unlike the abridgements, the abstract is printed with the published application, but it does not form part of the specification and may not be used for interpretation of the scope of protection. The USA and a number of other countries also require abstracts to be filed with the application or within a certain time after filing.

Unlike a journal article, the patent will generally contain no theoretical discussion of reaction mechanism or why the invention works; this is usually omitted in case it should be incorrect or, if correct, should make the invention seem obvious. The reader may also find non-standard nomenclature or even newly-coined technical terms; this is permissible in patent specifications so long as a definition is given.

There are also marked differences between the examples of a typical patent and the experimental section of a scientific paper, even if both are describing the synthesis of new compounds. As already described, the patent will normally give at least one example in full detail (often consideraby more detail than would be thought necessary for a scientific journal), followed by a list of other examples in tabular form. The practice in writing a scientific paper is normally to present all examples in essentially the same relatively short length.

Academic scientists are sometimes distrustful of patents as sources of scientific information, and this may well be due to the fact that many, if not most, chemical patents contain what we have called 'paper examples' which were never actually carried out. Of course, an author of a scientific publication who added 'paper examples' to his text would rightly be considered guilty of fraud on the scientific community, and it is perhaps natural for scientists to feel that the same should apply to authors of patents. The cases are not the same, however. The inclusion of a paper example in a patent is not a false representation that the compound has been made; it is an honest representation that it is predictable that the compound can be made in that way. The reader may be assured that in the vast majority of cases, examples in chemical patents which are given in full detail, with physical data such as melting points for the products, are completely reliable scientific information.

Industrial chemists and chemical engineers may also be sceptical about the value of patents as information sources because many patents do not contain sufficient information to put the invention into immediate commercial practice. This is particularly true for inventions relating to new compounds, and the reason is quite clear. The patent is normally written in the early stages of a project when the patentee himself has not scaled it up to industrial production. The synthesis described in the patent may be a good laboratory process, but may be found to be totally unsuitable for large-scale production. A great deal of further work, mostly of a routine nature, may be necessary before a commercially feasible manufacturing process can be developed. The patent is required to disclose the invention; it is not required to, and indeed can not, disclose all its subsequent development. A patent is not meant to be an operating manual, patent drawings are not engineering blueprints, and a patent example cannot necessarily be expected to work on a ten ton scale. However, where the patent relates to improvements in an established industrial process, it can reasonably be expected that the data it contains will be directly applicable to commercial practice.

Availability of patents

Copies of British patent specifications or published applications are sold by the publications branch of the Patent Office for a sum which is the same whether the specification consists of a single sheet or, as one patent dealing with computers, four volumes running to over 1000 pages. It is possible to subscribe to receive a copy of all patents issuing within a certain classification heading (see below) and copies of all patents within a broad technical category such as pharmaceuticals or agrochemicals can be supplied on microfilm by Derwent Publications.

Copies of all British patents and published applications are available for inspection on the shelves of the Science Reference Library (Holborn Branch), 25 Southampton Buildings, London WC2 (SRL). The SRL also has a full set of European and PCT published applications, and of granted European patents. It should be noted that a European patent designating the UK is not printed separately by the British patent office, and since the UK is one of the few EPC countries which does not require the text to be translated, these patents, equivalent in effect to British patents, may be published only in French or German. Similarly, a PCT application designating the UK is given a British application number when it enters the national phase, but a search under the application number will produce only a title page, with a reference to the PCT publication, which may be in French, German, Japanese, or Russian.

The SRL also has extensive collections of foreign patents from all major countries, as well as early-published applications from Germany, France, and Holland.

In addition to the SRL, a total of 27 libraries throughout the UK have various holdings of UK, European, PCT, and foreign patent publications, and in all of these, as in the SRL, copies may be inspected free of charge and photocopies may be taken on payment of a fee for each page copied.

Copies of US patents are similarly available from the US Patent Office and from a number of libraries throughout the country. The search room of the US Patent Office in Crystal City, Arlington, Virginia also has US patents arranged by classification to facilitate subject matter searches.

Information about patents

Subject matter searches
With the increasing quantity and diversity of patent literature and the increasing complexity of information retrieval systems, carrying out a full

patentability or infringement search is today a job for a professional
information scientist, and no more than a brief outline of some of the
available methods can be given here.

There are four main sources of information about patent literature
which are accessible on the basis of subject matter classification. These are
national patent offices, *Chemical Abstracts*, Derwent Publications, and
INPADOC.

The British Patent Office uses a classification system according to
which the technical subject matter is allocated to one of eight sections,
designated by letters A–H as follows:

A   human necessities;
B   performing operations;
C   chemistry;
D   textiles and paper;
E   engineering and building accessories;
F   mechanics, heating and lighting;
G   instrumentation; and
H   electricity

Each of these sections is divided into from two to eight divisions
(designated by number) and each division into a number of headings
(designated by letter again). There are a total of approximately 400
headings from A1A (fishing) to H5R (radiology and radiography). Further
subdivision is carried out to give a very large number of classmarks, which
go into considerable detail, and are updated from time to time.

The Patent Office publishes a guide to the classification system
including a Catchword Index by means of which the most relevant
classmark for a particular field of invention may be found. Searching may
then be carried out using collected volumes of abridgements of old Act
patents or abstracts of new Act applications and patents in which there is a
listing of the patent or application numbers classified under each
classmark. Alternatively, file lists can be purchased from the Patent Office;
these are computer print-outs of all patent and published application
numbers classified under any specified classmark. As most patents have
more than one classmark, cross-referencing can be done between two file
lists in order to find patents having both of two classmarks, and in some
areas this can be done directly by the Patent Office computer.

This file list service now includes EPC and PCT applications and
patents designating the United Kingdom, although since these originally
will have only the International Patent Classification (IPC), there is a time-
lag during which they are reclassified according to the British system.
British patents and applications are also allocated an IPC by the Patent
Office, but the IPC system is less detailed and less flexible than the British

one. This may be seen from a recent study comparing the classification of 250 British patents in one product area; an average of 6.4 British classmarks and only 1.6 IPCs were allocated to each patent. Other studies have shown that examiners in different countries are inconsistent in their use of IPC, and that searches based on IPC give poor results compared with either the British or US systems.

The British classification system was developed primarily for the use of Patent Office examiners in conducting novelty searches, but has also proved a very useful tool for outside searchers, both in patentability and infringement searches. One disadvantage of the system is that at certain times it has placed emphasis mainly on the classification of the inventive step rather than on the technical field of application of the invention, which can lead to what appear to be very odd classifications. It has been suggested that it would be useful if the published patent included a classification according to the Standard Industrial Classification (SIC) used in many countries to classify industrial products.

Since the 1977 Act came into force, a number of professional searchers have expressed fears that the high standard of the British classification system is being lowered. A possible reason for this is that now that examiners must search not only in a narrow field for novelty, but also more broadly in related fields for obviousness, there is no longer a need for so detailed a system within the Patent Office. At any rate it appears that the number of cross-references; i.e. the number of classmarks cited under different headings, is declining and this is making subject matter searches more difficult.

Today, the majority of patent searches are carried out by way of computer terminals which may be linked telephonically to any of a number of available databases. Some of these databases contain only bibliographic data and are of more use for equivalence searching (see below). Others store abstracts, claims, title pages, or even complete texts of patents.

Chemical Abstracts (CA), published by the Ohio State University, abstracts both patents and scientific literature in the chemical field. The information retrieval system is based on a CA registry number allocated to every published chemical compound; once this has been identified, abstracts of all patents or literature articles mentioning the compound can be listed, and printed out if required. In addition it is possible to use a graphics system in which a structure is drawn with a light pen on the screen of a suitable terminal, and abstracts relevant to the structure are identified by the system. The bound volumes of indexes of CA which are available in many libraries can be used by the individual scientist who does not have access to a computer-based information retrieval system.

Derwent Publications Ltd. provides a wide range of abstracting and information retrieval systems, including the WPI (World Patent Index) database. This includes all patents in the major countries issued since 1974, and in some areas includes patents of earlier date. Thus pharmaceutical patents are available from 1963, agrochemical from 1965, plastics and polymers from 1966, and all chemical patents from 1970. Patents published from 1981 onwards are in a separate database designated WPIL (L for latest). Searches can be made on the basis of keywords or of partial structures of chemical compounds. Derwent also have a database covering all publications and patents in the field of biotechnology since 1982.

For US patents only, Derwent has a database containing abstracts and all claims of all US patents issued from 1970 on. Similar US patent databases are Claims (IFI Plenum Data) which gives the abstract and main claim of chemical patents from 1950 and all US patents from 1963; Lexpat (Mead Data) from which the complete text of any US patent from 1975 onwards can be retrieved; and Video-Patsearch (Pergamon/Infoline), which stores the title page of each patent in video format.

For Japan, the database JAPIO has been available from the end of 1985, and gives English-language abstracts of all Japanese early-published applications from 1976 onwards. As of 1986, similar databases for German and British patents were being prepared.

Current awareness

Although a company library may receive copies of all British or other patents relevant to a particular area, it would be unduly time-consuming for the company's scientific employees to have to read through all of these in order to keep abreast of current developments. It is much more sensible to rely on an abstracting service such as *Chemical Abstracts*, Derwent, or one of the more specialized abstracting services specific to a particular industry. Here, Derwent certainly provides the greatest possibilities, with abstracts appearing 2–3 months after issue both in *Country Bulletins* for each of the major industrial countries and in *Alerting Bulletins* classified by subject matter. Abstracts can be provided in volumes, on file cards or microfilm, and various indexing systems are available.

An example of an abstracting service provided by a Research Association for a particular industry is that of the Rubber and Plastics Research Association (RAPRA). RAPRA has a database for computer searching, but relatively few patents are included.

In the USA, abstracts of each of the 2000 or so patents issued every Tuesday are published by the US Patent Office in the *Official Gazette*. Although they appear in numerical order, the patent numbers are assigned in such a way that they will appear in the order of the US classification system, so that patents relevant to a particular field can be located relatively easily.

The corresponding publication of the British Patent Office, the

Official Journal (Patents), does not publish abstracts, but unlike the *Official Gazette* it gives information (filing date, application no., applicant, title, and priority data) about new applications as well as more detailed information about newly published applications and granted patents. It can thus be useful as a current guide to the patenting activities of competitors.

Seven-figure publication numbers of published applications under the 1977 Act are, like US patent numbers, allocated so that they appear in order of classification headings when set out in numerical order. The *Official Journal* also indexes published applications by the original application number and by the name of the applicant, and lists applications which have been withdrawn or refused, patents which have been allowed to lapse or have expired and patents for which applications for amendment or revocation have been made. It contains official notices about Patent Office procedures and services, and is also the main vehicle for job advertisements within the British patent profession.

Journals similar to these are published by other national patent offices and by the EPO and by WIPO (for PCT applications).

Equivalence searches

For the purposes of an infringement search, it is often very important to locate equivalents of a given patent or application in other countries. This cannot be done immediately an early published application appears, but after about two years from the priority date it should be possible to locate all early published equivalent applications (e.g. in the United Kingdom, Germany, France, Holland, and Japan) and after about five years most granted equivalent patents should be locatable.

The best source of information on equivalents is the Inpadoc database, available through Pergamon/Infoline, which stores bibliographic data on all patents from 1974 onwards. By input of a single patent or application number for one country, a complete list of all published equivalents is printed out, together with title, applicant, inventors, priority dates, and cited prior art. For very recent publications a separate databank called Inpanew stores data on patents published within the last three months.

For patents older than 1974, Chemical Abstracts has published concordances of equivalent patents, although these are likely to be incomplete.

If the matter is important, it may be necessary to make enquiries through local agents in each country for which the information is needed.

Status searches

When relevant patent rights have been found in the course of an infringement search, the questions arise whether, in the case of an application, it has been granted and whether, in the case of a patent, it is still in force. Further information such as whether the patent has been amended, has been assigned or licensed, or has been endorsed 'licences of right' may also be necessary.

For each granted British patent, a new page is opened in the statutory Register of Patents, which contains the name of the patentee, the patent number, and data about filing dates, priorities claimed, publication date, etc. It does not contain any information about the technical content of the patent, other than the title. The date on which each renewal fee is paid is entered into the Register, and when the patent lapses for non-payment of renewal fees, this fact is recorded.

The Register, together with a subsidiary register listing all recorded assignments or licences under the patent, is available for inspection at the Patent Office, and copies of the Register for a particular patent may be obtained there or ordered by post. There is also a list of the status of granted patents which is kept in the SRL, and which does not have the statutory authority of the Register. A telephone inquiry to the SRL will be answered by checking the list there; the answer will very probably be correct, but as there is a time-lag between an entry in the main Register and its transmittal to the SRL list, it may not be wholly accurate. If the matter is important it is best to inspect the Register itself.

For a pending application, there is a card index in the SRL in which all the applications for each calendar year are arranged in alphabetical order of applicant. These lists go back seven years, by which time all applications must either have been granted, refused, or withdrawn. There is also a non-statutory applications register which notes whether applications are granted, abandoned, or void and also notes divisional applications. Information from this register can also be obtained by telephone, but inspection of the card index is more reliable. The pending applications index now includes European and PCT applications designating the United Kingdom; information about other European applications must be obtained from Munich.

As well as checking the current status of a British patent application at the Patent Office, one can also arrange to be informed when a particular application is granted or abandoned. This is generally referred to as 'filing a caveat', and requires a form to be filed and fee to be paid; the Patent Office will then notify the inquirer as soon as the information is available.

The European Patent Office now has a database which gives on-line information as to the status of European applications. Using this system, one can check, for example, whether a particular application is being examined, or has been granted, or refused. By enquiry to the Inpadoc database in Vienna, one can check whether any of the patents in a family of equivalents has been granted and whether or not it remains in force.

In the USA, there has up to now been little occasion for any status searching, since no information is given about the status of pending US applications and a patent once granted automatically remained in force. It might however have been voluntarily abandoned by being dedicated to the public, and this could be checked, although with some difficulty. Now that renewal fees are payable on US patents, the US Patent Office will no doubt keep some form of record of which patents are still in force.

Validity searches

In carrying out a search directed to determining whether or not a patent is valid, one needs in addition to a general patentability search some specific information about the patent in question. Essentially one needs to know what specific prior art was cited against the patent during examination, and how the patentee overcame the cited prior art in his arguments to the examiner.

In the majority of countries, the prior art cited in prosecution is listed with the published patent, either on the title page as in the USA or in an attached search report as in France. In the United Kingdom one used to be able to find out what prior art had been cited only by filing a form and paying a fee; and then nine times out of ten one found that no art had been cited at all. Now the documents cited in the British Search report are listed on the title page of the published application, together with a note of the one or two classification headings under which the search was carried out. One therefore knows the scope of the Patent Office search as well as its results.

Furthermore, the entire file of the prosecution of the application is now open to public inspection as of the date of publication of the application. Previously, only the priority document and patent forms filed after the publication date of the accepted specification could be inspected as of right, and the prosecution file could be inspected only by court order in the course of infringement or revocation proceedings. There is therefore considerably more information available now than there was before 1978 upon which an opinion as to the validity of a British patent can be based.

Copies of the prosecution file of published patents or applications can also be obtained in a number of countries including USA and Germany, as well as the European Patent Office.

PART IV

THE POLITICS OF PATENTS

20

SOME FUNDAMENTAL CONFLICTS

. . .every new invention is bought up and suppressed by Breakages,
Ltd.,. . .these people can afford to pay an inventor more for his machine
or process or whatever it may be than he could hope to make by a legitimate
use of it; and when they have bought it they smother it.

G. B. Shaw: *The Apple Cart*

Charges against the patent system

From the days of Queen Elizabeth I onwards, monopolies have been seen as an economic evil, and patent monopolies have been recognized, more or less grudgingly, as a limited exception to this rule. The distinction that because a patent gives a monopoly for a new invention it cannot take anything away from the public which it already has is not always appreciated. Accordingly, patents have been blamed for a whole series of economic ills, real or imaginary, including high prices, erection of barriers to free trade, foreign domination of national economies, exploitation of developing countries, suppression of worthwhile inventions, and others.

Some of these charges are obviously false; for example the patent system, because it involves publication of the invention, clearly cannot be used to suppress inventions. If Bernard Shaw's Breakages, Ltd., wanted to buy up and smother inconvenient inventions it could do so more easily in the absence of any kind of patent system.

Another charge, that of foreign domination by patents, is often heard even in industrialized countries when someone compares the number of patents in his home country granted to foreigners with the number granted to local nationals, and finds to his horror that the foreign patentees are in the majority.

In recent years in Canada and Australia such arithmetical exercises have led to serious proposals to abolish the patent system altogether in these countries, and even in the USA the Commissioner of Patents expressed alarm in 1978 because the proportion of US patents being granted to Americans was declining.

Yet the situation of 'foreign domination' of patents is true for every country in the world, with the exceptions of the USA and Japan. If we consider that there are perhaps 20 industrialized countries whose nationals regularly file patent applications abroad, it is only to be expected that in any one of them the patents granted to all the other 19 put together will outnumber those granted to the nationals of that one country.

Abuse of monopoly

A patent monopoly, even if it is not in itself objectionable (as a monopoly on existing products would be), is nevertheless capable of being used in ways which may be regarded as undesirable or even illegal by various national governments and supranational organizations such as the EEC. Practically all countries, as well as the EEC, have developed counter-measures against what are regarded as abuses of monopoly by patentees: these are sometimes referred to collectively as anti-trust laws, although this term properly applies only to the US Sherman and Clayton Acts. In the following chapters we shall look in some detail at the situations in the USA, the EEC, the socialist countries, and the developing countries, each of which have their own special problems, leading to particular types of restriction being placed upon the use of patent rights.

United Kingdom

It has already been mentioned that in the majority of countries it is regarded as abuse of monopoly to use a patent simply to exclude others, while refusing to work the invention oneself. This type of abuse is dealt with by provisions enabling compulsory licences to be granted if the patent is not worked within a certain time, normally three years after grant, or even by the lapse of a patent if it is not worked. In the United Kingdom, compulsory licences may also be granted if the patentee is abusing his monopoly by not meeting demand for the product upon reasonable terms, or is preventing the working of a dependent patent by refusing to grant a licence. In the latter case, the owner of the dependent patent has to be prepared to grant a cross-licence. Compulsory licensing in the United Kingdom may also result from an investigation of the Monopolies Commission into a monopoly situation or merger which is considered to be against the public interest, and where a market in patented products is involved.

The Patents Act 1977, like the 1949 Act, also prohibits tie-in clauses in contracts; for example a licence contract entitling the licensee to manufacture a patented compound cannot compel him to purchase unpatented starting material from the licensor, or forbid him to obtain it from others. Such tie-in clauses are seen as a clear abuse of the patent monopoly, and have the effect of rendering the patent unenforceable, since it is a defence in an infringement action to show that a contract containing such a clause has been made by the patentee; this is so even where the defendant was not a party to the contract. The only way in which a tie-in clause can be legally made is if the contract gives the licensee a reasonable alternative (for example a lower royalty rate if he buys the starting material from the licensor) and if he can change to the alternative which does not require him to purchase the material upon giving three months' notice to the licensor.

Another form of abuse of monopoly which is prevented by United Kingdom patent law is that of granting a licence only on condition that royalty payments must continue even after the patent expires. The Patents Act provides that no matter what the contract may say, any licence agreement may be terminated on three months' notice once all the patents existing at the time the contract was made have ceased to be in force.

Apart from these specific restrictions, United Kingdom law leaves patentees and licensees free to work out their own agreements and put any clauses they like into them. Nevertheless, EEC law now takes precedence over national law, and there are a number of types of clauses in licence agreements which are considered by the EEC Commission to be illegal as being in violation of the Treaty of Rome. Licence agreements made in the United Kingdom must therefore comply with EEC requirements, at least if there is any chance that trade between EEC member states may be affected. Where there is no such effect, as for example a licence agreement between two small United Kingdom firms, relating only to the United Kingdom market, EEC regulations need not be considered.

An example of a clause permissible under English but not EEC law is a clause forbidding the licensee from challenging the validity of the licensed patent. In fact, such a clause would according to English law be implied in a licence agreement; a licensee has always been considered as estopped from challenging validity just as someone who rents land is estopped from challenging the owner's title once he has entered into the agreement. In the USA and where EEC law applies, however, such no-contest clauses are considered impermissible.

USA

Although the USA does not oblige the patentee to work his patented invention and there are no compulsory licence provisions, US law has generally taken a stricter view than does United Kingdom law of attempts to extend the patent monopoly beyond its legal scope, and has placed more restrictions on the freedom of a licensor. There are two main sources of US law in such matters: one is the common law doctrine of patent misuse, which as we have seen stems from the equitable 'clean hands' concept, the other is the statute law, particularly the Sherman and Clayton anti-trust acts. The basis of these laws is that all monopolies are bad and that patents are a strictly limited exception. The fact that US judges tend to be more familiar with anti-trust law than with industrial property law has led to very narrow interpretations of the rights given by a patent.

Since 1980, however, the US government has had a more permissive attitude to anti-trust matters generally, and patent licensing in particular, and this less rigid attitude is beginning to influence the courts.

EEC

The basis for EEC law is the Treaty of Rome, which is concerned with establishing a common market and abolishing barriers to the freedom of movement of goods between member states. This principle is in fundamental conflict with the territorially limited nature of patent rights. Until the day when the Community Patent Convention comes into force and there is a single unitary patent for all of the EEC, the only patent rights within the EEC are national patents, and these can in principle be used to stop importation of patented goods. For example, if a product is on the market in Germany and is the subject of a French patent, then a priori the French patentee should be able to prevent importation of the product from Germany into France.

Nevertheless, the provisions of the Treaty of Rome have been interpreted by the European Court of Justice to mean that such importation cannot be prevented if the goods were put upon the market in Germany by the owner of the French patent or with his consent. Restrictions on the exercise of patent rights and on the types of clauses permissible in licence agreements within the EEC are dealt with more fully in Chapter 21.

Socialist countries

There would at first sight appear to be an irreconcilable conflict between a patent system and a fully socialist economy; if all enterprises are state-owned, then if an enterprise obtains a patent the state is merely granting to itself exclusive rights which it already has. In practice, most socialist countries have a dual system; inventor's certificates, giving no monopoly rights, are granted to their own nationals as a form of recognition, while foreign patentees can obtain patents of the traditional monopoly type, just as state-owned enterprises of socialist countries may obtain patents abroad.

Developing countries

In developing countries of the Third World, there are severe problems because the majority of these countries badly need imported technology in order to build up their own industrial base, and at the same time have little spare currency to pay for it. A conflict exists here between the attitude of the industrialized countries that technology is a commodity which must be paid for at the going rate, and the idea prevalent in some developing countries that technology is the common property of mankind and should be made available essentially free of charge. The traditional type of patent system, often a legacy from colonial times, reflects the first of these attitudes, and as a result many developing countries are abolishing or severely weakening patent protection, at least in some fields. Experience is showing that this approach is counter-productive, and suitable compromises have yet to be found.

It is, of course, not a self-evident proposition that a strong patent system such as now exists in most industrialized countries is in the public interest in these countries, still less that such a system is good for all countries in whatever stage of industrial development. Nevertheless, such evidence as there is tends to show that there is a positive correlation between strength of patent protection and level of industrial development, and, more convincingly, that in countries where patent protection in certain areas has been abolished or severely weakened, the results have been the opposite of what might have been expected.

It is a fact, for example, that the rapid industrial progress of the USA in the latter half of the nineteenth century followed the setting up of a strong patent system, although this is far from establishing any cause-and-effect relationship. Japan's rapid emergence since the last war as one of the world's leading industrial nations coincides with the establishment of a reasonably strong patent system, which has recently been strengthened further. Of course, many other factors are involved and we cannot know how these countries would have developed in the absence of patents. Japan, however, illustrates an interesting point shown also by a number of other countries, namely that when a country makes the transition from being predominantly an importer of technology, or an imitator of other's efforts, to being primarily an innovator rather than a copier, its patent laws are strengthened.

This may be seen also by the examples of Holland, which had no patents at all between 1860 and 1913, at a time when its industry was at a rudimentary level compared with the United Kingdom and Germany, but which developed a strong system thereafter. Also in the chemical area, the United Kingdom abolished product *per se* protection between 1919 and 1949, at a time when the British dyestuffs industry felt itself threatened by the more research-based German industry, and wished to be free to copy new dyes, so long as they could find a new process to make them. We should not then be surprised if certain developing countries reject an inherited patent system which is not appropriate to their level of industrial development, but this does not mean that it is in the interests of these countries to abolish patents altogether or to weaken them beyond a certain point.

Alternatives

We can imagine two clear alternatives to a classical monopoly patent system. One is the complete abolition of patents altogether, the other is a system in which patents give a right to a royalty, but no exclusive rights. We can take as models for these two alternatives the situation of pharmaceutical inventions firstly in Italy up to 1978 and secondly in India, Canada or, until recently the United Kingdom.

Abolition

As described in Chapter 3, Italy had no patent protection whatsoever for pharmaceutical inventions from 1939 to 1978. The proponents of the law of 1939 hoped that the abolition of patent protection for medicinals would bring down prices by opening up the possibility of competition for new drugs as well as old. The results did not justify these expectations. The structure of the Italian pharmaceutical industry in these years was one of very few research-based companies and a great number of small companies selling the same products and spending vast sums on advertizing. Thus, one new product originated in Italy over a period in which the United Kingdom and German industries each introduced approximately thirty new drugs, while advertising overheads, which unlike research costs are totally unproductive, resulted in drug prices in Italy being actually higher than in other European countries. Although some Italian companies could make money by pirating the inventions of research-based companies in other countries and exporting the products, the Italian public did not receive any benefit from the abrogation of pharmaceutical patents.

Compulsory licensing

The compulsory licence provisions for pharmaceutical patents presently in force in India and Canada and which existed before 1977 in the United Kingdom, provide a model for the alternative system in which patents would provide only the right to compensation of the patentee without giving him any monopoly. The object of such provisions was to make drugs more readily and cheaply available and, at least in India and Canada, to encourage local production of pharmaceuticals.

In the United Kingdom the relatively few compulsory licences which were actually granted eventually carried high royalty rates which took into account the research overheads which had to be carried by the patentee and were not incurred by the licensee. This rapidly discouraged imitator companies from seeking compulsory licences, since they could not pay the royalties and still undercut the prices charged by the patentee by an amount large enough to gain any significant amount of sales. To this extent the provision failed to achieve its object, but in any case the prices of pharmaceuticals in the United Kingdom were effectively controlled by the purchasing power of the National Health Service, so that the compulsory licence provisions for pharmaceuticals were superfluous. This was recognized by their abolition in the Patents Act 1977; of course the normal compulsory licence provisions in case of abuse of monopoly continue to apply to pharmaceutical patents as to any others.

In Canada the level of royalties for pharmaceuticals cannot be more than 4 per cent of net sales of finished product, and in India no more than 4 per cent of bulk sales price. The return to the patentee in Canada is inadequate and in India is derisory. The result in India has been that practically no pharmaceutical companies now file patents there, and such companies are most reluctant to invest money in the transfer of technology to India, since any such technology may be freely taken and copied. The results for India have certainly not been the rapid development of the Indian pharmaceutical industry which had been hoped for, but rather the stagnation of that industry as the basis for co-operation with foreign companies was destroyed.

Canada is in a somewhat special situation because although it is an industrially developed country, its industry is heavily dominated by its larger neighbour the USA. Provisions such as compulsory licences for pharmaceuticals have not improved the position of local industry, but rather the reverse. Because of this, extreme proposals have been made in Canada to the effect that complete abolition of the patent system is desirable in order to reduce foreign domination. Such proposals have recently been rejected by the Canadian Government, and although it is now proposed to retain the compulsory licence provisions, it is intended to increase the royalties on such licences as a function of the amount of investment the patentee company has made in local manufacturing and research. How this would work in practice we cannot yet say, but it is clear that the compulsory licensing of patents at artificially low royalty rates does not achieve the objectives of improved transfer of technology and low prices.

A strong patent system as in Western Europe, USA, and Japan may be open to abuse and cannot be proved to be in the public interest, although there is circumstantial evidence that it has been a factor in the industrial development of these countries. The potential abuses can readily be controlled by legal restraints upon actions considered to be abuse of monopoly, and the abolition of the existing system would almost certainly lead to real disadvantages.

There is a basic question of equity or fairness involved in any proposal to substantially weaken patent rights. To make and develop an invention costs effort and in some fields a great deal of money. In the pharmaceutical field, for example, it is estimated that to bring a new product on the market worldwide costs, for that product alone, approximately 50–60 million dollars, not to speak of the money spent upon development of products dropped before they get that far. Why, after all, should an imitator be permitted to take the benefit of all this investment while himself contributing nothing?

Without the protection for a limited period of time which is conferred by patent rights, and, of course, without the possibility of keeping the formula of a new drug as secret know-how, there is no way in which the enormous research costs of the pharmaceutical industry could be economically justified. One cannot pretend that every new pharmaceutical which appears on the market is a miracle drug; many are 'me-too' compounds similar to existing products and having only marginal advantages. Nevertheless, the miracle drugs are there, too: products which have saved, prolonged or made bearable the lives of millions of people, and products which have reduced overall health costs enormously; for example, by making unnecessary the long hospitalization previously needed in the treatment of tuberculosis and certain mental diseases. It is probably true to say that only in the last fifty years has the taking of medical treatment actually improved the patient's chances of recovery from illness. It is not an exaggeration to give at least some of the credit for this to the patent system.

21

THE EEC: PATENTS AND THE TREATY
OF ROME

The Treaty does not touch any of the matters which concern solely the mainland of England and the people in it. These are still governed by English law. They are not affected by the Treaty. But when we come to matters with a European element, the Treaty is like an incoming tide. It flows into the estuaries and up the rivers. It cannot be held back.

Lord Denning in *Bulmer* v. *Bollinger* (1974)

The organization of the EEC

The European Economic Community, although a supranational organization, has many of the features of a national government, and the closest analogy to the EEC is probably the government of the United States of America. The US government is based on a written constitution and has separate legislative, executive, and judicial branches each of which can act as a check on the others. In particular, the most important role of the judiciary is that of interpreter of the constitution, and it may declare a law passed by the legislature or an act of the executive as unconstitutional and void.

In very much the same way, the EEC has an executive branch, the Commission, and a judicial branch, the European Court of Justice (ECJ). The role of legislature is shared by two bodies, the Council of Ministers and the European Parliament. Up to now the European Parliament has played a very minor role, and all really important decisions have been taken by the Council composed of ministers of member state governments, but this may change in the future. The Commission is presided over by Commissioners appointed by the member states and staffed by EEC civil servants; it is divided up into various Directorates-General, including one dealing with competition within the EEC. The Commission implements the policies of the Council, but also has considerable powers to initiate policy on its own.

The 'constitution' of the EEC is the Treaty of Rome, signed in 1962 by the six original member states and adhered to in 1973 by the United Kingdom, Ireland, and Denmark, in 1981 by Greece, and by Spain and Portugal in 1986. The provisions of the Treaty of Rome, as well as regulations made under it by the Council or the Commission, are directly binding upon member states and in cases of conflict take precedence over national law. It is the main task of the ECJ to interpret the Treaty of Rome and apply its provisions to the cases which come up before it.

The ECJ has jurisdiction only in the following types of proceedings:

1. Proceedings against a member state for failure to fulfil its obligations under the Treaty. Such proceedings may be instituted by the Commission or by another member state.
2. Complaints that an act of the Council or Commission is illegal or that the Council or Commission has failed to act where it should. These proceedings may be brought by a member state, the Commission, or the Council, but also by any natural or legal person affected by the action (or inaction).
3. Preliminary rulings referred by a national court or tribunal concerning points of interpretation of the Treaty of Rome, or the interpretation and validity of acts (regulations, etc.) of Community institutions.
4. Disputes between the EEC and its employees.
5. In addition, conventions entered into by member states may provide that the ECJ has jurisdiction in certain matters. In particular, the Community Patent Convention provides that in revocation proceedings in relation to an EEC patent, there shall be a further appeal (on matters of law only) to the Court from the Revocation Boards, and that the Court can give a preliminary ruling on the interpretation of the Convention and on any provisions enacted under it. However, it is now proposed to give the appeal jurisdiction to the new Community Patents Appeal Court (COPAC).

These illustrate the wide variety of matters which may come before the Court. One day the judges may be giving a decision on a major dispute between the United Kingdom and France, the next they may have to decide whether some minor EEC official was unfairly passed over for promotion. As far as matters concerning industrial property are concerned, however, cases normally arise only under the second and third of the above headings. For example, a decision by the EEC Commission that a patent licence agreement violates the Treaty of Rome could be challenged in the Court by the party to whom the decision is addressed. As an example of a reference a national court could ask for a ruling on whether a national patent could be used to prevent importation of goods under certain circumstances. At present, these are essentially the only two types of cases involving industrial property (including copyright, design protection, and trademarks as well as patents) which can come before the Court. For the Treaty of Rome to be relevant, there must be trade between member states, so that questions of validity of a national patent, or its infringement where no importation is involved, cannot be heard by the Court. In no sense is the Court a supra-national court of appeal on general patent matters.

There do not appear to have been any examples of the first type of case (appeals from the Commission) which are directly concerned with patents, and it is perhaps unfortunate that there have not been more challenges in the Court to Commission decisions on patent licence agreements. Instead, the majority of industrial property cases which have come before the Court have been references from national courts. Here it should be noted that a court of first instance has the option whether or not to refer a point of interpretation of Community law to the ECJ, whereas the highest national court, from which there is no further appeal, *must* refer such a question if it arises.

Parallel importation

The great majority of the cases which have come before the Court have been concerned with the question of whether the holder of an industrial property right in one member state can use that right to prevent importation from a second member state of goods covered by that industrial property right which were legally on the market in the second member state, i.e. 'parallel importation'. Parallel importation is particularly a problem in the pharmaceutical industry: first, because the high value of pharmaceuticals per unit weight makes it worthwhile to transport this type of goods from one country to another to take advantage of even relatively small price differentials; secondly, because government action in some EEC countries to hold down pharmaceutical prices results in very large price differentials between certain countries.

Until the EEC patent and trademark become reality, industrial property rights are essentially national in character, and stop at national boundaries. The doctrine of exhaustion of patent rights which has long been recognized in Germany and other EEC countries (although not in the United Kingdom – see Chapter 7) cannot be extended to the proposition that the sale of goods under a patent in one country exhausts the patentee's rights under an equivalent patent in another country. Still less can the sale of the goods in a country in which there is no patent be said to exhaust rights in a patent which does exist elsewhere.

However, this principle of territoriality of industrial property rights conflicts with the objective of the Treaty of Rome which is to promote the free movement of goods within the EEC. Articles 30–34 of the Treaty prohibit quantitative restrictions on imports and exports within the EEC, and although Article 36 specifically exempts from such prohibition restrictions which are justified on certain grounds including the protection of industrial property, the last sentence of Article 36 states that such restrictions, which are in principle allowed, 'shall not constitute a means of arbitrary discrimination or a disguised restriction on trade between Member States'. Unfortunately, the ECJ has fastened on this sentence to reach the somewhat absurd conclusion that although the *existence* of industrial property rights such as patents is not affected by the Treaty of Rome, the *exercise* of these rights may in certain circumstances be incompatible with the Treaty and therefore prohibited.

The crucial decision of the Court came in 1974 as one of a series of cases in which the Dutch company Centrafarm was sued by various pharmaceutical manufacturers for infringing trade marks or patents by parallel importation of drugs from the United Kingdom into Holland.

At that time the combination of low sterling prices for drugs in the United Kingdom and the weak exchange rate of the pound made it very easy to Centrafarm to make money by buying drugs wholesale in the United Kingdom and reselling them in Holland.

Sterling Drug sued Centrafarm for infringement of a Dutch patent by importing into Holland a patented product produced and marketed in the United Kingdom by the United Kingdom subsidiary of Sterling under an equivalent United Kingdom patent. The Dutch court found infringement, but referred to the ECJ the question of whether national patents laws could be used to stop parallel importation in these circumstances. The Court, applying Articles 30–34 of the Treaty, held that they could not: once patented goods had been put on the market in any EEC country by the patentee or with his consent, and whether or not there was a patent in that country, then those same goods could be resold freely anywhere in the EEC, and national patent rights could not prevent this.[1] In other words, the effect is the same as if the doctrine of exhaustion of patent rights applied to the EEC as a whole. It should be noted, however, that on the accession of Spain and Portugal to the EEC, parallel imports from these countries may still be stopped by national patent rights for a period of 10 years, i.e. until 1996.

In 1985, parallel imports were still very much in the news, but the Centrafarm situation was reversed. That is, drugs were being purchased more cheaply in continental Europe and parallel imported into the UK, undercutting the prices of British suppliers. But in whichever direction the parallel import traffic flows, the situation is basically unfair to the pharmaceutical manufacturers. In effect, it means that if in one EEC country such as France, the government imposes very low prices for drugs, then drugs at these artificially low prices are made available in other countries also.

The principle of free movement of goods is an admirable one if free market conditions apply; however, this is not the case in the pharmaceutical field. The market is totally distorted by price control of varying degrees in different countries, and the issue is far too politically sensitive for the EEC Commission to take any action against member state governments. It is much easier to make the pharmaceutical companies carry the burden and allow the parallel importers to get rich quick by the good old principle of buying cheap and selling dear.

There has been one recent case in which the ECJ refused to make life even easier for the parallel importers. In Britain, under the Patents Act 1949 compulsory licences were readily available for pharmaceuticals, and a company called DDSA obtained a compulsory licence to market in the UK a drug patented by Hoechst. Another company, Pharmon, parallel imported this product into Holland, and Hoechst tried to use its Dutch patent to prevent this. After going through the Dutch courts for some years, the case finally reached the ECJ.[2] Pharmon argued that there was no difference in principle between a compulsory licence and any other, and even that by patenting the drug in a country where a compulsory licence was a possibility, Hoechst was giving implied consent to the sales by the eventual compulsory licensee. However, the ECJ held that a product sold under a compulsory licence was *not* on the market with the consent of the patentee, and the parallel importation could be stopped.

The same situation cannot arise under present conditions, since the Patents Act 1977 has no provisions for easy compulsory licences for pharmaceuticals, and no other EEC country has such a law at present. The decision is more of symbolic significance, and shows that there are some limits beyond which the ECJ is not prepared to go in the direction of weakening patent rights which conflict with free movement of goods. A rather similar situation does exist, however, with respect to the 'new existing patents' in the UK which were automatically extended from 16 years to 20 years term with the proviso that for the last four years they be treated as if endorsed 'licences of right'. It is not yet decided whether the *Hoechst* v. *Pharmon* decision would apply in this case. A normal 'licences of right' endorsement is clearly voluntary and the resulting licences are not compulsory licences; but if the endorsement itself is compulsory, it could certainly be argued that the end result is a compulsory licence.

The Patents Act 1977 states that a licence granted under the 'licences of right' provision may allow local manufacture but exclude importation. In a recent case[3] the House of Lords held that this was in order as long as imports from non-EEC countries were concerned, but referred to the ECJ the question of whether the Treaty of Rome forbids such a restriction on importation from EEC countries.

Patent licence agreements

The other main impact of EEC law upon matters relating to patents concerns restrictions upon the terms of patent licence agreements. A licence agreement is an agreement between undertakings which falls within the general scope of Article 85 of the Treaty of Rome. Paragraph 1 of this Article declares that agreements which prevent, restrict, or distort competition within the common market are prohibited. Paragraph 2 states that agreements so prohibited are automatically void, and paragraph 3 provides for exceptions in certain cases.

Although Article 85 (1) gives some examples of objectionable agreements, for example those which fix prices, control or share markets, or have tie-in provisions, no detailed guidance is given as to which clauses in a contract for the licensing of industrial property might be considered to contravene the Treaty. Similarly, Article 85 (3) is framed in very general language, and says in effect that agreements which *a priori* violate Article 85 (1) may be exempted if they contribute to the production or distribution of goods or to technical progress, give the consumer a fair share of the benefits, and do not include unnecessary restrictions or eliminate competition.

Notification

Until recently, there were no detailed rules as to what conditions were or were not considered permissible in patent licence agreements, and companies had to notify licence agreements individually to the Commission, a procedure which as we shall see is still necessary in some cases. The procedure for notification is laid down in EEC Regulation 17 of 1962; at the same time as notification is made, negative clearance may be requested. Negative clearance is a declaration by the Commission that the agreement does not conflict with Article 85 (1), whereas notification is a request for exemption under Article 85 (3) of an agreement which may fall under 85 (1).

The 'Christmas Message'

An early set of guidelines as to what was considered by the Commission to be acceptable terms in a patent licence agreement was contained in the Commission's announcement of 24 December 1962 – universally referred to as the 'Christmas Message'. The Christmas Message was indeed one of goodwill to all men – it stated that a whole list of licence provisions, including the grant of licences limited by territory or field of use, as well as grant of exclusive licences, would not normally bring a licence agreement within Article 85 (1).

Further developments

In 1965 the Council empowered the Commission to grant by Regulation a block exemption to patent licence agreements between two parties. However, it was not until 1976 that the first informal draft of such a Regulation was issued, and, after much discussion and several further drafts, the Regulation was adopted only on 23 July 1984, and came into force on 1 January 1985.

In the intervening time, the Commission issued a number of decisions in individual cases which showed a clear change of attitude from the permissiveness of the 'Christmas message'. Such decisions cast doubt on the legality of territorially limited licences, and even upon exclusive licences.[4] For some time, the Commission took the view that an exclusive licence was prima facie a violation of Article 85 (1) because it limited competition by preventing the patentee from granting further licences, and that such an agreement was illegal unless it could, on the facts, be excepted under 85 (3). This attitude was even more restrictive than that of US anti-trust law, under which the legality of exclusive licences has never seriously been questioned.

In 1976 the final text of the Community Patent Convention was negotiated, and the governments of the member states agreed that patent licences within the EEC, whether under an EEC patent or national patents, could be exclusive or non-exclusive, and could be territorially limited. The views expressed in the Convention could not take precedence over the ECJ's interpretation of the Treaty of Rome, but the text adopted for the Convention could be regarded as a warning that the member state governments felt that the Commission was going too far in the restrictions it was applying to the freedom of negotiating parties.

If it was meant as a warning, it fell on deaf ears. The Commission reconciled the Convention with its own views by assuming that the article specifically allowing exclusive licences referred only to those which could be exempted under Article 85 (3), which of course would leave the situation unchanged.

The group exemption for patent licence agreements

A regulation granting a group exemption for a certain category of agreements, such as patent licence agreements, has the effect that agreements in that category which meet certain clear conditions and do not contain specified objectionable clauses are automatically exempted under Article 85 (3), without the need for individual notification. Although the Christmas Message gave certain guidelines, it did not have the power of a Regulation to give automatic exemption. For some time in the early 1970s it was known that a Regulation on the group exemption of patent licence agreements was being prepared, and industry looked forward to a regulation which would resolve the uncertainties in the legal position and, it was hoped, take account of the views expressed in the Luxembourg Convention.

When the first draft of the Regulation appeared in December 1976 the disappointment was great. Far from providing clarification, the document needed clarification itself, as it was drafted in a most indirect and contradictory style. Thus, having stated in Article 1 that the presence of certain types of clauses was compatible with automatic exemption, the draft reversed itself in Article 2 by applying far-reaching restrictions to such clauses. Thus, clauses forbidding the licensee to sell in certain territories within the EEC were allowable, but only for a period of ten years from the date of application for the basic patent, and only if the patentee had an annual turnover below 100 million units of account (ECU). Similarly, minimum royalty clauses were allowable, but only for five years from the signing of the agreement. Such arbitrary limitations lacked any foundation in law or in logic. It was said at that time, not without reason 'In England everything which is not forbidden is allowed, in Germany everything which is not allowed is forbidden, but in the EEC everything which is allowed is also forbidden'.

The draft Regulation met with strong opposition both from industry and from member state governments, and in successive drafts culminating in the fourth draft which was the first officially published version (March 1979), the Commission made various minor improvements without changing its basic unsatisfactory approach. In particular, the Commission still maintained its view that exclusive licences were *per se* violations of Article 85 (1), and refused to give exemption to any large company (with total turnover of more than 100 million ECU), on the simple theory that 'big is bad'.

Acting on this principle, the Commission had decided in 1978 that an agreement between a German and a French company in which the former gave the latter an exclusive licence to sell certain types of maize seed in France violated Article 85 (1) and could not be exempted under 85 (3). The companies appealed to the ECJ, and although this case did not relate to patent licences, no further action was taken by the Commission on the draft group exemption until the ECJ gave its ruling on the status of exclusive licence agreements.

The judgement of the Court in the 'Maize Seeds' case[5] was finally given in 1982. Although the facts of the case are complex, and the Court's decision is by no means easy to follow, the conclusion did not support the Commission's position. The Court held that exclusive licences could violate Article 85 (1), but did not necessarily do so, and in particular that, at least for new products, an 'open exclusive licence' in which there was no absolute contractual prohibition of sales by one licensee to the territory of another and no attempt to prevent parallel imports, was acceptable.

In view of this decision, the Commission modified its views and produced further drafts in 1983 and early 1984 which were considerably more favourable to exclusivity than the early drafts had been. Finally, the group exception for patent licence agreements was adopted as Regulation 2349/84 in July 1984, in a form which apart from some minor matters is generally acceptable to industry, and should achieve its aim of making it unnecessary to notify the great majority of patent licence agreements.

The most important parts of the Regulation are the first three articles, which list what are usually referred to as 'grey', 'white', and 'black' clauses respectively. The grey clauses of Article 1 restrict competition and therefore violate 85 (1), but are by the regulation exempted under 85 (3). The white clauses of Article 2 are considered not to restrict competition and not to violate 85 (1), while the black clauses listed in Article 3 violate 85 (1) and cannot be exempted under 85 (3). Following the reasoning of the ECJ in the Maize Seed case, Article 1 allows complete exclusivity for the lifetime of the patents as between licensor and licensee, and allows the licensor to keep part of the EEC as his own exclusive territory. As between an exclusive licensee in one part of the EEC and a different exclusive licensee in another, agreements may oblige each licensee not to manufacture in the territory of the other, nor to actively market in the other's territory (e.g. by advertising or establishing branches or distribution depots) as long as parallel patents exist there. However, 'passive marketing', i.e. filling unsolicited orders from another licensee's territory, may be prohibited only for 5 years from first marketing of the product anywhere in the EEC.

The allowable 'white clauses' in Article 2 include provisions such as minimum royalties, field of use limitations, confidentiality of know-how, quality control, non-exclusive grant-back of rights to improvements, and obligations to mark the goods with the licensor's name or patent number. Even tie-ins are allowable to the extent they are necessary for a 'technically satisfactory exploitation of the invention'.

The eleven 'black clauses' of Article 3, whose presence in an agreement will rule out automatic exception are those which provide for:

(1) no challenge to patent validity (however, the licensor may terminate the licence if validity is challenged);
(2) automatic prolongation of the agreement by new patents, unless the licensee has the right to terminate annually;
(3) restrictions on competition other than those in Article 1;
(4) charging of royalty on non-patented products, or on know-how which is within the public domain;
(5) quantity control;
(6) price control;

(7) restricton to certain classes of customer;
(8) assignment back to improvements made by licensee;
(9) package licensing, i.e. the licensee being forced to accept additional licences he does not want;
(10) restriction on passive marketing for more than the 5 year period allowed by Article 1;
(11) restrictions on parallel imports.

The Regulation gives retrospective exemption to existing agreements meeting its conditions, and applies also to assignments of patents if these are for a royalty rather than a lump sum. It does not apply to agreements between more than two parties, cross-licensing agreements, patent pools or joint ventures.

If an agreement of the kind to which the Regulation applies contains restrictions on competition which go beyond those allowed in Articles 1 and 2 but do not contain any of the black clauses of Article 3, it is now possible to obtain individual exemption by an accelerated procedure. The notification is passed by the Commission to the member states; if neither the Commission nor any member state objects within six months, the exemption is automatically granted.

Negative features of the Regulation include the fact that it has effect for only 10 years, whereas most licence agreements will be of longer duration, and the potentially serious problem that an exemption given under the Regulation may be withdrawn if the agreement turns out in practice to have anti-competitive effects.

Individual notification

Individual notification of some agreements may still be desirable, either because they are outside the scope of Regulation 2349/84 (for example, because there are three parties to the agreement) or because the conditions for accelerated individual exemption apply to them. In either case, the work involved for the company notifying the agreement is considerable. The actual form (Form A/B) on which the request for negative clearance or exemption is made is simple enough, but answers to very detailed questions about the companies involved, their market shares, the projected markets for the licensed products and much more must be supplied with it. The new type of individual exemption provided for in the Regulation may be accelerated, but it is not simplified, at least as far as the initial application is concerned.

Notification is never compulsory, but if the agreement is of doubtful legality it is very useful as a form of insurance. A company entering into an agreement which violates Article 85 (1) is liable to heavy fines, but no fines can be imposed in respect of any period between notification and the issurance of a decision by the Commission.

The provision of Article 85 (2) that agreements which violate 85 (1) are void is less serious a problem. It appears that only the clauses which specifically offend against 85 (1) would be held invalid, and national courts could decide that the rest of the agreement would be enforceable. Unlike in the USA, where patent misuse renders the patent unenforceable, it would seem that violation of 85 (1) has no effect upon the enforceability of the licensed patent.

The powers of the Commission

Council Regulation 17 has given the Commission very extensive powers to investigate violations of Articles 85 and 86 of the Treaty of Rome. Article 85 does not deal only with written contracts, but also with concerted practices, such as unwritten 'gentlemen's agreements' to fix prices or share out markets. It is of course clear that if such illegal practices are to be stopped, there must be some powers of investigation, since the companies concerned are certainly not about to notify this type of agreement to the Commission of their own free will.

There are basically two different ways in which the Commission can obtain information. Under Article 11 of the Regulation the Commission may request information from any undertaking – not necessarily the one being investigated – and if the information is not provided or is incomplete, the Commission may issue a decision compelling the information to be produced, on penalty of fines. Furthermore, by Article 14, the Commission may send investigators to the premises of a company to examine business records, take copies of documents and ask for oral explanation.

The ECJ recently ruled[6] that an investigation under Article 14 does not have to be a two-stage procedure like that of Article 11. The company does not have to be given prior warning and the opportunity to comply voluntarily, but can be faced with a 'dawn raid' in which the investigators bring with them a Commission decision which must be complied with on penalty of heavy fines.

There has recently been considerable concern that in proceedings before the Commission the fundamental legal rights of the party whose conduct is being investigated may not be fully safeguarded. Thus when the action is the result of a complaint, the complainant may never be identified, and the accused may not be allowed to inspect the file to determine exactly on what basis an adverse decision was arrived at. There is no opportunity to cross-examine, and it is difficult to tell whether the right inferences are being drawn from the available evidence. Furthermore, it is not at all clear to what extent the Commission will respect legal privilege with respect to documents containing advice from lawyers or patent agents, particularly if these are company employees.

In a further decision on an appeal from the Commission, the ECJ laid down some rules of procedure which should avoid some of the worst inequities.[7] In particular, the Commission cannot use as evidence any document which it is not free to disclose to the accused party: the accused party must be able to see what exactly is being used as evidence against him.

The problem is more than just a procedural one; it is basically that the Commission is acting as investigator, prosecutor, judge and jury. Although appeal lies to the ECJ, the Court can only consider legal points and cannot properly review the economic evidence which led to the decision. It has been suggested either that there should be an intermediate appeal tribunal or, which would be easier to achieve, a strict separation of function within the Commission between the investigative department and the body which reaches a decision on the case.

22

THE USA: PATENTS AND ANTI-TRUST

> Business is a useful beast,
> We should not hate it in the least;
> Its profits should not be sequestered,
> And yet it should be mildly pestered.
> To pester, rather than to bust,
> Should be the aim of Anti-Trust.
> For business best can serve the nation
> When pushed by gentle irritation.

(Author unknown)

The anti-trust acts

The period after the Civil War in the USA was one of unrestrained capitalism in which trusts and cartels were set up in all major industries to fix prices and exclude unwanted competition. Public reaction against these abuses finally reached the point where the anti-trust forces were able to pass legislation to curb them. This took the form of the Sherman Act, passed in 1890, section 1 of which declares any contracts or combinations in restraint of trade to be illegal, and section 2 of which makes any attempt to monopolize any part of interstate or foreign trade a criminal offence.

It will be seen that whereas section 1 of the Sherman Act requires mutual action of at least two parties to make an illegal act, a section 2 offence may be committed by a single party. There are close parallels between these two sections and Articles 85 and 86 of the Treaty of Rome, and indeed these parts of the Treaty of Rome appear to have been modelled on the Sherman Act. This being the case, it is interesting to see whether competition law in the EEC has developed along parallel lines to US anti-trust law, or if their directions have diverged.

A further piece of US anti-trust law is the Clayton Act, of which section 3 prohibits tie-ins, section 4 gives individuals injured by any act forbidden by the anti-trust laws the right to sue the person responsible, and section 7 prohibits the acquisition of any assets of another company if this would create a monopoly or substantially lessen competition.

All of these provisions are expressed in very vague and general language, and it is not spelled out exactly what acts are to be forbidden. The Sherman and Clayton Acts do not mention patents at all, but quite clearly a patent licence agreement may be a contract contravening section 1 of the Sherman Act, and patents may be among the assets whose acquisition may violate section 7 of the Clayton Act.

The US patent law is equally vague about what types of restrictions may legally be made when a patent is licensed. In section 261, however, it is clearly stated that a patent may be exclusively licensed for the whole or part of the USA. Exclusive licences and territorial limitations as such are therefore statutorily allowed in the USA, and the Sherman Act, which is of equal status to the patent law, cannot overturn this.

This is in contrast to the situation in the EEC where although the Community Patent Convention also specifies that the EEC patent may be exclusively licensed for all or part of the Common Market, the Treaty of Rome, which is to the EEC what the Constitution is to the USA, could have been interpreted by the European Court so as to overrule this provision.

There is, of course, a conflict between the patent law, which grants limited monopolies to inventors, and the anti-trust laws which broadly condemn monopolies and restrictions on competition. Because the anti-trust laws are so broadly drafted it is perhaps inevitable that they should be seen as constituting a general principle, to which the patent law forms a strictly limited exception. Thus, considering the statutory right to grant a territorially limited licence, it should be noted that whereas a simple licence granting the licensee exclusive rights in, say, the USA west of the Mississippi is legal, a cross-licensing agreement whereby A licenses B in the West and B licenses A in the East could constitute a division of markets which would be illegal under section 1 of the Sherman Act.

Patent misuse and anti-trust violations

Apart from the anti-trust laws, under which certain acts may be illegal or even criminal, the other main restraint upon the patentee is that provided by the concept of patent misuse. A court may consider patent misuse to exist when a patentee attempts to extend the scope of his monopoly to areas outside of the bounds of the patent, for example by tying a licence to the purchase of unpatented goods. An action may be patent misuse without necessarily amounting to an anti-trust violation, and the distinction between the two is that patent misuse is not in itself illegal, but simply has as consequence the unenforceability of the patent under the 'clean hands' doctrine.

Thus, patent misuse disentitles the patentee to equitable relief for infringement and may be used as a defence by an alleged infringer. Anti-trust violations, on the other hand, give rise to a cause of action by the US Government or by any person who has suffered damage. If proven, the penalties may include an injunction against the action found to be illegal, the unenforceability of any relevant contract (as well as the patent itself), damages to the extent of three times the actual damage sustained, and in particularly flagrant cases, the possibility of a jail sentence. Clearly these are not the sort of consequences to be taken lightly.

Even the consequence of patent misuse, that the patent is unenforceable, is unduly harsh when it is considered that the misuse need not be shown to have any anti-competitive effect, and that the person raising the defence of patent misuse need not have been injured by it in any way. In 1983, legislation was proposed to reform the patent misuse doctrine by providing that the doctrine of patent misuse could not be applied by the courts unless it was proved that the alleged misuse would violate the anti-trust laws. As of 1985, however, no such legislation has been enacted, and the situation remains as before.

Patent misuse does not result in patent invalidity, but only in unenforceability, which may be only temporary. If the misuse is stopped, the patent may once against be enforced against infringers. On the other hand anti-trust violations enable the validity of the patent itself to be challenged, and even related patents not directly involved may be affected.

Fraud on the Patent Office may give rise to breach of the anti-trust laws. When a patent has been obtained by 'knowing and wilful fraud', then any attempt to enforce the patent may amount to an illegal attempt to monopolize, in violation of section 2 of the Sherman Act, the patent will be invalid, and the patentee will be liable for triple damages to the person against whom the patent was enforced. It could even be alleged that although the patent was not enforced, its mere existence kept competitors off the market and was in violation of the Sherman Act. Challenges to patent validity arising out of anti-trust suits by the US Justice Department were used frequently in recent years to bring about what is in effect compulsory licensing in a number of areas.

Patent licence agreements

The legality of specific types of restrictions which may be placed upon a licensee in a patent licence agreement is determined by rules which have developed through case law. A restriction may be regarded as *per se* illegal, or as subject to the 'rule of reason'. In the first category are restrictions which constitute antitrust violations which, in the words of the Supreme Court in *Northern Pacific Railway Co* v. *US* (1958) because of their 'pernicious effect on competition and lack of any redeeming virtue' are conclusively presumed to be 'illegal without elaborate inquiry as to the precise harm they have caused'.[1] Application of the 'rule of reason' requires an enquiry into the overall effect of the agreement. The restriction is not illegal if it is ancillary to carry out the lawful primary purpose of the agreement, if its scope and duration are no greater than necessary, and if it is otherwise reasonable in all the circumstances.

Restrictions which are *per se* illegal include tie-ins, which are specifically forbidden under the Clayton Act. However, the power to enforce a patent against contributory infringement, which by its nature involves a certain degree of control over the market in unpatented goods, is specifically allowed under the patent law, and this right has been upheld by the Supreme Court in the recent Rohm & Haas case (see p. 102), at least so long as the unpatented goods have no substantial non-infringing use.

Difficulties arise when the patent claims a new use for a material which already has other uses, and it is a real problem for the patentee to know how he can commercialize such a patent if he himself is selling the material in question. One possible method is the 'label licence' whereby the patentee sells the product with a statement on the label such as:

The purchase price includes a prepaid royalty of x ¢/lb. to use the process of US Patent No. . . . This will be refunded on request if the patented process is not used. The purchaser can use the products of other manufacturers upon payment of the same royalty.

This is all very well in theory but in practice if the patentee sells the product at x ¢/lb. more than the competition, the users will probably buy the competing product without paying the royalty, and enforcement of the patent against the users may well be counter-productive.

Also clearly illegal are 'tie-outs', that is, clauses forbidding the licensee to deal in competitors' products. Clauses requiring continued payment of royalties after the expiry of the patent are *per se* illegal, as are agreements in which the licensee is compelled to accept a licence under a whole package of patents when in fact he only needs a licence under some of them, or in which the licensee is compelled to pay royalties upon total sales of one type of product only some of which fall under the licensed patents.

In the second category of clauses are included price-fixing restrictions. It seems surprising that these should not be clearly illegal *per se*, but there is in fact an old (1926) Supreme Court decision[2] allowing such clauses, which is still good law, although it has been given a very restricted interpretation by the courts in later cases. In the 1970s the Antitrust Division of the Justice Department took an attitude similar to that of the EEC Commission in trying to impose more and more severe controls upon clauses of patent licence agreements, and stated that it considered not only price fixing, but also a number of other types of restriction previously subject to the 'rule of reason' to be *per se* illegal.

The Justice Department could not by itself change the law, nor compel the courts to follow its views, but it could decide whether or not to instigate an anti-trust suit or whether to intervene in a civil anti-trust action, so that its influence was very great. It would be a courageous, not to say foolhardy, businessman who would enter into an agreement containing one of the nine types of clauses which the Justice Department considered *per se* illegal – the list which became facetiously known as the 'nine no-no's' – whether or not they were really *per se* illegal under existing case law.

The 'nine no-no's' were:

(1) tie-ins;
(2) exclusive grant-back of improvements;
(3) restrictions on re-sale of patented products;
(4) tie-outs;
(5) licensee's veto on grant of future licences;
(6) mandatory package licensing;
(7) requirement to pay royalties not directly related to sales of patented products (e.g. royalties on total sales of products of the general type covered by the patent);
(8) restrictions on sales of unpatented products made by use of a patented process;
(9) price restrictions on sale of licensed products.

As will be seen, there are strong similarities between this list and that of the 'black clauses' of Art. 3 of the EEC Group Exemption Regulation.

Since 1981, however, there has been a complete change in the attitude of the Justice Department, as the Reagan administration appointed officials who adhered to the 'Chicago school' of *laisser-faire* economics rather than the 'Harvard school' which favoured an interventionist approach. The 'nine no-no's' have been repudiated, and the official line is that there should be no restrictions which are *per se* illegal, but that the rule of reason should be applied in all cases. The important distinction is seen as that between vertical agreements (e.g. as between a supplier and distributor) and horizontal agreements between actual or potential competitors. In the former case there should be little or no concern over restrictive clauses in the agreements; in the latter case where the danger of cartel-building exists, restraints should be viewed more harshly.

There has been one case so far in which an Appeal Court has decided[3] against *per se* illegality of one of the 'nine no-no's; the one listed as number (8) above. Studiengesellschaft Kohle (SG) had a patent for the only commercially feasible process for the manufacture of aluminium trialkyls, which were not patented products. Hercules had a non-exclusive licence to manufacture and an exclusive licence to sell the products in the USA. Certain other companies had non-exclusive licences to manufacture aluminium trialkyls for their own use, but were not allowed to sell them to others. This was a restriction on the sales of an unpatented product made by a patented process, and was held *per se* illegal by the District Court. On appeal, however, it was held that since SG would have been clearly within its rights to have granted only the single licence to Hercules, the grant of additional manufacturing licences was pro-competitive.

A legislative change which has already been made is the National Co-operative Research Act of 1984, which requires joint R & D agreements, including agreements to license the results of joint R & D, to be judged for anti-trust legality under the rule of reason, and eliminates the possibility of treble damages if the agreement is notified to the Attorney General and the Federal Trade Commission.

These moves to reverse the previous anti-patent views of the US executive and judiciary are very welcome, and have perhaps influenced the relaxation of attitude on the part of the EEC Commission. All in all, the position in USA and in Europe with respect to legal control over patent licence agreements looks much more favourable than it did only four years ago when the first edition of this work was written.

Validity challenges by licensees

An important change in licensing law in the USA in recent years relates to the question of whether a licensee can challenge the validity of the patent under which he is licensed. The law always used to be the same as in England; that a licensee was estopped from so doing because it was not just that he should be able to enjoy the protection of the patent for as long as it suited him and then be able to turn around and attack it. However, in 1969 this was overturned by the Supreme Court in the case of *Lear* v. *Adkins*.[4] The Supreme Court felt that the public interest in invalid patents being challenged outweighed the possible injustice to the patentee, and ruled that notwithstanding any clause in the agreement to the contrary, a licensee could at any time challenge the patent's validity.

In the years immediately following this decision the law was in a confused state and it was not clear how far *Lear* v. *Adkins* could be extended and what were the rights of the licensee if he did successfully challenge validity. At one time, indeed, it looked as if a licensee under a patent which was held invalid at the end of the patent term would be able to recover all the royalties he had paid. Fortunately a decision to this effect, which would have had a disastrous effect upon licensing activities, was overturned on appeal.[5]

The position has since been clarified somewhat, and now appears to be as follows. A licensee may at any time cease to pay royalties and seek a declaratory judgment of patent invalidity. If he wins, he has no further obligation to pay royalties, but cannot recover any royalties already paid.

On the other hand if the patent is invalidated by a third party, the licensee's freedom from royalty payments begins only when the patent is finally held invalid, unless the licensee himself stopped paying royalties earlier and made some contribution towards the resolving of the issue of validity.

Although the licensor can no longer have a 'no-contest' clause in the licence agreement, it is thought that he may at least have a clause specifically terminating the licence if the licensee challenges validity. If the licensee's challenge is unsuccessful, he will then be liable as an infringer for anything done after he stopped paying royalties. It also seems that the rule of *Lear* v. *Adkins* does not apply to patent assignments, even those made in return for a running royalty, nor does it apply to know-how agreements. In a recent Supreme Court case[6] a licensee who had signed a contract obliging him to pay royalties indefinitely on a know-how agreement (a patent was applied for but not granted) could not terminate the payment of royalties even though the know-how had entered the public domain. Thus in this case, the licensor was in a better position without a patent than she would have been with one.

23

THE SOCIALIST COUNTRIES: PATENTS
AND MARXISM

Foreigners enjoy civil rights in the Soviet Union to the same extent as
Soviet citizens. Special exceptions may be decreed by law of the USSR.
Civil Law of the USSR: Art. 122 para. 1 (1961)

Patents in socialist countries

Although Marx himself was silent on the subject of patents, one might
expect that countries with a socialized economy in which the state owns all
means of production and exchange would have no use for a patent system.
Isn't a patent a capitalist device created to reward entrepreneurs? On the
contrary, the socialist countries of East Europe (which we shall consider as
the USSR, Bulgaria, Czechoslovakia, the DDR, Hungary, Poland, and
Romania) all have a patent system which in theory at least is reasonably
strong and in fact is stronger than that in many developing countries.

Two further Eastern European countries, Albania and Yugoslavia,
are excluded from the following discussion. Albania exists in a state of
paranoid isolation from all other countries, and if it has a patent system at
all it is of interest to no one but itself. Yugoslavia, although an associate
member of the Council for Mutual Economic Assistance (COMECON)
prefers to see itself as a leader of the developing countries of the Third
World, and is dealt with as such in the following chapter.

Hungary and Poland have a single type of patent which is basically
similar to that in most Western European countries about 30 years ago,
while the remaining countries have some kind of a dual system in which
patents of the classical type co-exist with inventors' certificates or with
special categories of patent granted predominantly to local nationals.

Inventor's certificates in the USSR

This dual system is most fully developed in the USSR, where the two
alternatives are patents and inventor's certificates. Patents in the USSR are
similar to those elsewhere, although considerably weaker than in Western
Europe; the term of protection is 15 years from application, and for
chemical inventions there is only process protection available; the product
of the process is not covered. An inventor's certificate, on the other hand,
is a form of recognition granted to the inventor which gives him no

monopoly, since the invention is freely available for use by the state. Instead of monopoly rights, the inventor receives benefits such as cash awards, superior living accommodation, diplomas, further education opportunities, and the like.

Until recently an inventor's certificate did not have a fixed term, but in 1978 the law was changed so that certificates like patents now expire after 15 years. Certificates and patents are also equivalent for the purpose of claiming priority abroad, at least in countries which have ratified the Stockholm amendments to the Paris Convention, by which a patent application may claim priority from an application for inventor's certificate.

Despite such similarities, however, the basic distinction remains that in the USSR patents are, as elsewhere, a form of property giving monopoly rights while inventor's certificates are more like a nationwide bonus scheme for employee inventions and suggestions. The distinction is illustrated by the fact that it is possible to obtain inventor's certificates for unpatentable categories of inventions such as chemical products.

In theory any applicant may choose between an inventor's certificate and a patent. In practice, however, employees of state and co-operative enterprises may apply only for inventor's certificates for inventions made in connection with their work, and even those who make inventions independently stand to benefit more from an inventor's certificate than from a patent which they would have no opportunity to exploit. The result is that essentially all applications made by Soviet citizens are applications for inventor's certificates.

On the other hand, an inventor's certificate is of no interest to a foreign applicant in the USSR. He does not want 500 roubles and a larger flat, but industrial property rights which can be used as the basis for selling goods to the USSR or for licensing agreements. Foreign applicants, therefore, almost invariably file applications for patents rather than inventor's certificates in the USSR and this is true for applicants from other socialist countries as well as those from the West.

It may be asked why a country such as the USSR which has a planned, state-controlled economy should be willing to provide the means whereby foreign capitalist companies may obtain monopoly rights, however limited, within that economy. One answer is that the USSR, whatever its internal economic system, recognizes that in international trade there must be reciprocity of rights. Soviet enterprises apply for patents in capitalist countries,and could hardly do so without the USSR being prepared to grant equivalent rights to foreign applicants. This principle of reciprocity is enshrined in the Paris Convention, of which the USSR has been a member since 1965.

A further factor is that the USSR also realizes that patents form the most suitable basis for transfer of technology by means of licensing agreements, and indeed it is in these circumstances that a Russian patent is of most value to a foreign company. In this respect, the USSR and other socialist countries are much closer to the capitalist industrialized countries than to the developing countries, which to a large extent seem to have rejected patents as a basis for technology transfer.

Other COMECON countries

Bulgaria and Czechoslovakia, like the USSR have a dual system of patents and inventor's certificates. In the DDR and in Romania there are essentially two different types of patents; in the DDR these are known as *Ausschliessungspatente* (exclusion patents) and *Wirtschaftspatente* (economic patents) respectively. The exclusion patents are of the classical type, and are granted to foreign applicants; economic patents are granted to state-owned enterprises and may be used on request by other such enterprises. At first this was done on a royalty-free basis, but more recently the concept has developed that so long as state-controlled enterprises are in competition with each other to the extent that each is held accountable for its own profit or loss, a reasonable royalty rate should be paid by the licensee enterprise. If this were not so, then the enterprise using the invention freely would have an unfair advantage over the enterprise which invested its resources in research and development. In other words, even within a socialist economic system, patent rights are being recognized as a necessary incentive to investment in research.

Romania has normal patents and 'state patents' similar to the economic patents of the DDR. Both of these are quite distinct from inventor's certificates since they can be used as the basis for a licensing agreement. In their effect the state patents resemble a British patent which has been endorsed 'licenses of right'.

Both Hungary and Poland at one time had dual systems similar to that of the USSR, but both have changed towards a single 'classical' patent system. Hungary abolished the inventor's certificate in 1957; Poland still has inventor's certificates, but these are not alternatives to normal patents. Thus when a Polish employee of a state-owned enterprise makes an invention, he receives an inventor's certificate but the enterprise receives a patent for the same invention which it may license to other enterprises for a reasonable royalty, or even in certain circumstances refuse to license. Hungary has the strongest patent protection of any socialist country, providing for both product-by-process protection and reversal of onus of proof.

Within the COMECON bloc, the original intention was that member states would grant each other free licences on inventions which were the subject of inventor's certificates or patents. However, for the same reasons that a state-owned enterprise in the DDR was reluctant to give its inventions away free to other enterprises within the DDR, the idea of royalty-free transfer of technology did not prove practicable upon an international level either. Thus the great majority of applications filed within the USSR by enterprises of other COMECON countries are not applications for inventor's certificates, but for patents, since patents, but not certificates, can base a royalty-bearing transfer of technology which makes economic sense for both parties.

The Havana agreement

In 1976 the COMECON countries, together with Mongolia and Cuba, signed the Havana agreement which provides a system for the grant of patents in these countries which has some similarities to the European Patent Convention. Unlike the EPC, however, the Havana system applies only to inventions made within the member countries, so that it cannot be used by applicants in the West. There is no central examining office such as the EPO, but rather an application after being examined in the patent office of its home country may be registered in the other member countries without further examination. The application in countries with both patents and inventor's certificates may be for either type, but the procedure is easier and cheaper if an inventor's certificate is applied for rather than a patent.

Whereas the trend in Western industrialized countries is towards stronger patent protection and that in developing countries is towards a weakening of patent rights, such developments as there are in Eastern Europe are relatively minor and are contradictory in direction. The USSR made a step towards stronger protection by allowing certain categories of inventions to be protected by patents instead of only by inventor's certificates. At the same time, however, the practice of the Soviet Committee for Inventions and Discoveries, which is responsible for the granting of patents, has become more and more restrictive and it is becoming increasingly difficult to receive any meaningful scope of protection for chemical inventions. In Hungary also, patent rights have been weakened by recent court decisions holding agrochemical compositions to be unpatentable *per se*. There certainly does not appear to be any likelihood of product protection for chemicals being introduced in any of these countries in the foreseeable future.

The new Chinese patent law

Although the Peoples' Republic of China introduced temporary regulations on the protection of inventions in 1950, ony four patents were granted under this system, and in 1963 these regulations were replaced by an Awards to Inventors system, since at that time it was thought that a patent system was contrary to socialist principles. Only after the death of Mao Tse-Tung did the question of establishing a patent system arise again, and it became clear that a Chinese patent system was desirable both to encourage the introduction of foreign technology into China and also to protect Chinese inventions abroad through membership of the Paris Convention. After extensive consideration, including many visits of Chinese delegations to patent offices in other countries, the new Chinese law was enacted and came into force on 1 April 1985.

The law resembles the law of the European Patent Convention much more than it resembles the laws of the USSR and other Eastern European countries. There are no 'inventor's certificates' as such; the closest which the Chinese law comes to this concept is that an enterprise which is fully owned by the national or a provincial government is regarded as a patent 'holder', not as an 'owner', and is obliged to grant 'State Plan licences', for a fee, to other enterprises within the same administrative unit. Chinese individuals and collectively-owned enterprises can be subject to the same provisions, but only if the patent is of 'great significance to the interests of the State', and only by approval of the State Council at the request of a government department. For patents owned by foreigners or by Chinese/ foreign joint venture companies, the normal compulsory licence provisions for non-working apply, importation not being counted as working.

The patents will be subject to substantive examination and opposition before grant, and will have a term of 15 years from filing. The main weaknesses of the system are that there will be no patents for chemical and pharmaceutical products *per se*, and that importation of the product of a patented process will not constitute infringement. In spite of this, the new law seems to provide a sound basis which could be strengthened in future as China's industrial development increases.

The value of patents in socialist countries

The West European or American company which owns rights in an invention will want to know whether it is worthwhile to file patent applications in socialist countries, particularly in view of the relatively high costs in translation expenses, application fees, and renewal fees. Experience seems to suggest that it depends what one wants to do with the patent. In the USSR at least, it appears that owning a patent can be a valuable asset in negotiations for the supply of goods or, particularly, ventures such as setting up a chemical plant. If two Western companies are contending for this sort of contract, and one owns a relevant USSR patent, it is the patentee which will be favoured. A patentee in Hungary apparently has a reasonably good chance that his patent will be respected and he may be able to use it to prevent a Hungarian enterprise from imitating his product and exporting it to patent-free countries. As the chemical industry in Hungary is well developed in some areas, this may make patenting in Hungary worthwhile for an invention in such an area.

In most of these countries, however, and particularly in the DDR, a patentee is deceiving himself if he thinks he has any chance of enforcing his monopoly rights against a local enterprise which decides to imitate his invention. Patenting in the socialist countries should be considered on a very selective basis, bearing in mind that the costs-benefit ratio is generally very high. It is as yet too early to estimate the value of the patents newly granted by the People's Republic of China.

24

THE DEVELOPING COUNTRIES: PATENTS AND TRANSFER OF TECHNOLOGY

I have seen with real alarm, several recent attempts in quarters carrying some authority to impugn the principle of patents altogether – attempts which, if practically successful, would enthrone free stealing under the prostituted name of free trade.

John Stewart Mill: Speech in the House of Commons. *c*. 1860

Transfer of technology to developing countries

One of the major concerns of international politics in recent years has been the economic relations between the industrialized free enterprise countries and the developing countries of the Third World, often referred to as the North–South dialogue. On paper, there should be no great difficulty in this since each side has what the other needs. The industrialized countries have the technology which the developing countries need in order to establish local industry and raise their own per capita income. The developing countries own the bulk of the minerals and raw materials to which the industrialized countries need access.

Transfer of technology to developing countries is badly needed by those countries, and is also in the long-term interests of the industrialized countries themselves, since higher per capita income in the developing countries will give rise to more international trade. The problem is that the technology is not in the possession of governments who can simply transfer it as if it were cash. Technology, whether patented or in the form of know-how, is primarily in the possession of industrial companies existing within the framework of the free market economy.

To such companies, their technology is a valuable commodity which they have paid for by their investment in research and development, and which they simply cannot afford to give away without receiving a reasonable return on that investment. It is no criticism of these companies that they are profit oriented; given the structure of the economy in which they function, they have to be. A company which transferred its technology on any large scale to Third World countries free of charge because it sympathized with their problems would lose markets or face competition in other countries without any compensating return. If it continued to do so long enough it would decrease in size and eventually go out of business.

These basic facts of life in a market economy are ignored by those in Third World countries who argue that technology is part of the human heritage which should be freely available to all. It is simply not so, and rhetoric will not make it so.

The developing countries cannot afford to pay for all the technology which they require, and are extremely anxious to find ways in which technology can be transferred to them at affordable cost. The term transfer of technology is somewhat vague, but may be regarded primarily as the setting up of local industry capable of putting the technology into effect, and capable of both supplying the home market without reliance on imports and, hopefully, earning foreign exchange by exporting manufactured goods to other countries. This local industry is preferably fully locally owned, but may also include a local company partly or even wholly owned by a foreign company.

Between industralized countries, this form of transfer of technology is most frequently effected by means of a patent licence agreement. Strong patents are desirable both in order to secure the exclusive position of the licensee (which, except in a socialist system, he will need) and to define the rights granted by the licensor. In the developing countries, however, patents are regarded with suspicion for a number of reasons. One explanation may be that the patent systems of most developing countries were originally legacies of the colonial era. Because that era, rightly or wrongly, is thought of as one of exploitation, patents may be perceived as a tool of the ex-colonial powers to continue exploitation by other means.

A further reason is the fact that the great majority of patents in developing countries are owned by foreigners, and very few are locally worked. It is not appreciated that this is also true for almost all of the industrialized countries. Whatever the reason, many developing countries have the mistaken idea that patents are an impediment rather than an aid to the transfer of technology by licensing.

Another type of transfer is not of technology but of technological products. Here the sole concern of the developing country, if a necessary product must be imported, is to be able to import it at the lowest possible price. It cannot be denied that patent protection for the product serves the purpose of keeping out unauthorized imports and thus keeping the price higher than it might otherwise be. This is particularly the case for pharmaceuticals, where because the research overheads of an innovating company are so high, an imitator who has no research costs can always sell at well below the price of the research-based company.

It is clearly unfair that imitators who contribute nothing to the progress of pharmaceutical science should be able to reap the benefits of the inventions made by those who do, but the developing country importing the product may be excused for feeling that that is not its problem. Its problem is rather to get the drugs that its people need at the lowest price. However, a policy of weakening patent protection by abolishing patents for pharmaceuticals, or by making such patents ineffective against importation, acts to the disadvantage of local industry as soon as this has developed to the point where it can manufacture patented pharmaceutical products under licence. At that point local industry itself will be unprotected against cheap imports and will not be able to develop as it should.

It is also a fact which should be kept in mind that there are very few patents at all in developing countries. Figures recently given by Mr A. Laird, the head of ICI's Patent Department, show that of the patents owned by his company, representing the whole range of the chemical industry, no less than 85 per cent are held in 22 industralized market economy countries, 3 per cent in socialist countries, 6 per cent in the eight most important Third World countries and only 6 per cent in an additional 98 Third World countries. As Mr Laird points out, the number of patents in these countries is so small that it is hard to believe that the existence of patents is responsible in any way for their lack of development, on the contrary it is their low level of development which is the reason why so few 'patents are filed there.

Patent erosion

Whatever the reasons may be for the mistrust of patents which is prevalent in the Third World, the last decade or so has seen a very marked erosion of patent rights in these countries. This may be seen particularly in the pharmaceutical field, where protection has been totally or effectively abolished in a number of countries. In many countries the requirements for local working have been increased to the point where it is impossible to work a pharmaceutical invention within the stated time limits. These changes may be illustrated by the specific examples of India, Brazil, Argentina, the Andean Pact countries, Mexico, and Ghana.

India

The old Indian Patents and Designs Act of 1911 was closely based on the British law of that time. In 1970 a new law was enacted which, after some delays, came into force in April 1972. This represented a radical departure from the classic type of patent law which India previously had; it weakened patent protection quite generally, but for certain fields of inventive activity patent protection was effectively abolished.

General provisions applicable to all patents include the reduction of the patent term from 16 to 14 years, and a requirement that patentees and licensees must give annual reports on the working of the invention.

Provisions on Government use go further than normal in that Government use (which is broadly defined) is without compensation to the patentee, and that the Government can itself take over ownership of a patent.

The categories of patentable inventions were reduced, and claims to a chemical process no longer cover the product of the process; in other words patents cannot be used to prevent importation of chemical products. Furthermore all patents for chemical inventions are automatically endorsed 'Licences of Right' three years after grant.

The most extreme feature of the 1970 Act, however, is the special provisions for inventions relating to 'substances used or capable of being used as food or as medicine or drug', a category which is defined so broadly as to include not only medicines for human or animal use, but also substances used in diagnosis, insecticides, germicides, fungicides, weed-killers, all other substances intended to be used for the protection of preservation of plants, and intermediates used in the manufacture of any of these. Patents granted for processes for the manufacture of any of these substances have a term of only five years from sealing or seven years from the date of the patent, whichever is shorter, and the royalty payable on a licence granted on such a patent under the 'Licences of Right' provision must not exceed four per cent of the nett ex-factory bulk sales price of the product. Thus for this broad class of inventions not only is the patent life reduced to a point at which the patent will normally have expired before the product comes on the market, but if there is any patent term left, a competitor can operate under the patent on payment of a nominal royalty. As has often been stated, this amounts to abrogation of patent rights for this type of invention.

Brazil

The present Brazilian patent law has the effect of prohibiting any form of patent protection for pharmaceutical inventions, whereas processes for the preparation of non-pharmaceutical chemicals remain patentable. The term of patent protection was reduced from 15 years from grant to 15 years from application, a loss of term of about two years.

Compulsory licences are available if the patent is not locally worked within three years of grant (extensible to five years if licence negotiations are in progress). The patent lapses 'ex-officio' or on the petition of any interested party if it has not been worked within four years of grant (five years if a licence has been granted).

Argentina

Although the Argentine patent law itself has not changed in the last 15 years, its effect has been altered by court decisions, patent office rules, and legislation on transfer of technology.

In 1970, the Argentine Supreme Court ruled that it was not possible to patent all feasible processes for the preparation of a chemical compound, since this would be equivalent to product *per se* protection, which was not allowed by the patent law. This decision, of course, made process protection of very little value.

In 1974, the Patent Office promulgated a rule which laid down norms for disclosure and exemplification in chemical patent applications. As originally formulated, these rules placed an impossible burden on the applicant, who was expected to list each and every compound whose preparation was covered by the scope of the patent, and to give characterized examples for each and every substituent group which could be present in the molecule. It now appears that in practice these rules have been relaxed somewhat, although it is still very hard to obtain a reasonable scope of protection without having an unduly large number of examples.

The law in Argentina has provided for some time that a patent lapses unless worked within two years of grant, but nominal working was considered sufficient to meet this requirement. Recently, however, a number of Court decisions have held that nominal working is ineffective and there must be real local working; if confirmed by the Supreme Court, these decisions mean that most Argentinian patents will be invalid.

Andean Pact countries

Ecuador, Colombia, and Peru have amended their Patent Laws to implement Decision 85 of the Cartagena Agreement which draws up a model patent law for the Andean Pact countries. Bolivia and Venezuela are expected to follow shortly. Ecuador, the first state to ratify Decision 85, went even further than envisaged by the Decision itself. Decision 85 provides that pharmaceutical products shall not be patentable; in Ecuador this prohibition was interpreted to include processes for production of pharmaceuticals. Colombia and Peru still admit the possibility of patent protection for pharmaceutical processes, although in view of the other restrictions of the law, this protection is effectively non-existent.

The 1979 Patent Law of Peru is representative of laws implementing Decision 85. There is no product-by-process protection, and even for a patented product there is no protection against importation. If a corresponding patent application has been filed abroad, the Peruvian application must be filed within one year of the first filing, even though no priority under the Paris Convention can be claimed. Compulsory licences may be granted if there is no local working within three years of grant; nominal working is not effective. The patent term is initially only five years from grant, and this is extensible to ten years only if local working has been carried out.

The provisions for working are applied also to existing patents, which expired unless worked within two years of the entry into force of the new law, extensible by a further two years.

Mexico

The Mexican law of 1976 gives inventors the choice of a patent, giving exclusive rights to exploit the invention, or a certificate of invention giving only the right to receive compensation from anyone else who exploits it. However, the exclusivity granted by a patent is very limited, since it cannot be used to prevent importation, and is subject to compulsory licensing after three years from grant unless locally worked. Furthermore, for any invention relating to processes for the preparation of pharmaceuticals, drinks, foods, fertilizers, insecticides, herbicides, and fungicides, or to the preparation of chemical mixtures and alloys, or to nuclear energy and nuclear safety, no patents but only certificates of invention may be granted. It should be noted that the Mexican certificates of invention are not the same as inventor's certificates in Socialist countries, but are more or less equivalent to patents endorsed 'licences of right'.

The standards of patentability, the term and the renewal fees payable are the same for certificates as for patents. The term of patents is reduced from 15 years from application to 10 years from grant (an effective reduction of about two years), and the patent will lapse automatically if local working is not effected within four years of grant. Certificates of invention, on the other hand, remain in force even if not worked. The compensation payable to the certificate holder by a person who wishes to exploit the invention will be fixed by the authorities if agreement cannot be reached between the parties. The certificate holder is obliged to supply any know-how necessary for the exploitation of the invention.

Existing Mexican patents relating to pharmaceuticals had to be converted to certificates of invention when the new law came into force, and patents which related to other fields were supposed to lapse four years from the date of entry into force of the law unless they had been worked by then.

Ghana

In Ghana, reasonably strong patent protection is still available by registration of British patents. However, by the Patents Registration (Amendment) Decree of 1972, no registration of patents for pharmaceuticals is possible, and all such registrations existing at the time of the decree were cancelled.

Such changes in patent law have been the rule in developing countries in recent years, and some have carried the trend to ludicrous lengths. In Costa Rica, for example, a patent relating to a pharmaceutical must be locally worked within only one year of grant, and in the Dominican Republic not only are patents ineffective against importation, they are actually invalidated if the patentee imports the patented products.

It can be asked at this stage whether this weakening of patent protection has had the effects intended by the legislators. India is perhaps the best example to consider, as India is an important developing country and the changes to the Indian law were made earlier than elsewhere. The first and most obvious consequence of the change in the law is that foreign chemical companies generally no longer apply for patents in India. To do so is a pointless exercise in view of the negligible value any granted patents would have. It is possible that this consequence was intended, but if so it would have been simpler to abolish patents for chemical inventions entirely.

But has this absence of chemical patenting in India led to an upsurge of the local chemical industry? It must be said that there is no evidence whatsoever of any such effect. The Indian chemical industry, which although small is reasonably well developed and technically competent, is free to copy inventions described in foreign patents, but it appears that without the corresponding specific know-how this is of little use, and licence agreements which could transfer that know-how are inhibited in the absence of patents.

It may be imagined how much less a small and technologically backward country is able to take advantage of freedom from chemical patents.

Restrictions on licence agreements

In addition to the weakening of patent protection in developing countries, particularly for pharmaceuticals, a further development has been the framing of laws, regulations, and guidelines on the national or international level which seek to severely limit the freedom of contracting parties to reach a mutually acceptable licence agreement. Of course, one cannot quarrel with some degree of regulation to prevent abuse of monopoly at least to the same extent as provided by the US anti-trust laws and the laws of many industrialized countries. But some of the proposals, and even some of the laws already in force, practically go so far as to stipulate the terms of an 'agreement' so one-sided that all the rights and benefits are on the side of the licensee while all the obligations and liabilities are carried by the licensor (who is to receive no more than a nominal royalty).

Examples of such provisions on a national level are to be found in the Brazilian law; and on the level of a group of nations in the decisions of the Andean Pact Commission. On the broader international scene, a number of United Nations organizations have made proposals which are designed to improve the position of the recipient of technology transfer, but which are so extreme that if they were adopted they could result in there being little or no transfer of technology at all.

Brazil

The Brazilian law of 1975 governs licence agreements between Brazilian and foreign companies, and provides that these must be registered with the authorities. Among the provisions of the law are that the licensee must be free to continue his activities after the agreement ends, and confidentiality provisions cannot extend after termination. The ex-licensee is therefore free to sell confidential know-how to third parties. The agreement must specifically state that the licensee is free to export the licensed product to any part of the world, even if there is an exclusive licensee in another country.

As far as royalties are concerned, there is a general rule that maximum royalties on chemicals should be in the range 2–4 per cent, and no minimum royalty clauses are allowed. Royalties can be paid on a Brazilian patent only if a corresponding patent has been granted in the country of origin (a provision which favours Belgian over Dutch licensors for no logical reason), if the Brazilian patent was applied for within 12 months of the first application, and if the Brazilian patent is not the subject of nullity proceedings (which of course the licensee can institute).

Andean Pact countries

Decision 24 of the Commission of the Andean Pact sets guidelines for licensing agreements, but these guidelines can be interpreted and modified by the individual countries and do not have automatic legal effect. Indeed, Bolivia and Ecuador do not appear to have any effective regulatory authority as yet.

In Colombia, but not Venezuela, the Committee for Royalties must approve the royalty rate to be charged. Exclusive licences are not allowed, nor is licensing of only part of the scope of a patent. In Venezuela, the term of a registered agreement cannot exceed an initial period of five years, although this may be extended on application. A serious problem for the licensor in Venezuela, as in Brazil, is that the licensee cannot be prohibited from continuing manufacture or sale after the termination of the agreement, even if a patent is still in force.

United Nations organizations

UN Conference on Trade and Development (UNCTAD)

In 1972 this organization started to investigate the possibility of a Code of Conduct for the Transfer of Technology (TOT-Code), which would have the aim of preventing abuse of monopoly by licensors and generally shifting the balance of rights and obligations in favour of the developing countries. The experts working on this project divided themselves, as is usual in many United Nations matters, into three groups, those representing the so-called Group B countries (industrialized free market countries), Group D countries (industrialized socialist countries) and the 'Group of 77'. The latter term stands for the Third World Countries and is so called because at the time it was adopted there were 77 independent developing countries in the UN. The present figure stands at over 120, but the name remains.

In 1976, drafts for the TOT-Code were produced by Group B and the Group of 77, and subsequent drafts have only served to accentuate the differences between the two. The main difference is that the Group B countries want the TOT-Code to be in the form of guidelines whereas the Group of 77, supported by the Group D, want the Code to be legally binding.

UN Industrial Development Organization (UNIDO)

UNIDO has recently proposed a set of draft guidelines for pharmaceutical licensing agreements. While these are neither so far developed nor so important as the TOT-Code of UNCTAD, they illustrate even more clearly the extreme positions adopted by some UN organizations in attempting to change the world by decree.

This draft starts from the premise that patents in the pharmaceutical field are objectionable in themselves although as no evidence or arguments are brought to support this view, it is evidently to be accepted as an article of faith. Some of the most objectional provisions of the draft are listed below.

1. All pharmacological and medical information must be supplied, not only what is necessary for registration in the licensee's country.
2. All improvements must be supplied free of charge during the term of agreement.
3. The licence must be exclusive with the right to sublicense.
4. The royalty is to be limited to 2 per cent (in exceptional cases 3 per cent) for a maximum of 5 years and this is to be based on the selling price less the value of any basic drug supplied by the licensor.
5. Although the licensor must guarantee that he can supply the

licensee's requirements of the basic drug, the licensee is free to obtain it from other sources, i.e. from imitators.

6. The licensee has a right to use the licensor's trade mark, and is also free to use this trade mark on products he has bought from imitators.

7. The licensor must indemnify the licensee for any damages for patent infringement and, what is much worse, be fully liable for any loss or damage caused by the product.

8. Confidentiality terminates when the agreement terminates. All the information may be transferred to a sub-licensee during the agreement and sold freely to competitors afterwards.

9. The licensee must be free to export to any country, in other words to compete with the licensor in his home market.

This draft is an extreme, but not atypical, example of proposals made by those who do not realize that it needs two willing partners to make an agreement. Anyone can draw up a contract which is grossly biased in favour of one side or the other, but it is a different matter to find someone willing to sign it. There must be some incentive for the licensor, and he cannot be expected to agree to terms which not only give him no effective return on his investment, but also undermine his position in other countries.

Thus when, for a minimal 2 per cent return, the licensor is asked to accept that his licensee can sell, in the licensor's home market and under the licensor's own trade mark, drugs produced by an imitator, he can be excused for feeling that he is being asked to pay for the privilege of having his throat cut.

If guidelines such as these were made compulsory either by national law or international agreement, the result would be that no one would be found willing to be a licensor – and such a situation would be just as damaging to the developing countries as to the pharmaceutical industry.

Yugoslavia

Yugoslavia was not discussed in Chapter 23, because it considers itself as a leading member of the Group of 77 rather than as a minor member of Group D, and its economy is mixed rather than fully state-controlled. Because of Yugoslavia's leading position it is particularly unfortunate that it appears to be adopting both the policy of weakening of patent rights and that of imposing inequitable terms in licensing agreements, and both to a particularly extreme extent. These policies are set forth in the Medicinals Law, Long-Term Co-operation Law, and new Patent Law. According to the first of these, a medicinal product may be marketed under a trademark only if the Yugoslav organization marketing the product is the exclusive owner of the trademark. The second imposes terms similar to those of the UNIDO draft guidelines discussed above, and adds the further point that the Yugoslav partner is obliged to export at least 40 per cent of the products from his imported raw materials or intermediates. Finally the new Patent Law reduces the term of all patents to 7 years, which is too short a time to give any protection for pharmaceutical inventions.

Thus, 'co-operation' as envisaged by the Yugoslav authorities consists in a foreign licensor, in the absence of patent protection, giving all his know-how to a Yugoslav organization and accepting that this Yugoslav 'partner' can export to the licensor's own markets using his own trademark. It is hardly to be wondered that the reaction of potential licensors is that if this is co-operation they prefer to have none of it. If these laws are enforced in this form, there will be a practically complete halt to transfers of technology in the pharmaceutical field to Yugoslavia.

The World Intellectual Property Organization (WIPO)

The main function of WIPO is the administration of the Paris Convention, and more recently, of the Patent Co-operation Treaty. In recent years WIPO has proposed a Model Patent Law for developing countries, which is essentially classical in concept and would give strong patent protection. The Model Law has been used as a basis for the patent laws of some developing countries, notably Nigeria and the Sudan. Unfortunately, the latter at present has an excellent patent law but no patent office.

In WIPO, as in other international organizations, the Group 77 countries are now in a majority, and in consequence of this proposals are being made to amend the Paris Convention in ways which would abandon the principle of equal treatment on which the whole convention was based and replace this with the principle of a bias in favour of developing countries.

The Paris Convention has not, of course, remained unchanged. It has already been revised several times, most recently at London (1934), Lisbon (1958), and Stockholm (1967). One of the features of the Stockholm revision was a provision enabling inventor's certificates (e.g. in the USSR) to base a claim to priority for a patent application in other countries.

One of the revisions presently proposed is to grant equal status to inventor's certificates and to patents. This proposal sounds innocuous at first, but is in fact far from it. It would mean that a country could in effect abolish patents and grant only certificates giving no actual property right, while its nationals would still have the right to obtain patents under the Convention in other countries.

Up to now, revisions of the Convention have required unanimity among member countries, and it would seem that all the Group B countries needed to do was to refuse to change this rule. Instead of this, however, a compromise has been agreed to whereby a two-thirds majority suffices to carry a proposal if no more than twelve countries vote against it.

New developments in the 1980s

Since 1980, the position has improved slightly. No other major developing country has further weakened its patent protection, and some countries have actually improved it. For example, Sri Lanka introduced product *per se* protection in 1980, and in Africa the English Speaking Africa Regional Industrial Property Organisation (ESARIPO) has come into effect, and on 3 July 1985 granted its first patent (a pharmaceutical patent to the Wellcome Foundation). A single application to the ESARIPO office in Harare, Zimbabwe, enables a patent to be granted having effect in Botswana, Ghana, Kenya, Malawi, Sudan, Uganda, and Zimbabwe, the system being similar to that of the EPO. Even some major developing countries such as India seem to be having second thoughts about their policy of weakening patent protection.

It is also encouraging that unwelcome initiatives such as the UNCTAD TOT code seem unlikely ever to reach agreement. The Western industralized countries finally took firm action to defend their own interests and refused to give way to the unreasonable demands presented by the Group of 77 and Group D countries. The result is that after 10 years of discussion, TOT seems to be dead and unlamented. Equally, the proposals to destroy the reciprocity which is the basis of the Paris Convention appear to be getting nowhere.

The US government has indeed gone over to the attack and is threatening to remove from preferred status within the US Generalised System of Preferences countries which refuse to give adequate patent protection for inventions. Specifically mentioned were Mexico, Brazil, Argentina, South Korea and Taiwan. The 'big stick' approach could turn out to be counter-productive, but at least such action reminds the governments of these countries that they cannot expect to receive benefits and give none in return, just as a licensee cannot expect to receive everything and pay nothing.

The needs of developing countries

It is a mistake to talk of Third World countries as if they were all alike. In fact they cover a very wide range of developmental stages, and have differing needs corresponding to the stage of development in which they find themselves. Leaving out of consideration oil-rich countries, such as Saudi Arabia, which may not be highly developed but which can afford to buy the technology they want, we can distinguish three main stages of development:

1. The country has little or no industrial infrastructure and has no manufacturing capacity. All technological products must be imported, and local industry can arise only from the activities of foreign enterprises (e.g. many African countries).
2. The country has sufficient infrastructure and manufacturing capacity to produce some or all of its own requirements (e.g. many Latin American countries).
3. The country has the capability to export significant amounts of technological products (e.g. Brazil, India, Argentina, Mexico, and Yugoslavia).

Countries in the first stage are in the position of England in the fifteenth century when the first patents were granted to foreigners to bring certain types of industry into the country. Any foreign companies setting up local manufacturing subsidiaries in a developing country will want to be protected against imports of the same goods. The developing country has a need to import goods as cheaply as possible, and thus it would be unrealistic to expect it to grant patents which could be used by one importer purely to prevent imports by others. However, where local industry is being set up, protection of that industry against imported products would be in the interests of the developing country even if that local industry were wholly foreign owned. Thus it would be reasonable for such a country to grant a patent which would be effective only if locally worked. Such a patent could be subject to compulsory licensing at a reasonable royalty to other local manufacturers, but not to importers. If the patent is for a new invention there should be no unreasonably short period within which the invention has to be locally worked; but, as discussed below, there is no reason why this type of patent should be limited to new technology.

The major need for a new approach is in connection with countries in the second stage. Here it is know-how and technology which is required, but not necessarily the most up-to-date patented technology. One approach is the granting of patents of importation based upon granted foreign patents, valid only if locally worked and giving protection against importation. WIPO proposes something similar, the so-called Transfer of Technology Patent (TTP) which would be based upon a know-how agreement and be applied for jointly by the local licensee and the foreign licensor. Like most patents of importation, the novelty of a TTP would be destroyed only by prior local working of the invention. Such a patent could be tied to a foreign patent, but this may not be desirable since even unpatented know-how may be valuable.

The problem of transferring technology at an acceptable cost remains, and this is perhaps an area in which governments of Group B countries could help. Suppose in connection with a TTP the licensee can only afford to pay 2 per cent royalty while the licensor cannot afford to accept less than 4 per cent, it might be possible for the government of the licensor's home country to make the extra 2 per cent available as a form of aid. This would be politically very difficult, as it might appear that aid money was going not to the recipient country but to the donor's own industry. Nevertheless if the result was to make possible a transfer of technology which genuinely could not otherwise take place, it should be justifiable.

The types of patent suggested as appropriate for countries in the first and second stages of development should not be subject to the normal novelty requirements. It is ridiculous for such a country to have absolute novelty requirements, since this presupposes a level of technology such that the invention could be put into practice locally on the basis of a mere written description. This is by definition not the case; countries in the second group require detailed know-how and those in the first require equipment and personnel as well. Such patents should therefore be granted even if the subject matter is old, provided only that it has not previously been locally worked.

For the third group of countries, the way ahead lies in strengthening patent protection so as to be able to deal with industrialized countries on equal terms. This will in the long run bring far greater benefits to the country than an attempt to demand special privileges by legislation and claim the right to take all and give nothing in return. These countries should consider that no one can force anyone to transfer technology to them, and if the terms are not right no transfer will take place. They are in the position now that Japan was in not very long ago, and it is the example of Japan which they should follow if they wish to industralize. As part of this development they should eventually adopt product *per se* protection for all chemicals including pharmaceuticals, so that research based companies cannot be undermined by imitators able to export to other countries.

GLOSSARY OF PATENT TERMS AND JARGON

absolute novelty a system whereby any prior publication anywhere destroys the novelty of a patent.

abridgement a summary of the disclosure of a patent specification, formerly written by the UK Patent Office examiner.

abstract a summary of the disclosure of a patent specification, written by the applicant.

acceptance (UK) the formal decision by the Patent Office that a patent should be granted.

account of profits alternative to damages, based on profits made by infringer.

advisory action (USA) an official action issued by the US examiner when a final rejection is being maintained.

allowance (USA) see acceptance.

amendment alteration made to a patent specification during prosecution or after grant.

analogy process a non-inventive chemical process.

Andean Pact an association of smaller South American countries with common economic policies.

anticipation prior art which destroys the novelty of a claim by fully describing something falling within it.

anti-trust laws or regulations to prevent abuse of monopoly.

appeal brief (USA) a summary of arguments why the invention should be patentable, submitted to the Board of Appeals.

assignment transfer of ownership of a patent.

attorneys fees (USA) award of costs in US litigation (unusual).

belated opposition (UK) formerly, an application to the Patent Office for revocation of a newly-granted patent.

best mode requirement (USA) the obligation to describe the best way of carrying out the invention

blocking patent see defensive patent.

boilerplate standard clauses in contracts.

Cartagena Agreement the treaty setting up the Andean Pact (q.v.).

caveat a request to a patent office to be informed when some future event (e.g. the grant of a patent on another's application) occurs.

certificate of invention (Mexico) a weak form of industrial property giving the right to royalties but no monopoly.

certiorari (USA) a petition requesting the Supreme Court to review the decision of a lower court.

characterizing clause the part of a German or European-style claim which indicates the novel features of the invention.

Chartered patent agent (UK) a British-qualified patent agent who is a fellow of the Chartered Institute of Patent Agents.

Christmas Message (EEC)   the Commission's announcement of 24 December 1962 on patent licence agreements.

claim   the part of a patent specification which defines the scope of protection.

classmark (UK)   a combination of letters and numbers indicating a heading within the UK Patent Office classification system.

clean hands doctrine (USA)   the principle that equitable relief such as enforcement of patent rights can be granted only to one who has acted in good faith.

Clayton Act (USA)   one of the two major US anti-trust acts.

collateral estoppel (USA)   the principle that a judgment of patent invalidity is binding in subsequent infringement actions.

compulsory licence   a licence which government authorities or courts force the patentee to grant to a third party.

complete specification (UK)   formerly, a full description of an invention filed after an initial brief description.

conception (USA)   the mental part of the inventive process.

conflict (Canada)   proceedings in the Canadian Patent Office to determine priority of invention.

constructive reduction to practice (USA)   the filing of an adequate patent application as evidence of having fully worked out the invention.

continuation application (USA)   a new filing of a US application with unaltered specification to allow presentation of new claims.

continuation-in-part application (USA)   a new filing of a US application, with alterations or additions to the specification.

contributory infringement   infringement by supplying another with the means to infringe a patent.

convention country   a state which is a member of the Paris Convention for the Protection of Industrial Property.

convention year   a period of 12 months from a first application in a convention country within which applications having the effective date of the original filing may be filed in other convention countries.

declaratory judgment (USA)   a judgment on patent validity by a US court, initiated by a party in dispute with the patentee.

defensive patent   a patent which does not cover what the patentee is doing, but which helps to keep competitors away from his area of interest.

deferred examination   a system in which the examination of a patent application may be postponed for several years until requested by the applicant.

delivery up (UK)   a court order compelling an infringer to deliver infringing goods to the patentee for alteration or destruction.

dependent claim   a claim incorporating all the features of an earlier claim to which it refers.

depositions (USA)   in a US infringement suit, the pre-trial stage of taking down evidence on oath.

designation (EPO, PCT)   the naming of the countries for which a European or PCT application is being filed.

disclaimer   the exclusion of specific subject matter from the scope of protection claimed.

discovery   a court order to parties in an infringement action to produce relevant documents.

divisional application   an application claiming part of the subject matter originally in an earlier pending application.

early publication   publication of an application before examination.

enabling disclosure (USA)   a description sufficient to enable the reader to carry out the invention.

equivalence   the extension of the scope of a patent to cover something outside the literal wording of the claims.

estoppel   the barring of a person from claiming a legal right because of an earlier act incompatible with his claim.

Europatent   a patent in any member state of the EPC, granted by the European Patent Office.

European patent attorney   the English title for a professional representative on the register of the EPO.

European route   obtaining patents in EPC countries by a single application at the EPO.

examiner's answer (USA)   written in response to an appeal brief (q.v.).

exclusive licence   a licence which excludes all others, the patentee himself among them.

exhaustion of rights   the principle that when patented goods have been sold by the patentee, he has no further control over them.

extended technical arm (USA)   someone who helps to reduce an invention to practice, although not an inventor.

extension   prolongation of a normally fixed term such as the life of a patent.

fairly based   [of a claim] – supported by the descriptive part of the specification or by a priority document.

file history }   (USA)   the dossier containing all papers relevant to the prosecution
file wrapper   of an application.

file wrapper estoppel (USA)   a principle forbidding the patentee from asserting a scope broader than the literal wording of the claims if the claims were narrowed in prosecution to avoid prior art.

final rejection (USA)   an official action severely limiting further prosecution.

fingerprint claim   a claim characterizing a new product of unknown structure in terms of its properties.

foreign filing   filing in countries other than the country of first filing.

forum shopping (USA)   legal manoeuvring to try to have a suit heard by a court thought to be favourable to one's own side.

fraud on the Patent Office (USA)   obtaining a patent by concealment or misrepresentation of relevant facts.

free invention (Germany)   an invention made by an employee which does not belong to the employer.

generic claim   a claim which covers a number of compounds defined by common structural features.

genus   the group of compounds claimed in a generic claim.

grace period   a period of time before the filing date of an application during which certain types of publication do not invalidate the application.

grant-back   a clause in a licence agreement granting the licensor rights in developments made by the licensee.

Gillette defence (UK)   the argument that one cannot infringe a valid patent because what one is doing is essentially the same as the prior art.

importation invention (UK)   formerly, an invention known abroad but brought into the United Kingdom for the first time.

infringement   doing something forbidden by the grant of a patent to another.

injunction   a court order to cease doing something (e.g. infringing).

innocent infringer (UK)   an infringer who could not be expected to know of the existence of the patent, and who does not have to pay damages.

insufficiency   a ground of invalidity of a patent, if the description does not enable the reader to work the invention.

integer   a distinct feature of a claim.

interdict (Scotland)   see injunction.

interference (USA)   as conflict in Canada (q.v.), but more complex.

interlocutory injunction   a court order to stop alleged infringement pending the trial of the action.

internal priority   the possibility of filing, within 12 months, an application claiming priority from an earlier application in the same country.

international application   an application made under the provisions of the PCT.

inutility   a ground of invalidity of a patent, if the claimed product does not give the promised results.

inventor's certificate (USSR)   granted primarily to Soviet inventors, the rights in the invention being owned by the state.

Jepson claim (USA)   a claim in the German style which distinguishes the new from the old features.

junior party (USA)   the party in an interference who has the later US filing date.

know-how   unpatented technical or commercial information.

label licence (USA)   a statement that the purchase of the labelled goods gives a licence to use them in a patented process.

language of the proceedings (EPO)   the language (English, French, or German) in which a European patent application is filed.

letters patent   an 'open letter' from the sovereign to notify a grant, such as of a monopoly for a new invention.

licenses of right   an endorsement on a patent to the effect that anyone may have a licence upon reasonable terms.

local novelty   the principle that a patent can be invalidated by prior publication only if the publication was in the country granting the patent.

maintenance fees   annual fees payable to keep a patent application pending.

manner of manufacture (UK)   the term used in the Statute of Monopolies (q.v.) for the proper subject of a patent.

man skilled in the art   the hypothetical person to whom the patent specification is addressed.

Markush group (USA)   a group of compounds or substituents defined for the purpose of a patent claim and lacking a common generic description.

mixed novelty   the principle that a patent can be invalidated by a prior printed publication anywhere in the world, but by prior use only in the country granting the patent.

mosaicking   the combination of different pieces of prior art to put together all the features of claimed invention.

national route (EPC)   obtaining patents in EPC countries by separate applications at national patent offices.

negative clearance (EEC)   a statement by the EEC Commission that an agreement does not appear to contravene Article 85 (1) of the Treaty of Rome.

new existing patent (UK)   a British patent, in force on 1 June 1978 and dated on or after 1 June 1966, whose term was extended to 20 years by the 1977 Act.

new matter   material entered into a specification by amendment describing something not previously disclosed.

no-contest clause   a clause in a patent licence agreement in which the licensee agrees not to attack the validity of the licensed patent.

nominal working   an attempt to avoid working requirements (q.v.) by offering licences under the patent.

non-convention filing   an application which does not claim priority from an earlier application, although one exists.

non-exclusive licence   a licence which does not exclude the possibility of further licences being granted.

non-staple   an article of commerce whose only significant use is in a patented process.

non-unity   the condition of an application claiming more than one invention.

novelty   the essential condition for patentability, that what is claimed is new.

obiter   a judicial expression of opinion which does not constitute a precedent.

object clause   part of patent specification stating the object to be achieved by the invention.

obligation of candour (USA)   the obligation of the applicant and his attorney to inform the US Patent Office of all relevant facts.

obvious   capable of being performed by the average skilled man in possession of the prior art.

official action (USA) ⎫   communications from the patent office examiner raising
official letter (UK)   ⎭   objections to a patent application.

Official Gazette (USA) ⎫   publications of the respective patent offices giving inform-
Official Journal (UK) ⎭   ation about newly granted patents and other matters.

old existing patent (UK) a patent in force on 1 June 1978 and dated before 1 June 1966.

omnibus claim (UK) a claim claiming the invention as described with reference to the drawings or examples.

opposition proceedings before a patent office in which a third party raises objections to the grant of a patent.

paper example an example in a chemical patent specification which has not in fact been carried out.

parallel importation the unauthorized importation of patented goods from a country in which the goods are legally on the market.

partial validity the principle that a patent may be valid and enforceable in part, even if part of its scope is invalid.

patent agent (USA) a US patent practitioner who is not a lawyer.

patent agent (UK) see chartered patent agent.

Patentanwalt (Germany) a German patent practitioner in private practice.

Patentassessor (Germany) a German patent practitioner employed in industry.

patent attorney (USA) a US patent practitioner who is admitted to the bar.

patent misuse (USA) any attempt to extend the scope or effect of a patent beyond that granted by law.

patent of addition a patent for an improvement in, or modification of, the subject of an earlier patent, which expires with the earlier patent.

patent of importation }
patent of revalidation } patents granted by certain countries on the basis of patents already granted elsewhere, and protecting local manufacture only.

pith and marrow (UK) the essential features of an invention.

precharacterizing clause the part of a German or European-style claim which recites the features of the invention which are already known.

presumption of validity the rebuttable legal presumption that a granted patent is valid.

prior art all publications before the priority date which could be relevant to the novelty or unobviousness of an invention.

prior claiming the claiming of essentially the same invention in an earlier application which was not published at the priority date.

priority date the date on which an invention was first disclosed to a patent office in the application in question or in an earlier application from which it validly claims priority.

priority document a patent application from which subsequent applications claim priority.

prior use the use of an invention before the priority date of an application claiming it.

product-by-process claim a claim to a product when made by a specified process.

product *per se* claim a claim to a product irrespective of how it is made.

provisional specification (UK) formerly, a brief description of the invention filed with an application, to be followed by a complete specification.

Receiving Section (EPO)   the branch of the EPO at The Hague which deals with formal examination of applications.

reduction to practice (USA)   completion of the inventive act by carrying out the invention and finding a use for it.

re-examination (USA)   a new procedure whereby the patentee or a third party can ask the Patent Office to review a granted patent in the light of new prior art.

refiling   abandonment of a first filed application and filing a new application with essentially the same specification.

registration   obtaining patent protection in certain territories (e.g. Hong Kong) on the basis of a granted British patent.

reissue (USA)   a procedure whereby defects in a granted US patent may be corrected on application by the patentee.

renewal fee   a fee payable at intervals to maintain a granted patent in force.

request for reconsideration (USA)   a request to the Board of Appeals to reverse its own adverse decision.

restoration   proceedings to revive a patent which has lapsed by non-payment of renewal fees.

restriction requirement (USA)   a demand by the examiner that the applicant limit his application because of non-unity.

résumé (France)   formerly, a summary of the invention at the end of a French patent, in place of claims.

reversal of onus   the principle that, when a patent claims a process for making a new compound, the compound will be presumed to be made by the patented process unless proved otherwise.

revocation proceedings   proceedings before a patent office or a court to have a patent declared invalid.

right of prior use   the principle that a patent cannot be used to stop someone from continuing what he was doing before the priority date of the patent.

rule 60 application (USA)   see continuation application

Saccharin doctrine (UK)   the former principle that importation of a product made abroad from an intermediate infringes a UK patent for that intermediate.

scope   the total field encompassed by a claim.

Search Division (EPO)   the branch of the EPO at The Hague (formerly the IIB) which carries out searches on EP applications.

second (pharmaceutical) use claim   a claim which attempts to protect the invention that a compound already known as a pharmaceutical has a new unrelated pharmaceutical use.

secret use (UK)   the former ground of invalidity that the invention had been used (although not in public) before the priority date.

selection invention   an invention which selects a group of individually novel members from a previously known class, on the basis of superior properties.

semi-exclusive licence   a licence exclusive except that the patentee retains the right to use the invention.

senior party (USA)   the party in an interference who has the earlier US filing date.

serial number (USA)   a six-figure number allocated to an application on filing.

service invention (Germany)   an invention made by an employee which belongs to the employer (if claimed by him).

Sherman Act (USA)   the most important of the US anti-trust laws.

shop right (USA)   the right of an employer to a free licence under a patent belonging to an employee, if the invention was made using the employer's facilities.

showing (USA)   evidence of unexpected superiority filed to overcome an objection of obviousness over prior art.

sole licence   see semi-exclusive licence.

species claim (USA)   a claim to a single chemical compound, a member of a claimed genus.

specification   the description of the invention filed with a patent application.

statement of invention   the part of the specification corresponding to the main claim, summarizing the broadest aspect of the invention.

state of the art   the total information in the relevant field known to the hypothetical man skilled in the art.

Statute of Monopolies (UK)   the early English law banning monopolies except for those for new inventions.

sub-claim   see dependent claim.

substantive examination   examination for patentability, as distinct from formal matters.

swearing back (USA)   presenting evidence of an invention date in the USA earlier than the publication date of a cited reference.

synergism   what happens when two plus two makes five. In chemistry, the interaction of two or more compounds to give a superadditive effect. In mechanics, meaningless.

technical progress   formerly a requirement for patentability in some countries according to which an invention had to show advantages over the state of the art.

term   the lifetime of a patent (20 years in most countries).

Thornhill claim (UK)   a claim with exactly the same scope as a specific priority document.

threats action   a suit brought by a person threatened with an infringement action.

tie-in clause   a clause in a licence agreement requiring the licensee to buy unpatented materials from the licensor. Illegal.

tie-out clause   a clause in a licence agreement requiring the licensee not to buy unpatented materials from competitors. Illegal.

tort   a wrong for which remedies may be obtained by suit in the civil courts.

trailer clause   a clause in a contract of employment giving the employer rights to inventions made by the employee for a limited time after he leaves his job.

unit of account (EEC)   the monetary unit of EEC finances (and of fines levied by the Commission). In 1981, about 60p.

utility statement   the part of the specification which states what the invention is useful for.

venue (USA)   the part of the USA in which the Federal District Court has jurisdiction to hear a patent case.

whole contents approach   the principle that the whole contents (not just the claims) of an unpublished application may destroy the novelty of a later application.

working requirements   provisions that a patent will be subject to compulsory licensing or lapse unless the invention is operated commercially in the country in question.

writ (of summons) (UK)   the formal document initiating a suit.

LIST OF CASES REFERRED TO

4. General Mills (Miller's) Application (PAT) [1972] RPC 709
5. Spiro compounds/CIBA-GEIGY T 181/82 (Technical Board of Appeal, EPO) OJEPO 9/84 401
6. *du Pont* v. *Akzo*, reported as E.I. du Pont de Nemours & Co. (Witsiepe's) Application [1982] FSR 303
7. ICI's Application (1971) (unreported, but see Blanco White, *Patents for Inventions*, 4th Edition, p. 120 reference 61)
8. *In re May and Eddy* (USA, CCPA) 197 USPQ 601
9. Beecham Group Ltd's (Amoxycillin) Application (Court of Appeal) [1980] RPC 261
10. Egyt Gyogyszervegyeszeti Gyar's Patent [1981] RPC 99

Chapter 10
1. *Beecham* v. *Bristol Laboratories* (House of Lords) [1977] FSR 215
2. *Parke-Davis* v. *H.K. Mulford* (US Federal Court of Appeal 2nd circuit) 196 F 496
3. Pyrrolidone Derivatives/HOFFMAN-LA ROCHE T 128/82 (Technical Board of Appeal, EPO) OJEPO 4/84 164
4. Bayer's Application (Patents Court) IPD 6014 (1983).
5. Wellcome's Application (High Court, NZ) [1980] RPC 305.
6. Hydropyridine X ZB 4/83 (German Federal Supreme Court) IIC 2/84 215
7. Legal Advice from the Swiss Federal Intellectual Property Office 30 May 1984: OJEPO 11/84 581
8. e.g. EISAI Co. Ltd. Gr 05/83 (Enlarged Board of Appeal, EPO) 5 Dec 1984
9. Schering's Application (Patents Court) [1985] IPD 8032

Chapter 11
1. *Diamond* v. *Chakrabarty* (US Supreme Court) 206 USPQ 193
2. *In re Argoudelis* (USA, CCPA) 168 USPQ 99
3. *Ex parte Lundak* (USA, CAFC) 30 PCTJ 557
4. Bakers' yeast (Bäckerhefe) (German Federal Supreme Court) 6 IIC 207 [1975]
5. Wistar's Application (Patents Court) [1983] RPC 255
6. *Hybritech* v. *Monoclonal Antibodies Inc.* (USA, Federal District Court for Northern California) Newswatch 16 Sept 1985.

Chapter 13
1. *Electrolux* v. *Hudson* (High Court) [1977] FSR 312
2. *Patchett* v. *Sterling Engineering Co.* (House of Lords) 72 RPC 50
3. Harris' Application (Patents Court) [1985] RPC 19

Chapter 15
1. Control circuit/LANSING BAGNALL T 11/82 (Technical Board of Appeal, EPO) OJEPO 12/83 479
2. *In re Welstead* (USA, CCPA) 174 USPQ 449
3. Mobil Oil Corp's Application (PAT) [1970] FSR 265
4. *BASF* v. *Soc. Chim. du Rhône* (Court of Appeal) 15 RPC 359
5. Thornhill's Application (PAT) [1962] RPC 199
6. Daikin Kogyo (Shingu's) Application (Court of Appeal) [1974] RPC 559
7. Claim categories/IFF T 150/82 (Technical Board of Appeal, EPO) OJEPO 7/84 309

Abbreviations of journals:

CD	*Commissioner's Decisions*
CMLR	*Common Market Law Reports*
F	*Federal reports*
FSR	*Fleet Street Reports*
IIC	*International review of Industrial property and Copyright law*
IPD	*Intellectual Property Decisions*
OJEPO	*Official Journal, European Patent Office*

PTCJ	*Patents, Trademarks and Copyright Journal*
RPC	*Reports of Patent Cases*
US	*United States reports*
USPQ	*United States Patents Quarterly*
WPC	*Webster's Patent Cases*

INDEX